FRENCH-ENGLISH
ENGLISH-FRENCH
DICTIONARY

WEBSTER'S

FRENCH·ENGLISH

ENGLISH·FRENCH

DICTIONARY

1992 EDITION

P.S.I. & Associates, Inc.
13322 S.W. 128th Street
Miami, Florida 33186
305-255-7959

28206

ENGLISH-FRENCH

DICTIONARY

ABBREVIATIONS

adj. adjective	*pron*. pronoun
adv. adverb	*qch*. quelque chose
art. article	*qn*. qulqu'un
conj. conjunction	*rel*. relative
dem. demonstrative	*s*. substantive
f. feminine	*sing*. singular
fig. figurative	*s.o.* someone
impers. impersonal	*sth*. something
inf. infinitive	*v.a.* active verb
int. interjection	*v.a. & n.* active and neuter
m. masculine	verb
pers. person	*v. aux.* auxiliary verb
pl. plural	*v.n.* neuter verb
poss. possessive	* irregular verb
pp. past participle	*prep*. preposition

Pronunciation

We give below a short, simple guide to French pronunciation, giving the French sounds and their description. Vowels or consonants that are equivalent to the English ones are not indicated in this list.

Letters	French key word	Description
a, à, â	la, là, bâtir	between *bag* and *bug*
ai, aî	chaise, maîtr	resembles *ai* in *chair*
an	dans	between the vowels of *ah* and *oh* with *n* nasalised
au	pause	as in *oh* but with no final *u*
c	a) café	before *a, o, u* pronounced as *k*
	b) ici	before *e, i, y* pronounced *s* as in *say*
ç	français	as *s* in *say*
ch	chambre	as *sh* in *she*
e	a) le, petit	as the unstressed vowel of *the, standard*
	b) derriere, m	(in a closed syllable) as *e i deck*
é	été	as in *day* but with no final *i*

è, ê	père, fête	resembles the vowels in *pear* or *mare* without diphthongization
eau	eau	as in *oh* but with no final *u*
en	enfant	between *ah* and *oh* with *n* nasalized
er	donner	as in *day* but with no final
eu	jeudi, leur	closer than *earth* or *sir* pronounced with the lips pouted
g	a) rouge	before *e, i, y* pronounced as *s* in *measure, usual*
	b) grand	as *g* in *grand, good*
gn	signe	as in *new* or *lenient*
h	homme	it is never pronounced in French
i	a) ici	tenser than English short *i*
	b) mise	as *ee* in *meet*
î	île	as *ee* in *meet*
ille	fille	as in *key* with *y* at the end
in	vin	resembles the sound in *tan* pronounced through the nose
o	jour	as *s* in *usual*
jô	mot, côte	as in *oh* but with no final *u*
œ	œil	closer than *earth* pronounced with the lips pouted
oi	moi	as in *memoir* (memwaa[1])
on	non, son	between *ah* and *oh* with *n* nasalized
ou, oû	rouge, goûter	short or long *oo* as in *foot* or
qu	quand, question	as *k* in English
r	rare	as a slightly rolled English *r*
s	a) son	usually *s* as in *say*
	b) maison	(between two vowels) *z* as in *zero*
th	thé	as *t* in English
tion	nation	always *sio*+nasal *n*
u, û	sur, sûr	no equivalent in English: round lips for *oo* and try to pronounce *ee*
un	brun	the vowel of *her, earth* with a nasal *n*
w	wagon	as *v* in English
x	a) deuxième	as *z* in *zero*
	b) six	as *s* in *say*
y	y	as short *i* in English

FRENCH GRAMMAR

L i a i s o n.—Final consonants are not usually pronounced, but in most cases, when a word begins with a vowel (or the mute *h*), it is linked with the last consonant of the preceding word. In such cases final *c* and *g* are pronounced as *k*, final *s* and *x* as *z*, e.g. les_Anglais (lezangle).

S t r e s s.—In polysyllabic words stress usually falls on the last pronounced syllable, e.g. plusieurs, le docteur, la société.

The Article
The definite article is *le* (m.), *la* (f.), *les* (m. f. pl.). *Le*, *la* are shortened to *l'* before a vowel or mute *h*.

The indefinite article is *un* (m.), *une* (f.).

The Noun
The p l u r a l is generally formed in *s*. Nouns in *s*, *x*, and *z* do not change in the plural. Nouns in *au* and *eu* form their plurals in *x*, e.g. *joyau, joyaux, jeu, jeux*. Nouns in *al*, form their plurals in *aux*, e.g. *cheval, chevaux*.

There are two *genders* in French. Nearly all nouns ending in *e* mute are feminine, except those in *isme*, *age* and *iste*. Nearly all nouns ending in a consonant or a vowel other than *e* mute are masculine, except nouns in *tion* and *té*. Nouns in *er* form their f. in *ère* e.g. *laitier, laitière*. Nouns in *en, on* form their f. in *enne, onne*, e.g. *chien, chienne, lion, lionne*. Nouns in *eur* form their f. in *euse* except those in *ateur* which have *atrice*, e.g. *admirateur, admiratrice*.

The Adjective
The p l u r a l is generally formed in *s*. Adjectives in *s* or *x* do not change. Those in *al* usually form their plurals in *aux*, e.g. *principal, principaux*.

The f e m i n i n e is generally formed by adding *e* to the masculine form, e.g. *élégant, élégante*. Adjectives in *f* change *f* into *ve*, e.g. *vif, vive*. Those in *x* change *x* into *se*, e.g. *heureux, heureuse*. Adj. in *er* form their f. in *ère*, e.g. *amer, amère*. Those in *el, eil, en, et, on* double the final consonant before adding *e*, e.g. *bel, belle, bon, bonne*.

C o m p a r a t i v e.—'more ... than' or '... er than' is to be translated by 'plus ... que'; 'less ... than' by 'moins ... que'.

S u p e r l a t i v e.—'the most ... ' or 'the ... st' is to be translated by 'le plus ...', 'la plus ... ' or 'les plus ...'

The Pronoun
P e r s o n a l p r o n o u n s: je, tu, il, elle; nous, vous, ils, elles.—*Accusative:* me, te, le, la; nous, vous, les. *Dative:* me, te, lui; nous, vous, leur.—

After prep.. moi, toi, lui, elle; nous, vous, eux, elles.

Reflexive pronouns: me, te, se; nous, vous, se.

Possessive pronouns: le mien (la mienne, les miens, les miennes), le tien (la tienne, les tiens, les tiennes), le sien (la sienne, les siens, les siennes); le nôtre (la nôtre, les nôtres), le vôtre (la vôtre, les vôtres), le leur (la leur, les leurs).

Relative pronouns: who = qui, whom = que, whose = dont, which = qui or que, to whom = a qui.

Interrogative pronoun: who, whom = qui; what = que.

The Adverb
Most French adverbs are formed by adding *ment*, to the feminine form of the corresponding adjective, e.g. *facile*, *facile+ment, heureux, heureuse + ment*. Those in *ant* and *ent* form their adverbs in *amment* and *emment*, respectively, e.g. *patient—patiemment*.

The Verb
We give here the conjugation of the two auxilliaries (*avoir, être*) and of the verbs in -er, -ir, and -re, giving only the principal simple forms:

avoir *Pres. Ind.* j'ai, tu as, il a, nous avons, vous avez, ils ont; *Impf.* j'avais, tu avais, il avait, nous avions, vous aviez, ils avaient; *Fut.* j'aurai, tu auras, il aura, nous aurons, vous aurez, ils auront; *Cond.* j'aurais, tu aurais, il aurait, nous aurions, vous auriez, ils auraient; *Pres. Subj.* que j'aie, que tu aies, qu'il ait, que nous ayons, que vous ayez, qu'ils aient; *Imp.* aie, ayons, ayez; *Pres. Part.* ayant; *Past.Part.* eu.

être *Pres. Ind.* je suis, tu es, il est, nous sommes, vous êtes, ils sont; *Impf.* j'étais, tu étais, il était, nous étions, vous étiez, ils étaient; *Fut.* je serai, tu seras, il sera, nous serons, vous serez, ils seront; *Cond.* je serais, tu serais, il serait, nous serions, vous seriez, ils seraient; *Pres. Subj.* que je sois, que tu sois, qu'il soit, que nous soyons, que vous soyez, qu'il soient; *Imp.* sois, soyons, soyez; *Pres. Part.* étant; *Past. Part.* été.

donner *Pres. Ind.* je donne, tu donnes, il donne, nous donnons, vous donnez, ils donnent; *Impf.* je donnais, tu donnais, il donnait, nous donnions, vous donniez, ils donnaient; *Fut.* je donnerai, tu donneras, il donnera, nous donnerons, vous donnerez, ils donneront; *Cond.* je donnerais, tu donnerais, il donnerait, nous donnerions, vous donneriez, ils donneraient; *Pres. Subj.* que je donne, que tu donnes, qu'il donne, que nous donnions, que vous donniez, qu'ils donnent; *Imp.* donne, donnons, donnez; *Pres. Part.* donnant; *Past. Part.* donné.

finir *Pres. Ind.* je finis, tu finis, il finit, nous finissons, vous finnissez, ils finissent; finis, il finit, nous finissons, vous finissez, ils finissent; *Impf.* je finissais, tu finissais, il finissait, nous finissions, vous finissiez, ils finissaient; *Fut.* je finirai, tu finiras, il finira, nous finirons, vous finirez, ils finiront; *Cond.* je finirais, tu finirais, il finirait, nous finirions, vous finiriez, ils finiraient; *Pres. Subj.* que je finisse, que tu finisses, qu'il finisse, que nous finissions, que vous finissiez, qu'ils finissent; *Imp.* finis, finissons, finissez; *Pres. Part.* finissant; *Past Part.* fini.

rendre *Pres. Ind.* je rends, tu rends, il rend, nous rendons, vous rendez, ils rendent; *Impf.* je rendais, tu rendais, il rendait, nous rendions, vous rendiez, ils rendaient; *Fut.* je rendrai, tu rendras, il rendra, nous rendrons, vous rendrez, ils rendront; *Cond.* je rendrais, tu rendrais, il rendrait, nous rendrions, vous rendriez, ils rendraient; *Pres. Subj.* que je rende, que tu rendes, qu'il rende, que nous rendions, que vous rendiez, qu'ils rendent; *Imp.* rends, rendons, rendez; *Pres. Part.* rendant; *Past. Part.* rendu.

Irregular Verbs

Verbs in -*ger* add *e* before endings in *a* and *o*. Verbs in -*eler*, -*eter* double the *l* or *t* before a mute *e*. Verbs having an acute *é* in the last syllable but one change for a grave *e* when the ending begins with a mute *e*. Verbs in -*yer* change *y* into *i* before a mute *e*.

In the following list of the most frequent French irregular verbs (the root verbs only) the numbers indicate the principal tenses and forms in a fixed order: 1. Present Indicative; 2. Imperfect; 3. Future; 4. Present Subjunctive; 5. Imperative; 6. Present Participle; 7. Past Participle. (+ *être*, if *être* is used to form the past tenses e.g. je suis allé.)

absoudre 1. j'absous, tu absous, il absout, nous absolvons, vous absolvez, ils absolvent; 2. j'absolvais; 3. j'absoudrai; 4. que j'absolve; 5. absous, absolvons, absolvez; 6. absolvant; 7. absous, absoute.

acquérir 1. j'acquiers, tu acquiers, il acquiert, nous acquérons, vous acquérez, ils acquièrent; 2. j'acquérais; 3. j'acquerrai; 4. que j'acquière; 5. acquiers, acquérons, acquérez; 6. acquérant; 7. acquis.

aller 1. je vais, tu vas, il va, nous allons, vous allez, ils vont; 2. j'allais; 3. j'irai; 4. que j'aille, que nous allions, qu'ils aillent; 5. va, allons, allez; 6. allant; 7. allé (être).

assaillir 1. j'assaille, tu assailles, il assaille, nous assaillons, vous assaillez, ils assaillent; 2. j'assaillais; 3. j'assaillerai; 4. que j'assaille; 5. assaille, assaillons, assaillez; 6. assaillant; 7. assailli.

asseoir 1. j'assieds, tu assieds, il assied, nous asseyons, vous asseyez, ils assey-
ent *or* j'assois, tu assois, il
assoit, nous assoyons, vous
assoyez, ils assoient; 2.
j'assayais *or* j'assoyais; 3.
j'assiérai *or* j'assoierai; 4.
que j'asseye *or* que j'assoie;
5. assieds, asseyons *or* assoyons, asseyez *or* assoyez;
6. asseyant or assoyant; 7.
assis.

atteindre *as* **peindre.**

battre 1. je bats, tu bats, il
bat, nous battons, vous bat-
tez, ils battent; 2. je bat-
tais; 3. je battrai; 4. que je
batte; 5. bats, battons, bat-
tez; 6. battant; 7. battu.

boire 1. je bois, tu bois, il
boit, nous buvons, vous bu-
vez, ils boivent; 2. je bu-
vais; 3. je boirai; 4. que je
boive; 5. bois, buvons, bu-
vez; 6. buvant; 7. bu.

bouillir 1. je bous, tu bous, il
bout, nous bouillons, vous
bouillez, ils bouillent; 2. je
bouillais; 3. je bouillirai; 4.
que je bouille; 5. bous,
bouillons, bouillez; 6. bouil-
lant; 7. bouilli.

clore 1. je clos, tu clos, il clôt;
3. je clorai; 4. que je close;
7. clos.

concevoir 1. je conçois, tu
conçois, il conçoit, nous con-
cevons, vous concevez, ils
conçoivent; 2. je concevais;
3. je concevrai; 4. que je
conçoive; 5. conçois, con-
cevons, concevez; 6. con-
cevant; 7. conçu.

conclure 1. je conclus, tu
conclus, il conclut, nous
concluons, vous concluez, ils
concluent; 2. je concluais;
3. je conclurai; 4. que je
conclue; 5. conclus, concluons, concluez; 6. concluant;
7. conclu.

conduire 1. je conduis, tu
conduis, il conduit, nous
conduisons, vous conduisez,
ils conduisent; 2. je con-
duisais; 3. je conduirai;
4. que je conduise; 5. conduis, conduisons, conduisez;
6. conduisant; 7. conduit.

connaître 1. je connais, tu
connais, il connaît, nous
connaissons, vous connais-
sez, ils connaissent; 2. je
connaissais; 3. je connaîtrai;
4. que je connaisse; 5.
connais, connaissons, con-
naissez; 6. connaissant; 7.
connu.

conquérir *as* **acquérir.**

construire *as* **conduire.**

contraindre 1. je contrains,
tu contrains, il contraint,
nous contraignons, vous
contraignez, ils contrai-
gnent; 2. je contraignais;
3. je contraindrai; 4. que
je contraigne; 5. contrains,
contraignons, contraignez;
6. contraignant; 7. con-
traint.

coudre 1. je couds, tu couds,
il coud, nous cousons, vous
cousez, ils cousent; 2. je
cousais; 3. je coudrai; 4.
que je couse; 5. couds, cousons, cousez; 6. cousant;
7. cousu.

courir 1. je cours, tu cours, il
court, nous courons, vous
courez, ils courent; 2. je
courais; 3. je courrai; 4.
que je coure; 5. cours, cour-

ons, courez; **6.** courant; **7.** couru.

couvrir *as* **ouvrir.**

croire 1. je crois, tu crois, il croit, nous croyons, vous croyez, ils croient; **2.** je croyais; **3.** je croirai; **4.** que je croie; **5.** crois, croyons, croyez; **6.** croyant; **7.** cru.

croître 1. je crois, tu crois, il croit, nous croissons, vous croissez, ils croissent; **2.** je croissais; **3.** je croîtrai; **4.** que je croisse; **5.** crois, croissons, croissez; **6.** croissant; **7.** crû, crue.

cueillir 1. je cueille, tu cueilles, il cueille, nous cueillons, vous cueillez, ils cueillent; **2.** je cueillais; **3.** je cueillerai; **4.** que je cueille; **6.** cueillant; **7.** cueilli.

cuire 1. je cuis, tu cuis, il cuit, nous cuisons, vous cuisez, ils cuisent; **2.** je cuisais; **3.** je cuirai; **4.** que je cuise; **5.** cuis, cuisons, cuisez; **6.** cuisant; **7.** cuit.

déchoir 1. je déchois, tu déchois, il déchoit, nous déchoyons, vous déchoyez, ils déchoient; **2.** je déchoyais; **3.** je décherrai; **4.** que je déchoie; **7.** déchu.

déconfire *as* **confire.**

découvrir *as* **ouvrir.**

déduire, détruire *as* **conduire.**

devoir 1. je dois, tu dois, il doit, nous devons, vous devez, ils doivent; **2.** je devais; **3.** je devrai; **4.** que je doive; **5.** dois, devons, devez; **6.** devant; **7. du, due.**

dire 1. je dis, tu dis, il dit, nous disons, vous dites, ils disent; **2.** je disais; **3.** je

dirai; **4.** que je dise; **5.** dis, disons, dites; **6.** disant **7.** dit.

dissoudre 1. je dissous, tu dissous, il dissout, nous dissolvons, vous dissolvez, ils dissolvent; **2.** je dissolvais; **3.** je dissoudrai; **4.** que je dissolve; **5.** dissous, dissolvons, dissolvez; **6.** dissolvant; **7.** dissous, dissoute.

dormir 1. je dors, tu dors, il dort, nous dormons, vous dormez, ils dorment; **2.** je dormais; **3.** je dormirai; **4.** que je dorme; **5.** dors dormons, dormez; **6.** dormant; **7.** dormi.

échoir *or* **écheoir 1.** il échoit *or* il échet, ils échoient; **2.** il échoyait; **3.** il écherra, ils écherront; **4.** qu'il échoie; **6.** échéant; **7.** échu.

écrire 1. j'écris, tu écris, il écrit, nous écrivons, vous écrivez, ils écrivent; **2.** j'écrivais; **3.** j'écrirai; **4.** que j'écrive; **5.** écris, écrivons, écrivez; **6.** écrivant; **7.** écrit.

envoyer 1. j'envoie, tu envoies, il envoie, nous envoyons, vous envoyez, ils envoient; **2.** j'envoyais; **3.** j'enverrai; **4.** que j'envoie; **5.** envoie, envoyons, envoyez; **6.** envoyant; **7.** envoyé.

éteindre *as* **peindre.**

étreindre *as* **peindre.**

exclure *as* **conclure.**

faire 1. je fais, tu fais, il fait, nous faisons, vous faites, ils font; **2.** je faisais; **3.** je ferai; **4.** que je fasse; **5.** fais, faisons, faites; **6.** faisant; **7.** fait.

falloir 1. il faut; **2.** il fallait; **3.** il faudra; **4.** qu'il faille; **7.** fallu.

feindre as **peindre.**

frire 1. je fris, tu fris, il frit; **3.** je frirai; **5.** fris; **7.** frit.

fuir 1. je fuis, tu fuis, il fuit, nous fuyons, vous fuyez, ils fuient; **2.** je fuyais; **3.** je fuirai; **4.** que je fuie; **5.** fuis, fuyons, fuyez; **6.** fuyant; **7.** fui.

gésir 1. il git, nous gisons, vous gisez, ils gisent; **2.** je gisais; **6.** gisant.

haïr 1. je hais, tu hais, il hait, nous haïssons, vous haïssez, ils haïssent; **2.** je haïssais; **3.** je haïrai; **4.** que je haïsse; **5.** hais, haïssons, haïssez; **6.** haïssant, **7.** haï.

instruire as **conduire.**

joindre 1. je joins, tu joins, il joint, nous joignons, vous joignez, ils joignent; **2.** je joignais; **3.** je joindrai; **4.** que je joigne; **5.** joins, joignons, joignez; **6.** joignant; **7.** joint.

lire 1. je lis, tu lis, il lit, nous lisons, vous lisez, ils lisent; **2.** je lisais; **3.** je lirai; **4.** que je lise; **5.** lis, lisons, lisez; **6.** lisant; **7.** lu.

luire as **nuire.**

maudire 1. je maudis, tu maudis, il maudit, nous maudissons, vous maudissez, ils maudissent; **2.** je maudissais; **3.** je maudirai; **4.** que je maudisse; **5.** maudis, maudissons. maudissez; **6.** maudissant; **7.** maudit.

mentir as **sentir.**

mettre 1. je mets, tu mets, il met, nous mettons, vous mettez, ils mettent; **2.** je mettais; **3.** je mettrai; **4.** que je mette; **5.** mets, mettons, mettez; **6.** mettant; **7.** mis.

moudre 1. je mouds, tu mouds, il moud, nous moulons, vous moulez, ils moulent; **2.** je moulais; **3.** je moudrai; **4.** que je moule; **5.** mouds, moulons, moulez; **6.** moulant; **7.** moulu.

mourir 1. je meurs, tu meurs, il meurt, nous mourons, vous mourez, ils meurent; **2.** je mourais; **3.** je mourrai; **4.** que je meure; **5.** meurs, mourons, mourez; **6.** mourant; **7.** mort (être.)

mouvoir 1. je meus, tu meus, il meut, nous mouvons, vous mouvez, ils meuvènt; **2.** je mouvais; **3.** je mouvrai; **4.** que je meuve; **5.** meus, mouvons, mouvez; **6.** mouvant; **7.** mû, mue.

naître 1. je nais, tu nais, il nait, nous naissons, vous naissez, ils naissent; **2.** je naissais; **3.** je naîtrai; **4.** que je naisse; **5.** nais, naissons, naissez; **6.** naissant; **7.** né, née (être.)

nuire 1. je nuis, tu nuis, il nuit, nous nouisons, vous nuisez, ils nuisent; **2.** je nuisais; **3.** je nuirai; **4.** que je nuise; **5.** nuis, nuisons, nuisez; **6.** nuisant; **7.** nui.

offrir as **ouvrir.**

ouvrir 1. j'ouvre, tu ouvres, il ouvre, nous ouvrons, vous ouvrez, ils ouvrent; **2.** j'ouvrais; **3.** j'ouvrirai; **4.** que j'ouvre; **5.** ouvre, ouvrons, ouvrez; **6.** ouvrant; **7.** ouvert.

paître 1. je pais, tu pais, il paît, nous paissons, vous paissez, ils paissent; **2.** je paissais; **3.** je paîtrai; **4.** que je paisse; **5.** pais, paissons, paissez; **6.** paissant.

paraître 1. je parais, tu parais, il paraît, nous paraissons, vous paraissez, ils paraissent; **2.** je paraissais; **3.** je paraîtrai; **4.** que je paraisse; **5.** parais, paraissons, paraissez; **6.** paraissant; **7.** paru.

partir 1. je pars, tu pars, il part, nous partons, vous partez, ils partent; **2.** je partais; **3.** je partirai; **4.** que je parte; **5.** pars, partons, partez; **6.** partant; **7.** parti (être.)

peindre 1. je peins, tu peins, il peint, nous peignons, vous peignez, ils peignent; **2.** je peignais; **3.** je peindrai; **4.** que je peigne; **5.** peins, peignons, peignez; **6.** peignant; **7.** peint.

plaire 1. je plais, tu plais, il plaît, nous plaisons, vous plaisez, ils plaisent; **2.** je plaisais; **3.** je plairai; **4.** que je plaise; **5.** plais, plaisons, plaisez; **6.** plaisant; **7.** plu.

pouvoir 1. je peux *or* je puis, tu peux, il peut, nous pouvons, vous pouvez, ils peuvent; **2.** je pouvais; **3.** je pourrai; **4.** que je puisse; **6.** pouvant; **7.** pu.

prendre 1. je prends, tu prends, il prend, nous prenons, vous prenez, ils prennent; **2.** je prenais; **3.** je prendrai; **4.** que je prenne; **5.** prends, prenons, prenez; **6.** prenant; **7.** pris.

prescrire *as* **écrire.**

produire *as* **conduire.**

proscrire *as* **écrire.**

recevoir *as* **concevoir.**

reconstruire *as* **conduire.**

réduire *as* **conduire.**

repartir *as* **partir.**

reproduire *as* **conduire.**

résoudre 1. je résous, tu résous, il résout, nous résolvons, vous résolvez, ils résolvent; **2.** je résolvais; **3.** je résoudrai; **4.** que je résolve; **5.** résous, résolvons, résolvez; **6.** résolvant; **7.** résolu.

restreindre *as* **peindre.**

rire 1. je ris, tu ris, il rit, nous rions, vous riez, ils rient; **2.** je riais; **3.** je rirai; **4.** que je rie; **5.** ris, rions, riez; **6.** riant; **7.** ri.

savoir 1. je sais, tu sais, il sait, nous savons, vous savez, ils savent; **2.** je savais; **3.** je saurai; **4.** que je sache; **5.** sais, sachons, sachez; **6.** sachant; **7.** sus.

sentir 1. je sens, tu sens, il sent, nous sentons, vous sentez, ils sentent; **2.** je sentais; **3.** je sentirai; **4.** que je sente; **5.** sens, sentons, sentez; **6.** sentant; **7.** senti.

servir 1. je sers, tu sers, ils sert, nous servons, vous servez, ils servent; **2.** je servais; **3.** je servirai; **4.** que je serve; **5.** sers, servons, servez; **6.** servant; **7.** servi.

sortir 1. je sors, tu sors, il sort, nous sortons, vous sortez, ils sortent; **2.** je sortais;'

3. je sortirai; 4. que je sorte; 5. sors, sortons, sortez; 6. sortant; 7. sorti (être).

souffrir as **ouvrir.**

se souvenir *as* **venir.**

suffire 1. je suffis, tu suffis, il suffit, nous suffisons, vous suffisez, ils suffisent; 2. je suffisais; 3. je suffirai; 4. que je suffise; 5. suffis, suffisons, suffisez; 6. suffisant; 7. suffi.

suivre 1. je suis, tu suis, il suit, nous suivons, vous suivez, ils suivent; 2. je suivais; 3. je suivrai; 4. que je suive; 5. suis, suivons, suivez; 6. suivant; 7. suivi.

surseoir 1. je sursois, tu sursois, il sursoit, nous sursoyons, vous sursoyez, ils sursoient; 2. je sursoyais; 3. je surseoirai; 4. que je sursoie; 5. sursois, sursoyons, sursoyez; 6. sursoyant; 7. sursis.

taire *as* **plaire.**

teindre *as* **peindre.**

tenir 1. je tiens, tu tiens, il tient, nous tenons, vous tenez, ils tiennent; 2. je tenais; 3. je tiendrai; 4. que je tienne; 5. tiens, tenons, tenez; 6. tenant; 7. tenu.

traduire *as* **conduire.**

traire 1. je trais, tu trais, il trait, nous trayons, vous trayez, ils traient; 2. je trayais; 3. je trairai; 4. que je traie; 5. trais, trayons, trayez; 6. trayant; 7. trait.

vaincre 1. je vaincs, tu vaincs, il vainc, nous vainquons, vous vainquez, ils vainquent; 2. je vainquais: 3. je vaincrai; 4. que je vainque; 5. vaincs, vainquons, vainquez; 6. vaincant; 7. vaincu.

valoir 1. je vaux, tu vaux, il vaut. nous valons, vous valez, ils valent; 2. je valais, 3. je vaudrai; 4. que je vaille; 6. valant; 7. valu.

venir 1. je viens, tu viens, il vient, nous venons, vous venez, ils viennent; 2. je venais; 3. je viendrai; 4. que je vienne; 5. viens, venons, venez; 6. venant; 7. venu (être.)

vêtir 1. je vêts, tu vêts, il vêt, nous vêtons, vous vêtez, ils vêtent; 2. je vêtais; 3. je vêtirai; 4. que je vête; 5. vêts, vêtons, vêtez; 6. vêtant; 7. vêtu.

vivre 1. je vis, tu vis, il vit, nous vivons, vous vivez, ils vivent; 2. je vivais; 3. je vivrai; 4. que je vive; 5. vis, vivons, vivez; 6. vivant; 7. vécu.

voir 1. je vois, tu vois, il voit, nous voyons, vous voyez, ils voient; 2. je voyais; 3. je verrai; 4. que je voie; 5. vois, voyons, voyez; 6. voyant; 7. vu.

vouloir 1. je veux, tu veux, il veut, nous voulons, vous voulez, ils veulent; 2. je voulais; 3. je voudrai; 4. que je veuille, que nous voulions; 5. veuille, veuillions, veuillez *or* voulez; 6. voulant; 7. voulu.

PHRASES

Good morning. Good evening. Good-bye.
: Bonjour. Bonsoir. Au revoir.

I beg your pardon. Excuse me.
: Je vous demande pardon. Pardon.

How are you? Very well — and you?
: Comment allez-vous? Très bien — et vous?

How do you do (delighted to meet you).
: Enchanté (de faire votre connaissance) monsieur (madame, mademoiselle).

Allow me! You are very kind.
: Permettez-moi ! Vous étes très gentil.

It's all the same to me.
: Cela m'est égal.

Your good health.
: A votre santé.

Allow me to introduce you to . . .
: Permettez-moi de vous présenter à . . .

It is fine (bad) weather.
: Il fait beau (mauvais) temps.

You are right. You are wrong.
: Vous avez raison. Vous avez tort.

It is not my fault.
: Ce n'est pas ma faute.

To do one's best.
: Faire son possible.

It is very annoying.
: C'est très ennuyeux.

You're pulling my leg.
: Vous vous moquez de moi.

So much the better (worse).
: Tant mieux (pis).

He's a jolly nice fellow.
: C'est un chic type.

To put one's foot in it.
: Mettre les pieds dans le plat.

Things are going badly.
: Rien ne va bien. Tout va mal.

I am an Englishmen (Englishwoman).
: Je suis anglais (anglaise).

I cannot speak French.
: Je ne parle pas français.

I am looking for . . .
: Je cherche . . .

I don't understand you.
: Je ne vous comprends pas.

Please speak slowly!
: Parlez lentement, s'il vous plait!

Is there anyone here who speaks English?
: Y-a-t-il quelque'un qui parle anglais?

Where is the British Consulate?
: Où est le consulat britannique?

It is wonderful, splendid !
: C'est épatant, formidable !

No . . . Trespassers will be prosecuted.
: Défense de . . . sous peine d'amende.

No entry.	Entrée interdite.
Lavatory.	Les toilettes, les lavabos, les cabinets.
What time is it?	Quelle heure est-il?
It is five past one.	Il est une heure cinq.
We are in a hurry.	Nous sommes pressés.
How long does it take to . . . ?	Combien de temps faut-il pour . . . ?
This evening, tonight. Last night.	Ce soir. Hier soir.
How long have you been here?	Depuis quand êtes-vous ici?
I have been here a month.	Je suis ici depuis un mois.
Can we lunch (dine) here?	Est-ce qu'on peut déjeuner (dîner) ici?
There are four of us.	Nous sommes quatre.
We only want a snack.	Nous voudrions seulement un casse-croûte.
Please give us the menu.	Voulez-vous nous donner le menu, s'il vous plaît.
Bring us the wine list, please.	Apportez-nous la carte des vins, s'il vous plaît.
We would like black coffee (white coffee).	Nous voudrions du café noir (café au lait).
The bill, please.	L'addition, s'il vous plaît.
I want some petrol (oil, water).	Je voudrais de l'essence (de l'huile, de l'eau).
I have had a breakdown.	Je suis en panne.
My car is on the road two kilometres from here.	Mon auto est sur la route à deux kilomètres d'ici.
Do you know the road to . . . ?	Connaissez-vous a route de . . . ?
Is the post office (bank) near here?	Y a-t-il un bureau de poste (bureau de change) près d'ici?
Are there any letters for me?	Y a-t-il des lettres pour moi?
Do you sell . . . ?	Est-ce que vous vendez . . . ?
You have given me the wrong change.	Vous vous êtes trompé en me rendant la monnaie
Have you anything to declare?	Avez-vous quelque chose à déclarer?
I cannot find my ticket.	Je ne peux pas trouver mon billet.
I have left something in the train.	J'ai laissé quelque chose dans le train.
I have a train to catch.	J'ai un train à prendre.
What time is the first (last) train for . . . ?	A quelle heure est le premier (dernier) train pour . . . ?

From which platform?	Sur quel quai?
Where do I change for . . .?	Où est-ce que je change pour . . .?
Is there a hotel where I can stay the night?	Est-ce qu'il y a un hôtel où je peux passer la nuit?
The last train has gone	Le dernier train est parti.
I do not feel well.	Je ne me sens pas bien.
I want to get off at . . .	Je veux descendre à . . .
Do you go near . . .?	Allez-vous près de . . .?
Can I have a room for the night?	Puis-je avoir une chambre pour la nuit?
I am only staying for two or three days.	Je reste deux ou trois jours seulement.
I want a room with a double bed.	Je désire une chambre avec un grand lit.
Can you put me up for the night?	Pouvez-vous me donnez une chambre pour la nuit?
I shall be back at three.	Je serai de retour à trois heures.
Have you any English newspapers?	Avez-vous des journaux anglais?
What does it cost to send a letter to . . .?	Combien met-on sur une lettre pour . . .?
Where can I buy . . .?	Où puis-je acheter . . .?
Will you reserve this place for me?	Voulez-vous me reserver cette place?
Will you take a traveller's cheque?	Acceptez-vous un cheque de voyage?
Will you have letters sent on to this address?	Voulez-vous faire suivre mon courrier à cette adresse?
I need a guide who speaks English.	J'ai besoin d'un guide qui parle anglais.
Is this the right road for . . .?	Est-ce bien la route pour . . .?
How far is it from here to . . . ?	Combien de kilomètres d'ici à . . .?
Have you any post-cards?	Avez-vous des cartes postales?
Have you a map (plan)?	Avez-vous une carte (un plan)?
Do you know what is on at the cinema (theatre)?	Savez-vous ce qu'on donne au cinéma (Théatre)?
Where does this road lead?	Ce chemin, ou mène-t-il?

Can you recommend a cheap restaurant?	Pouvez-vous recommander un restaurant pas trop cher?
It is too dear. Have you anything cheaper?	C'est trop cher. Avez-vous quelque chose de meilleur marché?
We are lost.	Nous sommes perdus.
Have you any identification papers?	Avez-vous une pièce d'identite?
Have you a carrier bag?	Avez-vous un sac en papier?
Here is my address.	Voici mon adresse.
That's all right.	Je vous en prie.
Don't mention it.	Il n'y a pas de quoi.
Take my seat, madame.	Prenez ma place, madame.
Can I help you?	Puis-je vous aider?
Am I disturbing you?	Est-ce que je vous dérange?
I am terribly sorry.	Je suis navré (désolé).
Thank you for your hospitality.	Je vous remercie de votre hospitalité.
We had a very good time.	Nous nous sommes bien amusés.
It's too much. It's too dear.	C'est trop. C'est trop cher.
Look out!	Attention!
You are right. You are wrong.	Vous avez raison. Vous avez tort.
Listen. Look.	Ecoutez. Regardez.
What is the matter?	Qu'est-ce qu-il y a?
Please speak slowly.	Parlez lentement, s'il vous plait.
Wait, I am looking for the phrase in this book.	Attendez, je cherche la phrase dans ce livre.
I have already paid you.	Je vous ai déjà payé.
It's terribly funny.	C'est tordant, c'est rigolo.
You don't say!	Sans blague!
You are joking. Joking apart.	Vous plaisantez. Blague à part.
Agreed. O.K.	Entendu. D'accord.
What a pity!	Quel dommage!
Do not touch.	Ne pas toucher.
Wet paint.	Prenez garde à la peinture.
You have plenty of time.	Vous avez tout le temps.
I have no time.	Je n'ai pas le temps.
The day before yesterday.	Avant-hier.
The day after tomorrow.	Après-demain.

Waiter, bring us some bread, please.	Garçon apportez-nous du pain, s'il vous plaît.
A little more . . .	Encore un peu de . . .
What would you like to drink?	Que désirez-vous boire (comme boisson)?
Is the service (the cover charge) included?	Le service (le couvert), est-il compris?
Keep the change.	Vous pouvez garder la monnaie.
There is a mistake in the bill.	Il y a une erreur dans l'addition.
Please don't mention it.	Je vous en prie.
Is the garage open all night?	Est-ce que le garage est ouvert la nuit?
I want to leave early tomorrow.	Je veux partir demain de bonne heure.
How long shall I have to wait?	Combien de temps faut-il attendre?
Can you lend me . . . ?	Pouvez-vous me prêter . . . ?
How much do I owe you?	Combien est-ce que je vous dois?
I have two first class (second class) seats reserved.	J'ai deux places réservées en première (en seconde).
Excuse me, sir, that seat is mine.	Pardon monsieur, cette place est à moi.
Porter I want to put this luggage in the cloak-room (left-luggage office).	Porteur, je veux mettre ces bagages à la consigne.
I am coming with you.	Je vous suis.
Is there a porter from the . . . Hotel here?	Est-ce qu'il y a un porter de l'hôtel . . . ici?
Where is the enquiry office?	Où est le bureau de renseignements?
When do we get to . . . ?	A quelle heure arrive-t-on à . . .?
How long does the train stop here?	Combien de temps le train s'arrête-t-il ici?
The plane for . . . is twenty minutes late already.	L'avion pour . . . a déjà vingt minutes de retard.
The . . . plane is announced.	L'avion de . . . est signalé.
Where is the Airline Office?	Où est le bureau de la compagnie aérienne?
I want to reserve a seat on the plane leaving tomorrow for . .	Je voudrais réserver une place dans l'avion qui part demain pour . .

Is there a plane for ... today?	Est-ce qu'il y a un avion pour ... aujourd'hui?
I do not feel well.	Je ne me sens pas bien.
Bring me some coffee (brandy, a glass of water), please.	Apportez-moi du café (cognac, un verre d'eau), s'il vous plait.
Put out your cigarettes and fasten your seatbelts, please.	Eteignez vos cigarettes et attachez vos ceintures, s'il vous plait.
Call me a taxi.	Appelez-moi un taxi.
Go quickly, I am in a great hurry.	Dépêchez-vous, je suis très pressé.
Please wait here for a few minutes.	Attendez-moi ici quelques minutes, s'il vous plaît.
Where is the office?	Où est le bureau?
Have you a room with a private bathroom?	Avez-vous une chambre avec salle de bains?
What is the price of a room per night?	Quel est le prix d'une chambre par nuit?
I am expecting a gentleman (a lady, a young lady).	J'attends un monsieur (une dame, une demoiselle).
Give me two 25 centime stamps and two at 15 centimes.	Donnez-moi deux timbres de vingt-cinq centimes et deux de quinze.
I want to send a telegram.	Je voudrais envoyer une dépêche.
Have you the time-table of trains for ... ?	Avez-vous l'horaire des trains pour ... ?
Can we have an English breakfast?	Peut-on avoir un petit déjeuner anglais?
Order a taxi for 9.30, please.	Commandez un taxi pour neuf heures et demie, s'il vous plaît.
Please have my bill made out.	Préparez la note, s'il vous plaît.
We want to be together.	Nous voudrions être ensemble.
How far it to ... ?	Quelle distance d'ici à ... ?
What is the name of this town· (village)?	Quel est le nom de cette ville (ce village)?
Where is the market place?	Où est le marché?
Weather permitting, we hope to leave at dawn.	Si le temps le permet, nous comptons partir à l'aube.
Get me Molitor 44—94,	Voulez-vous me demander

please.	Molitor quarante-quatre, quatre-vingt quatorze, s'il vous plaît.
How much do I owe you for the call?	Combien vous dois-je pour la communication?
Can I make an appointment?	Puis-je prendre un rendezvous?
Can I have something to read?	Puis-je avoir de la lecture?
Can you make up this prescription, please?	Pouvez-vous faire cette ordonnance, s'il vous plaît?
Can you give me something for insect (ant, mosquito) bites?	Pouvez-vous me donner quelque chose pour les piqûres d'insects (de fourmis, de moustiques)?
My skin is smarting; have you anything to soothe it?	La peau me cuit; avez-vous quelque-chose de calmant?
For external use.	Pour l'usage externe.
I want a reversal (negative) colour film.	Je voudrais un film en couleur inversible (negatif).
Do you sell . . .?	Est-ce que vous vendez . . .?
Have you anything cheaper (better)?	Avez-vous quelque chose de moins cher (de meilleure qualité)?
I want something like this (that).	Je voudrais quelque chose comme ceci (cela).
Can you order it for me?	Pouvez-vous le (la) commander?
Will you send it to this address?	Voulez-vous l'envoyer à cette adresse?
That's exactly what I want.	Voilà ce qu'il me faut.
You have given me the wrong change.	Vous vous êtes trompé en me rendant la monnaie.
Can you change it?	Pouvez-vous le changer?
Do you sell English cigarettes (tobacco)?	Est-ce que vous vendez des cigarettes anglaises (du tabac anglais)?
There has been an accident.	Il y a eu un accident.
Is there a doctor near here?	Y a-t-il un médecin près d'ici?
Welcome to England (France).	Je vous souhaite la bienvenue en Angleterre

(France).

Avez-vous fait un bon voyage?	Did you have a good journey?
A quelle heure est le petit déjeuner (le déjeuner, le goûter, le dîner)?	What time is breakfast (lunch, tea, dinner)?

NUMBERS

1 *one*, un.	1st *first*, premier.
2 *two*, deux.	2nd *second*, deuxième.
3 *three*, trois.	3rd *third*, troisième.
4 *four*, quatre.	4th *fourth*, quatrième.
5 *five*, cinq.	5th *fifth*, cinquième.
6 *six*, six.	6th *sixth*, sixième.
7 *seven*, sept.	7th *seventh*, septième.
8 *eight*, huit.	8th *eighth*, huitième.
9 *nine*, neuf.	9th *ninth*, neuvième.
10 *ten*, dix.	10th *tenth*, dixième.
11 *eleven*, onze.	11th *eleventh*, onzième.
12 *twelve*, douze.	12th *twelfth*, douzième.
13 *thirteen*, treize.	13th *thirteenth*, treizième.
14 *fourteen*, quatorze.	14th *fourteenth*, quatorzième.
15 *fifteen*, quinze.	15th *fifteenth*, quinzième.
16 *sixteen*, seize.	16th *sixteenth*, seizième.

a, an, *art.* un, -e.

abandon, *v. a.* abandonner.

abate, *v. a. & n.* diminuer; se calmer, s'apaiser.

abbey, *s.* abbaye *f.*

abbot, *s.* abbé *m.*

abbreviate, *v. a.* abréger.

abbreviation, *s.* abréviation *f.*

abdicate, *v.a. & n.* abdiquer.

abdomen, *s.* abdomen *m.*

abhor, *v. a.* détester, abhorrer.

ability, *s.* capacité *f.*, habilité *f.*

able, *adj.* capable.

aboard, *adv.* à bord.

abode, *s.* demeure *f.*

abolish, *v.a.* abolir; supprimer.

abominable, *adj.* abominable.

abound, *v.n.* abonder (de).

about, *adv. & prep.* autour (de); environ, presque; au sujet de.

above, *adv. & prep.* au-dessus (de); *(in book)* ci-dessus.

abroad, *adv.* à l'étranger.

absence, *s.* absence *f.*, éloignement *m.*

absent, *adj.* absent.

absolute, *adj.* absolu.

absolve, *v.a.* absoudre; relever de; remettre, pardonner.

absorb, *v. a.* absorber.

abstain, *v.n.* s'abstenir de.

abstract, *adj.* abstrait.

abstraction, *s.* abstraction *f.*

absurd, *adj.* absurde; ridicule.

abundance, *s.* abondance *f.*

abundant, *adj.* abondant.

abusive, *adj.* abusif; injurieux; offensant.

academic, *adj.* académique.

academy, *s.* académie *f.*

accelerate, *v.a.* accélérer; *v.n.* s'accélérer.

accent, *s.* accent *m.*

accept, *v.a.* accepter

access, *s.* accès *m.*

accessible, *adj.* accessible.

accessory, *s. & adj.* accessoire *(m.).*

accident, *s.* accident *m.*

accidental, *s.* accidentel.

accommodate, *v.a.* accommoder; loger; ~ *oneself to* s'accommoder à.

accommodation, *s.* ajustement *m.*, adaptation *f.*; commodité *f.*; logement *m.*

accompany, *v.a.* accompagner.

accomplish, *v.a.* accomplir, achever.

accomplishment, *s.* accomplissement *m.*; talent *m.*

accord, *s.* accord *m.*, consentement *m.*

according: ~ *to* selon, d'après.

accordingly, *adv.* donc; en conséquence.

account, *s.* compte *m.*; *(narration)* récit *m.*; *on* ~ *of* à cause de; *on no* ~ dans aucun cas; *take into* ~ tenir compte de; — *v.n.* ~ *for* expliquer; rendre compte de.

accuracy, *s.* exactitude *f.*

accusation, *s.* accusation *f.*

accuse, *v.a.* accuser; incriminer.

accustom, *v.a.* accoutumer (à).

ache, *s.* douleur *f.*

achieve, *v.a.* accomplir, achever; atteindre.

acknowledge, *v.a.* reconnaître; accuser réception de.

acquaint, *v.a.* informer (de); faire part à.

acquaintance, *s.* connaissance *f.*

acquire, *v.a.* acquérir.

acre, *s.* arpent *m.*

across, *prep.* à travers; en croix.

act, *s.* action *f.*; *(law)* loi *f.*; *(theatre)* acte *m.*; — *v.n.* agir; *v.a.* jouer.

action, *s.* action *f.*; acte *m.*; *(war)* combat *m.*

active, *adj.* actif.

activity, *s.* activité *f.*

actor, *s.* acteur *m.*

actress, *s.* actrice *f.*

actual, *adj.* réel.

actually, *adv.* en fait.

adapt, *v.a.* adapter.

add, *v.a.* ajouter; additionner.

addition, *s.* addition *f.*; *in ~ to* en plus de.

additional, *adj.* additionnel; supplémentaire.

address, *s.* adresse *f.*; — *v.a.* adresser.

adequate, *adj.* suffisant.

adjust, *v.a.* ajuster, régler.

administer, *v.a. & n.* administrer.

administration, *s.* administration *f.*

admirable, *adj.* admirable.

admiral, *s.* amiral *m.*

admiration, *s.* admiration *f.*

admire, *v.a.* admirer.

admission, *s.* admission *f.*; entrée *f.*

admit, *v.a.* admettre; laisser entrer.

adopt, *v.a.* adopter.

adoption, *s.* adoption *f.*

adore, *v.a.* adorer.

adult, *adj. & s.* adulte *(m.f.)*

advance, *v. n.* avancer; — *s.* avance *f.*; progrès *m.*

advantage, *s.* avantage *m.*

adventure, *s.* aventure *f.*

adversary, *s.* adversaire *m.*

adverse, *adj.* adverse.

adversity, *s.* adversité *f.*

advertise, *v.a.* annoncer; faire de la réclame (pour).

advertisement, *s.* annonce *f.*; réclame *f.*

advice, conseil *m.*; avis *m.*

advise, *v.a.* conseiller.

aerial, *s.* antenne *f.*

aerodrome, *s.* aérodrome *m.*

aeroplane, *s.* avion *m.*

affair, *s.* affaire *f.*

affect, *v.a.* affecter.

affection, *s.* affection *f.*

affectionate, *adj.* affectueux.

affirmative, *adj.* affirmatif; — *s.* affirmative *f.*

afford, *v.a.* donner, fournir, accorder; *can ~* avoir les moyens de.

afraid, *adj.* effrayé; *be ~ of* avoir peur de.

African, *adj.* africain; — *s.* Africain, -e.

after, *prep. & adj.* après.

afternoon, *s.* après-midi *m.* or *f.*

afterwards, *adv.* après, ensuite.

again, *adv.* encore une fois, de nouveau.

against, *prep.* contre.

age, *s.* âge *m.*

agency, *s.* agence *f.*

agent, *s.* agent *m.*

aggression, *s.* agression *f.*

ago, *adv.* il y a.

agony, *s.* agonie *f.*

agree, *v.n.* s'accorder, être d'accord; ~ (up-) on convenir sur; ~ *to* consentir à; ~ *with* entrer dans les idées de.

agreeable, *adj.* agréable.

agreement, *s.* accord *m.*

agricultural, *adj.* agricole.

agriculture, *s.* agriculture *f.*

ahead, *adv.* en avant.

aid, *s.* aide *f.*; — *v.a.* aider, assister.

aim, *s.* but *m.*; objectif *m.*; visée *f.*; — *v.a.* & *n.* viser.

air. *s.* air *m.*

air-conditioning, *s.* conditionnement d'air *m.*; climatisation *f.*

aircraft, *s.* avion *m.*

air-line, *s.* ligne *f.* aérienne.

air-mail *s.* poste aérienne; *by* ~ par avîon.

airport, *s.* aéroport *m.*,

alarm, *v.a.* alarmer; —*s.* alarme *f.*

alcoholic, *adj.* alcoolique.

ale, *s.* bière *(f.)* anglaise.

alike, *adj.* semblable; — *adv.* également.

alive, *adj.* vivant.

all, *pron. s., adv. & adj.* tout; *not at* ~ pas du tout.

allege, *v.a.* alléguer.

alley, *s.* ruelle *f.*

allow, *v.a.* permettre; laisser; admettre.

allude, *v.n.* faire allusion.

ally, *v.a.* allier; *v.n.*

s'allier; — *s.* allié, -e.

almost, *adv.* presque; à peu près.

alone, *adj.* & *adv.* seul.

along, prep. le long de.

aloud, *adv.* à haute voix.

already, *adv.* déjà.

also, *adv.* aussi.

altar, *s.* autel *m.*

alter, *v.a.&n.* changer.

alternate, *adj.* alternatif; — *v.n.* alterner.

although, *conj.* quoique; bien que.

altitude, *s.* altitude *f.*, élévation *f.*

altogether, *adv.* tout à fait; entièrement.

always, *adv.* toujours.

amaze, *v.a.* frapper d'étonnement, frapper de stupeur.

amazing, *adj.* étonnant.

ambassador, *s.* ambassadeur *m.*

ambassadress, *s.* ambassadrice *f.*

ambition, *s* ambition *f.*

ambitious, *adj.* ambitieux.

ambulance, *s.* ambulance (automobile) *f.*

amend, *v.a.* amender.

amends: *make* ~ *for* dédommager de.

American, *adj.* américain; — *s.* Américain, -e.

among, prep. parmi; chez.

amount, *s.* somme *f.*; *(total)* montant *m.*; — *v.n.* ~ *to* monter à.

ample, *adj.* ample.

amplifier, *s.* amplificateur *m.*

amuse, *v.a.* amuser; divertir.

amusement, *s.* amusement *m.*; divertissement *m.*

an *see* a.

analogy, *s.* analogie *f.*

analyse, *v.a.* analyser.
analysis, analyse *f.*
anarchy, *s.* anarchie *f.*
anatomy, *s.* anatomie *f.*
ancestor, *s.* ancêtre *m. f.*
anchor, *s.* ancre *f.*
ancient, *adj.* ancien; antique.
and, *conj.* et.
anecdote, *s.* anecdote *f.*
angel, *s.* ange *m.*
anger, *s.* colère. *f.*
angle, *s.* angle *m.*
angler, *s.* pêcheur *m.*

Anglican, *adj.* anglican.
angry, *adj.* fâché, irrité.
animal, *s.* animal *m. (pl.* -aux).
ankle, *s.* cheville *f.*
anniversary, *s.* anniversaire *m.*
announce, *v.a.* annoncer.
announcement, *s.* annonce.
announcer, *s.* speaker *m.*
annoy, *v.a.* ennuyer; contrarier; gêner.
annoying, *adj.* contrariant; ennuyeux.
annual, *adj.* annuel.
annul, *v.a.* annuler.
another, *pron. & adj.* un autre, une autre.
answer, *s.* réponse *f.;* — *v.a.&n.* répondre.
ant, *s.* fourmi *f.*
antelope, *s.* antilope *f.*
antibiotic, *s.* antibiotique *m.*
anticipate, *v.a.* anticiper.
antipathy, *s.* antipathie *f.*
antiquated, *adj.* vieilli.
antiquity, *s.* antiquité *f.*
anvil, *s.* enclume *f.*
anxiety, *s.* anxiété *f.*
anxious, *adj.* inquiet; désireux; be ~ to désirer faire qch.
any, *adj. & pron.* quelque; *(at all)* n'importe quoi/qui/quel; *(some, in*

question) du, de la; *have you* ~? en avez vous; *not* ~ ne ... pas de; ~ *more* encore du.
anybody, *pron.* quelqu'un; *(at all)* n'importe qui.
anyhow, *adv.* n'importe comment.
anyone *see* anybody.
anything, *pron.* quelque chose; *(at all)* n'importe quoi.
anyway, *see* anyhow.
anywhere, *adv.* n'importe où.
apart, *adv.* à part; de côté; ~ *from* en dehors de.
apartment, *s.* logement *m.;* appartement *m.*
apologize, *v.n.* faire des excuses, s'excuser.
apology, *s.* excuse *f.*
apostle, *s.* apôtre *m.*
appalling, *adj.* épouvantable.
apparatus, *s.* appareil *m.*
apparent, *adj.* manifeste.
appeal, *s.* appel *m.;* — *v.n.* en appeler (à).
appear, *v.n.* (ap)paraître; *(seem)* sembler.
appearance, *s.* apparition *f.; (look)* air *m.*
appendicitis, *s.* appendicite *f.*
appendix, *s.* appendice *m.*
appetite, *s.* appétit *m.*
applaud, *v.n.* applaudir.
applause, *s.* applaudissement *m.*
apple, *s.* pomme *f.*
appliance, *s.* appareil *m.*
applicant, *s.* postulant, -e.
application, *s.* demande *f.; (use)* application *f.*
apply, *v.a.* appliquer; — *v.n.* avoir rapport à; ~ *for* solliciter.
appoint, *v.a.* nommer; désigner.

appointment, *s.* nomination *f.*; emploi *m.*; rendez-vous *m.*

appreciate, *v.a.* apprécier.

appreciation, *s.* appréciation *f.*

apprehend, *v.a.* appréhender; *(understand)* comprendre.

apprentice, *s.* apprenti *m.*

approach, *s.* approche *f.*; — *v. a. & n.* (s')approcher (de).

appropriate, *adj.* approprié, convenable.

approval, *s.* approbation *f.*

approve, *v.a. & n.* approuver.

approximate, *adj.* approximatif.

approximation, approximation *f.*

apricot, *s.* abricot *m.*

April, *s.* avril *m.*

apron, *s.* tablier *m.*

aptitude, *s.* aptitude *f.*

Arab, *s.* Arabe *m.*

Arabian, *adj.* arabe.

arbitrary, *adj.* arbitraire.

arcade, *s.* arcade *f.*

arch, *s.* arche *f.*; arc *m.*

archaeology, *s.* archéologie *f.*

archbishop, *s.* archevêque *m.*

architect, *s.* architecte *m.*

architecture, *s.* architecture *f.*

area, *s.* surface *f.*; aire *f.*

Argentine, *adj.* argentine.

argue, *v.n.* argumenter; *v.a.* discuter.

argument, *s.* argument *m.*; discussion *f.*

arise, *v. n.* se lever; *(emerge)* surgir; *(come from)* résulter de.

aristocratic, *adj.* aristocratique.

arm[1], *s.* bras *m.*

arm[2], *s.(pl)*. arme(s) *f.*

armament, *s.* armement *m.*

armchair, *s.* fauteuil *m.*

armour, *s.* armure *f.*

army, *s.* armée *f.*

around, *adv. & prep.* autour (de).

arouse, *v.a.* réveiller.

arrange, *v.a.* arranger.

arrangement, *s.* arrangement *m.*; ~s mesures *f. pl.*

array, *s.* ordre *m.*

arrears, *s. pl.* arriéré *m.*

arrest, *v.a.* arrêter; — *s.* arrestation *f.*

arrival, *s.* arrivée *f.*

arrive, *v.n.* arriver.

arrow, *s.* flèche *f.*

art, *s.* art *m.*

artery, *s.* artère *f.*

article, *s.* article *m.*

artificial, *adj.* artificiel.

artillery, *s.* artillerie *f.*

artist, *s.* artiste *m.*

artistic, *adj.* artistique.

as, *adv. & conj.* comme; *(like a)* en; *(when)* comme; ~ ... ~ aussi ... que.

ascend, *v.n.* monter.

ash(es), *s. (pl.)* cendre *f.*

ashamed, *adj.* honteux; be ~ of avoir honte de.

ashore, *adv.* à terre.

ash-tray, *s.* cendrier *m.*

Asiatic, *adj.* asiatique.

aside, *adv.* de côté.

ask, *v. a.* demander (à + qn., de + *inf.*); ~ about se renseigner sur; ~ for demander.

asleep, *adj.* endormi; fall ~ s'endormir.

aspect, *s.* aspect *m.*; *(look)* air *m.*

aspire, *v.n.* aspirer à.

ass, *s.* âne *m.*
assail, *v. a.* assaillir.
assault, *s.* assaut *m.*
assemble, *v. a.* assembler;
v.n. s'assembler.
assembly, *s.* assemblée *f.;*
~ *hall* halle *f.* de
montage; ~ *line* chaîne
f. de montage.
assert, *v.a.* affirmer.
assess, *v.a.* cotiser.
assets, *s. pl.* actif *m.*
assign, *v. a.* assigner;
céder.
assignment, *s.* cession *f.*
assist, *v.a.* aider.
assistance, *s.* aide *f.*
associate, *v.a.* associer;
— *s.* associé, -e *m. f.*
association, *s.* association
f.
assume, *v.a.* prendre;
assumer; supposer.
assumption, *s.* supposi-
tion *f.*
assurance, *s.* assurance *f.*
assure, *v.a.* assurer.
astonish, *v. a.* étonner.
astonishment, *s.* étonnement *m.*
astronomy, *s.* astronomie
f.
at, *prep.* *(place, time)* à;
(house, shop) chez.
athletic, *adj.* athlétique.
athletics, *s.* athlétisme *m.*
at-home, *s.* réception *f.*
atlas, *s.* atlas *m.*
atmosphere, *s.* atmos-
phère *f.*
atom, *s.* atome *m.*
atomic, *adj.* atomique; ~

bomb bombe *f.* atomi-
que; ~ *energy* énergie
f. atomique.
attach, *v.a.* attacher.
attaché, *s.* attaché *m.;*
~ *case* petite valise *f.*
attachment, *s.* attache-
ment *m.*
attack, *v.a.* attaquer; —

s. attaque *f.*
attain, *v.a.* atteindre.
attainment, *s.* réalisa-
tion *f.;* connaissances
f. pl.
attempt, *s.* tentative *f.;*
— *v.a.* tenter; entre-
prendre.
attend, *v.a.* suivre; *(look
after)* soigner; — *v.i.*
faire attention à; as-
sister.
attendance, *s.* présence *f.;*
(persons present) as-
sistance *f.*
attendant, *s.* serviteur *m.;*
employé *m.;* ouvreuse
f.
attention, *s.* attention *f.*
attitude, *s.* attitude *f.*
attorney, *s.* avoué *m.*
attract, *v.a.* attirer.
attraction, *s.* attraction *f.*
attractive, *adj.* attrayant.
attribute, *v.a.* attribuer.
auction, *s.* vente *f.*
audience, *s.* auditoire *m.*
audio-visual, *adj.* audiovisuel.
auditorium, *s.* salle *f.* (de
cours).
August, *s.* août *m.*
aunt, *s.* tante *f.*
Australian, *adj.* australien
— *s.* Australien, -ne *m.*
f.
Austrian, *adj.* autrichien;

— *s.* Autrichien, -enne
m. f.
authentic, *adj.* authen-
tique.
author, *s.* auteur *m.*
authority, *s.* autorité *f.*
authorize, *v.a.* autoriser·
automatic, *adj.* automa-
tique.
autonomy, *s.* autonomie
f.
autumn, *s.* automne *m.*
avail, *s. be of no* ~ ne
servir à rien; — *v.a.*

~ *oneself of* profiter
de.
available, *adj.* disponible;
sous la main.
avalanche, *s.* avalanche *f.*
avenge, *v.a.* venger.
avenue, *s.* avenue *f.*
average, *s.* moyenne *f.;*
— *adj.* moyen.
aversion, *s.* aversion *f.*
avoid, *v.a.* éviter.
await, *v.a.* attendre.
awake, *v. a.* éveiller; *v. n.*
s'éveiller; — *adj.* éveil-
lé.
awaken, *v.a.* éveiller.
award, *v.a.* accorder.
aware, *adj. be ~ of* avoir
conscience de, savoir
bien.
away, *adv.* (au) loin;
carry ~ enlever; *go ~*
partir.
awful, *adj.* terrible.
awhile, *adv.* pendant quelque temps, un moment.
awkward, *adj. (pers.)*
gauche;   maladroit;
(things) gênant, embar-
rassant.
axe, *s.* hache *f.*
axis, *s.* axe *m.*

axle, *s.* essieu *m.*

B

babble, *s.* babil *m.; —*
v.n. babiller.
baby, *s.* bébé *m.*
baby-sitter, *s.* garde-bébé
m.
bachelor, *s.* célibataire;
(arts) licencié *m.*
back, *s.* dos *m.; (hand)*
revers *m.; (football)*
arrière *m.;* — *adj.* de
derrière; arriéré; —
adv. en arrière; *be ~*
être de retour; — *v.a.*
soutenir,   seconder;
(bet) parier pour; *v.n.*

reculer.
background, *s.* fond *m.;*
arrière-plan *m.*
backstairs, *s. pl.* escalier
m. de service.
backward, *adj.* arriéré.
backwards, *adv.* en arrière; à reculons.
bacon, *s.* lard *m.*
bad, *adj.* mauvais.
badge, *s.* insigne *m.*
badger, *s.* blaireau *m.*
badly, *adv.* mal.
bag, *s.* sac *m.; (large)*
valise *f.*
baggage, *s.* bagage *m.*
bait, *s.* amorce *f.*
bake, *v.a.* cuire;   faire
cuire.
baker, *s.* boulanger *m.*
bakery, *s.* boulangerie *f.*
balance,   *s.   (weighing,*
account) balance *f.;*
(bank) solde *m.; (equi-*
librium) équilibre *m.;*
— *v.a.* balancer; *v.n.* se
balancer.
balcony, *s.* balcon *m.*
bald, *adj.* chauve; plat.
ball, *s. (games)* balle *f.*
ballon *m.; (bowl)* boule
f.; (dance) bal *m.*
ball-bearings, *s. pl.* roulement *m.* à billes.
ballet, *s.* ballet *m.*
balloon, *s.* ballon *m.*
ball(-point) pen, *s.* stylo
m. à bille.
bamboo, *s.* bambou *m.*
banana, *s.* banane *f.*
band, *s. (people)* troupe
f.; bande *f.;* orchestre
m.; (ribbon, tie) ruban
m.; lien *m.*
bandage, *s.* bandage *m.*
bandit, *s.* bandit *m.*
bang, *s.* coup *m.;* claquement *m.*
banish, *v.a.* bannir.
banister, rampe *f.*
bank[1], *s. (river)* rive *f.;*

(earth) talus *m.*

bank², *s.* banque *f.*

bank-holiday, *s.* (jour *m.* de) fête *f.* légale.

banknote, *s.* billet *m.* (de banque).

bankruptcy, *s.* banque-route *f.;* faillite *f.*

banner, *s.* bannière *f.*

banquet, *s.* banquet *m.*

baptism, *s.* baptême *m.*

baptize, *v.a.* baptiser.

bar, *s. (iron, tribunal, music)* barre *f.; (rail-way)* barrière *f.; (ob-stacle)* obstacle *m.; (lawyers)* barreau *m.; (counter place for drink)* comptoir *m.,* débit *m.* (de boissons), bar *m.*

barber, *s.* coiffeur *m.*

bare, *adj.* nu; *(mere)* seul.

barefoot, *adj.* nu-pieds.

barely, *adv.* à peine.

bargain, *s.* marché *m.;* — *v.n.* marchander.

bark, *s.* aboiement *m.;* — *v.n.* aboyer.

barley, *s.* orge *f.*

barmaid, *s.* demoiselle *f.* de comptoir, barmaid *f.*

barman, *s.* garçon *m.* de comptoir, barman *m.*

barn, *s.* grange *f.*

barometer, *s.* baromètre *m.*

baron, *s.* baron *m.*

baroness, *s.* baronne *f.*

barracks, *s. pl.* caserne *f.*

barrel, *s.* tonneau *m.*

barren, *adj.* stérile.

barrier, *s.* barrière *f.*

barrister, *s.* avocat *m.*

bartender *see* **barman.**

barter, *s.* échange *m.;* — *v.a.* échanger.

base, *s.* fondement *m.;* base *f.*

basement, *s.* sous-sol *m.*

bashful, *adj.* timide.

basic, *adj.* fondamental; basique.

basin, *s.* bassin *m.;* cu-vette *f.*

basis, *s.* base *f.*

basket, *s.* panier *m.*

basket-ball, *s.* basket-ball *m.*

bass, *s.* basse *f.*

bat¹, *s.* chauve-souris *f.*

bat², *s.* batte *f.*

bath, *s.* bain *m.; (tub)* baignoire *f.*

bathe, *v.n.* se baigner; *v.a.* baigner.

bathing-costume, *s.* cos-tume *m.* de bain(s).

bathroom, *s.* salle *f.* de bain.

battery, *s. (military)* bat-terie *f.; (electr.)* pile *f.*

battle, *s.* bataille *f.*

bay, *s.* baie *f.*

be, *v. n.* être; *(be situated)* se trouver; *there is* il y a.

beach, *s.* plage *f.*

bead, *s. (string of)* col-lier *m.*

beak, *s.* bec *m.*

beam, *s. (timber)* poutre *f.; (light)* rayon *m.*

bean, *s.* fève *f.*

bear¹, *s.* ours *m.*

bear², *v.a.* porter; soute-nir; supporter.

beard, *s.* barbe *f.*

bearing, *s.* rapport *m.*

beast, *s.* bête *f.*

beat, *v.a.* battre; frap-per; — *s.* battement *m.*

beautiful, *adj.* beau, bel, belle.

beauty, *s.* beauté *f.*

beaver, *s.* castor *m.*

because, *conj.* parce que; ~ *of* à cause de.

beckon, *v.n.* faire signe (à).

become, *v. n.* devenir.

bed, *s.* lit *m.*

bed-clothes, *s. pl.* couvertures *f. pl.*

bedroom, *s.* chambre *f.* à coucher.

bee, *s.* abeille *f.*

beech, *s.* hêtre *m.*

beef, *s.* bœuf *m.*

beef-steak, *s.* bifteck *m.*

beer, *s.* bière *f.*

beetle, *s.* scarabée *m.*

beetroot, *s.* betterave *f.*

before, *prep.(time)* avant; *(space)* devant; — *adv.* avant; *(in front)* en avant.

beforehand, *adv.* d'avance; en avance.

beg, *v.a.* demander, prier; *v. n.* mendier; *I ~ your pardon!* excusez-moi!; pardon!

beget, *v.a.* engendrer.

beggar, *s.* mendiant, -e.

begin, *v. a. & n.* commencer.

beginner, *s.* commençant, -e *m. f.*

beginning, *s.* commencement *m.*

behalf, *s. on ~ of* de la part de; *in ~ of* en faveur de.

behave, *v.n.* se conduire.

behaviour, *s.* conduite *f.*

behind, *prep.* derrière.

Belgian, *adj.* belge; — *s.* Belge *m. f.*

belief, *s.* croyance *f.*

believe, *v.a. & n.* croire.

bell, *s.* cloche *f.*

belly, *s.* ventre *m.*

belong, *v.n. ~ to* appartenir à.

belongings, *s. pl.* effets *m.;* biens *m.*

below, *adv.* au-dessous; en bas; — *prep.* au-dessous de.

belt, *s.* ceinture *f.*

bench, *s.* banc *m.; (working)* établi *m.*

bend, *v. a.* courber; tendre

fléchir; *v.n.* se courber; — *s.* courbure *f.; (road)* tournant *m.*

beneath *see* below.

benefit, *s.* bienfait *m.; (gain)* bénéfice *m.*

bent, *s.* penchant *m.*

berry, *s.* baie *f.; (coffee)* grain *m.*

berth, *s.* couchette *f.; (for ship)* mouillage *m.*

beseech, *v. a.* supplier.

beside, *prep.* auprès de, à côté de.

besides, *adv.* en outre.

best, *adj.* le meilleur; *do one's ~* faire tout son possible (pour).

bestow, *v. a.* conférer (à).

bet, *v.a.* parier.

betray, *v. a.* trahir.

better, *adj.* meilleur; *adv.* mieux.

between, *prep* entre.

beyond, *prep.* au delà de.

bias, *s.* biais *m.; (fig.)* préjugé *m.*

Bible, *s.* bible *f.*

bibliography, *s.* bibliographie *f.*

bicycle, *s.* bicyclette *f.*

big, *adj.* grand; gros.

bill, *s. (hotel)* note *f.; (restaurant)* addition *f.; (invoice)* facture *f.; (of exchange)* lettre *f.* de change; *(of fare)* carte *f.,* menu *m.; (poster)* affiche *f.;(parliament)* projet *m.* de loi.

bin, *s.* huche *f.,* coffre *m.*

bind, *v.a.* lier; *(book)* relier.

biological, *adj.* biologique.

biology, *f.* biologie *f.*

birch, *s.* bouleau *m.*

bird, *s.* oiseau *m.*

birth, *s.* naissance *f.*

birthday, *s.* anniversaire *m.*

birth-place, s. lieu m. de naissance.

biscuit, s. biscuit m.

bishop, s. évêque m.

bit[1], s. morceau m.; (drill) mèche f.; a ~ un peu (de).

bit[2], s. (horse) mors m.

bite, v. a. & n. mordre.

bitter, adj. amer; mordant; (cold) âpre.

bitterness, s. amertume f.

black, adj. noir.

blackbird, s. merle m.

blackmail, s. chantage m.

blacksmith, s. forgeron m.

bladder, s. vessie f.

blade, s. lame f.

blame, s. blâme m.; — v. a. blâmer, accuser qn.

blameless, adj. innocent.

blank, adj. blanc; nu; — s. blanc m.

blanket, s. couverture f.

blast, s. rafale f.; coup m. de vent; souffle m.; — v.a. faire sauter; détruire.

blaze, s. flamme f.; — v.n. flamber.

bleak, adj. lugubre.

bleed, v.a. & n. saigner.

blend, s. mélange m.; — v.a. fondre; mêler.

bless, v.a. bénir.

blessing, s. bénédiction f.

blind[1], adj. aveugle.

blind[2], s. store m.

blindness, s. cécité f.

blink, v. n. clignoter.

bliss, s. félicité f.

blister, s. ampoule f.

block, s. bloc m.; (wood) billot m.; (buildings) pâté m.; (traffic) encombrement m.

blond adj. blond.

blood, s. sang m.

bloody, adj. sanglant.

bloom, s. fleur f.; — v. n. fleurir.

blossom, s. fleur f.

blot, s. tache f.; pâté m.

blouse, s. blouse f.

blow[1], v. a. (trumpet) sonner; (glass) souffler; ~ out éteindre; ~ up faire sauter; v.n. (wind) souffler.

blow[2], s. coup m.

blue, adj. bleu.

blunder, s. bévue f.; — v. n. faire une bévue

blunt, adj. émoussé; (person) brusque.

blush, v.n. rougir.

board, s. planche f.; (meals) pension f.; (council) conseil m.; (paper) carton m.; (theatre) ~s planches; ~ and lodging pension f. et chambre(s); on ~ (ship) à bord d'un navire; — v.n. prendre pension chez; v.a. monter à bord de.

boarder, s. pensionnaire m. f.

boarding-house, s. pension f.

boarding-school, s. pensionnat m.

boast, s. vanterie f.; — v. n. se vanter (de).

boat, s. bateau m.

body, s. corps m.

bog, s. marécage m.

boil[1], v.a. faire bouillir; (cook) faire cuire; v. n. bouillir.

boil[2], s. furoncle m.

boiler, s. chaudière f.

bold, adj. hardi; effronté.

boldness, s. hardiesse f.; effronterie f.

bolt, s. verrou m.; — v. a. verrouiller; v. n. filer.

bomb, s. bombe f.

bond, s. lien m.

bone, s. os m.; (fish)

arête *f.*

bonnet, *s.* chapeau *m.;* bonnet *m.;* *(motor)* capot *m.*

bony, *adj.* osseux; maigre.

book, *s.* livre *m.;* – *v.a* prendre (un billet); retenir.

bockcase, *s.* bibliothèque *f.*

booking-office, *s.* guichet *m.*

book-keeper, *s.* teneur *m.* de livres.

book-keeping, *s.* compatibilité *f.*

booklet, *s.* livret *m.*

bookseller, *s.* libraire *m.*

bookshelf, *s.* rayon *m.*

bookshop, *s.* librairie *f.*

book-stall, *s.* bibliothèque (de gare) *f.*

boot, *s.* bottine *f.;* brodequin *m.*

booth, *s.* baraque *f.*

booty, *s.* butin *m.*

border, *s.* bord *m.;* frontiere *f.*

bore, *v. a.* ennuyer, raser; –*s.* raseur *m.*

boring, *adj.* ennuyeux, assommant.

born, *pp.* né; *be* ~ naître.

borrow, *v. a.* emprunter.

bosom, *s.* sein *m.*

boss, *s.* patron *m.*

botanical, *adj.* botanique.

botany, *s.* botanique *m.*

both, *pron. & adj.* l'un(e) et l'autre; tous (les) deux; ~ ... *and* et ... et ...

bother, *v.a.* tracasser.

bottle, *s.* bouteille *f.*

bottom, *s.* bas *m.;* fond *m.;* derrière *m.*

bough, *s.* rameau *m.*

bound, *pp.* ~ *for* à destination de, en route pour.

boundary, *s.* borne *f.*

bounty, *s.* générosité *f.*

bouquet, *s.* bouquet *m.*

bow[1], *s.* arc *m.;* *(violin)* archet *m.;* *(knot)* nœud *m.*

bow[2], *v.a.* incliner; courber; *v.n.* s'incliner; se courber; – *s.* salut *m.;* *(ship)* avant *m.*

bowels, *s. pl.* entrailles *f.*

bowl, *s.* bol *m.,* jatte *f.*

box, *s.* boîte *f.,* caisse *f.;* *(horse)* stalle *f.;* *(theatre)* loge *f.;* *(on the ears)* soufflet *m.;* – *v. n.* boxer.

box-office, *s.* bureau *m.* de location.

boy, *s.* garçon *m.;* ~ *scout* boy-scout *m.,* éclaireur *m.*

bra, *s.* soutien-gorge *m.*

brace, *s.* couple *f.;* lien *m.;* ~s bretelles *f. pl.*

bracelet, *s.* bracelet *m.*

brain, *s.* cerveau *m.;* ~s cervelle *f.*

brainy, *adv.* intelligent.

brake, *s.* frein *m.*

branch, *s.* branche *f.*

brand, *s.* tison *m.;* marque *f.;* – *v.a.* marquer.

brandy, *s.* cognac *m.*

brass, *s.* cuivre jaune *m.*

brave, *adj.* brave.

brawl, *s.* querelle *f.*

bread, *s.* pain *m.*

breadth, *s.* largeur *f.*

break, *v.a.* briser, casser; *(law)* violer; *(promise)* manquer; *(news)* apprendre à; *v. n.* se casser; se briser; ~ *down* abattre; s'effondrer; *(motor)* avoir une panne; ~ *in* dresser; ~ *up* lever; – *s.* interruption *f.;* pause *f.*

break-down, *s.* *(motor)* panne *f.;* *(health)* débâcle; ~ *lorry* dépanneuse *f*.

breakfast, *s*. déjeuner *m*.

breast, *s*. poitrine *f*., sein *m*.

breath, *s*. haleine *f*.; souffle *m*.

breathe, *v.a.* & *n*. respirer.

breathless, *adj*. essoufflé; sans souffle.

breeches, *s. pl*. culotte *f*.

breed, *s*. race *f*.; — *v.a.* élever.

breeze, *s*. brise *f*.

breezy, *adj*. venteux.

brew, *v.a.* brasser.

bribe, *s*. pot-de-vin *m*.; — *v.a.* corrompre.

brick, *s*. brique *f*.

bricklayer, *s*. maçon *m*.

bride, *s*. mariée *f*.

bridegroom, *s*. marié *m*.

bridge, *s*. pont *m*.

bridle, *s*. bride *f*.

brief, *adj*. bref.

briefcase, *s*. serviette *f*.

briefly, *adv*. brièvement.

briefs, *s. pl*. slip *m*.

bright, *adj*. brillant; vif; clair; éclatant.

brighten, *v.a.* faire briller; égayer.

brightness, *s*. éclat *m*.

brilliant, *s*. brillant *m*.

brim, *s*. bord *m*.

bring, *v.a.* amener; apporter; ~ *about* amener; ~ *back* rapporter; ~ *forth* produire; ~ *up* élever.

brink, *s*. bord *m*.

brisk, *adj*. vif; actif.

bristle, *s*. *(brush)* poil *m*.

British, *adj*. britannique.

brittle, *adj*. cassant.

broad, *adj*. large; vaste.

broadcast, *v.a.* radiodiffuser.

broadcasting, *s*. radiodiffusion *f*.

broken, *adj*. brisé.

bronze, *s*. bronze *m*.

brooch, *s*. broche *f*.

brood, *s*. couvée *f*.; — *v.n.* couver.

brook, *s*. ruisseau *m*.

broom, *s*. balai *m*.

brother, *s*. frère *m*.

brother-in-law, *s*. beau-frère *m*.

brow, *s*. sourcil *m*.

brown, *adj*. brun.

bruise, *s*. contusion *f*.; — *v.a.* meurtrir.

brush, *s*. brosse *f*.; pinceau *m*.; balai *m*.; — *v.a.* brosser; ~ *up* donner un coup de brosse à.

brutal, *adj*. brutal, q

brutality, *s*. brutalit

bubble, *s*. bulle *f*.; — bouillonner.

buck, *s*. daim *m*.

bucket, *s*. seau *m*.

buckle, *s*. boucle *f*.

bud, *s*. bourgeon *m*.

budget, *s*. budget *m*.

buffet, *s*. soufflet *m*.

bug, *s*. punaise *f*.

build, *v.a.* bâtir; construire; sur; ~ *up* établir.

builder, *s*. entrepreneur *m*. de bâtiments; constructeur *m*.

building, *s*. bâtiment *m*.

bulb, *s*. bulbe *m*.; *(lamp)* ampoule *f*.

bulge, *v.n.* bomber.

bulk, *s*. masse *f*.; volume *m*.

bull, *s*. taureau *m*.

bullet, *s*. balle *f*.

bulletin, *s*. bulletin *m*.

bump, *s*. bosse *f*.; collision *f*.; coup *m*.

bumper, *s*. pare-choc *m*.

bun, *s*. brioche *f*.

bunch, *s*. bouquet *m*.; botte *f*.; grappe *f*.

bundle, *s*. botte *f*.; paquet

m.; fagot *m.*

bunk, *s.* couchette *f.*

buoy, *s.* bouée *f.*

burden, *s.* charge *f.;* far-deau *m.*

burglar, *s.* cambrioleur *m.*

burial, *s.* enterrement *m.*

burn, *v.a. & n.* brûler.

bursary, *s.* bourse *f.*

burst, *v.n.* éclater; crever; exploser; *v.a.* faire éclater; rompre; crever; — *s.* éclat *m.;* explosion *f.*

bury, *v.a.* enterrer.

bus, *s.* autobus *m.*

bush, *s.* buisson *m.*

business, *s.* affaires *f. pl.;* profession *f.;* on ~ pour affaires; ~ *hours* heures *(f. pl.)* d'ouverture.

businessman, *s.* homme *m.* d'affaires.

bus-stop, *s.* arrêt *m.* d'autobus.

busy, *adj.* occupé, affairé.

but, *conj.* mais.

butcher, *s.* boucher *m.;* ~'*s (shop)* boucherie *f.*

butter, *s.* beurre *m.*

butterfly, *s.* papillon *m.*

buttock, *s.* fesse *f.,* derrière *m.*

button, *s.* bouton *m.*

buy, *v.a.* acheter.

buyer, *s.* acheteur *m.*

by, *prep.* par; *de;* ~ *Monday* d'ici à lundi.

bystander, *s.* spectateur, -trice *m. f.*

C

cab, *s.* taxi *m.;* fiacre *m.*

cabbage, *s.* chou *m.*

cabin, *s.* cabane *f.; (ship)* cabine *f.*

cabinet, *s. (politics)* cabinet *m.*

cable, *s.* câble *m.*

cablegram. *s.* câblo-gramme *m.*

café, *s.* café(-restaurant) *m.*

cage, *s.* cage *f.*

cake, *s.* gâteau *m.*

calculate, *v.a.&n.* calculer.

calculation, *s.* calcul *m.*

calendar, *s.* calendrier *m.*

calf, *s.* veau *m.; (leg)* mollet *m.*

call, *v. a. & n.* appeler; ~ *for,* réclamer; ~ *on* faire visite à; — *s.* appel *m.;* cri *m.; (visit)* visite *f.*

call-box, *s.* cabine *f.* téléphonique.

calm, *adj.* calme.

calorie, *s.* calorie *f.*

camel, *s.* chameau, -elle *m. f.*

camera, *s.* appareil *m.* (photographique).

camp, *s.* camp *m.*

campaign, *s.* campagne *f.*

camping, *s.* camping *m.*

can[1], *s.* broc *m.;* pot *m.*

can[2], *v. aux.* pouvoir; savoir.

canal, *s.* canal *m.*

canary, *s.* canari *m.*

cancel, *v.a.* annuler.

cancer, *s.* cancer *m.*

candle, *s.* chandelle *f.;* bougie *f.*

cannon, *s.* canon *m.*

canoe, e *s.* canoë *m.*

canteen, *s.* cantine *f.*

canvas, *s.* toile *f.*

cap, *s.* bonnet *m.;* casquette *f.*

capable, *adj.* capable (de).

capacity, *s.* capacité *f.*

cape, *s. (land)* cap *m.; (cloak)* pèlerine *f.;* cape *f.*

capital, *s. (city)* capitale *f.; (letter)* majuscule *f.* *(commerce)* capital *m;*

capsule, *s.* capsule *f.*

captain, *s.* capitaine *m.*

caption, *s.* sous-titre *m.*

captivate, *v.a.* captiver.

capture, *v.a.* capturer; — *s.* capture *f.*

car, *s.* voiture *f.*, auto *f.*

caravan, *s.* roulotte *f.* (de camping), caravane *f.*

carbon-paper, *s.* papier *m.* carbone.

carburetter, *s.* carburateur *m.*

card, *s.* carte *f.*

cardboard, *s.* carton *m.*

cardinal, *adj. m.* cardinal *m.*

care, *s.* attention *f.;* soin *m.; souci m.; ~ of aux* bons soins de; *take ~ of* prendre soin de; — *v.n. ~ for* se soucier de; *~ to* aimer.

career, *s.* carrière *f.*

careful, *adj.* soigneux.

careless, *adj.* insouciant, négligent.

caress, *v.a.* caresser.

cargo, *s.* cargaison *f.*

caricature, *s.* caricature *f.*

carnation, *s.* œillet *m.*

carpenter, *s.* charpentier *m.*

carpet, *s.* tapis *m.*

carriage, *s.* voiture *f.;* (transport) transport *m.*

carriage-way, *s.* chaussée *f.*

carrier, *s.* voiturier *m.*

carrot, *s.* carotte *f.*

carry, *v.a.* porter; transporter; *~ on* exercer; *~ out* mettre à exécution.

cart, *s.* charrette *f.*

cartridge, *s.* cartouche *f.*

carve, *v. a.& n.* sculpter; (meat) découper.

case, *s.* (box) étui *m.*, caisse *f.; (instance)* cas *m.; cause f.*

casement, *s.* croisée *f.*

cash, *s.* espèces *f. pl.*

cash-book, *s.* livre *m.* de caisse.

cashier, *s.* caissier, -ère *m. f.*

cash-register, *s.* caisse *f.* enregistreuse.

cask, *s.* tonneau *m.*

cast, *v.a.* jeter; (metal) fondre; — *s.* coup *m.; (theatre)* distribution *f.*

castle, *s.* château *m.*

casual, *adj.* casuel.

casualty, *s.* accident *m.*

cat, *s.* chat, -te *m. f.*

catalogue, *s.* catalogue *m.*

catastrophe, *s.* catastrophe *f.*

catch, *v.a.* saisir; attraper; (eye) frapper; *~ up* rattraper; — *s.* prise *f.;* attrape *f.*

category, *s.* catégorie *f.*

cater, *v.n.* pourvoir à.

caterpillar, *s.* chenille *f.*

cathedral, *s.* cathédrale *f.*

catholic, *adj.* catholique.

catholicism, *s.* catholicisme *m.*

cattle, *s.* bétail *m.* (pl. bestiaux).

cauliflower, *s.* chou-fleur *m.*

cause, *s.* cause *f.;* motif *m.; — v.a.* causer.

caution, *s.* prudence *f.*

cautious, *adj.* prudent.

cave, *s.* caverne *f.*

cavity, *s.* cavité *f.*

cease, *v.a. & n.* cesser.

ceiling, *s.* plafond *m.*

celebrate, *v.a.* célébrer.

celebration, *s.* célébration *f.;* commémoration *f.*

celery, *s.* céleri *m.*

cell, *s.* cellule *f.*

cellar, *s.* cave *f.*

cello, *s.* violoncelle *m.*

cellophane, *s.* cellophane

f.

cement, *s.* ciment *m.;*
— *v.a.* cimenter.

cemetery, *s.* cimetière *m.*

centenary, *s.* centenaire
m.

central, *adj.* central.

centre, *s.* centre *m.*

century, *s.* siècle *m.*

cereal, *s.* céréale *f.*

ceremony, *s.* cérémonie *f.*

certain, *adj.* certain.

certainly, *adj.* certainement; sans doute

certainty, *s.* certitude *f.*

certificate, *s.* certificat *m.*

certify, *v.a.* certifier.

chain, *s.* chaîne *f.*

chair, *s.* chaise *f.; (pro-
fessorship)* chaire *f.;
take the* ~ présider.

chairman, *s.* président *m.*

chalk, *s.* craie *f.*

challenge, *s.* défi *m.;*
— *v.a.* défier; pro-
voquer.

chamber, *s.* chambre *f.;*
~*s* étude *f.;* apparte-
ment *m.*

champagne, *s.* champagne
m.

champion, *s.* champion *m.*

championship, *s.* cham-
pionnat *m.*

chance, *s.* chance *f.;*
bv ~ par hasard.

chancellor, *s.* chancelier
m.

chancery, *s.* chancelle-
rie *f.*

change, *s.* changement
m.; (money) monnaie *f.;*
— *v.a.&n.* changer.

channel, *s.* canal *m.;
m.; the English Chan-
nel* la Manche.

chap, *s.* type *m.*

chapel, *s.* chapelle *f.*

chaplain, *s.* chapelain *m.*

chapter, *s.* chapitre *m.*

character *s.* caractère *m.;*
(theatre) personnage

m.

characteristic, *adj.* caractéristique; — *s.* trait
m. caractéristique.

charcoal, *s.* charbon *m.*
de bois

charge, *s.* charge *f.;*
(price) prix *m.; (ac-
cusation)* accusation *f.;*
— *v.a.* charger (de);
(price) demander; fai-
re payer; *(accuse)* ac-
cuser (de).

charity, *s.* charité *f.*

charm, *s.* charme *m.*

charming, *adj.* charmant.

chart, *s.* carte *f.* marine.

charter, *s.* charte *f.*

charwoman, *s.* femme *f.*
de ménage.

chase, *v.a.* chasser; poursuivre; — *s.* chasse *f.*

chassis, *s.* châssis *m.*

chat, *s.* causette *f.; —
v. n.* causer.

chatter, *v.n.* babiller;
(teeth) claquer.

cheap, *adj.* bon marché.

cheat, *v.a.* tromper; tricher; — *s.* tromperie
f.; tricherie; *(pers.)*
fourbe *m.*

check, *v.a.* contrôler,
vérifier; *(stop)* arrê-
ter; — *s.* vérifica-
tion *f.,* contrôle *m.*

checkmate, *s.* échec et
mat *m.*

check-up, *s.* examen *m.*
médical.

cheek, *s.* joue *f.*

cheeky, *adj.* impertinent.

cheer, *v.a.* réjouir,
encourager; accla-
mer; *v.n.* ~ up re-
prendre sa gaieté; cou-
rage!; — *s.* joie *f.;* ~*s*
acclamations *f.*

cheerful, *adj.* joyeux.

cheese, *s.* fromage *m.*

chemical, *adj.* chimique.

chemist, *s.* chimiste *m.;*

pharmacien *m.;* ~'s *(shop)* pharmacie *f.*

chemistry, *s.* chimie *f.*

cheque, *s.* chèque *m.; traveller's* ~ chèque *m.* de voyage.

cheque-book, *s.* carnet *m.* de chèques.

cherish, *v. a.* soigner; *(hope)* caresser.

cherry, *s.* cerise *f.*

chess, *s.* échecs *m. pl.*

chess-board, *s.* échiquier *m.*

chest, *s.* coffre *m.; (part of body)* poitrine *f.;* ~ *of drawers* commode *f.*

chestnut, *s.* châtaigne *f.*

chew, *v.a.* mâcher.

chicken, *s.* poulet *m.*

chief, *adj.* principal; — *s.* chef *m.*

chiefly, *adv.* principalement.

child, *s.* enfant *m.f.*

childhood, *s.* enfance *f.*

childish, *adj.* enfantin.

childless, *adj.* sans enfant.

chill, *s.* coup *m.* de froid; — *v.a.* refroidir, glacer.

chilly, *adj. (weather)* frais; (un peu) froid.

chimney, *s.* cheminée *f.*

chin, *s.* menton *m.*

china, *s.* porcelaine *f.*

Chinese, *adj.* chinois; — *s.* Chinois, -e.

chip, *s.* éclat *m.;* copeau *m.;* ~s frites *f. pl.*

chirp, *v.n.* gazouiller.

chisel, *s.* ciseau *m.;* — *v.a.* ciseler.

chivalry, *s.* chevalerie *f.*

chocolate, *s.* chocolat *m.*

choice, *s.* choix *m.*

choir, *s.* chœur *m.*

choke, *v.a. & n.* étouffer.

choose, *v.a.* choisir.

chop, *s.* côtelette *f.*

chorus, *s.* chœur *m.*

Christian, *adj.* chrétien; ~ *name* prénom *m.*

Christianity, *s.* christianisme *m.*

Christmas, *s.* Noël *m.;* ~ *eve* veille *f.* de Noël.

chuckle, *v.n.* rire tout bas; — *s.* rire étouffé.

church, *s.* église *f.*

churchyard, *s.* cimetière *m.*

cider, *s.* cidre *m.*

cigar, *s.* cigare *m.*

cigarette, *s.* cigarette *f.*

cigarette-case, *s.* étui *m.* à cigarettes.

cigarette-holder, *s.* porte-cigarette *m.*

cinders, *s.pl.* cendres *f.*

cine-camera, *s.* camera *f.*

cinema, *s.* cinéma *m.*

cinerama, *s.* cinérama *m.*

circle, *s.* cercle *m.*

circuit, *s.* circuit *m.;* détour *m.;* tournée *f.*

circular, *adj.* circulaire.

circulate, *v.n.* circuler; *v.a.* faire circuler.

circulation, *s.* circulation *f.*

circumstance, *s.* circonstance *f.*

circus, *s.* cirque *m.*

cistern, *s.* citerne *f.*

citation, *s.* citation *f.*

cite, *v. a.* citer.

citizen, *s.* citoyen, -ne *m. f.,* habitant *m.*

citizenship, *s.* droit *m.* de cité.

city, *s.* ville *f.; the City* Cité *f.*

civil, *adj.* civil; *(polite)* poli; ~ *servant* fonctionnaire *m.*

civilization, *s.* civilisation *f.*

civilize, *v.a.* civiliser.

claim, *s.* demande *f.,* réclamation *f.;* droit *m.;* — *v.a.* revendiquer, réclamer.

clamp, *s.* crampon *m.*

clang, *s.* bruit *m.* métallique; — *v.n.* retentir.

clap, *s.* battement *m.;* applaudissements *m. pl.;* — *v.n.* applaudir.

clash, *v.a.* choquer; *v.n.* s'entre-choquer.

clasp, *s.* agrafe *f.;* fermoir *m.;* — *v.a.* agrafer; joindre.

class, *s.* classe *f.*

classic(al), *adj.* classique.

classify, *v.a.* classifier.

class-room, *s.* classe *f.*

clatter, *s.* bruit *m.;* fracas *m.;* — *v.n.* faire du bruit.

clause, *s.* clause *f.*, article *m.*

claw, *s.* griffe *f.;* serre *f.;* ongle *m.*

clay, *s.* glaise *f.;* argile *f.*

clean, *adj.* propre; blanc; pur; — *v.a.* nettoyer.

cleanse, *v.a.* nettoyer.

clear, *adj.* clair; — *v.a.* déblayer; éclaircir; *v.n.* s'éclaircir; ∼ *away* enlever; ∼ *out* filer.

clearly, *adv.* clair, clairement; évidemment.

cleave, *v.a.* fendre; *v.n.* se fendre.

clergy, *s.* clergé *m.*

clergyman, *s.* ministre *m.*

clerk, *s.* employé *m.,* commis *m.*

clever, *adj.* habile, adroit; intelligent.

client, *s.* client *m.*

cliff, *s.* falaise *f.*

climate, *s.* climat *m.*

climb, *v.a. & n.* grimper.

cling, *v.n.* ∼ *to* se cramponner à.

clinic, *s.* clinique *f.*

clip, *s.* pince; — *v.a.* tondre; couper; rogner; *(tickets)* poinconner.

cloak, *s.* manteau *m.*

cloak-room, *s.* consigne *f.;* vestiaire *m.*

clock, *s.* horloge *f.;* pendule *f.; it is 10 o'clock* il est dix heures.

close, *v.a. (shut)* fermer; *(end)* terminer; *v.n.* (se) fermer; se terminer; — *adj.* fermé; *(narrow)* étroit; *(relations)* proche; intime; — *adv.* tout près; — *s.* enclos *m.; (end)* fin *f.*

closely, *adv.* de près; étroitement.

closet, *s.* cabinet *m.;* armoire *f.*

cloth, *s.* drap *m.; (table)* nappe *f.*

clothe, *v.a.* vêtir.

clothes, *s.pl.* habits *m.pl.*

clothing, *s.* vêtements *m. pl.*

cloud, *s.* nuage *m.*

cloudy, *adj.* couvert.

clover, *s.* trèfle *m.*

club, *s. (stick)* massue *f.; (people)* cercle *m.,* club *m.,* société *f.; (cards)* trèfle *m.*

clue, *s.* fil *m.; (crossword)* définition *f.*

clumsy, *adj.* gauche.

cluster, *s.* grappe *f.*

clutch, *v.a.* empoigner; *m.* pour empoigner; *(motor)* embrayage *m.*

coach, *s.* voiture *f.;* wagon *m.;* autocar *m.; (sports)* entraîneur *m.*

coal, *s.* charbon *m.*

coal-mine, *s.* mine *f.* de houille.

coarse, *adj.* grossier; vulgaire.

coast, s. côte f.

coat, s. (jacket) veston m.; (top) pardessus m., manteau m.

cock, s. coq m., mâle m.; (gun) chien m.; (tap) robinet m.

cocktail, s. cocktail m.

cocoa, s. cacao m.

cod, s. morue f.

code, s. code m.

coffee, s. café m.

coffee-pot, s. cafetière f.

coffin, s. cercueil m.

cog-wheel, s. roue f. dentée.

coil, s. rouleau m.; bobine f.; — v.a. lover; enrouler.

coin, s. pièce f.

coincidence, s. coïncidence f.

coke, s. coke m.

cold, adj. froid; be ~ (pers.) avoir froid; (weather) faire froid; — s. froid m.; (in the head) rhume m.; catch a ~ s'enrhumer.

collaborate, v. n. collaborer.

collaborator, s. collaborateur, -trice m.f.

collapse, v.n. s'effondrer; (pers.) s'affaisser; — s. effondrement m.; (pers.) affaissement m. subit.

collar, s. col m.; collet m.

colleague, s. collègue m. f.

collect, v.a. rassembler; recueillir.

collection, s. collection f.; collecte f.; (mail) levée f.

college, s. collège m.

collide, v.n. se heurter (contre), entrer en collision.

colliery, s. houillère f.; mine f.

collision, s. collision f.

colon, s. deux points m. pl.

colonel, s. colonel m.

colony, s. colonie f.

colour, s. couleur f.

colourful, adj. coloré.

colourless, adj. terne, pâle.

column, s. colonne f.

comb, s. peigne m.; — v.a. peigner.

combat, s. combat m.

combination, s. combinaison f.

combine, v.a. combiner.

come, v.n. venir, arriver; ~ across rencontrer; ~ back revenir; ~ by obtenir; passer; ~ down descendre; ~ in entrer; ~ off avoir lieu; se détacher; ~ out sortir; ~ up monter.

comedian, s. comédien m.

comedy, s. comédie f.

comely, adj. avenant, bienséant.

comfort, s. consolation f.; bien-être m.; — v.a. consoler.

comfortable, adj. confortable; commode; be ~ être à l'aise.

comic, adj. comique.

comma, s. virgule f.

command, s. ordre m.; — v.a. commander.

commander, s. commandant m.

commandment, s. commandement m.

commemorate, v.a. commémorer.

commence, v.a.& n. commencer.

commend, v.a. recommander; louer.

comment, s. commentaire *m.;* — *v.n.* commenter.

commentary, *s.* commentaire *m.*

commerce, *s.* commerce *m.*

commercial, *adj.* commercial; ~ *traveller* voyageur *m.* de commerce.

commission, *s.* commission *f.;* commande *f.*

commissioner, *s.* commissaire *m.*

commit, *v.a.* commettre; confier; ~ *oneself* se compromettre.

commitment, *s.* engagement *m.*

committee, *s.* comité *m.*

commodity, *s.* marchandise *f.,* article *m.*

common, *adj.* commun.

commonwealth, *s.* the British Commonwealth commonwealth *m.*

communicate, *v. a. & n.* communiquer.

communication, *s.* communication *f.*

communication-cord, *s.* signal *m.* d'alarme.

communion, *s.* communion *f.*

communiqué, *s.* communiqué *m.*

community, *s.* communauté *f.*

compact, *s.* pacte *m.;* poudrier *m.;* — *adj.* compact; concis.

companion, *s.* compagnon, -agne *m. f.*

company, *s.* compagnie *f.;* société *f.*

comparatively, *adv.* comparativement.

compare, *v.a.* comparer

(to à, *with* avec).

comparison, *s.* comparaison *f.*

compartment, *s.* compartiment *m.*

compass, *s. (mariner's)* boussole *f.; (pair of)* ~*es* compas *m.*

compassion, *s.* compassion *f.*

compel, *v.a.* forcer.

compete, *v.n.* faire concurrence (à); concourir.

competence, *s.* compétence *f.;* capacité *f.*

competent, *adj.* capable.

competition, *s.* concurrence *f.;* concours *m.;* compétition *f.*

competitor, *s.* concurrent *m.*

compilation, *s.* compilation *f.*

compile, *v.a.* compiler.

complain, *v.n.* se plaindre

complaint, *s.* plainte *f.;* maladie *f.;* réclamation *f.*

complement, *s.* complément *m.*

complete, *v.a.* compléter, achever; — *adj.* complet.

complicated, *adj.* compliqué.

complication, *s.* complication *f.*

compliment, *s.* compliment *m.*

comply, *v.n.* ~ *with* se conformer à.

component, *adj. & s.* composant *(m.).*

compose, *v.a.* composer; *be* ~*d of* se composer de.

composer, *s.* compositeur *m.*

composition, *s.* composition *f.;* dissertation *f.*

compound, *s. & adj.* composé *(m.);* — *v.a.* composer.

comprehend, *v.a.* comprendre.

comprehension, *s.* compréhension *f.*

compress, *v.a.* comprimer.

compromise, *s.* compromis *m.; —* *v.a.* compromettre.

compulsory, *adj.* obligatoire.

compute, *v.a.* calculer, computer.

computer, *s.* calculateur *m.* (électronique).

comrade, *s.* camarade *m.*

conceal, *v. a.* cacher.

conceit, *s.* vanité *f.*

conceive, *v.a.* concevoir.

concept, *s.* concept *m.*

concern, *v.a.* concerner; regarder; *be* ~*ed (in, with)* s'intéresser (à); *(about)* s'inquiéter (de); *— s.* affaire *f.;* entreprise *f.;* anxiété *f.*

concerning, *prep.* concernant.

concert, *a.* concert *m.*

concession, *s.* concession *f.*

conciliation, *s.* réconciliation *f.*

concise, *adj.* concis.

conclude, *v.a. &n.* conclure.

conclusion, *s.* conclusion *f.; in* ~ pour conclure.

concrete, *s.* béton *m.; — adj.* concret.

condemn, *v.a.* condamner.

condense, *v.a.* condenser.

condition, *s.* condition *f.;* état *m.; on* ~ *that* à condition que.

conduct, *s.* conduite *f.; — v. a.* conduire; diriger.

conductor, *s.* receveur *m.;* chef *m.* d'orchestre.

cone, *s.* cône *m.*

confederacy, *s.* confédération *f.*

confer, *v.a. & n.* conférer.

conference, *s.* conférence *f.*

confess, *v.a.* avouer; confesser.

confession, *s.* confession *f.*

confidence, *s.* confiance *f.*

confident, *adj.* confiant.

confidential, *adj.* confidentiel.

confine, *v.a.* confiner, enfermer; *be* ~*d to bed* être alité.

confirm, *v. a.* confirmer.

confirmation, *s.* confirmation *f.*

conflict, *s.* conflit *m.*

confound, *v. a.* confondre.

confront, *v.a.* être en face; confronter.

confuse, *v.a.* brouiller, mettre en désordre.

confusion, *s.* confusion *f.*

congratulate, *v.a.* féliciter (de).

congratulation, *s.* félicitations *f. pl.*

congregation, *s.* assemblée *f.,* congrégation *f.*

congress, *s.* congrès *m.*

conjunction, *s.* conjonction *f.*

connect, *v.a.* joindre, lier; associer.

connection, *s.* connexion *f.;* rapport *m.; (railw.)* correspondance *f.*

conquer, *v.a.* vaincre; conquérir.

conqueror, *s.* vainqueur *m.;* conquérant *m.*

conscience, *s.* conscience *f.*

conscious *adj.* *be* ~ (= *not fainting)* avoir connaissance; *be* ~ *of* avoir la conscience de.

consciousness, *s.* connaissance *f.;* conscience *f.*

conscript, *adj. & s.* conscrit *(m.).*

consent, *s.* consentement; *— v.n.* consentir.

consequence, *s.* consé-
quence *f.*

consequent, *adj.* consé-
quent.

consequently, *adv.* par
conséquent.

conservation, *s.* conservation *f.*

consider, *v.a.* considérer.

considerable, *adj.* considérable.

considerate, *adj.* attentif; réfléchi.

consideration, *s.* considération *f.; (money)*
rémunération *f.*

consign, *v.a.* livrer; consigner, expédier.

consignment, *s.* expédi-
tion *f.;* envoi *m.*

consist, *v. n.* ~ *of* se composer de, consister en.

consistent, *adj.* consé-
quent.

consolation, *s.* consolation *f.*

consonant, *s.* consonne *f.*

conspicuous, *adj.* en vue;
frappant.

conspiracy, *s.* conspiration *f.*

conspire, *v. a. & n.* conspirer.

constable, *s.* agent *m.*
(de police).

constant, *adj.* continuel;
constant.

constipation, *s.* constipation *f.*

constitute, *v.a.* constituer.

constitution, *s.* constitution *f.*

constrain, *v.a.* contraindre (à).

constraint, *s.* contrainte *f.*

construct, *v. a.* construire.

construction, *s.* construction *f.*

consul, *s.* consul *m.*

consulate, *s.* consulat *m.*

consult, *v.a. & n.* con-
sulter.

consultation, *s.* consultation *f.;* ~ *room* cabi-
net *m.* (de consultation).

consume, *v.a. (destroy)*
consumer; *(use up)* con-
sommer.

consumer, *s.* consomma-
teur, -trice *m.f.;* ~
goods articles *m.* de
grande consommation.

consumption, *s.* consom-
mation *f.; (disease)*
phtisie *f.*, tuberculose *f.*

contact, *s.* contact *m.;*
— *v.a.* entrer en rela-
tions avec.

contain, *v.a.* contenir.

container, *s.* récipient *m.*

contemplate, *v.a.* con-
templer; projeter.

contemplation, *s.* con-
templation *f.*

contemporary, *adj. & s.*
contemporain *(m.).*

contempt, *s.* mépris *m.*

contemptuous, *adj.* mé-
prisant.

contend, *v.n.* lutter contre (pour).

content, *s.* contentement
m.; ~*s* contenu *m.; table
of* ~*s* table *f.* des matières; — *adj.* content.

contest, *s.* lutte *f.; (sport)*
rencontre *f.*, match *m.;*
(dispute) contestation
f.; — *v. a.* contester.

continent, *s.* continent *m.*

continental, *adj.* continental.

continual, *adj.* continuel.

continuation, *s.* conti-
nuation *f.;* suite *f.*

continue, *v.a. & n.* continuer.

continuous, *adj.* continu.

contract, *s.* contrat *m.;*
— *v.a.* contracter.

contractor, *s.* entrepreneur *m.*

contradiction, *s.* contradiction *f.*

contrary, *adj.* contraire; — *adv.* contrairement.

contrast, *s.* contraste *m.;* — *v.a.* mettre en contraste.

contribute, *v. a. & n.* contribuer.

contribution, *s.* contribution *f.;* article *m.*

contributor, *s.* contribuant *m.;* collaborateur *m.*

contrive, *v.a.* inventer.

control, *s.* autorité *f.;* maîtrise *f.;* direction *f.,* commande *f.;* — *v.a.* gouverner, commander, maîtriser, diriger; contrôler.

controversy, *s.* polémique *f.,* controverse *f.*

convenience, *s.* commodité *f.,* convenance *f.;* *public* ~ cabinets *m. pl.* d'aisances.

convenient, *adj.* commode; *be* ~ *to s.o.* convenir à qn.

conversation, *s.* conversation *f.*

converse, *v.n.* converser; causer.

convert, *v.a.* convertir.

convey, *v.a.* transporter; transmettre; présenter.

conveyance, *s.* transport *m.;* voiture *f.,* véhicule *m.*

conveyer, *s.* porteur *m.;* ~ *belt* bande *f.* transporteuse.

convict, *s.* forçat *m.;* — *v.a.* convaincre (de), condamner.

convince, *v. a.* convaincre (de).

convoy, *s.* convoi *m.*

cook, *s.* cuisinier, -ière *m. f.;* *head* ~ chef *m.;*

— *v.a.* faire cuire; *v.n.* cuire.

cooking, *s.* cuisine *f.*

cool, *adj.* frais *(f.* fraîche); *(fig.)* calme; — *v.a.* rafraîchir.

co-operate, *v.n.* coopérer.

co-operation, *s.* coopération *f.*

copper, *s.* cuivre *m.*

copy, *s.* copie *f.;* exemplaire *m.;* numéro *m.* — *v. a.* copier.

copy-book, *s.* cahier *m.*

copyright, *s.* droit *m.* d'auteur.

coral, *s.* corail *m.*

cord, *s.* corde *f.*

cordial, *adj.* cordial.

cork, *s.* bouchon *m.*

corkscrew, *s.* tire-bouchon *m.*

corn, *s.* grain *m.;* grains *m. pl.;* *(wheat)* blé *m;* *(maize)* maïs *m.*

corner, *s.* coin *m.*

corporal, *adj.* corporel; — *s.* caporal *m.*

corporation, *s.* corporation *f.*

corps, *s.* corps *m.*

corpse, *s.* cadavre *m.*

correct, *adj.* correct; exact; — *v.a.* corriger, rectifier.

correction, *s.* correction *f.;* rectification *f.*

correspond, *v.n.* correspondre; être conforme (à).

correspondence, *s.* correspondance *f.*

correspondent, *s.* correspondant *m.*

corresponding, *adj.* correspondant.

corridor, *s.* corridor *m.;* couloir *m.*

corridor-train, *s.* train *m.* à couloir.

corrupt, *adj.* corrompu

cosmetics, *s. pl.* cosmétiques *m. pl.*, produits *m.pl.* de beauté.

cosmonaut, *s.* cosmonaute *m.*

cost, *s.* coût *m.*, frais *m. pl.*; prix *m.; ~ of living* coût de la vie; *at the ~ of* au prix de; — *v.n.* coûter.

costly, *adj.* coûteux.

costume, *s.* costume *m.*

cosy, *adj.* confortable.

cottage, *s.* chaumière *f.*

cotton, *s.* coton *m.*

couch, *s.* canapé *m.*, divan *m.*

cough, *s.* toux *f.;* — *v.n.* tousser.

council, *s.* conseil *m.*

councillor, *s.* conseiller *m.*

counsel, *s.* conseil *m.;* avocat *m.*

count[1], *s.* compte *m.; (title)* comte *m.*

count[2], *v.a. & n.* compter.

countenance, *s.* visage *m.;* air· *m.*

counter, *s.* comptoir *m.*, guichet *m.;* jeton *m.*

counterfoil, *s.* souche *f.*

countersign, *v.a.* contresigner.

countess, *s.* comtesse *f.*

countless, *adj.* innombrable.

country, *s.* pays *m.; (not town)* campagne *f.*

countryman, *s.* campagnard *m.*

countryside, *s.* (les) campagnes *f.pl.*

countrywoman, *s.* paysanne *f.*

county, *s.* comté *m.*

couple, *s.* couple *f.*

courage, *s.* courage *m.*

courageous, *adj.* courageux.

course, *s.* cours *m.:* route *f.; (meal)* service *m.*, plat *m.; of ~* bien entendu.

court, *s.* cour *f.;* tribunal *m.;* court *m.* (de tennis); — *v.a.* faire la cour à.

courteous, *adj.* courtois.

courtesy, *s.* courtoisie *f.*

courtship, *s.* cour *f.*

courtyard, *s.* cour *f.*

cousin, *s.* cousin, -e *m. f.*

cover, *s.* couverture *f.;* couvercle *m.; (meal)* couvert *m.; (post)* enveloppe *f.;* — *v.a.* couvrir.

cow, *s.* vache *f.*

coward, *s. & adj.* lâche *m.*

crab, *s.* crabe *m.*

crack, *s.* craquement *m.;* — *v.a.* faire craquer; *v.n.* craquer; se fêler.

cradle, *s.* berceau *m.*

craft, *s.* habileté *f.;* embarcation *f.;* métier *m.;* profession *f.*

craftsman, *s.* artisan *m.*

cram, *v.a.* fourrer; bourrer.

crane, *s.* grue *f.*

crash, *s.* fracas *m.;* débâcle; atterrissage brutal, collision; *v.n,* tomber avec fracas; s'écraser sur le sol.

crash-helmet, *s.* serretête *m.*

crave, *v.n. ~ for* désirer ardemment.

crawl, *v.n.* ramper; *(pers.)* se traîner.

crayon, *s.* crayon *m.*

craze, *s.* manie *f.*

crazy, *adj.* fou, toqué.

creak, *s.* cri *m.*, grincement *m.;* — *v. n.* crier, grincer.

cream, *s.* crème *f.*

crease, *s.* (faux) pli *m.*

create, *v.a.* créer.

creation, *s.* création *f.*

creature, *s.* créature *f.*

credit, *s.* crédit *m.;* mérite *m.;* honneur *m.;* on ~ à terme: *give* ~ *to* ajouter foi à; — *v.a.* ajouter foi à, créditer.

creditor, *s.* créancier *m.*

creek, *s.* crique *f.*

creep, *v.n.* ramper; se glisser.

crew, *s.* équipage *m.;* équipe *f.*

crib, *s.* mangeoire *f.;* lit *m.* d'enfant; berceau *m.*

cricket, *s.* *(game)* cricket *m.*

crime, *s.* crime *m.*

criminal, *adj.* & *s.* criminel, -elle.

cripple, *s.* estropié *m.*

crisis, *s.* crise *f.*

crisp, *adj.* croquant, croustillant; *(air)* vif.

critic, *s.* critique *m.*

critical, *adj.* critique.

criticize, *v.a.* critiquer.

critique, *s.* critique *f.*

croak, *v.n.* croasser.

crochet, *s.* crochet *m.*

crop, *s.* récolte *f.;* cueillette *f.*

cross, *s.* croix *f.;* — *v.a.* croiser, traverser.

crossing, *s.* passage *m.;* *(sea)* traversée *f.;* *level* ~ passage à niveau.

cross-question, *s.* contre-interrogatoire *m.;* — *v.a.* contre-interroger.

cross-reference, *s.* renvoi *m.*

crossroad, *s.* chemin *m.* de traverse; ~s carrefour *m.*

cross-section, *s.* coupe *f.* en travers.

cross-word (puzzle) *s.* mots *m.pl.* croisés.

crouch, *v. n.* se blottir.

crow, *s.* corneille *f.*

crowd, *s.* foule *f.;* tas *m.*

crowded, *adj.* encombré, comble.

crown, *s.* couronne *f ;* — *v.a.* couronner.

crucial, *adj.* décisif.

crude, *adj* brut; cru; grossier.

cruel, *adj.* cruel.

cruelty, *s.* cruauté *f.*

cruet, *s.* burette *f.*

cruise, *v.n.* croiser; — *s.* voyage *m.*

cruising, *adj.* ~ *speed* vitesse *f.* de croisière.

crumb, *s.* mie *f.;* miette *f.*

crumble, *v.a.* émietter; *v.n.* s'émietter.

crusade, *s.* croisade *f.*

crush, *s.* écrasement *m.;* cohue *f.;* — *v.a.* écraser.

crust, *s.* croûte *f.*

crutch, *s.* béquille *f.*

cry, *s.* cri *m.;* — *v.a.* crier; ~ *down* décrier; *v.n.* crier; *(weep)* pleurer.

crystal, *s.* cristal *m.*

cub, *s.* petit *m.;* *(boy scout)* louveteau *m.*

cube, *s.* cube *m.*

cuckoo, *s.* coucou *m.*

cucumber, *s.* concombre *m.*

cue, *s.* réplique *f.*

cuff, *s.* poignet *m.*, manchette *f.*

cuff-links, *s. pl.* boutons *m.pl.* de manchette.

culminate, *v.n.* se terminer.

culprit, *s.* accusé, -e *m. f.*

cultivate, *v.a.* cultiver.

cultural, *adj.* cultural.

culture, *s.* culture *f.*

cunning, *s.* ruse *f.*, finesse *f.;* — *adj.* rusé.

cup, *s.* tasse *f.;* gobelet *m.*

cupboard, s. armoire f.; placard m.

curate, s. vicaire m.

curb, s. gourmetté f.

curd, s. (lait) caillé m.

curdle, v.a. cailler; v.n. se cailler.

cure, s. guérison f.; cure f.; remède m.; — v.a. guérir.

curiosity, s. curiosité f.

curious, adj. curieux.

curl, s. boucle f.; — v.a. & n. boucler, friser; ~ up s'enrouler.

curly, adj. bouclé, frisé.

currant, s. black ~ cassis m.; red ~ groseille f. rouge.

currency, s. circulation f., cours m.; terme m. d'échéance; unité f. monétaire, monnaie f.; foreign ~ monnaie étrangère.

current, adj. courant, en cours; in ~ use d'usage courant; ~ events actualités f.; ~ account compte m. courant; — s. courant m.; cours m.

curse, s. malédiction f.; — v.a. maudire; v.n. blasphémer.

curtain, s. rideau m.

curve, s. courbe f.

cushion, s. coussin m.

custom, s. coutume f.; ~s douane f.; ~s duties droits m. de douane; ~s declaration déclaration f. de douane; ~s formalities la visite de la douane.

customary, adj. coutumier; accoutumé.

customer, s. client m., acheteur m.

custom-house, s. douane f.; ~ officer douanier m.

cut, v.a. couper; trancher; tailler; hacher; ~ down abattre, couper; réduire; ~ off couper; ~ out tailler; ~ up couper, débiter; — s. (knife) coup m.; (wound) coupure f.; (clothes) coupe f.; (meat) morceau m.; (in wages) réduction f.

cutlery, s. coutellerie f.

cutlet, s. côtelette f.

cutter, s. tailleur m.; coupeur m.

cycle, s. cycle m.; bicyclette f.; — v.n. pédaler.

cycling, s. cyclisme m.

cylinder, s. cylindre m.

cynic, adj. & s. cynique m.

Czech, adj. tchèque; — s. Tchèque m.

D

dad, daddy, s. papa m.

dagger, s. poignard m.

daily, adj. journalier, quotidien; — s. (journal) quotidien m.

dainty, adj. friand, délicat; gentil; — s. friandise f.

dairy, s. laiterie f.

daisy, s. marguerite f.

dam, s. barrage m.; digue f.

damage, s. dommage m.; préjudice m.; ~s dommages-intérêts m.

damn, v.a. condamner; — s. juron m.

damp, adj. humide; — s. humidité f.; — v. a mouiller, humecter.

dance, s. danse f.; bal m.; v.n. & a. danser.

dancer, s. danseur, -euse m. f.

dancing-hall, *s.* salle *f.* de danse; dancing *m.*

dancing-shoes, *s.pl.* souliers *m.* de bal, escarpins *m.*

Dane, *s.* Danois, -e *m. f.*

danger, *s.* danger *m.*

dangerous, *adj.* dangereux.

Danish, *adj.* danois; — *s. (language)* danois *m.*

dare, *v. aux. & a.* oser.

daring, *adj.* audacieux.

dark, *adj.* obscur, sombre; *(colour)* foncé; *(fig.)* triste; *be* ~ faire sombre; — *s.* obscurité *f.;* *in the* ~ dans l'obscurité.

darken, *v.a.* obscurcir.

darkness, *s.* obscurité *f.*

darling, *adj. & s.* chéri, -e.

darn, *v.a.* repriser.

darning, *s.* reprise *f.*

dart, *s.* dard *m.;* ~*s* *(game)* fléchettes *f.pl.*

dash, *v.a.* lancer; flanquer (par terre); ~ *to pieces* briser en morceaux; *v.n.* ~ *against* se heurter contre; ~ *at* se précipiter sur — *s. (with pen)* trait *m.,* tiret *m.; (vigour)* élan *m.,* fougue *f.;* attaque *f.* soudaine.

dash-board, *s.* tablier *m.;* tableau *m.* de bord.

data, *s. pl.* données *f.*

date¹, *s.* date *f.;* millésime *m.; be up to* ~ être à la page; — *v.a. & n.* dater.

date², *s.* datte *f.*

daughter, *s.* fille *f.*

daughter-in-law, *s.* belle-fille *f.*

dawn, *s.* point *m.* du jour; aube *f.*

day, *s.* jour *m.; (whole day)* journée *f.*

daylight, *s.* jour *m.*

daytime, *s.* jour *m.,* journée. *f.*

daze, *v.a.* étourdir; éblouir.

dazzle, *v.c.* éblouir.

deacon, *s.* diacre *m.*

dead, *adj.* mort; *the* ~ les morts *m.pl.*

deadly, *adj.* mortel.

deaf, *adj.* sourd; ~ *and dumb* sourd-muet.

deal, *v.a.* ~ *out* distribuer; donner; *v.n.* ~ *with* traiter qn; commercer, traiter avec qn; traiter (d'un sujet); ~ *in* commercer de; — *s. (cards)* donne *f.;* *(commerce)* affaire *f.;* *a good* ~, *a great* ~ beaucoup (de).

dealer, *s.* marchand *m.* *(in* de).

dean, *s.* doyen *m.*

dear, *s. & adj.* cher *m.,* chère *f.*

death, *s.* mort *f.*

debate, *s.* débat *m.,* discussion *f.;* — *v.a.* discuter, mettre en discussion.

debt, *s.* dette *f.*

debtor, *s.* débiteur, -trice *m. f.*

decay, *s.* décadence *f.;* — *v.n.* tomber en décadence; pourrir.

decease, *s.* décès *m.;* — *v.n.* décéder.

deceit, *s.* déception *f.;* tromperie *f.*

deceive, *v.a.* tromper; décevoir.

December, *s.* décembre *m.*

decent, *adj.* décent; assez bon.

deception, *s.* déception *f.*

decide, *v.a.* décider.

decision, *s.* décision *f.*

decisive, *adj.* décisif.

deck, *s.* pont *m.*

deck-chair, *s.* transatlantique *f.*

declaration, *s.* déclaration *f.*

declare, *v.a.* déclarer.

decline, *s.* décadence *f.;* — *v.a.* décliner; *v.n.* baisser.

decorate, *v.a.* décorer (de).

decoration, *s.* décoration *f.*

decrease, *v.a. & n.* diminuer; — *s.* diminution *f.*

decree, *s.* décret *m.*

dedicate, *v.a.* dédier.

deed, *s.* action *f.;* acte *m.*

deem, *v.a.* juger.

deep, *adj.* profond; *ten feet* ~ dix pieds de profondeur.

deer, *s.* cerf *m.*

deface, *v.a.* défigurer.

defeat, *s.* défaite *f.;* — *v.a.* vaincre.

defect, *s.* défaut *m.*

defence, *s.* défense *f.*

defend, *v.a.* défendre.

defender, *s.* défenseur *m.*

defer, *v.a.* retarder, ajourner; ~ *to* déférer à.

defiance, *s.* défi *m.; set at* ~ défier.

deficiency, *s.* manque *m.*

deficient, *adj.* insuffisant.

defile, *s.* défilé *m.;* — *v.n.* défiler; *v.a.* souiller.

define, *v.a.* définir.

definite, *adj.* déterminé, défini.

definition, *s.* définition *f.*

defy, *v.a.* défier; braver.

degrade, *v.a.* dégrader.

degree, *s.* degré *m.; (university)* grade *m.,;* diplôme *m.*

delay, *s.* retard *m.,* délai *m.;* — *v.a.* retarder; différer; *v.n.* tarder.

delegate, *s.* délégué *m.*

delegation, *s.* délegation *f.*

deliberate, *adj.* délibéré; — *v.a. & n.* délibérer.

delicacy, *s.* délicatesse *f.*

delicate, *adj.* délicat.

delicious, *adj* délicieux.

delight, *v.a. be* ~ed *at* être enchanté de.

delightful, *adj.* déliceux.

delinquent, *s.* délinquant *m.*

deliver, *v.a. (letters)* distribuer, *(goods etc.)* livrer, *(message)* remettre; *(speech)* faire, prononcer; *(free)* délivrer; *be* ~ed *of* accoucher de.

delivery, *s. (letters)* distribution *f., (message)* remise *f., (goods)* livraison *f.; (speech)* prononciation *f.,* débit *m.*

delusion, *s.* illusion *f.*

demand, *s.* demande, *f.* réclamation *f.;* — *v. a.* demander, réclamer.

democracy, *s.* démocratie *f.*

democrat, *s.* démocrate *m.*

democratic, *adj.* démocratique.

demolish, *v.a.* démolir.

demonstrate, *v.a.* démontrer.

demonstration, *s.* démonstration *f.*

den, *s.* antre *m.;* repaire *m.*

denial, *s.* dénégation *f.*

denomination, *s.* dénomination *f.;* secte *f.*

denote, *v.a.* dénoter.

denounce, *v.a.* dénoncer.

dense, *adj.* dense, épais.

density, *s.* densité *f.*

dentist, *s.* dentiste *m.*

denture, *s. (artificial)* dentier *m.*

deny, *v.a.* nier.

depart, *v.n.* partir.

department, *s.* département *m.*

departure, *s.* départ *m.*

depend, *v.n.* dépendre (de), compter (sur).

dependence, *s.* dépendance *f.*

dependent, *adj.* dépendant.

deplore, *v.a.* déplorer.

deposit, *s.* dépôt *m.;* — *v.a.* déposer.

depot, *s.* dépôt *m.*

depression *s.* abattement *m.*

deprive, *v.a.* priver (de).

depth, *s.* profondeur *f.*

deputy, *s.* délégué *m.;* vice-, sous-.

derive, *v.a.* retirer (de); be ~d from dériver de.

descend, *v.n.* descendre.

descendant, *s.* descendant, -e *m. f.*

descent, *s.* descente *f.*

describe, *v.a.* décrire.

description, *s.* description *f.;* sorte *f.*

desert, *s.* désert *m.;* — *v.a.* déserter.

deserve, *v.a.* mériter.

design, *s.* dessein *m.;* projet *m.;* dessin *m.;* — *v.a.* dessiner.

desirable, *adj.* désirable.

desire, *s.* désir *m.;* — *v.a.* désirer.

desk, *s.* bureau *m.*

desolation, *s.* désolation *f.*

despair, *s.* désespoir *m.;* — *v.n.* désespérer.

despatch *see* dispatch.

desperate, *adj.* désespéré.

despise, *v.a.* mépriser.

despite, *prep.* ~ (of) en dépit de.

dessert, *s.* dessert *m.*

destination, *s.* destination *f.*

destine, *v.a.* destiner.

destiny, *s.* destin *m.* destinée *f.*

destroy, *v.a.* détruire.

destruction, *s.* destruction *f.*

detach, *v.a.* détacher.

detachment, *s.* détachement *m.*

detail, *s.* détail *m.*

detain, *v.a.* retenir; détenir.

detect, *v.a.* découvrir.

detective, *s.* détective *m.*

detention, *s.* détention *f.*

detergent, *s.* détergent *m.*

deteriorate, *v.n.* se détériorer.

determination, *s.* détermination *f.*

determine, *v.a. & n.* déterminer, décider.

detrimental, *adj.* préjudiciable.

develop, *v.a.* développer; *v.n.* se développer.

development, *s.* développement *m.*

deviation, *s.* déviation *f.*

device, *s* expédient *m.;* invention *f.*

devil, *s.* diable *m.*

devilish, *adj.* diabolique.

devise, *v.a.* combiner; tramer.

devote, *v.a.* consacrer.

devoted, *adj.* dévoué.

devotion, *s.* dévotion *f.;* dévouement *m.*

devour, *v.a.* dévorer.

dew, *s.* rosée *f.*

diagnosis, *s.* diagnostic *m.*

diagram, *s.* diagramme *m.*

dial, *s.* cadran *m.;* — *v.a.* composer un numéro.

dialogue, *s.* dialogue *m.*

diameter, *s.* diamètre *m.*

diamond, *s.* diamant *m.;* (cards) carreau *m.*

diaper, *s.* couche *f.*

diarrhoea, *s.* diarrhée *f.*

diary, *s.* journal *m.;* agenda *m.*

dictate, *v.a.* dicter; *v.n.* ~ *to* donner des ordres à.

dictation, *s.* dictée *f.*

dictator, *s.* dictateur *m.*

dictionary, *s.* dictionnaire *m.*

die¹, *s.* dé *m.*

die², *v.n.* mourir.

Diesel engine, *s.* moteur *m.* Diesel; diesel *m.*

diet, *s.* alimentation *f.;* régime *m.*

differ, *v.n.* différer.

difference, *s.* différence *f.*

different, *adj.* différent.

difficult, *adj.* difficile.

difficulty, *s.* difficulté *f.*

diffuse, *adj.* diffus.

dig, *v.a.* bêcher.

digest, *v.a.* digérer.

digestion, *s.* digestion *f.*

dignity, *s.* dignité *f.*

diligent, *adj.* diligent.

dim, *adj.* faible, pâle, obscur.

dimension, *s.* dimension *f.*

diminish, *v. a. & n.* diminuer.

dimple, *s.* fossette *f.*

dine, *v.n.* dîner.

dining-car, *s.* wagon-restaurant *m.*

dining-hall, *s.* salle *f.* à manger; réfectoire *m.*

dining-room, *s.* salle *f.* à manger.

dinner, *s.* dîner *m.*

dinner-jacket, *s.* smoking *m.*

dip, *v.a. & n.* plonger.

diploma, *s.* diplôme *m.*

diplomacy, *s.* diplomatie *f.*

diplomat, *s.* diplomate *m.*

diplomatic, *adj.* diplomatique.

direct, *adj.* direct; — *v. a.* diriger; commander; adresser.

direction, *s.* direction *f;* instructions *f. pl.*

directly, *adv.* directement; tout de suite.

director, *s.* directeur *m.*

directory, *s.* annuaire *m.;* Bottin *m.*

dirt, *s.* saleté *f.;* boue *f.,* crotte *f.;* crasse *f.*

dirty, *adj.* sale; crotté; crasseux.

disadvantage, *s.* désavantage *m.*

disagree, *v.n.* différer; se brouiller; ne pas convenir (à).

disagreeable, *adj.* désagréable.

disappear, *v. n.* disparaître

disappearance, *s.* disparition *f.*

disappoint, *v.a.* désappointer; tromper.

disappointment, *s.* désappointement *m.*

disapprove, *v.n.* ~ *of* désapprouver qch.

disaster, *s.* désastre *m.*

disastrous, *adj.* désastreux.

disc *see* **disk.**

discern, *v.a.* discerner.

discharge, *v. a.* décharger; *(employee)* congédier; renvoyer; *(prisoner)* élargir; *(gas)* dégager; *(debt)* liquider; *(duty)* s'acquitter de; — *s.* décharge *f.; (employee)* congé *m.; (prison)* elargissement *m.*

discipline, *s.* discipline *f.*

disclose, *v.a.* découvrir.

discontented, *adj.* mécontent (de).

discourage, *v. a.* décourager.

discouragement, *s.* découragement *m.*

discourse, *s.* discours *m.*

discover, *v.a.* découvrir.

discovery, *s.* découverte *f.*

discredit, *s.* discrédit *m.;*
— *v.a.* discréditer.

discreet, *adj.* discret.

discretion, *s.* discrétion
f.; prudence *f.*

discuss, *v.a.* discuter.

discussion, *s.* discussion *f.*

disdain, *v.a.* dédaigner;
— *s.* dédain *m.*

disease, *s.* maladie *f.*

disembark *v.a. & n.* débarquer.

disgrace, *s.* disgrâce *f.;*
— *v.a.* disgracier.

disgraceful, *adj.* honteux.

disguise, *s.* déguisement;
— *v.a.* déguiser.

disgust, *s.* dégoût *m.;*
— *v.a.* dégoûter.

disgusting, *adj.* dégoûtant

dish, *s.* plat *m.;* mets *m.;*
wash up the ~es laver la
vaisselle.

dishonest, *adj.* malhonnête.

dishonour, *s.* déshonneur
m.; — *v.a.* déshonorer
(bill) ne pas honorer.

disinfect, *v.a.* désinfecter.

disk, *s.* disque *m.*

dislike, *s.* aversion *f.,*
dégoût *m.;* — *v.a.* ne
pas aimer.

dismal, *adj.* lugubre, sombre.

dismay, *s.* consternation
f.

dismiss, *v.a.* congédier;
bannir, écarter.

disobedience, *s.* désobéissance *f.*

disobedient, *adj.* désobéissant.

disobey, *v. a.* désobéir (à).

disorder, *s.* désordre *m.*

dispatch, *s.* expédition
f.; dépêche *f.*

dispensary, *s.* pharmacie
f.

dispense, *v.a.* dispenser;
préparer; *v.n. ~ with*
se disposer de.

disperse, *v.a.* disperser.

displaced, *adj. ~ person*
personne *f.* déplacée.

displacement, *s.* déplacement *m.*

display, *v.a.* exposer;
étaler; déployer, faire
preuve de; — *s.* exposition *f.;* étalage *m.;*
parade *f.*

displease, *v.a.* déplaire à

disposal, *s.* at *s.o.'s ~*
à la disposition de qn.

dispose, *v.n. ~ of* disposer de; vendre.

disposition, *s.* disposition
f.

dispute, *s.* dispute *f.* discuission *f.;* — *v.a* discuter; *v. n.* se disputer.

disqualify, *v.a.* disqualifier.

dissatisfy, *v.a.* mécontenter.

dissolve, *v.a.* dissoudre;
v.n. se dissoudre.

distance, *s.* distance *f.*

distant, *adj.* lointain; éloigné.

distil, *v. a. & n.* distiller.

distinct, *adj.* distinct (de);
marqué.

distinction, *s.* distinction
f.

distinguish, *v.a.* distinguer.

distract, *v.a.* distraire.

distraction, *s.* distraction
f.; confusion *f.*

distress, *s.* détresse *f.;*
— *v.a.* affliger.

distribute, *v. a.* distribuer.

distribution, *s.* distribution *f.*

district, *s.* région *f.,*
contrée *f.;* district *m.*

disturb, *v.a.* troubler; déranger.

disturbance, *s.* trouble *m.*, dérangement *m.*

ditch, *s.* fossé *m.*

dive, *v.n.* plonger (into dans).

diver, *s.* plongeur *m.*, scaphandrier *m.*

divergent, *adj.* divergent.

diversion, *s.* déviation *f.*

divide, *v.a.* diviser.

dividend, *s.* dividende *m.*

divine, *adj.* divin.

divinity, *s.* théologie *f.*

division, *s.* division *f.*

divorce, *s.* divorce *m.*; — *v. a.* divorcer (d'avec).

dizzy, *adj.* feel ~ avoir le vertige.

do, *v. a.* faire; finir; ~ away with supprimer; ~ up envelopper; ~ with se contenter de.

dock, *s.* bassin *m.*

doctor, *s.* docteur *m.*; médecin *m.*

doctrine, *s.* doctrine *f.*

document, *s.* document *m.*

dog, *s.* chien *m.*

dogma, *s.* dogme *m.*

doll, *s.* poupée *f.*

dollar, *s.* dollar *m.*

domestic, *adj. & s.* domestique (*m. f.*).

domicile, *s.* domicile *m.*

dominate, *v.a. &. n.* dominer.

dominion, *s.* domination *f.*; ~s colonies *f.*

donkey, *s.* âne *m.*

doom, *s.* sentence *f.*; — *v.a.* condamner; ~ed to voué à.

door, *s.* porte *f.*; (vehicle) portière *f.*

dormitory, *s.* dortoir *m.*

dose, *s.* dose *f.*

dot, *s.* point *m.*

double, *adj. & s.* double (*m.*).

doubt, *s.* doute *m.*; no ~ sans doute; — *v.a. & n.* douter.

doubtful, *adj.* douteux.

doubtless, *adj.* sans doute.

dough, *s.* pâte *f.*

dove, *s.* colombe *f.*

down, *adv.* à bas, en bas, par en bas; be ~ with (illness) être au lit avec; fall ~ tomber à terre; go ~ aller en bas; — *prep.* le long de; ~ the river en aval; ~ the street plus bas dans la rue.

downhill, *s.* pente *f.*; — *adv.* en pente, en descendant.

downstairs, *adv.* en bas.

downwards, *adv.* en bas.

dozen, *s.* douzaine *f.*

draft, *s.* projet *m.*; (letter) minute *f.*; (troops) détachement *m.*; (drawing) esquisse *f.*

drag, *v.a.* traîner; tirer.

drain, *s.* égout *m.*, canal *m.*; — *v.a.* drainer; vider.

drama, *s.* drame *m.*; théâtre *m.*

dramatic, *adj.* dramatique.

draper, *s.* marchand *m.* d'étoffes, (marchand) drapier *m.*; ~'s magasin *m.* de nouveautés.

draught, *s.* tirage *m.*; (drink) trait *m.*; (air) courant *m.* d'air.

draw, *v.a.* (pull) tirer, traîner; (tooth) arracher; (sketch) dessiner; ~ down baisser; ~ on tirer; ~ out prolonger; — *v. n.* tirer; ~ near s'approcher.

drawer, *s.* tiroir *m.*

drawing, *s.* dessin *m.*

drawing-pin, *s.* punaise *f.*

drawing-room, *s.* salon *m.*

dread, *v.a.* redouter.

dreadful, *adj.* redoutable.

dream, *s.* rêve *m.;* — *v.a. & n.* rêver.

dress, *s.* habits *m.pl.;* robe *f.;* — *v. a.* habiller; *v.n.* s'habiller; ∼ *a wound* panser.

dress-circle, *s.* (premier) balcon *m.*

dressing-gown, *s.(woman)* peignoir *m., (man)* robe *f.* de chambre.

dressmaker, *s.* couturière *f.*

drift, *v.n.* flotter; dériver; — *s.* dérive *f.;* amoncellement *m.*

drill, *s.* foret *m.; (soldiers)* exercice *m.*

drink, *s.* boisson *f.;* — *v.a.* boire.

drip, *v.n.* dégoutter.

drive, *v.a.* conduire; ∼ *in (nail)* enfoncer; *v.n.* conduire; aller en voiture.

driver, *s. (engine)* mécanicien *m.; (bus)* conducteur *m.; (car)* chauffeur *m.*

driving, *s.* conduite *f.;* ∼ *licence* permis *m.* de conduire.

drop, *s.* goutte *f.;* — *v.a.* laisser tomber; abandonner; *v.n.* (dé)-goutter; ∼ *in* entrer en passant.

drown, *v.a.* noyer; *v.n.* se noyer.

drug, *s.* drogue *f.*

druggist, *s.* droguiste *m.*

drum, *s.* tambour *m.*

drunk, *adj.* ivre.

dry, *adj.* sec, sèche; aride; tari; — *v.a.* sécher.

dry-clean, *v.a.* nettoyer à sec.

dual, *adj.* double.

dub, *v.a.* doubler.

duchess, *s.* duchesse *f.*

duck, *s.* cane *f.;* canard *m.*

due, *adj. (proper)* dû; *(owing)* exigible; échéant, payable; *in* ∼ *form* en bonne et due forme; *in* ∼ *time* en temps voulu; ∼ *to* causé par, par suite de; *the train is* ∼ *at* le train arrive à; — *s.* dû *m.;* droit *m.*

duke, *s.* duc *m.*

dull, *adj.* borné; ennuyeux; *(colour)* terne; *(weather, sad)* triste.

dumb, *adj.* muet.

dummy, *s.* mannequin *m.; (cards)* mort *m.*

dung, *s.* fumier *m.*

dupe, *s.* dupe *f.;* — *v.a.* duper.

duplicate, *s.* duplicata *m.;* — *adj.* en double; — *v.a.* faire en double.

during, *adv.* pendant, au cours de.

dusk, *s.* crépuscule *m.*

dust, *s.* poussière *f.*

dustbin, *s.* poubelle *f.*

dusty, *adj.* poussiéreux, poudreux.

Dutch, *adj.* hollandais.

Dutchman, *s.* Hollandais *m.*

duty, *s.* devoir *m.; (customs)* droit *m.; (task)* tâche *f.,* fonction(s) *f.(pl.); be on* ∼ être de service.

duty-free, *adj.* exempt de droits, en franchise.

dwarf, *s.* nain, -e *m. f.*

dwell, *v.n.* habiter; ∼ *(up)on* s'appesantir sur.

dwelling, *s.* habitation *f.*

dwelling-house *s.* maison *f.* d'habitation.

dwindle, *v.n.* diminuer.

dye, *s.* teinte *f.*, teinture *f.*; — *v.a.* teindre.

dynasty, *s.* dynastie *f.*

E

each, *pron.* chacun, -e; ~ *other* l'un l'autre; — *adj.* chaque.

eager, *adj.* ardent.

eagle, *s.* aigle *m.*

ear, *s.* oreille *f.*

earl, *s.* comte *m.*

early, *adv.* de bonne heure — *adj.* précoce; premier.

earn, *v. a.* gagner; mériter

earnest, *adj.* sérieux.

earnings, *s.pl.* salaire *m.*

earth, *s.* terre *f.*

earthenware, *s.* poterie *f.*

earthquake, *s.* tremblement *m.* de terre.

ease, *s.* aise *f.*; repos *m.*; *at one's* ~ à son aise; *with* ~ avec facilité.

east, *s.* est *m.*; — *adj.* d'est, de l'est; — *adv.* à l'est (de).

Easter, *s.* Pâques *m. pl.*

eastern, *adj.* (de l')est, oriental.

eastwards, *adv.* vers l'est.

easy, *adj.* facile.

easy-chair, *s.* fauteuil *m.*

easy-going, *adj.* nonchalant.

eat, *v.a.* manger; ~ *up* finir; dévorer.

ebb, *s.* reflux *m.*

ecclesiastic, *adj. & s.* ecclésiastique *(m.).*

economic, *adj.* économique.

economical, *adj.* économe

economics, *s.* économie *f.* politique.

economize, *v.n.* faire des économes.

economy, *s.* économie *f.*

ecstasy, *s.* extase *f.*

edge, *s.* tranchant *m.*, fil *m.*; bord *m.*

edition, *s.* édition *f.*

editor, *s.* rédacteur *m.*

editorial, *s.* article *m.* de fond.

educate, *v.a.* élever.

education, *s.* éducation *f.*

effect, *s.* effet *m.*

effective, *adj.* efficace; effectif.

efficiency, *s.* efficacité *f*

efficient, *adj.* capable.

effort, *s.* effort *m.*

egg, *s.* œuf *m.*; *boiled* ~ œuf à la coque; *fried* ~ œuf sur le plat.

Egyptian, *adj.* égyptien; — *s.* Egyptien, -enne *m. f.*

eight, *adj. & s.* huit.

eighteen, *adj. & s.* dix-huit.

eighteenth, *adj.* dix-huitième.

eighth, *adj.* huitième.

eighty, *adj. & s.* quatre-vingt(s).

either, *pron. & adj.* l'un ou l'autre; chacun; chaque; ~ ... *or* ou ... ou.

elaborate, *v.a.* élaborer; — *adj.* minutieux.

elastic, *adj.* élastique.

elbow, *s.* coude *m.*

elderly, *adj.* d'un certain âge.

elect, *v.a.* choisir; élire.

election, *s.* élection *f.*

electric(al), *adj.* électrique; ~*al engineer* (ingénieur) électricien *m.*

electricity, s. électricité f.
electron, s. électron m. ·
electronic, adj. électronique.
elegance, s. élégance f.
elegant, adj. élégant.
element, s. élément m.
elementary, adj. élémentaire.
elephant, s. éléphant m.
elevate, v.a. élever.
eleven, adj. & s. onze.
eleventh, adj. onzième.
elm, s. orme m.
else, adj. autre; anything ~, madam? encore quelque chose, Madame?; — adv. or ~ ou bien, autrement.
elsewhere, adv. ailleurs.
embankment, s. remblai m.
embark, v.a. embarquer; v.n. s'embarquer.
embarrass, v.a. embarrasser.
embassy, s. ambassade f.
embrace, v.a. embrasser.
embroidery, broderie f.
emerge, v.n. émerger; apparaître.
emergency, s. circonstance f. critique; in case of ~ en cas d'accident or d'urgence; ~ exit sortie f. de secours.
emigrant, s. émigrant, -e m. f.
emigrate, v.n. émigrer.
emigration, s. émigration f.
eminent, adj. éminent.
emit, v.a. émettre.
emotion, s. émotion f.
emphasis, s. accent · m., force f.; lay ~ on appuyer sur.
emphasize, v. a. appuyer sur.
empire, s. empire m.
employ, v.a. employer.

employee, s. employé m.
employer, s. employeur m.
employment, s. emploi m.
empty, adj. vide.
enable, v. a. rendre capable.
enclose, v.a. entourer (de); joindre (à une lettre).
encounter, v.a. affronter; rencontrer.
encourage, v.a. encourager.
encouragement, s. encouragement m.
encyclopaedia, s. encyclopédie f.
end, s. bout m.; fin f.; — v.a.&n. finir; ~ in finir en.
endeavour, s. effort m.; — v. n. s'efforcer (à or de).
ending, s. terminaison f.; fin f.
endless, adj. sans fin.
endorse, v.a. endosser.
endorsement, s. endossement m.
endow, v.a. doter (de).
endure, v.a. supporter, endurer.
enemy, s. ennemi, -e m. f.
energetic, adj. énergique.
energy, s. énergie f.
enforce, v.a. imposer; (law) faire exécuter.
engage, v.a. engager; fiancer; be ~d être occupé; être fiancé(e).
engagement, s. engagement m.; fiançailles f. pl.
engine, s. machine f.
engine-driver, s. mécanicien m.
engineer, s. ingénieur m.
English, adj. anglais.
Englishman, s. Anglais m.

Englishwomen, s. Anglaise f.

enjoy, v. a. jouir de; trouver bon; ~ oneself s'amuser.

enjoyment, s. jouissance f.

enlarge, v.a. agrandir.

enlist, v.a. enrôler.

enormous, adj. énorme.

enough, adj. & adv. assez (de).

enquire see inquire.

enrage, v.a. exaspérer.

enrol(l), v.a. enrôler.

ensign, s. (flag) drapeau m., pavillon m.; (pers.) porte-drapeau m.

ensue, v.n. s'ensuivre.

enter, v.a. entrer (dans); (in list) inscrire.

enterprise, s. entreprise f.

entertain, v.a. amuser; recevoir; avoir (une opinion).

entertainment, s. divertissement m.; amusement m.; hospitalité f.

enthusiasm, s. enthousiasme. m.

enthusiastic, adj. enthousiaste.

entire, adj. entier.

entirely, adv. entièrement.

entitle, v.a. be ~d to avoir droit à.

entrance, s. entrée f.; ~ examination examen d'entrée m.

entreat, v.a. supplier.

entry, s. entrée f.; inscription f.

enumerate, v.a. énumérer.

envelope, s. enveloppe f.

envious, adj. envieux (de).

enviromment, s. milieu m.

envy, s. envie f.; — v.a. envier.

epidemic, s. épidémie f.

equal, adj. égal.

equality, s. égalité f.

equation, s. équation f.

equip, v.a. équiper.

equipment, s. équipement m.

erase v.a. effacer.

erect, adj. droit ; — v.a. dresser; ériger.

err, v.n. errer.

error, s. erreur f.

escalator, s. escalator m., escalier m. roulant.

escape, v. n. (s')échapper; — s. fuite f.

escort, s. escorte f.; — v.a. escorter.

essay, s. essai m., composition f.

essential, adj. essentiel.

establish, v.a. établir.

establishment, s. établissement m.

estate, s. propriété f.; biens m. pl.

esteem, s. estime f.; — v.a. estimer.

estimate, s. estimation f.; évaulation f.; — v.a. estimer.

eternal, adj. éternel.

eucharist, s. eucharistie f.

European, adj. européen.

evacuate, v.a. évacuer.

even, adj. uni; égal; pair; — adv. même; ~ if même si.

evening, s. soir m.; (party) soirée f.

event, s. événement m.

eventual, adj. éventuel.

ever, adv. toujours; (any time) jamais.

evermore, adv. toujours.

every, adj. (all) tous; (each) chaque; ~ day tous les jours.

everybody, pron. tout le monde.

everyday, adj. de tous les jours.

everyone see everybody.

everything, pron. tout m.

everywhere, *adv.* partout.

evidence, *s.* évidence *f.*

evident, *adj.* évident.

evil, *s.* mal *m.;* — *adj.* mauvais.

evolution, *s.* évolution *f.*

ewe, brebis *f.*

exact, *adj.* exact.

exactly, *adv.* exactement.

exaggerate, *v.a.* exagérer.

exaggeration, *s.* exagération *f.*

examination, *s.* examen *m.*

examine, *v.a.* examiner; vérifier; *(customs)* visiter.

example, *s.* example *m.;* for ~ par exemple.

excavation, *s.* fouille *f.*

exceedingly, *adv.* excessivement.

excel, *v. a.* surpasser; *v. n.* exceller à.

excellent, *adj.* excellent.

except, *v.a.* excepter; — *prep.* excepté; sauf; ~ for exception faite pour.

exception, *s.* exception *f.*

exceptional, *adj.* exceptionnel.

excess, *s.* excès *m.;* ~ luggage excédent *m.* de bagages.

excessive, *adj.* excessif.

exchange, *s.* échange *m.;* *(telephone)* bureau central *m.; foreign* ~ change *m.;* — *v.a.* échanger.

excite, *v.a.* exciter.

excitement, *s.* excitation *f.*

exclaim, *v.n.* s'écrier.

exclamation, *s.* exclamation *f.*

exclude, *v.a.* exclure.

exclusive, *adj.* exclusif.

excursion, *s.* excursion *f.*

excuse, *s.* excuse *f.;* — *v.a.* excuser.

execute, *v.a.* exécuter.

execution, *s.* exécution *f.*

executive, *adj. & s.* exécutif *m.;* agent *m.* d'exécution

exempt, *adj.* exempt (de); *v.a.* exempter (de).

exercise, *s.* exercice *m.;* — *v.a.* exercer.

exertion, *s.* effort *m.*

exhaust, *v.a.* épuiser.

exhaust-pipe, *s.* tuyau *m.* d'échappement.

exhibit, *v. a.* présenter, exhiber; exposer.

exhibition, *s.* exhibition *f.;* exposition *f.*

exist, *v.n.* exister.

existence, *s.* existence *f.*

exit, *s.* sortie *f.*

expand, *v.a.* étendre; dilater.

expansion, *s.* expansion *f.*

expect, *v.a.* attendre, s'attendre à; *(think)* croire.

expedient, *s.* expédient *m.*

expedition, *s.* expédition *f.*

expel, *v.a.* expulser.

expense, *s.* dépense *f.*

expensive, *adj.* coûteux, cher.

experience, *s.* expérience *f.;* — *v.a.* éprouver.

experiment, *s.* expérience *f.;* — *v.n.* faire des expériences, expérimenter.

experimental, *adj.* expérimental.

expert, *s.* expert *m.*

expire, *v.n.* expirer.

explain, *v.a.* expliquer.

explanation, *s.* explication *f.*

exploration, *s.* exploration.

explore, *v.a.* explorer.

explosion, *s.* explosion *f.*

export, *s.* exportation *f.;* ~s articles *m.pl.* d'exportation; — *v.a.* exporter.

exporter, *s.* exportateur *m.*

expose, *v.a.* exposer.

exposure, *s.* exposition *f.*; révélation *f.*

express, *adj.* exprès; formel; exact; ~ *letter* lettre *f.* par exprès; — *s. (train)* express *m.*; — *v.a.* exprimer.

expression, *s.* expression *f.*

exquisite, *adj.* exquis.

extend, *v.a.* étendre; prolonger.

extension, *s.* extension *f.*; prolongation *f.*

extensive, *adj.* étendu, vaste.

extent, *s.* étendue *f.*

extinguish, *v.a.* éteindre.

extra, *adj.* supplémentaire.

extract, *s.* extrait *m.*; — *v.a.* extraire.

extraordinary, *adj.* extraordinaire.

extravagant, *adj.* extravagant.

extreme, *adj. & s.* extrême *(m.).*

extremely, *adv.* extrêmement.

extremity, *s.* extrémité *f.*

eye, *s.* œil *m.*

eyebrow, *s.* sourcil *m.*

eyelid, *s.* paupière *f.*

eyepiece, *s.* oculaire *m.*

F

fable, *s.* fable *f.*

fabric, *s.* tissu *m.*; textile *m.*

face, *s.* visage *m.*; face *f.*; figure *f.*; *in ~ of* devant; — *v.a.* affronter, faire face à, braver.

facility, *s.* facilité *f.*

fact, *s.* fait *m.*; *in ~* de fait; en effet.

factor, *s.* facteur *m.*; élément *m.*

factory, *s.* fabrique *f.*; usine *f.*

faculty, *s.* faculté *f.*

fade, *v.n.* se faner; ~ *away* s'évanouir.

fail, *v.n.* manquer (de); *(not succeed)* échouer, *(in an exam)* être refusé.

failure, *s.* insuccès *m.*

faint, *v.n.* s'évanouir.

fair, *adj.* beau; bel, belle; *(hair)* blond; *(just)* juste; *(weather)* clair; ~ *play* jeu loyal *m.*

fairly, *adv.* assez bien.

faith, *s.* foi *f.*

faithful, *adj.* fidèle.

falcon, *s.* faucon *m.*

fall, *v.n.* tomber; baisser; ~ *back on* avoir recours à; ~ *in* s'effondrer; ~ *off* se déprécier; ~ *under* être compris dans; — *s.* chute *f.*; baisse *f.*

false, *adj.* faux; artificiel.

falter, *v.n.* hésiter.

fame, *s.* réputation *f.*; renommée *f.*

familiar, *adj.* familier, intime (avec).

family, *s.* famille *f.*

famous, *adj.* célèbre, fameux.

fan[1], *s.* éventail *m.*; ventilateur *m.*

fan[2], *s.* passionné, -e *m. f.*, fervent *m.*

fancy, *s.* fantaisie *f.*, imagination *f.*

fantastic, *adj.* fantastique; fantasque.

far, *adv.* loin; ~ *off* au loin; *as ~ as* autant que; *by ~* de beaucoup; *how ~ is it?* à

quelle distance est-ce?;
— *adj.* lointain.
fare, *s.* prix de (la) place
m.; (taxi) prix de la
course*m.; (food)* chère *f.*
farewell, *s.* adieu *m.; bid*
~ *to* dire adieu à.
farm, *s.* ferme *f.*
farmer, *s.* fermier *m.*
farming, *s.* agriculture *f.*
farmyard, *s.* cour *f.* de
ferme.
farther, *adv.* plus loin
(que).
fashion, *s.* mode *f.;*
manière *f.*
fashionable, *adj.* élégant.
fast, *adj.* vite, rapide;
be ~ *(clock)* avancer;
— *adv.* vite.
fasten, *v.a.* attacher.
fastener, *s.* attache *f.;*
agrafe *f.; zip* ~ ferme-
ture éclair *f.*
fat, *adj.* gros, gras; — *s.*
gras *m.;* graisse *f.*
fatal, *adj.* fatal.
fate, *s.* destin *m.,* sort *m.*
father, *s.* père *m.*
father-in-law, *s.* beau-
père *m.*
fatigue, *s.* fatigue *f.*
fault, *s.* défaut *m.;* faute
f.
faultless, *adj.* sans faute.
faulty, *adj.* défectueux.
favour, *s.* faveur *f.; in* ~
of en faveur de; *do a* ~
rendre un service (à).
favourable, *adj.* favorable.
favourite, *adj.* favori.
fear, *s.* crainte *f.;* —
v.a.& n. craindre.
fearful, *adj.* affreux,
effrayant.
feast, *s.* fête *f.;* festin *m.*
feat, *s.* exploit *m.*
feather, *s.* plume *f.*
feature, *s.* trait *m.;* caractéristique *f.;* ~ *film* le

grand film.
February, *s.* février *m.*
federal, *adj.* fédéral.
federation, *s.* fédération *f.*
fee, *s.* honoraires *m. pl.;*
(school) ~*s* frais *m. pl.*
feeble, *adj.* faible.
feed, *v. a.* nourrir; paître.
feel, *v.n.&a.* (se) sentir;
éprouver, ressentir,
(with hand) toucher;
tâter; ~ *cold* avoir
froid.
feeling, *s.* sentiment *m.*
fellow, *s.* camarade *m.;*
compagnon *m.;* gar-
çon *m.; (of a society)*
membre *m., (univer-
sity)* agrégé *m.*
fellowship, *s.* camaraderie
f.; communauté *f.*
female, *adj.* féminin;
(animal) femelle; — *s.*
femme *f.;* femelle *f.*
feminine, *adj.* féminin.
fence, *s.* clôture *f.;* pa-
lissade *f.;* — *v.a.*
enclore; *v. n.* faire de
l'escrime.
fencing, *s.* escrime *f.*
fender, *s.* pare-choc(s) *m.*
ferry, *s.* (passage *m.* en)
bac *m.*
ferry-boat, *s.* bac *m.*
fertile, *adj.* fertile.
fertilize, *v.a.* fertiliser.
festival, *s.* festival *m.*
fetch, *v.a.* aller chercher;
apporter.
feudal, *adj.* féodal.
fever, *s.* fièvre *f.*
few, *pron. & adj.* peu
(de); *a* ~ quelques-
(-uns).
fiancé, -e, *s.* fiancé, -e
m. f.
fibre, *s.* fibre *f.*
fiction, *s.* fiction *f.;*
(novels) romans *m. pl.*
field, *s.* champ *m.;*
(sport) terrain *m.*
fierce, *adj.* cruel, violent,

féroce.

fiery, *adj.* de feu; ardent.

fifteen, *adj. & s.* quinze *(m.).*

fifteenth, *adj.* quinzième.

fifth, *adj.* cinquième; cinq.

fiftieth, *adj.* cinquantième.

fifty, *adj. & s.* cinquante *(m.).*

fig, *s.* figue *f.*

fight, *s.* combat *m.;* lutte *f.*

fighter, *s.* combattant *m.;* avion *m.* de chasse.

figure, *s.* figure *f.; (arithm.)* chiffre *m.*

file[1], *s. (tool)* lime *f.;* — *.a.* limer.

file[2], *s.* classeur *m.,* dossier *m.;* liasse *f.; (people)* file *f.;* — *v.a.* classer; enregistrer.

filing-cabinet, *s.* cartonnier *m.,* fichier *m.*

fill, *v.a.* remplir; occuper; ~ *in,* up remplir.

film, *s. (photo)* pellicule *f.; (cinema)* film *m.*

filter, *s.* filtre *m.;* — *v.a.* filtrer.

filthy, *adj.* sale; *(fig.)* obscène.

fin, *s.* nageoire *f.*

final, *adj.* final.

finally, *adv.* enfin.

finance, *s.* finance *f.*

financial, *adj.* financier.

find, *v.a.* trouver; ~ *out* inventer, découvrir.

fine[1], *s. (penalty)* amende *f.;* — *v.a.* mettre à l'amende.

fine[2], *adj.* fin; beau.

finger, *s.* doigt *m.; first* ~ index *m.*

finger-print, *s.* empreinte *f.* digitale.

finish, *v. a.* finir; terminer.

Finnish, *adj.* finlandais.

fir, *s.* sapin *m.*

fire, *s.* feu *m.; on* ~ en feu; — *v.a.* mettre feu à; *(gun)* tirer; *v.n.* tirer.

fire-arm, *s.* arme *f.* à feu.

fire-brigade, *s.* les pompiers *m. pl.*

fire-engine, *s.* pompe *f.* à incendie.

fire-escape, *s.* escalier *m.* de sauvetage.

fireplace, *s.* cheminée *f.*

fire-station, *s.* poste *m.* d'incendie.

fireworks, *s.pl.* feu *m.* d'artifice.

firm[1], *s.* maison *f.* (de commerce).

firm[2], *adj.* ferme.

firmament, *s.* firmament *m.*

firmness, *s.* fermeté *f.*

first, *adj.* premier; — *adv.* premièrement; d'abord; *(railway)* en première; *at* ~ d'abord.

firstly, *adv.* premièrement.

first-rate, *adj.* de premier ordre.

fish, *s.* poisson *m.;* — *v. a. & n.* pêcher.

fisher(man), *s.* pêcheur *m.*

fishmonger, *s.* poissonnier *m.*

fist, *s.* poing *m.*

fit[1], *s.* attaque *f.;* accès *m.*

fit[2], *adj.* convenable, bon, propre; en état (de), capable (de).

five, *adj. & s.* cinq *(m.).*

fix, *v.a.* fixer; ~ *up* arranger.

flag, *s.* drapeau *m.; (navy)* pavillon *m.*

flagrant, *adj.* flagrant.

flake, *s.* flocon *m.*

flame, *s*. flamme *f*.
flannel, *s*. flanelle *f*.
flap, *s*. coup *m*., tape *f*.
flare, *v.n*. flamboyer.
flash, *s*. éclair *m*.; —
v.n. jeter des éclairs,
étinceler.
flashlight, *s*. flash (électronique) *m*.
flat¹, *adj*. plat; insipide;
(postitive) formel, net;
— *s*. plat *m*.; *(music)*
bémol *m*.
flat², *s*. appartement *m*.;
étage *m*.
flatter, *v.a*. flatter.
flattery, *s*. flatterie *f*.
flavour, *s*. saveur *f*.,
goût *m*., arome *m*.
flax, *s*. lin *m*.
flea, *s*. puce *f*.
flee, *v.a*. & *n*. fuir, se
sauver.
fleece, *s*. toison *f*.
fleet, *s*. flotte *f*.
flesh, *s*. chair *f*.; viande *f*.
flexible, *adj*. flexible.
flight, *s*. vol *m*. *(birds,
stairs)* volée *f*.; *(fleeing)* fuite *f*.
flimsy, *adj*. ténu; fragile;
frivole.
fling, *v.a*. jeter.
flirt, *s*. coquette *f*.; —
v.n. flirter.
float, *v.n*. flotter; *v.a*.
faire flotter.
flock, *s*. troupeau *m*.,
troupe *f*.
flood, *s*. inondation *f*.;
(tide) flux *m*.; — *v.a*.
inonder.
flood-light, *v.a*. illuminer
par projecteurs.
floor, *s*. plancher *m*.,
parquet *m*.; *(storey)*
étage *m*.
flour, *s*. farine *f*.
flourish, *v.n*. fleurir;
prospérer.
flow, *v.n*. couler, s'écouler; — *s*. flux *m*.; cours

m.
flower, *s*. fleur *f*.
flower-bed, *s*. plate-bande
f.
flu, *s*. grippe *f*.
flue, *s*. tuyau *m*.
fluent, *adj*. facile, cou-
lant.
fluid, *adj*. & *s*. fluide *(m.)*.
fluorescent, *adj*. ～ *lamp
tube* *m*. fluorescent.
flush, *v.a*. inonder; nettoyer avec une chasse
d'eau; *v. n*. rougir.
flute, *s*. flûte *f*.
flutter, *s*. voltigement *m*.;
— *v. a*. agiter; *v. n*. voltiger.
fly¹, *s*. mouche *f*.
fly², *v.n*. voler; prendre
l'avion (pour).
foam, *s*. écume *f*.; *(beer)*
mousse *f*.
focus, *s*. foyer *m*.
fodder, *s*. fourrage *m*.
fog, *s*. brouillard *m*.
foil¹, *s*. feuille *f*.; tain *m*.
foil², *s*. *(fencing)* fleuret
m.
fold, *s*. pli *m*.; — *v.a*.
plier; envelopper;
(arms) croiser; ～ *up*
replier.
folding, *adj*. pliant.
foliage, *s*. feuillage *m*.
folk, *s*. gens *m*. *pl*.
follow, *v.a*. suivre; accompagner; *v.n*. sui-
vre; s'ensuivre; *as* ～*s*
comme suit.
follower, *s*. suivant *m*.,
compagnon *m*., parti-
san *m*.
following, *adj*. suivant;
the ～ ce qui suit.
folly, *s*. sottise *f*.
fond, *adj*. *be* ～ *of* aimer.
food, *s*. nourriture *f*.,
aliments *m*. *pl*.
fool, *s*. sot *m*.
foolish, *adj*. sot; fou.

foot, s. pied *m.; on* ~ à
pied.

football, s. football *m.;*
ballon *m.*

foot-brake, s. frein *m.* à
pied

foot-note, s. note *f.* (au
bas de la page).

footstep, s. pas *m.*

for[1], *prep.* pour; *(in exchange for)* contre; *(because of)* à cause de;
(time) pendant; *(in
spite of)* malgré.

for[2], *conj.* car.

forbid, *v.a.* défendre;
interdire.

force, s. force *f.;* violence
f.; — *v.a.* forcer.

forearm, s. avant-bras
m.

forecast, s. prévision *f.;* —
v.a. prévoir.

forefinger, s. index *m.*

foreground, s. premier
plan *m.*

forehead, s. front *m.*

foreign, *adj.* étranger.

foreigner, s. étranger, -ère
m. f.

foremost, *adj.* premier; —
adv. first and ~ tout
d'abord.

foresee, *v.a.* prévoir.

forest, s. forêt *f.*

foretell, *v.a.* prédire.

foreword, s. avant-propos
m.

orge, *v.a.* forger.

forgery, s. contrefaçon
f.; faux *m.*

forget, *v.a.* oublier.

forgetful, *adj.* oublieux.

forgive, *v.a.* pardonner.

fork, s. fourchette *f.;*
(hay) fourche *f.*

form, s. torme *f.; (bench)*
banc *m.; (class)* classe
f.; (paper) formule *f.;*
~ *of government* régime
m.; — *v.a.* former.

formal, *adj.* formel.

formality, s. formalité *f.*

former, *pron.* le premier,
la première; celui-là,
celle-là; — *adj.* pre-
mier, -ère; précédent.

formerly, *adv.* autrefois.

formula, s. formule *f.*

forsake, *v. a.* abandonner.

fortieth, *adj.* quarantième.

fortification, s. fortification *f.*

fortify, *v.a.* fortifier.

fortnight, s. quinze jours
m. pl.

fortress, s. forte sse *f.*

fortunate, *adj.* ureux.

fortunately *ad* heureuse-
ment

fortune, s. fortune *f*

forty, *adj. & s.* quarante
(m.).

forward, *adv.* en avant; *go*
~ (s')avancer; — *adj.*
avancé; — *v.a.* faire
suivre; expédier.

forwarding, s. expédition
f.; ~ *agency* entreprise
f. de transport.

forwards, *adv.* en avant.

foul, *adj.* sale; impure;
(language) ordurier.

found, *v. a.* fonder.

foundation, s. fondation *f.*

founder, s. fondateur *m.*

fountain, s. fontaine *f.*

fountain-pen, s. stylo-
(graphe) *m.*

four, *adj. & s.* quatre
(m.).

fourteen, *adj. & s.* quatorze *(m.).*

fourth, *adj.* quatrième;
quatre.

fowl, s. poule *f.*

fox, s. renard *m.*

fraction, s. fraction *f.*

fracture, s. fracture *f.*

fragile, *adj.* fragile.

fragment, s. fragment *m.*

fragrant, *adj.* parfumé.

frame, s. (picture) cadre m.; (structure) charpente f.; (window) châssis m.

framework, s. charpente f.

frank, adj. franc.

frankness, s. franchise f.

fraud, s. fraude f.

free, adj. libre; ~ of, from exempt de.

freedom, s. liberté f.

freely, adv. librement; gratis.

freeze, v.a. geler.

freight, s. fret m.

French, adj. français; — s. (language) le français; the ~ les Français m. pl.

French-bean(s), s. (pl.) haricots m. pl. verts.

Frenchman, s. Français m.

Frenchwoman, s. Française f.

frequent, adj. fréquent; — v. a. fréquenter.

frequently, adv. fréquemment.

fresh, adj. frais, fraîche; nouveau, nouvel, -elle.

friar, s. moine m.

fricassee, s. fricassée f.

friction, s. friction f.

Friday, s. vendredi m.

fridge, s. frigo m.

friend, s. ami, -e m. f.

friendly, adj. aimable; ami; amical.

friendship, s. amitié f.

fright, s. peur f.; take ~ prendre peur.

frighten, v.a. effrayer.

frightful, adj. affreux; effrayant.

frock, s. robe f.

frog, s. grenouille f.

frolic, s. ébats m. pl.; — v.n. folâtrer, gambader.

from, prep. (place) de; (time) depuis; (separation) de, à; (change) de.

front, s. front m.; devant m.; façade f.; in ~ of en face de, en avant de; — adj. de devant.

front-door, s. porte f. d'entrée.

frontier, s. frontière f.

frost, s. gelée f.

frosty, adj. de gelée; fig. froid.

frown, v.a. & n. froncer les sourcils.

frozen, adj. gelé.

fruit, s. fruit m.

fruitful, adj. fructueux.

fruit-tree, s. arbre fruitier m.

frustrate, v.a. déjouer; décevoir; contrecarres.

fry, v. a. & n. (faire) frire.

frying-pan, s. poêle (à frire) f.

fuel, s. combustible m.

fulfil, v.a. accomplir.

full, adj. plein; complet; ~ name les nom et prénoms m. pl.; ~ stop point m.

full-time, adj. de toute la journée.

fully, adv. pleinement.

fume, s. fumée f.

fun, s. amusement m.; for ~ pour rire.

function, s. fonction f.

fund, s. fonds m.

fundamental, adj. fondamental.

funeral, s. funérailles f. pl.

funnel, s. entonnoir m.; (steamer) cheminée f.

funny, adj. drôle.

fur, s. fourrure f.

fur-coat, s. manteau m. de fourrure.

furious, adj. furieux.

furnace, s. fourneau m.

furnish, v. a. pourvoir (de), fournir; meubler (de).

furniture, s. meubles m. pl., ameublement m.;

piece of ~ meuble *m.*
furrier, *s.* fourreur *m.*
furrow, *s.* sillon *m.*
further, *adv.* plus loin;
(any longer) davanta-
ge; — *adj.* ultérieur;
autre; plus lointain;
supplémentaire, nou-
veau.
furthermore, *adv.* en
outre, de plus.
fury, *s.* fureur *f.; (pers.)*
furie *f.*
fuss, *s.* embarras *m.;*
bruit *m.; make a* ~
faire des embarras; —
v. n. faire des embarras;
~ *about* faire l'affairé.
future, *s.* avenir *m.;*
(gramm.) futur *m.; in
the* ~ à l'avenir; — *adj.*
futur.

G

gain, *s.* gain *m.;* — *v.a.*
gagner.
gait, *s.* allure *f.*
gala, *s.* gala *m.*
gale, *s.* grand vent *m.*
gall, *s.* bile *f.;* fiel *m;*
amertume *f.*
gallant, *adj.* brave; galant.
gallery, *s.* galerie *f.*
gallon, *s.* gallon *m.*
gallop, *s.* galop *m.;* —
v.n. galoper.
gamble, *v. n.* jouer; — *s.*
jeu *m.*
game, *s.* jeu *m.;* partie *f.;*
(animal) gibier *m.*
gamekeeper, *s.* garde-
chasse *m.*
gang, *s.* bande *f.;* équipe *f.*
gangway, *s.* passage *m.*
gaol *see* **jail.**
gap, *s.* trou *m.;* brèche *f.;*
vide *m.*
gape, *v.n.* bâiller; *stand
gaping* gober des mou-
ches; ~ *at* regarder
bouche bée.
garage, *s.* garage *m.*

garden, *s.* jardin *m.*
gardener, *s.* jardinier *m.*
garlic, *s.* ail *m.*
garment, *s.* vêtement *m.*
garnish, *s.* garniture *f.;* —
v.a. garnir.
garter, *s.* jarretière *f.*
gas, *s.* gaz *m.*
gasp, *s.* soupir *m.*
gas-works, *s. pl.* usine *f.*
à gaz.
gate, *s.* porte *f.*
gateway, *s.* portail *m.*
gather, *v.a.* réunir; amasser; cueillir; *(under-
stand)* conclure; *v.n.*
s'assembler.
gathering, *s.* rassemble-
ment *m.;* abcès *m.*
gauge, *s.* jauge *f.;* calibre
m.; indicateur *m.;* —
v.a. jauger; calibrer.
gauze, *s.* gaze *f.*
gay, *adj.* gai.
gear, *s.* attirail *m.,* appareil *m.; (motorcar)*
vitesse *f.*
gear-box, *s.* boîte *f.* des
vitesses.
gear-lever, *s.* levier *m.* des
vitesses.
general, *adj.* général; — *s.*
général *m. (pl.* géné-
raux).
generation, *s.* génération *f.*
generator, *s.* générateur
m.
generosity, *s.* générosité *f.*
generous, *adj.* généreux.
genial, *adj.* doux, douce;
bienfaisant.
genius *s.* génie *m.*
gentle, *adj.* doux, douce.
gentleman, *s.* gentleman
m.
genuine, *adj.* authentique; vrai.
geographical, *adj.* géographique.
geography, *s.* géographie *f*
geology, *s.* géologie *f.*
geometric(al), *adj.* géomé-

trique.

geometry, *s.* géométrie *f.*

germ, *s.* germe *m.*

German, *adj.* allemand; — —*s.* Allemand, -e *m.f.*

gesticulate, *v.n.* gesticuler.

gesture, *s.* geste *m.*

get, *v.a.* obtenir, procurer, trouver, recevoir; — *v.n.* arriver; *(become)* devenir; ~ *at* parvenir (à); ~ *in* entrer;

~ *off* partir; ~ *on* prospérer; *(agree)* s'accorder (avec); ~ *out of* sortir (de); ~ *over* surmonter; *(illness)* se remettre; ~ *up* se lever.

geyser, *s.* chauffe-bain *m.*

ghost, *s.* esprit *m.;* revenant *m.*, fantôme *m.*

giant, *s.* géant *m.*

gift, *s.* don *m.*

gifted, *adj.* bien doué.

gills, *s. pl.* ouïes *f.*

gin, *s.* genièvre *m.;* gin *m.*

giraffe, *s.* girafe *f.*

girdle, *s.* ceinture *f.;* — *v.a.* ceinturer.

girl, *s.* jeune fille *f.*

give, *v. a.* donner; ~ *up* renoncer à; livrer; *v.n.* ~ *in* céder (à).

glacier, *s.* glacier *m.*

glad, *adj.* heureux; content; joyeux.

gladness, *s.* joie *f.*

glance, *s.* coup *m.* d'œil,; — *v. n.* ~ *at* jeter un regard sur.

glare, *s.* lumière *f.* éblouissante; clinquant *m.;* — *v.n.* briller d'un éclat éblouissant.

glass, *s.* verre *m.;* *(pane)* vitre *f.;* ~*es* lunettes *f. pl.*

glazier, *s.* vitrier *m.*

gleam, *s.* lueur *f.;* — *v. n.* luire.

glide, *v. n.* glisser; planer.

glider, *s.* planeur *m.*

glimmer, *s.* lueur *f.;* — *v.n.* jeter une lueur faible.

glimpse, *s.* coup *m.* d'œil (rapide).

glitter, *v.n.* étinceler.

globe, *s.* globe *m.*

gloomy, *adj.* sombre.

glorious, *adj.* glorieux.

glory, *s.* gloire *f.*

glove, *s.* gant *m.*

glow, *v.n.* luire rouge; *(joy)* rayonner; *(coal)* être rouge; — *s.* chaleur *f.;* lumière *f.; fig.* ardeur *f.*

glue, *s.* colle (forte) *f.;* — *v.a.* coller.

gnat, *s.* cousin *m.;* moustique *f.*

gnaw, *v.a. & n.* ronger.

go, *v. n.* aller; ~ *away* s'en aller; ~ *back* retourner; ~ *back on one's word* reprendre sa parole; ~ *down* descendre; baisser; ~ *in for* s'occuper de, s'adonner à, faire (de); ~ *into* entrer dans; ~ *off* s'en aller; ~ *on* continuer; *(happen)* se passer; ~ *out* sortir; ~ *over*, *through* traverser; *(read)* parcourir; ~*up* monter; ~ *with* accompagner; ~ *without* se passer de; *let* ~ lâcher prise.

goal, *s.* but *m.*

goalkeeper, *s.* gardien (de but) *m.*

goat, *s.* bouc *f.*, chèvre *f.*

God, *s.* Dieu *m.*

god-child, *s.* filleul, -e *m. f.*

godfather, *s.* parrain *m.*

godmother, *s.* marraine *f.*

goggles, *s. pl.* bésicles *f.*

gold, *s.* or *m.*

golden, *adj.* d'or, en Or.

golf, *s.* golf *m.*

good, *adj.* bon; ~ *evening!* bonsoir!; ~ *morning!* bonjour!; *be so* ~ *as to* avoir la bonté de; *make* ~ remplir; indemniser de; — *s.* bien *m.*; ~s marchandise *f.*; ~s *station* gare *f.* de marchandises; ~s *train* train *m.* de marchandises.

good-bye, *int.* & *s.* adieu (*m.*).

good-looking, *adj.* de belle mine, beau.

goodness, *s.* bonté *f.*

good-tempered, *adj.* de caractère facile, de bonne humeur.

goodwill, *s.* bonne volonté *f.*

goose, *s.* oie *f.*

gooseberry, *s.* groseille *f.* à maquereau.

gospel, *s.* évangile *m.*

gossip, *s.* bavardage *m.*; racontar *m.*, cancan *m.*; *(pers.)* compère *m.*; commère *f.*; — *v.n.* bavarder.

Gothic, *adj.* gothique.

govern, *v.a.* & *n.* gouverner.

governess, *s.* gouvernante *f.*

government, *s.* gouvernement *m.*

governor, *s.* gouverneur *m.*

gown, *s.* robe *f.*

grace, *s.* grâce *f.*

graceful, *adj.* gracieux.

gracious, *adj.* gracieux.

grade, *s.* grade *m.*; classe *f.*

gradual, *adj.* graduel.

graduate, *s.* gradué, -e *m. f.*; — *v.a.* graduer; *v.n.* prendre ses diplômes.

grain, *s.* grain *m.*

grammar, *s.* grammaire *f.*

grammar-school, *s.* lycée *m.*, collège *m.*

grammatical, *adj.* grammatical.

gram(me), *s.* gramme *m.*

gramophone, *s.* gramophone *m.*, phonographe *m.*

gramophone-record, *s.* disque *m.*

grand, *adj.* grand; magnifique; ~ *stand* tribune *f.*

grandchild, *s.* petit-fils *m.*, petite-fille *f.* (*pl.* petits-enfants *m.*)

granddaughter, *s.* petite-fille *f.*

grandfather, *s.* grand-père *m.*

grandmother, *s.* grand'mère *f.*

grandson, *s.* petit-fils *m.*

granite, *s.* granit *m.*

granny, *s.* grand'maman *f.*

grant, *v.a.* accorder, concéder; accéder; ~ *that* admettre que; — *s.* don *m.*, concession *f.*; subside *m.*

grape, *s.* grain *m.* de raisin; *bunch of* ~s grappe *f.* de raisin.

grape-fruit, *s.* pamplemousse *f.*

graph, *s.* graphique *m.*, courbe *f.*

graphic, *adj.* graphique.

grasp, *v.a.* saisir; comprendre; — *s.* prise *f.*, étreinte *f.*

grass, *s.* herbe *f.*; gazon *m.*

grasshopper, *s.* sauterelle *f.*

grate, *s.* grille *f.*; — *v.a.*

râper; faire grincer; *v.n.* grincer.

grateful, *adj.* reconnaissant (à).

gratitude, *s.* reconnaissance *f.*

grave[1], *s.* tombe *f.*, tombeau *m.*

grave[2], *adj.* grave.

gravel, *s.* gravier *m.*

gravy, *s.* jus *m.*

gray, *adj.* gris.

graze, *v.n.* paître.

grease, *s.* graisse *f.*; — *v.a.* graisser.

great, *adj.* grand; *a ~ many* beaucoup (de).

greatly, *adj.* très; beaucoup.

greatness, *s.* grandeur *f.*

greed, *s.* avidité *f.*

greedy, *adj.* avide.

Greek, *adj.* grec, grecque; —*s.* Grec *m.*, Grecque *f.*

green, *adj.* vert.

greengrocer, *s.* fruitier, -ère *m. f.*

greenhouse, *s.* serre *f.*

greet, *v.a.* saluer.

greeting, *s.* salutation *f.*

grey, *adj.* gris.

grief, *s.* chagrin *m.*

grieve, *v.a.* affliger; *v.n.* s'affliger.

grill, *s.* gril *m.*; — *v.a.* griller.

grim, *adj.* sévère, menaçant. sinistre.

grin, *v.n.* grimacer; *~ at* faire des grimaces à; — *s.* rire *m.*; grimace *f.*

grind, *v.a.* moudre.

grinder, *s.* (*tooth*) molaire *f.*

grindstone, *s.* meule *f.*

grip, *s.* étreinte *f.*; prise *f.*; — *v.a.* saisir, étreindre.

groan, *v. n.* gémir; — *s.* gémissement *m.*

grocer, *s.* épicier, -ère *m.*

f.; ~'s (*shop*) épicerie *f.*

grocery, *s.* épicerie *f.*

groove, *s.* rainure *f.*

gross, *adj.* gros; grossier; (*weight*) brut.

ground, *s.* terre *f.*; terrain *m.*; (*reason*) raison *f.*; ~s jardins *m. pl.*; — *v.a.* fonder.

group, *s.* groupe *m.*

grow, *v.a.* cultiver; *v.n.* (*pers.*) grandir; (*plant*) croître; (*become*) devenir.

growl, *s.* grondement *m.*; — *v.n.* gronder.

grown-up, *s.* grande personne *f.*

growth, *s.* croissance *f.*; culture *f.*; récolte *f.*

grudge, *s.* rancune *f.*; — *v.a.* donner à contrecœur à.

grumble, *v.n.* grommeler; — *s.* grognement *m.*

grunt, *s.* grognement *m.*; — *v.n.* grogner.

guarantee, *s.* garantie *f.*; (*pers.*) garant, -e *m. f.*; — *v.a.* garantir.

guard, *s.* garde *f.*; (*train*) conducteur *m.*; — *v.a.* garder; *v.n.* ~ *against* se garder.

guardian, *s.* gardien, -enne *m. f.*

guess, *v.a. & n.* deviner; conjecturer; — *s.* conjecture *f.*

guest, *s.* invité *m.*, convive *m.*; hôte, -esse *m. f.*

guide, *s.* guide *m.*; — *v. a.* guider.

guide-book, *s.* guide *m.*

guilt, *s.* culpabilité *f.*

guilty, *adj.* coupable (de).

guitar, *s.* guitare *f.*

gulf, *s.* golfe *m.*

gull, *s.* mouette *f.*

gullet, *s.* gosier *m.*

gum¹, *s.* gomme *f.;* — *v.a.* gommer.

gum², *s.* *(teeth)* gencive *f.*

gun, *s.* fusil *m.;* canon *m.*

gush, *v.i.* jaillir; — *s.* jaillissement *m.*

gutter, *s.* *(street)* ruisseau *m.*

gymnasium, *s.* gymnase *m.*

gymnastics, *s.* gymnastique *f.*

H

haberdashery, *s.* mercerie *f.*

habit, *s.* habitude *f.*

hail, *s.* grêle *f.;* — *v.n.* grêler.

hair, *s.* *(single)* cheveu *m.;* *(whole)* cheveux *m. pl.;* *(animal)* poil *m.*

hairdresser, *s.* coiffeur, -euse *m. f.*

half, *s.* moitié *f.;* demi *m.;* — *adj.* demi; ∼ *an hour* une demi-heure *f.*

half-time, *s.* mi-temps *m.*

half-way, *adv.* à mi-chemin; à moitié chemin; à mi-distance.

hall, *s.* *(grande)* salle *f.;* *(college)* réfectoire *m.;* *(house)* vestibule *m.;* *(hotel)* hall *m.*

halt, *s.* halte *f.;* *v.a.* faire arrêter; *v.n.* faire halte; boiter.

ham, *s.* jambon *m.*

hammer, *s.* marteau *m.*

hand, *s.* main *f.;* *(pers.)* ouvrier *m.;* *(clock)* aiguille *f.;* on the one ∼ ...on the other d'une part ... d'autre part.

handbag, *s.* sac (à main) *m.*

handbook, *s.* manuel *m.*

handkerchief, *s.* mouchoir *m.*

handle, *s.* manche *m.*, anse *f.;* poignée *f.;* bras *m.;* — *v.a.* manier; traiter.

hand-made, *adj.* fait à la main.

handsome, *adj.* joli.

handwriting, *s.* écriture *f.*

handy, *adj.* *(pers.)* adroit; *(thing)* commode.

hang, *v.a.* pendre; *(with tapestry)* tendre; ∼ *up* accrocher; *v. n.* pendre; dépendre (de).

hanger, *s.* crochet *m.;* cintre *m.*

happen, *v.n.* arriver; se trouver; *I* ∼*ed to be present* je me trouvais là par hasard.

happiness, *s.* bonheur *m.*

happy, *adj.* heureux.

harbour, *s.* port *m.*

hard, *adj.* dur; difficile; sévère; ∼ *up* gêné; — *adv.* durement; *work* ∼ travailler dur.

hardly, *adv.* à peine.

hardware, *s.* quincaillerie *f.*

hare, *s.* lièvre *m.*

harm, *s.* mal *m.;* tort *m.;* *do* ∼ *to* nuire à.

harmful, *adj.* nuisible.

harmless, *adj.* inoffensif.

harmony, *s.* harmonie *f.*

harness, *s.* harnais *m.*

harp, *s.* harpe *f.*

harsh, *adj.* revêche; âpre; rigoureux.

hart, *s.* cerf *m.*

harvest, *s.* moisson *f.;* *(crop)* récolte *f.*

haste, *s.* hâte *f.;* *make* ∼ se dépêcher.

hasten, *v.a.* hâter; *v. n.* se dépêcher.

hasty, *adj.* précipité.

hat, *s.* chapeau *m.*

hate, *v: a.* haïr; — *s.* haine *f.*

hateful, *adj.* odieux.

hatred, *s.* haine *f.*

haul, *v.a.* traîner; haler; — *s.* traction *f.*

haulage, *s.* roulage *m.*; frais *m.pl.* de roulage.

haunch, *s.* hanche *f.*

haunt, *v.a.* fréquenter; hanter.

have, *v.a.* avoir; *(food)* prendre; ~ *to* il faut que, il faut (+ *inf.*); *had rather* préférer (+ *inf.*); ~ *on* *(clothes)* porter.

haversack, *s.* havresac *m.*

hawk, *s.* faucon *m.*

hay, *s.* foin *m.*

hazard, *s.* hasard *m.*

hazy, *adj.* brumeux; *(fig.)* vegue.

he, *pron.* il, *(alone)* lui; ~ *who* celui qui

head, *s.* tête *f.*; *chief)* chef *m.*; *(river)* source *f.*; — *v.a.* être en tête de; — *adj.* principal.

headache, *s.* mal *m.* de tête.

heading, *s.* en-tête *m.*

headlight, *s.* phare *m.*, projecteur *m.*

headline, *s.* manchette *f.*

headmaster, *s.* directeur *m.*

headquarters, *s. pl.* quartier *m.* général.

heal, *v.a.* guérir; *v.n.* se guérir.

health, *s.* santé *f.*

healthy, *adj.* bien portant; sain.

heap, *s.* amas *m.*, tas *m.*; — *v.a.* ~ *up* entasser.

hear, *v.a.* entendre; *(listen to)* écouter; *v. n.* entendre; ~ *from* recevoir une lettre de; ~ *of* avoir des nouvelles de; entendre parler de.

heart, *s.* cœur *m.*; *by* ~ par cœur.

hearth, *s.* foyer *m.*

hearty, *adj.* cordial.

heat, *s.* chaleur *f.*; *(anger)* colère *f.*; — *v.a.&n.* chauffer.

heating, *s.* chauffage *m.*

heave, *v.a.* lever; pousser; jeter; *v.n.* se soulever.

heaven, *s.* ciel *m.*

heavy, *adj.* pesant; lourd.

hedge, *s.* haie *f.*

hedgehog, *s.* hérisson *m.*

heed, *s.* attention *f.*; *take* ~ *to* faire attention à.

heedless, *adj.* insouciant; inattentif.

heel, *s.* talon *m.*

height, *s.* hauteur *f.*

heir, *s.* héritier *m.*

heiress, *s.* héritière *f.*

helicopter, *s.* hélicoptère *m.*

hell, *s.* enfer *m.*

hello, *int.* allô!

helm, *s.* barre (du gouvernail) *f.*

helmet, *s.* casque *m.*

help, *v.a.* aider; secourir; ~ *oneself* se servir; — *s.* aide *f.*

helpful, *adj.* *(pers.)* serviable; *(thing)* utile.

helping, *s.* portion *f.*

helpless, *adj.* sans secours.

hem, *s.* ourlet *m.*; bord *m.*

hen, *s.* poule *f.*

hence, *adv.* *(place, time)* d'ici; *(reason)* de là.

her, *pron.* *(acc.)* la; *(dat.)* lui; *(alone)* elle.

herb, *s.* herbe *f.*

herd, *s.* troupeau *m.*

here, *adv.* ici; *from* ~ d'ici; *look* ~! dites donc!; ~ *he is!* le voici!

heritage, *s.* héritage *m.*

hermit, *s.* ermite *m.*

hero, *s.* héros *m.*

heroic, *adj.* héroïque.

heroine, *s.* héroïne *f.*

herring, s. hareng m.

hers, pron. à elle; le sien, la sienne, les siens, les siennes.

herself, pron. elle-même; (reflex.) se.

hesitate, v.n. hésiter.

hew, v.a. couper.

hiccough, hiccup, s. hoquet m.

hide, v.a. cacher; v.n. se cacher.

hideous, adj. hideux; horrible.

high, adj. haut; (speed) grand; (price) élevé; — adv. haut.

highness, s. altesse f.

highroad, highway, s. grande route f.

hike, v.n. faire du tourisme à pied.

hiker, s. touriste f., randonneur, -euse (à pied) m. f.

hill, s. colline f.

hilly, adj. montueux.

him, pron. (acc.) le; (dat.) lui; (alone) lui.

himself, pron. lui-même; (reflex.) se; by ~ tout seul.

hinder, v.a. empêcher.

hindrance, s. empêchement m.

hinge, s. gond m.; charnière f.; — v.n. tourner (sur).

hint, s. allusion f.; avis m.; — v.n. ~ at faire allusion à.

hip, s. hanche f.

hire, s. louage m.; for ~ à louer; — v.a. & n. louer.

his, pron. son, sa; ses.

hiss, s. sifflement m.; — v. a. & n. siffler.

historic(al), adj. historique.

history, s. histoire f.

hit, v.a. frapper; at-

teindre; trouver; — s. coup m.; succès m.

hitch-hike, v.n. faire de l'auto-stop.

hive, s. ruche f.

hoard, s. magot m., amas m.; — v. a. thésauriser; entasser.

hoarse, adj. raque.

hobby, s. dada m.

hockey, s. hockey m.

hoe, s. houe f.

hog, s. porc m.

hoist, v.a. hisser; —s. monte-charge m.

hold, v.a. tenir; retenir; maintenir; contenir; (consider) tenir (pour); ~ back retenir; ~ out tendre; offrir; ~ that soutenir que; — v.n. tenir; (be true) être vrai; ~ on ne pas lâcher prise; ~ out durer.

holder, s. possesseur m.

hole, s. trou m.

holiday, s. fête f., jour m. férié; (holidays) vacances f. pl., congé m.; be on être en congé, en vacance(s).

hollow, adj. reux, -euse; fig. faux, fausse.

holy, adj. saint; bénit.

home, s. foyer m., demeure f.; at ~ chez soi, à la maison; — adv. chez soi; come, go ~ rentrer; — adj. domestque; de l'intérieur.

homeless, adj. sans asile.

homely, adj. simple; modeste.

homesickness, s. mal du pays m.

homeward, adv. vers la maison; ~ bound en retour.

honest, adj. honnête.

honesty, s. honnêteté f.

honey, s. miel m.

honeymoon, s. lune f. de miel.

honour, s. honneur m.; — v.a. honorer.

hood, s. capuchon m.; capeline f.; (motor) capote f.

hoof, s. sabot m.

hook, s. crochet m., croc m.; (fishing) hameçon m.

hoop, s. cercle m.

hoot, v.a. huer; v.n. corner; — s. huée f.

hooter, s. sirène f.; corne f., trompe f.

hop, v.n. sautiller.

hope, s. espérance f.; espoir m.; — v.n. espérer.

hopeful, adj. plein d'espoir.

hopeless, adj. sans espoir

horizon, s. horizon m.

horizontal, adj. horizontal.

horn, s. corne f.; trompe f.

horrible, adj. affreux, -euse.

horse, s. cheval m. (pl. chevaux).

horseback: on ~ à cheval.

horseman, s. cavalier m.

horse-race, s. course f. de chevaux.

horseshoe, s. fer m. à cheval.

hose, s. bas m. pl.

hospitable, adj. hospitalier.

hospital, s. hôpital m.

hospitality, s. hospitalité f.

host, s. hôte m.

hostel, s. pension f. pour étudiants, hôtellerie f.

hostess, s. hôtesse f.

hostile, adj. hostile (à).

hostility, s. hostilité f.

hot, adj. chaud.

hotel, s. hôtel m.

hour, s. heure f.

house, s. maison f.; (theatre) salle f.

household, s. ménage m.

housekeeper, s. gouvernante f.

housekeeping, s. ménage m.

housewife, s. ménagère f.

housework, s. travaux (m. pl.) domestiques; do the ~ faire le ménage.

how, adv. comment; ~ many, much? combien de?; ~ long? combien de temps?; ~ are you? comment allez-vous?

however, adv. de quelque manière que...; toutefois, cependant.

howl, v. a. & n. hurler; — s. hurlement m.

hue, s. couleur f.; cri m.

hug, v.a. serrer dans les bras.

huge, adj. énorme.

hullo, int. ho là!; allô!

hum, v. n. bourdonner; — s. bourdonnement m.

human, adj. humain.

humanity, s. humanité f.

humble, adj. humble.

humorous, adj. amusant; humoristique; drôle.

humour, s. humour m.; be in a ~ to être d'humeur à.

hundred, s. cent m.

hundredth, adj. centième.

hundredweight, s. quintal m.

Hungarian, adj. hongrois; — s. Hongrois, -e m. f.

hunger, s. faim f.; — v.n. avoir faim.

hungry, adj. affamé; be ~ avoir faim.

hunt, v.a. & n. chasser; (with hounds) chasser à courre; — s. chasse (à courre) f.

hunter, s. chasseur m.

hurl, *v.a.* jeter; lancer.

hurry, *s.* hâte; *be in a* ~ *to* être pressé de; — *v.n.* se presser; ~ *up!* pressez-vous!; *v.a.* presser, hâter.

hurt, *v.a.* faire mal à; blesser; *(feelings)* froisser.

husband, *s.* mari *m.*

hush, *int.* chut!; — *s.* calme *m.;* — *v.a.* calmer.

husk, *s.* cosse *f.;* glume *f.;* — *v. a.* écosser, monder.

hut, *s.* cabane *f.*

hydrogen, *s.* hydrogène *m.*

hygiene, *s.* hygiène *f.*

hymn, *s.* hymne *m.*

hyphen, *s.* trait d'union *m.*

hypnotize, *v.a.* hypnotiser.

hypocrisy, *s.* hypocrisie *f.*

hysterical, *adj.* hystérique.

I

I, *pron.* je; moi.

ice, *s.* glace *f.*

ice-cream, *s.* glace *f.*

icy, *adj.* glacial.

idea, *s.* idée *f.*

ideal, *adj. & s.* idéal *(m.).*

identical, *adj.* identique.

identity, *s.* identité *f.;* ~ *card* carte *f.* d'identité.

idle, *adj.* désœuvré;*(lazy)* paresseux; — *v.a.* ~ *away* perdre.

idleness, *s.* oisiveté *f.;* paresse *f.*

if, *conj.* si; *as* ~ comme si.

ignition, *s.* ignition *f.;* *(motor)* allumage *m.*

ignorant, *adj.* ignorant; *be* ~ *of* ignorer.

ignore, *v.a.* refuser de connaître.

ill, *adj.* malade; *(bad)* mauvais; *be taken* ~ tomber malade; ~ *luck* malheur *m.;* — *adv.* mal; — *s.* mal *m.*

illegal, *adj.* illégal.

illegitimate, *adj.* illégitime.

illicit, *adj.* illicite.

illness, *s.* maladie *f.*

illusion, *s.* illusion *f.*

illustrate, *v.a.* illustrer.

illustration, *s.* illustration *f.;* exemple *m.*

image, *s.* image *f.*

imagination, *s.* imagination *f.*

imagine, *v. a.* imaginer; se figurer.

imitate, *v.a.* imiter.

immediate, *adj.* immédiat.

immense, *adj.* immense.

immigrant, *adj. & s.* immigrant, -e *(m. f.).*

immigrate, *v. n.* immigrer

immigration, *s.* immigration *f.*

immoral, *adj.* immoral.

immortal, *adj.* immortel.

impatience, *s.* impatience *f.*

impatient, *adj.* impatient.

impediment, *s.* obstacle *m.*

impel, *v.a.* forcer; pousser.

imperfect, *adj. & s.* imparfait *(m.).*

imperial, *adj.* impérial.

impertinent, *adj.* impertinent.

implement, *s.* outil *m.,* ustensile *m.*

implication, *s.* implication *f.*

implore, *v.a.* implorer.

imply, *v.a.* impliquer; donner à entendre.

import, *v.a.* importer; *(mean)* signifier; — *s.* *(usu. pl.)* importation(s) *f.*

importance, *s.* importance *f.*

important, *adj.* important.

importer, *s.* importateur *m.*

impose, *v.a.* imposer (à).

impossibility, *s.* impossibilité *f.*

impossible, *adj.* impossible.

impression, *s.* impression *f.*

imprison, *v.a.* emprisonner.

imprisonment, *s.* emprisonnement.

improbable, *adj.* improbable.

improper, *adj.* impropre; inconvenant.

improve, *v.a.* améliorer; perfectionner; *v.n.* s'améliorer.

improvement, *s.* amélioration *f.;* progrès *m.*

impulse, *s.* impulsion *f.*

in, *prep.* dans; en; à; ～ *the morning* le matin; ～ *the evening* le soir; ～ *time* à temps; ～ *spring* au printemps.

inadequate, *adj.* insuffisant.

incapable, *adj.* incapable (de).

incense, *s.* encens *m.*

inch, *s.* pouce *m.*

incident, *s.* incident *m.*

incidental, *adj.* fortuit; incidental.

incline, *v. a. & n.* incliner.

include, *v.a.* comprendre; renfermer.

inclusive, *adj.* inclusif; ～ *of* y compris.

income, *s.* revenu *m.*

income-tax, *s.* impôt *m.* sur (le) revenu.

incompatible, *adj.* incompatible.

incompetent, *adj.* incom-

pétent.

inconsistent, *adj.* inconséquent.

inconvenient, *adj.* incommode, gênant.

increase, *v.a.&n.* augmenter; — *s.* augmentation *f.*

incredible, *adj.* incroyable.

incur, *v. a.* contracter; encourir; s'attirer.

incurable, *adj.* incurable.

indebted, *adj.* endetté.

indeed, *adv.* de fait; vraiment.

independence, *s.* indépendance *f.*

independent, *adj.* indépendant.

index, *s.* index *m.; (on dial)* aiguille *f.; (math.)* exposant *m.;* ～ *finger* index *m.*

Indian, *adj.* indien; des Indes; ～ *corn* maïs *m.* — *s.* Indien, -enne *m. f.*

India-rubber, *s.* gomme *f.*

indicate, *v.a.* indiquer.

indicator, *s.* indicateur *m.*

indifference, *s.* indifférence *f.*

indifferent, *adj.* indifférent (à).

indigestion, *s.* indigestion *f.*

indignant, *adj.* indigné.

indirect, *adj.* indirect.

indiscreet, *adj.* indiscret.

indiscretion, *s.* indiscrétion *f.;* imprudence *f.*

indispensable, *adj.* indispensable.

individual, *adj.* individuel; — *s.* individu *m.*

indoor, *adj.* d'intérieur.

indoors, *adv.* à la maison; *stay* ～ ne pas sortir.

induce, *v.a.* persuader; *(cause)* occasionner.

inducement, *s.* encouragement *m.* ～s attraits

m. pl.

indulge, *v. a.* se livrer (à); caresser; *v.n.* ~ *in* s'abandonner à; se laisser aller à.

indulgence, *s.* indulgence *f.;* laisser-aller *m.*

industrial, *adj.* industriel.

industrious, *adj.* travailleur.

industry, *s.* industrie *f.*

inefficient, *adj.* incapable; inefficace.

inestimable, *adj.* inestimable.

inevitable, *adj.* inévitable.

inexpensive, *adj.* peu coûteux, peu cher, bon marché.

inexperienced, *adj.* inexpérimenté.

inexplicable, *adj.* inexplicable.

infallible, *adj.* infaillible.

infamous, *adj.* infâme.

infant, *s.* enfant *m. f.*

infantry, *s.* infanterie *f.*

infant-school, *s.* école *f.* maternelle.

infection, *s.* infection *f.*

infer, *v.a.* conclure, déduire.

inferior, *adj.* inférieur.

infinitive, *s.* infinitif *m.*

infirm, *adj.* infirm.

infirmary, *s.* infirmerie *f.*

inflame, *v.a.* enflammer

inflammable, *adj.* inflammable.

inflate, *v.a.* gonfler.

inflexion, *s.* inflexion *f.*

inflict, *v.a.* infliger; imposer à.

influence, *s.* influence *f.;* — *v.a.* influencer.

influenza, *s.* grippe *f.*

inform, *v.a.* informer.

informal, *adj.* sans cérémonie.

information, *s.* information *f.;* renseignements

m. pl.

ingenious, *adj.* ingénieux.

ingenuity, *s.* ingéniosité *f.*

ingredient, *s.* ingrédient *m.*

inhabit, *v.a.* habiter.

inhabitant, *s.* habitant *m.*

inherit, *v.a. & n.* hériter (de).

inheritance, *s.* héritage *m.*

initial, *s.* initiale *f.*

initiative, *s.* initiative *f.*

injection, *s.* injection *f.*

injure, *v.a.* nuire à; blesser.

injury, *s.* préjudice *m.;* dommage *m.;* blessure *f.*

injustice, *s.* injustice *f.*

ink, *s.* encre *f.*

inland, *s. & adj.* intérieur *(m.).*

inn, *s.* auberge *f.;* taverne *f.*

inner, *adj.* intérieur.

innocence, *s.* innocence *f.*

innocent, *adj.* innocent.

innumerable, *adj.* innombrable.

inoculate, *v.a.* inoculer.

inquire, *v.n.* ~ *about* s'enquérir, se renseigner sur; ~ *after* demander après, demander des nouvelles de.

inquiry, *s.* demande *f.;* recherche *f.; make inquiries about* s'informer de; ~ *office* bureau *m.* des renseignements.

insane, *adj.* fou, fol, folle.

inscription, *s.* inscription *f*

insect, *s.* insecte *m.*

insecure, *adj.* peu sûr, mal assuré.

insensible, *adj.* sans connaissance; insensible.

inseparable, *adj.* inséparable.

insert, *v. a.* insérer (dans).

inside, *s. & adj.* intérieur

(m.); — adv. à l'intérieur.

insignificant, adj. insignifiant.

insist, v.n. insister (on sur).

insistence, s. insistance f.

inspect, v.a. inspecter.

inspection, s. inspection f.

inspector, s. inspecteur m.

inspiration, s. inspiration f.

inspire, v.a. inspirer.

install. v.a. installer.

instalment, s. fraction f., acompte m.

instance, s. exemple m.; cas m.; for ~ par exemple.

instant, adj. urgent; — s. instant m.

instead, adv. ~ of au lieu de.

instinct, s. instinct m.

institute, s. institut m.; — v.a. instituer.

institution, s. institution f.

instruct, v. a. instruire.

instruction, s. instruction f.

instructive, adj. instructif.

instrument, s. instrument m.

instrumental, adj. instrumental.

insufficiency, s. insuffisance f.

insufficient, adj. insuffisant.

insult, s. insulte f.; — v.a. insulter.

insurance, s. assurance f.

insure, v. a. (faire) assurer.

integral, adj. intégral; — s. intégrale f.

integrity, s. intégrité f.

intellectual, adj. intéllectuel.

intelligence, s. intelligence f.; (information) renseignements m.pl.

intelligent, adj. intelligent.

intend, v. a. avoir l'intention de (faire qch.), se proposer de; destiner qn., qch. (à); vouloir dire.

intense, adj. intense.

intensity, s. intensité f.

intent, s. intention f.; — adj. ~ on absorbé dans.

intention, s. intention f.

intercontinental, adj. intercontinental.

interest, s. intérêt m.; — v.a. intéresser.

interesting, adj. intéressant.

interfere, v. n. intervenir; ~ with gêner; se mêler de.

interior, adj. & s. intérieur (m.).

intermediate, adj. intermédiaire.

intermission, s. interruption f., pause f.

internal, adj. interne; intérieur.

international, adj. international.

interpret, v.a. interpréter.

interpretation, s. interprétation f.

interpreter, s. interprète m.

interrogation, s. interrogation f.

interrupt, v.a. interrompre.

interruption, s. interruption f.

interval, s. intervalle m.

intervention, s. intervention f.

interview, entrevue f.; interview m. f.

intimate, adj. intime.

into, prep. dans; en.

intolerable, adj. intolérable.

introduce, v.a. introduire; (pers.) présenter.

introduction, *s.* introduction *f.; (pers.)* présentation *f.*

invade, *v.a.* envahir.

invalid¹, *s.* malade *m. f.*

invalid², *adj.* invalide.

invasion, *s.* invasion *f.*

invent, *v.a.* inventer.

invention, *s.* invention *f.*

inverted, *adj.* ~ *commas* guillemets *m.*

invest, *v.a.* *(money)* placer.

investigate, *v.a.* rechercher.

investigation, *s.* investigation *f.*

investment, *s.* placement *m.*

invisible, *adj.* invisible.

invitation, *s.* invitation *f.*

invite, *v.a.* inviter.

invoice, *s.* facture *f.*

involuntary, *adj.* involontaire.

involve, *v.a.* envelopper (dans); impliquer (dans); entraîner.

inward, *adj.* intérieur; interne.

inwards, *adv.* intérieurement; en dedans.

Irish, *adj.* irlandais

iron, *s.* fer *m.* — *v.a.* repasser.

ironical, *adj.* ironique.

ironware, *s.* quincaillerie *f.*

ironworks, *s.* ferronnerie *f.*

irony, *s.* ironie *f.*

irregular, *adj.* irrégulier.

irrelevant, *adj.* non pertinent; hors de la question; inapplicable (à).

irresolute, *adj.* irrésolu.

irritate, *v.a.* irriter.

island, *s.* île *f.; (street)* refuge *m.*

isle, *s.* île *f.*

isolate, *v.a.* isoler.

isotope, *s.* isotope *m.*

issue, *s.* *(way out)* sortie *f.; (end)* issue *f.,* fin *f.,* résultat *m.; (publication)* publication *f.,* édition, *(paper)* numéro *m.,* *(money)* émission *f.;* — *v. a.* émettre; publier.

it, *pron.* il, elle; *(acc.)* le, la; *of it* en; *to* ~ y.

Italien, *adj.* italien; — *s.* Italien, -enne *m.f.*

itch, *s.* démangeaison *f.;* — *v.n.* démanger.

itchy, *adj.* galeux.

item, *s.* article *m.,* détail *m.*

its, *pron.* son, sa, *pl.* ses.

itself, *pron.* lui-même, elle-même; se; *(emphatic)* même.

ivory, *s.* ivoire *m.*

ivy, *s.* lierre *m.*

J

jack, *s.* *(cards)* valet *m.; (lifting)* cric *m.,* lève-auto *m.*

jackal, *s.* chacal *m.*

jacket, *s.* veston *m.*

jail, *s.* prison *f.*

jam¹, *s.* confiture *f.*

jam², *v.a.* serrer; coincer; encombrer; — *s.* encombrement *m.*

January, *s.* janvier *m.*

Japanese, *adj.* japonais.

jar, *s.* jarre *f.;* bocal *m.*

javelin, *s.* javeline *f.*

jaw, *s.* mâchoire *f.*

jealous, *adj.* jaloux.

jealousy, *s.* jalousie *f.*

jelly, *s.* gelée *f.*

jerk, *s.* saccade *f.;* secousse *f*

jersey, *s.* jersey *m.*

jet, *s.* jet *m.; (gas)* bec *m.;* ~ *plane* avion *m.* à réaction.

Jew, *s.* Juif *m.*

jewel, *s.* bijou *m.*

jeweller, *s.* bijoutier *m.;* ~'s *shop* bijouterie *f.*

jewellery, *s.* bijouterie *f.*

jib, *s.* foc *m.*

job, *s.* tâche *f.;* travail *m.* (*pl.* -aux); emploi *m.;* *odd* ~s petits travaux *m.*

join, *v.a.* joindre; unir; se joindre (à); *v.n.* se joindre; s'unir; ~ *in* prendre part à.

joiner, *s.* menuisier *m.*

joint, *s.* joint *m.;* articulation *f.;* (*meat*) gros morceau *m.;* — *adj.* commun; indivis; co-; ~-*stock company* société *f.* par actions.

joke, *s.* plaisanterie *f.*

jolly, *adj.* joyeux; jovial.

journal, *s.* journal *m.* (*pl.* -aux).

journalist, *s.* journaliste *m.*

journey, *s.* voyage *m.*

joy, *s.* joie *f.*

joyful, *adj.* joyeux.

judge, *s.* juge *m.;* — *v.a.&n.* juger.

judg(e)ment, *s.* jugement *m.*

jug, *s.* cruche *f.;* pot *m.*

juggler, *s.* jongleur *m.*

Jugoslav, *adj.* yougoslave.

juice, *s.* jus *m.*

July, *s.* juillet *m.*

jump, *s.* saut *m.;* — *v.n. & a.* sauter.

junction, *s.* jonction *f.;* (gare *f.* d')embranchement. *m.*

June, *s.* juin *m.*

jungle, jungle *f.*

junior, *adj.* jeune.

jury, *s.* jury *m.*

juryman, *s.* juré *m.*

just, *adj.* juste; — *adv.* (*exactly*) juste; (*barely*) à peine; ~ *now*

il n'y a qu'un instant; ~ *so* précisément.

justice, *s.* justice *f.*

justification, *s.* justification *f.*

justify, *v.a.* justifier.

jut, *v.n.* ~ *out* faire saillie.

juvenile, *adj.* juvénile; d'enfants.

K

kangaro, *s.* kangourou *m.*

keel, *s.* quille *f.*

keen, *adj.* aigu; tranchant; (*mind*) pénétrant; *be* ~ *on* être enthousiaste de, avoir la passion de.

keep, *v.a.* tenir; garder; maintenir; observer; ~ *back* retenir; ~ *up* soutenir; — *v. n.* rester; ~ *on* continuer à.

keeper, *s.* gardien *m.*

kerb, *s.* bordure *f.*

kernel, *s.* amande *f.*

kettle, *s.* bouilloire *f.*

key, *s.* clé *f.;* (*piano*) touche *f.;* (*music*) ton *m.*

keyboard, *s.* clavier *m.*

kick, *v.a.* donner un coup de pied (à); *v.n.* ruer; — *s.* coup *m.* de pied.

kid, *s.* chevreau *m.;* (*child*) gosse *m. f.*

kidney, *s.* rein *m.;* (*food*) rognon *m.*

kill, *v.a. & n.* tuer; abattre.

kilogram(me), *s.* kilogramme *m.*

kilometre, *s.* kilomètre *m.*

kind, *adj.* bon; bienveillant; aimable.

kindle, *v.a.* allumer; exciter; enflammer; *v.n.* s'enflammer.

kindly, *adj.* bon; doux.

kindness, *s.* bonté *f.;* bienveillance *f.*

kindred, *s.* parenté *f.;* parents *m.pl.*

king, *s.* roi *m.*

kingdom, *s.* royaume *m.*

kinsman, *s.* parent *m.*

kiss, *s.* baiser *m.; v.a.* embrasser; baiser.

kit, *s.* fourniment *m.*

kitchen, *s.* cuisine *f.*

kite, *s.* cerf-volant *m.*

kitten, *s.* petit chat *m.*

knapsack, *s.* havresac *m.*

knee, *s.* genou *m.* *(pl. -x).*

kneel, *v.n.* s'agenouiller; ~ *down* se mettre à genoux.

knife, *s.* couteau *m.*

knight, *s.* chevalier *m.;* *(chess)* cavalier *m.*

knit, *v. a.* tricoter; *(brow)* froncer.

knob, *s.* bosse *f.;* bouton *m.*

knock, *s.* coup *m.;* — *v.a.* & *n.* frapper; ~ *down* renverser.

knocker, *s.* marteau *m.*

knot, *s.* nœud *m.;* *v.a.* nouer; *v.n.* se nouer.

know, *v.a.* savoir; connaître; reconnaître; ~*n for* connu pour; — *v.n.* savoir; ~ *of* avoir connaissance de; *let* ~ prévenir.

knowledge, *s.* connaissance *f.;* *(acquired)* savoir *m.*

knuckle, *s.* articulation *f.* de doigt.

L

label, *s.* étiquette *f.;* — *v.a.* étiqueter.

laboratory, *s.* laboratoire *m.*

labour, *s.* travail *m.;* ~ *(e)exchange* bureau *m.* de placement; — *v.n.* travailler.

labourer, *s.* travailleur *m.*

lace, *s.* dentelle *f.*

lack, *s.* manque; — *v.a.* & *n.* ~ *(for)* manquer (de).

lad, *s.* jeune garçon *m.*

ladder, *s.* échelle *f.*

lading, *s.* chargement *m.*

ladle, *s.* louche *f.*

lady, *s.* dame *f.; young* ~ jeune dame *f.;* demoiselle *f.,* jeune fille *f.*

lag, *v.n.* ~ *behind* rester en arrière.

lake, *s.* lac *m.*

lamb, *s.* agneau *m.*

lame, *adj.* boiteux.

lamp, *s.* lampe *f.*

lamp-shade, *s.* abat-jour *m.*

land, *s.* *(not sea)* terre *f.;* *(country)* pays *m.;* — *v.n.* & *a.* débarquer; *(plane)* atterrir.

landing, *s.* débarquement *m.;* *(plane)* atterrissage *m.*

landing-strip, *s.* piste *f.* d'atterrissage.

landlady, *s.* propriétaire *f.;* aubergiste *f.*

landlord, *s.* propriétaire *m.;* aubergiste *m.*

landscape, *s.* paysage *m.*

lane, *s.* ruelle *f.;* chemin *m.*

language, *s.* langue *f.;* *(expression)* langage *m.*

lap[1], *s.* genoux *m. pl.;* *(coat)* pan *m.;* *(sports)* tour (de piste) *m.*

lap[2], *v. a.* envelopper (de); laper.

lapse, *s.* faute *f.;* chute *f.;* lapsus *m.;* *(time)* laps *m.;* — *v.n.* retomber (dans); *(time)* s'écouler; *(fail)* faire un faux pas.

lard, *s.* saindoux *m.*

larder, *s.* dépense *f.*

large, *adj.* gros, grand; considérable; *at* ~ en liberté, en général.

lark, *s.* alouette *f.*

last, *adj.* dernier; — *adv.* dernièrement, en dernier lieu; — *v.n.* durer.

lasting, *adj.* durable.

latch, *s.* loquet *m.*

latch-key, *s.* clef *f.* de porte.

late, *adj.* tardif; *be* ~ être en retard; — *adv.* tard; ~*r on* par la suite; plus tard.

lately, *adv.* dernièrement, recemment.

latest, *adj.* récent, le dernier; *at (the)* ~ au plus tard.

lathe, *s.* tour *m.*

lather, *s.* mousse *f.*

Latin, *adj.* latin; — *s.* latin *m.*

latter, *adj.* dernier; *the* ~ ce dernier; celui-ci, celle-ci, ceux-ci.

laugh, *v.n.* rire *(at* de); — *s.* rire *m.*

laughter, *s.* rire *m.*

launch, *v.a.* lancer.

launching, *adj.* ~ *site* rampe *f.* à fusées.

laundry, *s.* buanderie *f.*, blanchisserie *f.*

lavatory, *s.* lavabo *m.* cabinet *m.* de toilette,

lavish, *adj.* prodigue (de). — *v.a.* prodiguer.

law, *s.* loi *f.*; droit *m.*

law-court, *s.* cour *f.* de justice, tribunal *m.*

lawful, *adj.* légal; permis; légitime.

lawn, *s.* pelouse *f.*

lawn-mower, *s.* tondeuse *f.*

lawsuit, *s.* procès *m.*

lawyer, *s.* homme *m.* de loi avoué *m.; avocat *m.*

lay, *v.a.* coucher, poser, étendre; ~ *aside, by* mettre de côté; *(money)* réserver; ~ *down* poser; ~ *on* appliquer; *be laid up* être alité.

lay-by, *s.* refuge *m.*, garage *m.*

layer, *s.* couche *f.*

lazy, *adj.* paresseux.

lead[1], *s. (metal)* plomb *m.*

lead[2], *v.a. & n.* mener, conduire; ~ *the way* montrer le chemin.

leader, *s.* conducteur *m.; (newspaper)* éditorial *m.*

leadership, *s.* conduite *f.;* direction *f.*

leaf, *s.* feuille *f.; (book)* feuillet *m.;* page *f.*

leak, *s.* fuite *f.;* voie d'eau *f.;* — *v.n.* fuir.

lean, *adj.* maigre.

leap, *v. n. & a.* sauter; — *s.* saut *m.*

learn, *v.a. & n.* apprendre.

learning, *s.* savoir *m.*, science *f.*

leash, *s.* laisse *f.*

least, *adj.* le plus petit; le moindre; — *adv.* le moins; — *s.* moins *m.; at* ~ au moins, à tout le moins; *not in the* ~ pas le moins du monde.

leatner, *s.* cuir *m.*

leave, *v. a.* laisser; quitter; *be left* rester; — *s.* permission *f.;* congé *m.; on* ~ en congé.

lecture, *s.* conférence *f.* *(on* sur); — *v.n.* faire des conférences.

lecturer, *s.* conférencier

m.; *(univ.)* professeur
m. (de faculté).

left, *adj. & s* gauche *(f.)*.

left-luggage office, *s.*
consigne *f.*

leg, *s.* jambe *f.; patte f.*

legal, *adj.* légal.

legislature, *s.* législature
f.

legitimate, *adj.* légitime.

leisure, *s.* loisir *m.; be
at ~* être de loisir.

lemon, *s.* citron *m.*

lemonade, *s.* limonade *f.*

lend, *v.a.* prêter.

length, *s.* longueur *f.;
(time)* durée *f.*

lengthen, *v.a.* allonger;
prolonger.

lens, *s.* lentille *f.*

leopard, *s.* léopard *m.*

less, *adj.* moindre; moins
de; — *adv.* moins; ~
than moins de.

lessen, *v. a. & n.* diminuer.

lesson, *s.* leçon *f.*

lest, *conj.* de peur que.

let, *v.a.* laisser, permettre
à; *(house)* louer; *~ me
go* laisse-moi aller; ~
down laisser tomber
(à); *~ in* laisser entrer.

letter, *s.* lettre *f.; ~s*
belles-lettres *f. pl.*

lettuce, *s.* laitue *f.*

level, *s.* niveau *m.;* — *adj.*
uni; plat; horizontal;
— *v.a.* niveler; pointer.

lever, *s.* levier *m.*

levy, *s.* levée *f.;* — *v.a.*
lever.

lexicon, *s.* lexique *m.*

liability, *s.* responsabilité
f.; liabilities passif *m.*

liable, *adj.* responsable
(de); sujet (à).

liar, *s.* menteur, *m.*

liberal, *adj.* libéral; généreux.

liberty, *s.* liberté *f.*

librarian, *s.* bibliothécaire
m. f.

library, *s.* bibliothèque *f.*

licence, *s.* permission *f.;*
permis *m.,* patente *f.;
(excess of liberty)* li-
cence *f.*

license, *v.a.* accorder un
permis (à).

lick, *v.a.* lécher.

lid, *s.* couvercle *m.*

lie¹, *s.* mensonge *m.;* —
v.n.&a. mentir.

lie², *v.n.* être couché;
(dead) reposer; *(be
situated)* se trouver; ~
down se coucher; *it ~s
with you* cela dépend
de vous.

lieutenant, *s.* lieutenant
m.

life, *s.* vie *f.*

life-insurance, *s.* assurance *f.* sur la vie.

lifeless, *adj.* inanimé.

lift, *v.a.* lever; *fig.* élever;
~ up soulever; — *s.
(apparatus)* ascenseur
m.; give s. o. a ~ faire
monter qn (dans sa
voiture).

light¹, *s.* lumière *f.;* éclairage *f.;* jour *m.;* lampe
f.; (fire) feu *m.; come
to ~* se révéler; — *v. a.*
allumer; éclairer; *v.n.*
s'éclairer; — *adj.* clair;
éclairé.

light², *adj.* léger; *make
~ of* faire peu de cas de.

lighten¹, *v.a.* éclairer;
v.n. faire des éclairs.

lighten², *v.a.* alléger.

lighter, *s.* briquet *m.*

lighthouse, *s.* phare *m.*

lighting, *s.* éclairage *m.*

lightning, *s.* éclair *m.*

like¹, *adj.* semblable, pareil, ressemblant; —
prep. comme.

like², *v.a.* aimer; *I should
~ to* je voudrais +
inf.

likely, *adv*. probable.
likeness, *s*. ressemblance *f.*; portrait *m*.
lily, *s*. lis *m*.
limb, *s*. membre *m*.
limit, *s*. limite *f.*; *v.a.* limiter.
limited, *adj.* ~ *liability company* société anonyme *f*.
line, *s*. ligne *f.*; *(poetry)* vers *m.*; *railw.*) voie *f.*; — *v.a. (garment)* doubler; *v.n.* ~ *up* s'aligner; faire la queue.
linen, *s*. toile *f.*; ligne *m*.
lining, *s*. doublure *f*.
link, *s*. chaînon *m.*, *fig.* lien *m.*; — *v.a.* lier; unir.
lion, *s* lion *m*.
lip, *s*. lèvre *f*.
lipstick, *s*. rouge *m*. à lèvres.
liquid, *adj..* & *s*. liquide *(m.)*.
list, *s*. liste *f.*; — *v.a.* enregistrer.
listen, *v.n.* (also ~ *in*) écouter.
listener, *s*. auditeur, -trice *m. f*.
literary, *adj.* littéraire.
literature, *s*. littérature *f*.
litter, *s*. litière *f*.
little, *adj.* petit; peu de.
live, *v.n.* vivre; *(reside)* habiter, demeurer; ~ *on* vivre de.
lively, *adv.* vivant, gai.
liver, *s*. foie *m*.
living-room, *s*. salle *f*. de séjour.
load, *s*. charge *f.*; fardeau *m.*; — *v.a.* charger.
loaf, *s*. pain *m*.
loan, *s*. prêt *m.*; emprunt *m*.
loathe, *v.a.* détester.
lobby, *s*. couloir *m.*, vestibule *m*.

lobster, *s*. homard *m*.
local, *adj.* local.
location, *s*. emplacement *m.*; situation *f*.
lock[1], *s*. serrure *f*.
lock[2], *s*. *(hair)* boucle *f*.
locksmith, *s*. serrurier *m*.
lodger, *s*. locataire *m. f*.
lodging, *s*. logement *m*. *furnished* ~s garni *m*.
log, *s*. bûche *f.*; bille *f*.
logical, *adj.* logique.
loin, *s*. *(pork)* longe *f.*; *(beef)* aloyau *m.*; rein *m*.
lonely, *adj.* solitaire.
long[1], *adj.* long; *a* ~ *time (since)* depuis longtemps; *be* ~ *in* être long à; — *adv.* longtemps; *how* ~? combien de temps?; ~ *ago* il y a longtemps.
long[2], *v.n.* ~ *for* désirer qch., soupirer après.
long-distance, *adj.* à (longue) distance.
long-play(ing), *adj.* ~ *record* microsillon *m*.
look, *v. n.* & *a.* regarder; ~ *after* soigner; ~ *at* regarder; ~ *back* regarder en arrière; ~ *for* chercher; ~ *into* examiner; ~ *out* être sur ses gardes, *int.* gare!; ~ *over* parcourir; ~ *up* chercher; — *s*. regard *m.*; air *m.*; aspect *m*.
looking-glass, *s*. miroir *m*.
loom, *s*. métier *m*. de tisserand
loop, *s*. boucle .
loose, *adj.* lâche; délié; détaché; vague.
loosen, *v.a.* desserrer.
lord, *s*. maître *m.*; seigneur *m*.
lorry, *s*. camion *m*.
lose, *v.a.* & *n*. perdre.

loss, s. perte f.

lot, s. sort m.; (portion) partage m.; a ~ of beaucoup de.

lottery, s. loterie f.

loud, adj. fort; bruyant.

loud-speaker, s. haut-parleur m.

lounge, s. (grand) vestibule m.; foyer m., hall m.; – v.n. flâner.

lounge-suit, s. complet veston m.

love, s. amour m.; – v.a. aimer.

lovely, adj. beau, bel, belle; charmant.

lover, s. amoureux m.; amant m.

low, adj. & adv. bas.

lower, adj. inférieur; (deck) premier (pont); – v.a. baisser; (flags, sails) amener.

loyal, adj. loyal; fidèle.

loyalty, s. loyauté f.

lubricate, v.a. lubrifier.

luck, s. chance f.; bad ~ malchance f.

lucky, adj. heureux.

luggage, s. bagages m. pl.

luggage-van, s. fourgon m. (aux bagages).

lump, s. morceau m.

lunch, s. déjeuner m.; – v.n. déjeuner.

lung, s. poumon m.

lute, s. luth m.

luxurious, adj. luxueux.

luxury, s. luxe m.

lyre, s. lyre f.

lyric, adj. lyrique.

M

machine, s. machine f.

machinery, s. machines f.pl.; fig. mécanisme m.

mackintosh, s. imperméable m.

mad, adj. fou, fol, folle.

madam, s. madame f.

magazine, s. revue f.; (rifle) magasin m.

magic, adj. magique.

magistrate, s. magistrat m.

magnet, s. aimant m.

magnetic, adj. magnétique.

magnificent, adj. magnifique.

maid, s. (jeune) fille f.; bonne f.

mail, s. courrier m.

mail-boat, s. paquebot-poste m.

mail-van, s. wagon-poste m.

main, adj. principal.

mainland, s. terre f. ferme.

mainly, adv. principalement.

mains, s. secteur (de courant) m.

maintain, v.a. maintenir; soutenir.

maintenance, s. entretien m.

majesty, s. majesté f.

major, s. commandant m.; – adj. majeur.

majority, s. majorité f.; plupart f.

make, v.a. & n. faire; rendre; ~ away with détruire; ~ for se diriger vers; ~ off décamper; ~ out comprendre; prouver; ~ over céder; ~ up (list) dresser; (invent) inventer; ~ up for compenser; – s. forme f., fabrication f.

male, adj. mâle; masculin; – s. mâle m.

malice, s. méchanceté

f.

man, *s.* homme *m.*

manage, *v. a.* conduire, diriger, gérer, gouverner; *I shall* ~ *it* j'en viendrai à bout.

management, *s.* direction *f.;* gérance *f.*

manager, *s.* directeur *m.;* gérant *m.*

manicure, *s.* manicure *n. f.*

manifest, *adj.* manifeste; — *v.a .* manifester.

manipulate, *v.a.* manipuler.

manner, *s.* manière *f.;* air *m.;* ~*s* manières *f. pl.;* *(morals)* mœurs *f. pl.*

manœuvre, *s.* manœuvre *f.;* — *v.a.* faire manœuvrer.

manor, *s.* manoir *m.*

manual, *adj. & s.* manuel *(m.).*

manufacture, *s.* manufacture *f.;* — *v.a.* fabriquer.

manufacturer, *s.* manufacturier *m.;* fabricant *m.*

manure, *s.* fumier *m.*

manuscript, *s.* manuscrit *m.*

many, *adj.* beaucoup de.

map, *s.* carte *f.* géographique.

marble, *s.* marbre *m.*

march, *s.* marche *f.;* — *v.n.* marcher.

March, *s.* mars *m.*

mare, *s.* jument *f.*

margarine, *s.* margarine *f.*

marine, *s.* marine *f.;* — *adj.* marin; maritime.

mariner, *s.* marin *m.*

mark, *s.* marque *f.; (aim)* but *m.; (school)* point *m.; (coin)* marc *m.;* — *v.a.* marquer; souligner.

market, *s.* marché *m.*

market-price, *s.* prix *m.* courant.

marmalade, *s.* marmelade *f.* (d'oranges).

marriage, *s.* mariage *m.*

married, *adj.* marié.

marry, *v. a.* épouser; *v. n. (get married)* se marier.

marsh, *s.* marais *m.*

marshal, *s.* maréchal *m.;* — *v.a.* ranger; conduire.

martial, *adj.* martial.

martyr, *s.* martyr *m.*

marvel, *s.* merveille *f.;* — *v.n.* s'étonner (de).

marvellous, *adj.* merveilleux.

masculine, *adj.* mâle; masculin.

mask, *s.* masque *m.*

mason, *s.* maçon *m.*

mass¹, *s.* masse *f.;* majorité *f.*

mass², *s. (eccles.)* messe *f.*

mast, *s.* mât *m.*

master, *s.* maître *m.;* — *v. a.* maîtriser

mat, *s. (door)* paillasson *m.; (table)* dessous de plat, *m.*

match¹, *s.* égal, -e *m.f.,* pareil, -le *m. f.,* mariage *m.; (pers.)* parti *m.; (sport)* match *m.;* — *v.a.* assortir; *v.n.* s'assortir.

match², *s.* allumette *f.*

mate, *s.* camarade *m.; (birds)* mâle *m.,* femelle *f.; (chess)* mat *m.; (ship)* second *m.;* — *v.a.* marier (à); *v.n.* s'accoupler.

material, *s.* matière *f.;* — *adj.* matériel.

maternal, *adj.* maternel.

mathematical, *adj.* mathématique.

mathematics, *s.* mathématiques *f. pl.*

matinée, *s.* matinée *f.*

matron, *s.* mère de famille, *f.; (hospital)* infirmière-en-chef *f.;* surveillante *f.*

matter, *s.* matière *f.;* affaire *f.;* sujet *m.;* chose *f.; as a ~ of fact* en fait; *what is the ~?* qu'est-ce qu'il y a?; — *v.n.* importer; *it does not ~* n'importe.

mattress, *s.* matelas *m.; spring ~* sommier *m.,* matelas *m.* à ressort.

mature, *adj.* mûr; — *v.a.* & *n.* mûrir.

maturity, *s.* maturité *f.*

May, *s.* mai *m.*

may, *v. aux.* pouvoir; *~ I?* vous permettez?

maybe, *adv.* peut-être.

mayor, *s.* maire *m.*

me, *pron. (acc.)* me; *(alone, with prep.)* moi.

meadow, *s.* pré *m.*

meal, *s.* repas *m.*

mean[1], *s.* moyen terme, *m.; (math.)* moyenne *f.; ~s* moyens *m. pl.,* *(way to do)* moyen *m.; by ~s of* au moyen de: *by all ~s* mais certainement; *by no ~s* en aucune façon; — *adj.* moyen.

mean[2], *v.a. (signify)* vouloir dire, signifier: *(wish)* vouloir (faire), avoir l'intention (de); destiner; *what does that word ~?* que signifie ce mot?; *what do you ~ by that?* qu'entendez-vous par là?

mean[3], *adj.* misérable, pauvre; bas, vil; ladre.

meaning, *s.* intention *f.;* sens *m.*

meantime, ~while, *adv.* *(in the ~)* dans l'intervalle, pendant ce temps-là.

measure, *s.* mesure *f.;* — *v.a.* mesurer.

meat, *s.* viande *f.; (food)* nourriture *f.*

mechanic, *s.* artisan *m.,* mécanicien *m.*

mechanical, *adj.* mécanique.

mechanics, *s.* mécanique *f.*

mechanism, *s.* mécanisme *m.*

mechanize, *v.a.* mécaniser.

medal, *s.* médaille *f.*

medical, *adj.* médical; *~ student* étudiant *m.* en médecine.

medicine, *s.* médecine *f.*

meditate, *v.a.* & *n.* méditer.

medium, *s.* moyen terme *m.;* milieu *m.;* — *adj.* moyen.

meet, *v.a.* rencontrer (qn.), se rencontrer avec (qn.); *(face)* affronter; *(expenses)* faire face à; *~ sy at the station* aller recevoir qn. à la gare; — *v. n.* se rencontrer; *~ with* rencontrer; éprouver.

meeting, *s.* rencontre *f.;* réunion *f.*

mellow, *adj.* mûr; moelleux.

melody, *s.* mélodie *f.*

melon, *s.* melon *m.*

melt, *v.a.* fondre.

member, *s.* membre *m.*

memorial, *s.* monument *m.;* mémorial *m.*

memory, *s.* mémoire *f.;* souvenir *m.*

mend, *v. a.* raccommoder; réparer; corriger.

mental, *adj.* mental.

mention, *v. a.* mentionner; citer; *don't ~ it* il n'y a pas de quoi.

merchandise, *s.* marchandise *f.*

merchant, *s.* négociant *m.;* commerçant *m.*

merciful, *adj.* miséricordieux.

mercy, *s.* pitié *f.;* miséricorde *f.*

mere, *adj.* seul.

merely, *adv.* purement; simplement.

merit, mérite *m.;* — *v.a.* mériter.

merry, *adj.* gai.

mess, *s.* gâchis *m.; make a ~ of* gâcher.

message, *s.* message *m.*

messenger, *s.* messager *m.*

metal, *s.* métal *m.*

meteorology, *s.* météorologie *f.*

method, *s.* méthode *f.*

metre, *s.* mètre *m.*

microphone, *s.* microphone *m.*

microscope, *s.* microscope *m.*

middle, *s.* milieu *m.;* — *adj.* du milieu; moyen.

midnight, *s.* minuit *m.*

might, *s.* force *f.;* puissance *f.*

mighty, *adj.* fort; puissant

migrate, *v.n.* émigrer.

mild, *adj.* doux; bénin.

mile, *s.* mille *m.*

mileage, *s.* parcours *m.;* *(expense)* prix *m.* par mille.

military, *adj.* militaire.

milk, *s.* lait *m.*

milkman, *s.* laitier *m.*

mill, *s.* moulin *m.;* fabrique *f.*

miller, *s.* meunier *m.*

milliner, *s.* modiste *f.*

million, *s.* million *m.*

mince, *s.* hachis *m.;*

v.a. hacher.

mind, *s.* esprit *m.; (remembrance)* souvenir *m.; (opinion)* pensée *f.,* avis *m.; change one's ~* changer d'avis; *make up one's ~ to* se décider à, se résigner à; — *v.a.* faire attention à, prendre garde à; écouter; *(look after)* garder; *(trouble about)* s'inquiéter de; *do you ~ my smoking?* est-ce que cela vous gêne que je fume?; *I don't ~* cela m'est égal; *never ~* ça ne fait rien.

mine¹, *s.* mine *f.;* — *v.a.* miner.

mine², *pron.* à moi; le mien.

miner, *s.* mineur *m.*

mineral, *adj.* & *s.* minéral *(m.).*

minister, *s.* ministre *m.*

ministry, *s.* ministère *m.*

minor, *adj.* mineur.

minority, *s.* minorité.

mint, *s.* Hôtel *m.* de la Monnaie; *(plant)* menthe *f.*

minus, *adj.* en moins; — *adv.* moins.

minute, *s.* minute *f.;* petit moment, *m.; ~ hand* grande aiguille *f.*

miracle, *s.* miracle *m.*

mirror, *s.* miroir *m.*

miscarry, *v.n.* avorter.

miscellaneous, *adv.* divers.

mischief, *s.* mal *m.;* méchanceté *f.*

miser, *s.* avare *m.*

miserable, *adj.* misérable; malheureux.

misery, *s.* misère *f.*

misfortune, *s.* malheur *m.*

miss¹, *v.a.* manquer; ne pas entendre; ne pas voir; s'apercevoir de l'absence (de); ~ out omettre; be ~ing manquer.

miss², s. mademoiselle f.

missile, s. projectile m.

mission, s. mission f.

missionary, s. missionnaire m. f.

mist, s. brouillard m., brume f.

mistake, s. erreur f., méprise f.; faute f.; — v.a. se tromper de; ~ for prendre pour; be ~n se tromper.

mistress, s. maîtresse f. (de maison).

mistrust, s. méfiance f.

misty, adj. brumeux.

misunderstand, v. a. comprendre mal.

mitten, s. mitaine f.

mix, v.a. mêler; mélanger; be ~ed up in être mêlé à.

mixture, s. mélange m.; mixture f.

moan, v.n. gémir; — s. gémissement m.

mob, s. foule f., populace f.

mobilization, s. mobilisation f.

mobilize, v.a. mobiliser.

mock, s. moquerie f.; — adj. faux; — v.a. railler.

mockery, s. moquerie f.

model, s. modèle m.

moderate, adj. modéré; — v.a. modérer.

moderation, s. modération f.

modern, adj. moderne.

modest, adj. modeste.

modesty s. modestie f.

modify, v.a. modifier.

moist, adj. moite, humide.

moisten, v.a. humecter.

moisture, s. humidité f.

molecule, s. molécule f.

moment, s. moment m.

momentary, adj. momentané.

monarch, s. monarque m.

monarchy, s. monarchie f.

Monday, s. lundi m.

money, s. argent m.; monnaie f.

money-order, s. mandat m.

monk, s. moine m.

monkey, s. singe m.

monopolize, v.a. monopoliser.

monopoly, s. monopole m.

monotonous, adj. monotone.

monstrous, adj. monstrueux.

month, s. mois m.

monthly, adj. mensuel; — adv. mensuellement.

monument, s. monument m.

monumental, adj. monumental.

mood, s. humeur f.; mode m.

moon, s. lune f.

moonlight, s. clair m. de lune

moor, s. bruyère f.

mop, balai m.; — v.a. (also ~ up) éponger, essuyer.

moral, s. morale f.; ~s moeurs f. pl.; — adj. moral; de morale.

more, adj. & pron. plus de; davantage de; ~ than plus que; some ~ en ... davantage; no ~ n'en ... pas davantage, ne ... plus; — adv. plus; davantage; ~ and ~ de plus en plus.

moreover, adv. de plus.

morning, s. matin m.; in the ~ le matin; — adj. du matin.

mortal, *adj*. & *s*. mortel (*m., f.*).

mortality, *s*. mortalité *f*.

mortgage, *s*. hypothèque *f*.; — *v. a*. hypothéquer.

mosquito, *s*. moustique *f*.

moss, *s*. mousse *f*.

most, *adj*. & *pron*. le plus (de), la plupart (de); *at the* ~ tout au plus; ~ *people* la plupart des gens; *make the* ~ *of* tirer le meilleur parti de; — *adv*. très, fort, bien.

mostly, *adv*. pour la plupart; principalement; la plupart du temps.

motel, *s*. motel *m*.

moth, *s*. mite *f*.

mother, *s*. mère *f*.

mother-in-law, *s*. belle-mère *f*.

mother-tongue, *s*. langue *f*. maternelle.

motion, *s*. mouvement *m*.: signe *m*.; (*proposal*) motion *f*.

motionless, *adj*. immobile.

motive, *s*. motif *m*.

motor, *s*. moteur *m*.

motor-bus, *s*. autobus *m*.

motor-car, *s*. auto(mobile) *f*.

motor-coach, *s*. autocar *m*.

motor-cycle, *s*. motocyclette *f*.

motor-scooter, *s*. scooter *m*.

motorway,, *s*. autoroute *f*.

mould, *s*. moule *m*.; — *v.a*. mouler.

mount, *s*. mont *m*.; — *v.a*. & *n*. monter.

mountain, *s*. montagne *f*.

mountaineering, *s*. alpinisme *m*.

mountainous, *adj*. montagneux.

mourn, *v. n*. & *a*. pleurer, (se) lamenter.

mouse, *s*. souris *f*.

moustache, *s*. moustache *f*.

mouth, *s*. bouche *f*.; (*beast*) gueule *f*.

move, *s*. mouvement *m*.; (*chess*) coup *m*.; — *v.a*. remuer; déplacer; (*goods*) transporter; (*affect*) émouvoir; (*motion*) proposer ~ *house* (*also*: ~) déménager; — *v.n*. se mouvoir, se déplacer; s'avancer; (*chess*) jouer; ~ *forward* s'avancer; ~ *in* emménager; ~ *out* déménager; ~ *on* avancer; *int*. circulez!

movement, *s*. mouvement *m*.

mow, *v.a*. faucher; tondre.

mower, *s*. faucheur *m*.; faucheuse (à moteur) *f*.

much, *adj*. & *pron*. beaucoup; — *adv*. beaucoup; très; *too* ~ trop.

mud, *s*. boue *f*.

muddle, *s*. fouillis *m*.; — *v.a*. embrouiller.

muddy, *adj*. boueux.

mug, *s*. timbale *f*.

mule, *s*. mulet *m*., mule *f*.

multiple, *adj*. multiple.

multiplication, *s*. multiplication *f*.

multiply, *v.a*. multiplier.'

multitude, *s*. multitude *f*.

municipal, *adj*. municipal.

murder, *s*. meurtre *m*.

murderer, *s*. meurtrier *m*.

murmur, *s*. murmure

m.

muscle, *s.* muscle *m.*

museum, *s.* musée *m.*

mushroom, *s.* champignon *m.*

music, *s.* musique *f.*

musical, *adj.* musical; ~ *instrument* instrument *m.* de musique.

music-hall, *s.* café *m.* concert.

musician, *s.* musicien, -enne *m. f.*

must, *v. aux.* il faut que; devoir.

mustard, *s.* moutarde *f.*

mute, *adj.* muet.

mutter, *s.* murmure *m.;* — *v. n.* murmurer.

mutton, *s.* mouton *m.*

mutual, *adj.* mutuel.

my, *pron.* mon, ma; mes *(pl.).*

myself, *pron.* moi-même; *by* ~ seul.

mysterious, *adj.* mystérieux.

mystery, *s.* mystère *m.*

mystic, *adj.* mystique.

myth, *s.* mythe *m.*

N

nail, *s. (to hammer)* clou *m.; (on fingers)* ongle *m.;* — *v.a.* clouer.

nail-brush, *s.* brosse *f.* à ongles.

naked, *adj.* nu; dénudé.

name, *s.* nom *m.;* — *v.a.* nommer; désigner.

namely, *adv.* savoir.

nap, *s.* somme *m.*

napkin, *s.* serviette *f.; (infant)* couche *f.*

narrate, *v. a.* raconter.

narrow, *adj.* étroit.

nation, *s.* nation *f.*

national, *adj.* national.

nationality, *s.* nationalité

f.

nationalize, *v.a.* nationaliser.

native, *adj. & s.* natif, -ive *(m. f.).*

natural, *adj.* naturel.

naturalize, *v.a.* naturaliser.

nature, *s.* nature *f.*

naughty, *adj.* méchant.

nava l. *adj.* naval

navigate, *v.n.* naviguer.

navigator, *s.* navigateur *m.*

navy, *s.* marine *f.*

near, *adv.* près, proche; — *prep.* près de, auprès de; — *adj.* proche.

nearly, *adv. (almost)* presque.

neat, *adj.* propre; élégant.

necessary, *adj.* nécessaire.

necessity, *s.* néccesité *f.*

neck, *s.* cou *m.*

necklace, *s.* collier *m.*

necktie, *s.* cravate *f.*

need, *s.* besoin; — *v.a.* avoir besoin (de); demander.

needle, *s.* aiguille *f.*

needless, *adj.* inutile.

needy, *adj.* nécessiteux.

negative, *adj.* négatif; — *s.* négative *f.; (photo)* cliché *m.; in the* ~ négativement.

neglect, *v. a.* négliger (de).

negligence, *s.* négligence *f.*

negotiation, *s.* négociation *f.*

negro, -ess *s.* nègre *m.,* négresse *f.*

neighbour, *s.* voisin, -e *m. f.*

neighbourhood, *s.* voisinage *m.*

neither, *pron. & adj.* ni l'un ni l'autre.

nephew, *s.* neveu *m.*

nerve, *s.* nerf *m.*

nervous, *adj.* nerveux.

nest, *s.* nid *m.*

net¹, s. filet m.
net², adj. net.
network, s. réseau m.
neutral, adj. neutre.
never, adj. (ne ...) jamais..
nevertheless, adv. néan-
moins.
new, adj. neuf, neuve;
nouveau, -el, -elle; *New
Year* Nouvel An.
news, s. nouvelle f.
newspaper, s. journal
m.
next, adj. le plus proche;
prochain, suivant; ~
door to à côté de; adv.
ensuite, après; — prep.
~ *to* à côté de.
nice, adj. agréable, bon;
gentil.
niece, s. nièce f.
night, s. nuit f.; soir m.;
by ~ de nuit; *good* ~*l*
bonne nuit!
nightingale, s. rossignol
m.
nine, adj. & s. neuf (m.).
nineteen, adj. & s. dix-
neuf (m.).
ninety, adj. & s. quatre-
-vingt-dix (m.).
ninth, adj. neuvième;
neuf.
nip, v.a. pincer.
nitrogen, s. azote m.
no, adj. ne ... pas (de),
ne ... aucun.
noble, adj. noble.
nobleman, s. gentilhomme
m.
nobody, no one, pron.
personne ne (+ *verb*).
noise, s. bruit m.
noisy, adj. bruyant.
none, pron. ne ... aucun;
personne ne (+ *verb*.)
nonsense, s. bêtise; m. *no*
~ pas de bêtises
non-smoker, s. comparti-
ment m. pour non-
fumeurs.

non-stop, adj. & adv.
sans arrêt; sans escale.
noon, s. midi m.
nor, conj. ni; (*and* ...
not) et ne ... pas,
non plus.
normal, adj. normal.
north, s. nord m.; — adj.
du nord.
north-east, adj. & s.
nord-est m.
northern, adj. du nord.
north-west, adj. & s.
nord-ouest m.
nose, s. nez m.
nostril, s. narine f.
not, adv. ne ... pas, ne
... point.
notable, adj. notable.
note, s. note f.; (*letter
and money*) billet m.;
(*tone*) ton m.; — v.a.
noter; remarquer.
note-book, s. carnet m.
noted, adj. distingué.
nothing, pron. rien; ne ...
rien.
notice, s. avis m.; attention f.; connaissance
f.; *take* ~ *of* faire
attention à.
notify, v.a. avertir, noti-
fier.
notion, s. idée f.
noun, s. nom m.
nourish, v.a. nourrir.
novel, s. roman m.
novelist, s. romancier m.
novelty, s. nouveauté f.
November, s. novembre m.
now, adv. maintenant.
nowadays, adv. de nos
jours.
nowhere, adv. ne ... nulle
part.
nuclear, adj. nucléaire; ~
energy énergie f. nu-
cléaire; ~ *physics*
physique f. nucléaire;
~ *power station* centrale
f. nucléaire.
nuisance, s. (*pers.*) peste

f.; (thing) ennui *m.*

number, *s.* nombre *m.,* numéro *m.*

number-plate, *s.* plaque *f.* matricule.

numerous, *adj.* nombreux.

nun, *s.* religieuse *f.*

nurse, *s.* nourrice *f.,* bonne (d'enfant) *f.; (hospital)* infirmier, -ère *m. f.; — v.a. (suckle)* allaiter; *(the sick)* soigner.

nursery, *s.* chambre *f.* des enfants.

nut, *s.* noix *f.,* noisette *f.*

nylon, *s.* nylon *m.; ~ stockings* (or *~s*) bas nylons *m. pl.*

O

oak, *s.* chêne *m.*

oar, *s.* rame *f.*

oat(s) *s. (pl).* avoine *f.*

oath, *s.* serment *m.*

obedience, *s.* obéissance *f.*

obedient, *adj.* obéissant.

obey, *v.a. & n.* obéir (à)·

object, *s.* objet *m.;* but *m.; (gramm.)* régime *m.; — v.a.* objecter; *v.n.* s'opposer (à).

objection, *s.* objection *f.*

objective, *adj. & s.* objectif *(m.).*

obligation, *s.* obligation *f.*

oblige, *v.a.* obliger.

obscure, *adj.* obscur.

observation, *s.* observation *f.*

observe, *v.a. & n.* observer.

obstacle, *s.* obstacle *m.*

obstinate, *adj.* obstiné.

obtain, *v.a.* obtenir.

obvious, *adj.* évident.

occasion, *s.* occasion *f.*

occasional *adj.* occasionnel.

occasionally, *adv.* de temps en temps.

occupation, *s.* occupation *f.*

occupy, *v.a.* occuper; *~ oneself with* s'occuper de.

occur, *v.n.* arriver; se trouver; *it ~red to me* il m'est venu à l'idée que.

occurrence, *s.* événement *m.*

ocean, *s.* océan *m.*

October, *s.* octobre *m.*

odd, *adj.* impair; dépareillé, déparié; *(strange)* non usuel, bizarre.

odds, *s. pl.* avantage *m.;* chances *f. pl.*

of, *prep.* de.

off, *adv.* à ... de distance; *be ~* s'en aller; *be well ~* être à l'aise; — *prep.* de.

offence, *s* offense *f.*

offend, *v. a. & n.* offenser.

offensive, *s.* offensive *f.*

offer, *s.* offre *f.; — v.a.* offrir.

office, *s.* bureau *m.; (of pers.)* charge *f.;* fonction *f.*

officer, *s.* officer *m.; (police)* agent *m.*

official, *adj.* officiel; — *s.* fonctionnaire *m. f.*

often, *adv.* souvent.

oil, *s.* huile *f.;* pétrole *m.*

ointment, *s.* onguent *m.*

old, *adj.* vieux, -eil, -eille; âgé; ancien; *how ~ are you?* quel âge avez-vous?; *~ age* vieillesse *f.; grow ~* vieillir.

old-fashioned, *adj.* à l'ancienne mode.

omission, *s.* omission *f.*

omit, *v.a.* omettre (de).

on, *prep.* sur; *(prep. omitted with days etc.); ~ Monday* lundi; *~*

time à la minute.

once, *adv.* une fois; autre-fois; *at* ~ tout de suite.

one, *adj. & s.* un, une; — *pron.* (~, ~s omitted if preceded by adj.); (peo-ple, they) on; *this* ~ celui-ci; *that* ~ ce-lui-là; ~'s son, sa, ses; *which* ~? le-quel ...?

oneself, *pron.* soi-même; *by* ~ tout seul.

onion, *s.* oignon *m.*

onlooker, *s.* spectateur, -trice *m. f.*

open, *adj.* ouvert; dé-couvert; public; franc; — *v.a.* ouvrir; *v.n.* s'ouvrir.

opening, *s.* ouverture *f.*

opera, *s.* opéra *m.*

operate, *v.a. & n.* opérer; ~ *on* opérer (qn).

operating-theatre, *s.* salle *f.* d'opération.

operation, *s.* opération *f.*

operative, *adj.* actif.

opinion, *s.* opinion *f.; in my* ~ à mon avis.

opponent, *s.* adversaire *m.*

opportunity, *s.* occasion *f.*

oppose, *v.a.* s'opposer à; ~d *to* opposé à.

opposition, *s.* opposition *f.*

optional, *adj.* facultatif.

or, *conj.* ou; *whether* ... ~ ou ... ou.

oral, *adj.* oral.

orange, *s.* orange *f.*

orchard, *s.* verger *m.*

orchestra, *s.* orchestre *m.*

order, *s.* ordre *m.; (com-merce)* commande *f.; (ruling)* règlement *m.;* — *v.a.* ordonner; *(goods)* commander.

order-form, *s.* bon *m.* commande.

ordinary, *adj.* ordinaire *m.*

ore, *s.* minerai *m.*

organ, *s.* organe *m.; (music)* orgue *m.*

organic, *adj.* organique.

organization, *s.* organisa-tion. *f*

organize, *v.a.* organiser.

oriental, *adj.* oriental.

origin, *s.* origine *f.*

original, *adj.* original.

ornament, *s.* ornement *m.;* — *v.a.* orner.

ornamental, *adj.* orne-mental.

orphan, *adj. & s.* orphelin, -e *(m. f.).*

other, *adj. & pron.* autre.

otherwise, *adv.* autre-ment.

ought, *v. aux.* devoir.

ounce, *s.* once *f.*

our, *adj.* notre, *(pl.)* nos.

ours, *pron.* le, la nôtre; les nôtres.

ourself, *pron.* nous(-mê-mes); *ourselves* nous-(-mêmes); *by ourselves* seul, -s.

out, *adv.* dehors; — *prep.* ~ *of* hors de.

outdoors, *adv.* dehors, en plein air.

outfit, *s.* trousseau *m.*

outing, *s.* excursion *f.*

outline, *s.* contour *m.;* aperçu *m.;* — *v.a.* es-quisser.

outlive, *v.a.* survivre à.

outlook, *s.* perspective *f.*

output, *s.* production *f.*

outrageous, *adj.* outra-geant; atroce.

outset, *s.* début *m.; at the* ~ dès le commence-ment.

outside, *adv.* au dehors; — *prep.* en dehors de; — *adj.* du dehors; — *s.* extérieur.

outskirts, *s. pl.* banlieue

f.; lisière *f.*

outstanding, *adj.* non réglé, à payer; saillant; éminent.

outward, *adj.* extérieur.

outwards, *adv.* à l'extérieur, en dehors.

oven, *s.* four *m.*

over, *prep.* au-dessus de; *(motion)* par dessus; *(superior)* sur; *(more than)* plus de; *(across)* par; — *adv. (more)* davantage; *(finished)* fini, passé; *(too)* trop.

overcoat, *s.* pardessus *m.*

overcome, *v.a.* surmonter; vaincre.

overcrowded, *adj.* surpeuplé.

overdo, *v.a.* faire trop cuire; exagérer.

overexpose, *v.a.* surexposer.

overflow, *s.* débordement *m.;* — *v.a.* inonder; *v.n.* déborder.

overlook, *v.a. (look on to)* avoir vue sur; *(neglect)* négliger; *(superintend)* surveiller.

overpower, *v.a.* accabler; subjuguer.

oversea, *adj.* d'outre-mer; ∼*s (adv.)* outre-mer.

oversight, *s.* inadvertence *f.*

overtake, *v.a.* rattraper; surprendre (par).

overthrow, *s.* renversement *m.;* — *v.a.* renverser.

overtime, *s.* heures *f. pl.* supplémentaires.

overwhelming, *adj.* accablant.

owe, *v.a.* devoir (à); être redevable (à).

owing, *adj.* ∼ *to* à cause de.

owl, *s.* hibou *m.*

own, *adj.* propre; *of my* ∼ à moi; — *v.a.* posséder.

owner, *s.* propriétaire *m. f.*

ox, *s.* bœuf *m.*

oxygen, *s.* oxygène *m.*

oyster, *s.* ñuître *f.*

P

pace, *s.* pas *m.;* *v.a.* arpenter; *v.n.* aller au pas.

pack, *s.* paquet; *(cards)* jeu *m.;* *(wool)* balle; *(hounds)* meute *f.;* — *v.a.* emballer; faire: ∼ *off* expédier.

package, *s.* colis *m.;* paquet *m.*

packet, *s.* paquet *m.*

pact, *s.* pacte *m.*

pad, *s.* bourrelet *m.;* tampon *m.;* bloc *m.;* *blotting* ∼ buvard *m.*

paddle, *v.n.* pagayer.

page, *s.* page *f.*

pail, *s.* seau *m.*

pain, *s.* douleur *f.; take* ∼*s* se donner de la peine.

painful, *adj.* douloureux.

paint, *s.* peinture *f.;* — *v. a.* peindre.

painter, *s.* peintre *m.*

painting, *s.* peinture *f.*

pair, *s.* paire *f.;* couple *m.*

palace, *s.* palais *m.*

palate, *s.* palais *m.*

pale, *adj.* pâle; *grow* ∼ pâlir.

palm, *s.* palme *f.*

pan, *s.* poêle *f.*

pane, *s.* vitre *f.*

panel, *s.* panneau *m.*

panorama, *s.* panorama *m.*

pansy, *s.* pensée *f.*

pantry, *s.* office *f.*

pants, *s.pl.* caleçon *m.;* pantalon *m.*

paper, *s.* papier *m.;*

(newspaper) journal *m.; (essay)* étude *f.; (exam)* composition *f.*

parade, *s.* parade *f.;* — *v.n.* parader.

paraffin, *s.* pétrole *m.*

paragraph, *s.* paragraphe *m.*

parallel, *s. (line)* parallèle *f.; (comparison)* parallèle *m.;* — *adj.* parallèle.

paralysis, *s.* paralysie *f.*

parcel, *s.* paquet *m.*

pardon, *s.* pardon *m.; I beg your* ~ je vous demande pardon; *(I beg your)* ~? comment (dites-vous)?, pardon?; — *v.a.* pardonner.

parents, *s. pl.* père *m.* et mère *f.,* parents.

parish, *s.* paroisse *f.*

Parisian, *adj.* parisien; — *s.* Parisien, -enne *m.f.*

park, *s.* parc *m.; (car)* (parc de) stationnement *m.;* — *v.a.* garer; stationner; *no* ~*ing* stationnement interdit.

parliament, *s.* parlement *m.*

parliamentary, *adj.* parlementaire.

parlour, *s.* petit salon *m.*

parrot, *s.* perroquet *m.*

part, *s.* part *f.;* partie *f.; (theatre)* rôle *m.; (region)* région *f.; on my* ~ de ma part; *take* ~ *in* prendre part à; — *v.a.* diviser; séparer; *v.n.* se diviser; *(pers.)* se séparer (de).

partial, *adj. (unfair)* partial; *(incomplete)* partiel.

participant, *s.* participant *m.*

participate, *v.n.* ~ *in* prendre part à.

participation, *s.* participation *f.*

participle, *s.* participe *m.*

particular, *adj.* particulier; — *s.* détail *m.*

partly, *adv.* en partie.

partner, *s.* associé, -e *m. f.;* partenaire *m. f.*

partridge, *s.* perdrix *f.*

party, *s.* parti *m.;* partie *f.;* groupe *m.;* réception *f.,* soirée *f.*

pass, *v.a.* passer; dépasser; surpasser; *(law)* voter; *(resolution)* prendre; *(exam)* être reçu (à); — *v. n.* passer; — *s.* défilé *m.;* laisser-passer *m.*

passage, *s.* passage *m.;* couloir *m.*

passenger, *s.* voyageur, -euse *m. f.;* passager, -ère *m. f.*

passer-by, *s.* passant *m.*

passion, *s.* passion *f.*

passionate, *adj.* passionné.

passive, *adj. & s.* passif *(m.).*

passport, *s.* passeport *m.*

past, *adj.* passé; dernier; — *s.* passé *m.*

paste, *s.* pâte *f.*

pastime, *s.* passe-temps *m*

pastry, *s.* pâtisserie *f.*

patch, *s.* pièce *f.*

patent, *s.* brevet *m.* d'invention.

path, -way, *s.* sentier *m.*

patience, *s.* patience *f.*

patient, *s.* malade *m. f.;* — *adj.* patient.

patriot, *s.* patriote *m. f.*

patrol, *s.* patrouille; — *v.n.* aller en patrouille.

patron, *s.* patron *m.;* client *m.*

pattern, *s.* modèle *m.*

pause, *s.* pause *f.;* — *v.n* faire une pause.

pave, *v.a.* paver.

pavement, *s.* trottoir *m.*

pavilion, s. pavillon m.
paw, s. patte f.
pay, v.a. payer; (visit) faire; ~ off acquitter; v.n. payer; — s. paye f., salaire m.
payable, adj. payable (à).
payment, s. payement m.
pea, s. pois m.
peace, s. paix f.
peaceful, adj. paisible.
peach, s. pêche f.
peacock, s. paon m.
peak, s. pic m., cime f.
pear, s. poire f.
pearl, s. perle f.

peasant, s. paysan, -anne m. f.
pebble, s. caillou m.
peck, s. coup m. de bec.
peculiar, adj. particulier.
pedestrian, s. piéton m.
peel, s. pelure f.; — v.a. peler.
peer, s. pair m.
peg, s. pince f.; piquet m.
pen, s. stylo m.
penalty, s. peine f.
pencil, s. crayon m.
penicillin, s. pénicilline f.
penknife, s. canif m.

penny, s. penny m.
pension, s. pension f.
people, s. peuple m.; gens m. pl. [f. with adj. before it]; famille f.
pepper, s. poivre m.
per, prep. par; ~ cent pour cent.
perceive, v.a. percevoir.
perch, s. perchoir m.; — v.n. se percher.
perfect, adj. parfait; — v.a. rendre parfait; achever.
perform, v.a. accomplir, exécuter.
performance, s. représentation f.
perfume, s. parfum m.

perhaps, adv. peut-être.
peril, s. péril m.
period, s. période f.
periodical, s. périodique m.
perish, v.n. périr.
perishable, adj. périssable.
permanent, adj. permanent.
permission, s. permission f.
permit, s. permis m.; — v.a. permettre.
persecution, s. persécution f.
Persian, adj. persan.
persist, v.n. persister.
person, s. personne f.
personal, adj. personnel.
personality, s. personnalité f.
perspiration, s. transpiration f.
persuade, v.a. convaincre (de), persuader.
pertain, v.n. appartenir (à).
pet, s. enfant m.f. gâté, -e; — adj. favori; ~ dog chien m. familier.
petrol, s. essence f.
petroleum, s. pétrole m.
petticoat, s. jupon m.
phase, s. phase f.
pheasant, s. faisan, -e m. f.
phenomenon, s. phénomène m.
philosopher, s. philosophe m.
philosophy, s. philosophie f.
phone, s. téléphone m.; — v.a. & n. téléphoner.
photo(graph), s. photographie f. — v.a. photographier.
phrase, s. phrase f.
physical, adj. physique.
physician, s. médecin m.
physicist, s. physicien m.

physics, *s.* physique *f.*

pianist, *s.* pianiste *m. f*

piano, *s.* piano *m.*

pick, *v. a.* cueillir; picoter; *(teeth)* curer; *(bone)* ronger; *(choose)* choisir; ~ *out* choisir; ~ *up* ramasser; prendre.

pickle, *s.* marinade *f.* ~s pickles *m.*

picnic, *s.* pique-nique *m.*

picture, *s.* tableau *m.*; portrait *m.*; film *m.*; ~s cinéma *m.*

pie, *s.* pâté *m.*

piece, *s.* morceau *m.*; partie *f.*; pièce *f.*; ~ *of news* nouvelle *f.*; ~ *of work* ouvrage *m.*

pier, *s.* jetée *f.*

pierce, *v.a.* percer.

pig, *s.* cochon *m.*

pigeon, *s.* pigeon *m.*

pile¹, *s.* tas *m.*; — *v.a.* (also ~ *up)* entasser, amasser.

pile², *s.* pieu *m.*, pilot *m.*

pill, *s.* pillule *f.*

pillar, *s.* pilier *m.*

pillar-box, *s.* boîte *f.* aux lettres.

pillow, *s.* oreiller *m.*

pilot, *s.* pilote *m.*

pin, *s.* épingle *f.*

pinch, *v.a.* pincer.

pine, *s.* pin *m.*

pineapple, *s.* ananas *m.*

pink, *adj. & s.* rose *(m.).*

pint, *s.* pinte *f.*

pious, *adj.* pieux.

pipe, *s.* tuyau *m.*; *(smoking)* pipe *f.*

pistol, *s.* pistolet *m.*

pit, *s.* fosse *f.*; creux *m.*; *(theatre)* parterre *m.*

pitch, *s.* degré *m.*; ton *m.*; *v.a. (tent)* dresser; *(camp)* asseoir.

pity, *s.* pitié *f.*; dommage *m.*

place, *s.* lieu *m.*, endroit *m.*; place *f.*; emploi *m.*; — *v.a.* mettre.

plain, *adj.* uni; simple; évident; ordinaire.

plait, *s.* tresse *f.*

plan, *s.* plan *m.*; projet *m.*; — *v.a.* faire le plan (de).

plane, *s.* plan *m.*; *(tool)* rabot *m.*; *(aero-)* avion *m.*; — *v.a.* raboter.

planet, *s.* planète *f.*

plank, *s.* planche *f.*

plant, *s.* plante *f.*; *(works)* usine *f.*, fabrique *f.*; — *v.a.* planter.

plantation, *s.* piantation *f.*

plaster, *s.* (em)plâtre *m.*

plastic, *adj.* plastique; ~s plastiques *m. pl.*

plate, *s.* plaque *f.*; planche *f.*; *(china)* assiette *f.*; *(silver)* vaisselle *f.*

platform, *s.* quai *m.*

platinum, *s.* platine *m.*

platter, *s.* plat *m.*

play, *s.* jeu *m.*; pièce *f.* de théâtre; — *v.a. & n.* jouer.

player, *s.* joueur, -euse *m. f.*

playground, *s.* cour *f.* de récréation.

plea, *s.* excuse *f.*; défense *f.*

plead, *v.a.&n.* plaider

pleasant, *adj.* agréable.

please, *v.a. & n.* plaire (à); *be* ~*ed with,* to être content de; *as you* ~ comme vous voulez; *if you* ~ s'il vous plaît.

pleasure, *s.* plaisir *m.*

pledge, *s.* gage *m.*; — *v.a.* mettre en gage.

plenty, *s.* abondance *f.*; ~ *of* quantité de,

beaucoup de.

plot, *s. (land)* terrain *m.; (story)* intrigue *f.; (conspiracy)* complot *m.; v. n.* conspirer.

plough, *s.* charrue *f.;* — *v.a.&n.* labourer.

plug, *s.* tampon *m.;* prise *f.* de courant; — *v.a.* tamponner.

plum, *s.* prune *f.*

plume, *s.* plume *f.;* plumet *m.*

plunder, *v.a.* piller; — *s.* pillage *m.*

plunge, *v.a. & n.* plonger; — *s.* plongeon *m.*

plural, *s. & adj.* pluriel *(m.).*

plus, *prep.* plus.

ply, *v.a.* manier; s'appliquer (à); *v.n.* faire le service (entre).

pocket, *s.* poche *f.*

pocket-book, *s.* carnet *m.;* portefeuille *m.*

poem, *s.* poème *m.*

poet, *s.* poète *m.*

poetic(al), *adj.* poétique

poetry, *s.* poésie · *f.*

point, *s.* point *m ;* pointe *f.;* — *v.a. & n.* ~ *out* montrer du doigt; faire valoir (un fait); ~ *to* indiquer.

poison, *s.* poison *m.; v.a.* empoisonner.

poisonous, *adj.* vénéneux.

pole, *s.* pôle *m.*

Pole, *s.* Polonais, -e *m. f.*

police, *s.* police *f.*

policeman, -officer, *s.* agent (de police) *m.*

police-station, *s.* poste (de police) *m.*

policy, *s.* politique *f.; (insurance)* police *f.*

polish, *s.* poli *m.; fig.* politesse *f.;* — *v. a.* polir.

Polish, *adj.* polonais.

polite, *adj.* poli.

political, *adj.* politique.

politician, *s.* politique *m.;* politicien *m.*

politics, *s.* politique *f.*

poll, *s.* vote *m.;* liste *f.* (électorale); scrutin *m.*

pool¹, *s.* mare *f.*

pool², *s.* pool *m.*

poor, *adj.* pauvre; *(bad)* mauvais.

pope, *s.* pape *m.*

popular, *adj.* populaire.

popularity, *s.* popularité *f.*

population, *s.* population *f.*

pork, *s.* porc *m.;* ~ *butcher* charcutier *m.*

port, *s.* port *m.; (ship)* bâbord *m.*

portable, *adj.* portatif.

porter, *s.* portier *m.; (railw.)* porteur *m.*

portfolio, *s.* serviette *f.*

portion, *s.* portion *f.;* — *v.a.* partager.

portrait, *s.* portrait *m.*

Portuguese, *adj.* portugais; — *s.* Portugais, -e *m. f.*

position, *s.* position *f.*

positive, *adj. & s.* positif *(m.).*

possess, *v.a.* posséder.

possession, *s.* possession *f.*

possibility, *s.* possibilité *f.*

possible, *adj.* possible.

post¹, *s.* poteau *m.;* — *v.a.* afficher, placarder.

post², *s.* poste *f.;* courrier *m.* — *v.a.* mettre à la poste.

postage, *s.* port *m.,* affranchissement; ~ *paid* port payé.

postal, *adj.* postal; ~ *order* mandat (de poste) *m.*

poster, *s.* affiche *f.*

post-free, *adj.* franco.

postman, *s.* facteur *m.*

post(-)office, *s.* bureau *m.* de poste

postpone, *v.a.* remettre.

postscript, ● post-scriptum *m.*

pot, *s.* pot *m.*

potato, *s.* pomme *f.* de terre.

pottery, *s.* poterie *f.*

pouch, *s.* blague *f.*

poultry, *s.* volaille *f.*

pound, *s.* livre *f.*

pour, *v.a.* verser.

pouring, *adj.* torrentiel.

poverty, *s.* pauvreté *f.*

powder, *s.* poudre *f.*

power, *s.* pouvoir *m.;* puissance *f.;* force *f.*

powerful, *adj.* puissant.

power-plant, -station, *s.* centrale *f.* électrique.

practical, *adv.* pratique.

practice, *s.* pratique *f.;* exercise *m.*

practise, *v.a.* pratiquer, exercer; étudier.

praise, *s.* louange *f.;* — *v.a.* louer.

pray, *v.a. & n.* prier.

prayer, *s.* prière *f.*

preach, *v.a. & n.* prêcher.

preacher, *s.* prédicateur *m.*

precede, *v.a.* précéder.

preceding, *adj.* précédent.

precious, *adj.* précieux.

precision, *s.* précision *f.*

predecessor, *s.* prédécesseur *m.*

predict, *v.a.* prédire.

prefabricated, *adj.* préfabriqué.

preface, *s.* préface *f.*

prefer, *v.a.* préférer *(to* à), aimer mieux.

preferable, *adj.* préférable (à).

preference, *s.* préférence *f.*

pregnant, *adj.* enceinte.

prejudice, *s.* préjugé *m.*

preliminary, *adj.* préliminaire.

premature, *adj.* prématuré.

premier, *s.* premier ministre *m.,* (in France) président *m.* du conseil.

premises, *s. pl.* lieux *m. pl.;* local *m.,* immeuble *m.*

premium, *s.* prime *f.*

preparation, *s.* préparation *f.*

prepare, *v.a.* préparer, apprêter; — *v.n.* se préparer.

preposition, *s.* préposition *f.*

Presbyterian, *adj.* presbytérien.

prescribe, *v.a.* prescrire, ordonner; *v.n.* ~ *for* faire une ordonnance pour.

prescription, *s.* prescription *f.;* (medical) ordonnance *f.*

presence, *s.* présence *f.*

present[1], *adj.* présent; actuel; — *s.* présent *m.;* *at* ~ à présent.

present[2], *s.* (gift) cadeau *m.,* présent *m.;* — *v.a.* présenter; donner.

presently, *adv.* tout à l'heure.

preserve, *v.a.* préserver; (fruits) conserver; — *s.* confiture *f.;* conserve *f.*

president, *s.* président *m.*

press, *s.* presse *f.;* — *v.a.* presser; serrer.

pressure, *s.* pression *f.*

presume, *v.a.* présumer.

presumption, *s.* présomption *f.*

pretend, *v. a. & n.* feindre,

faire semblant; pré-
tendre (à).

pretention, s. prétension
f.

pretty, adj. joli.

prevail, v.n. prévaloir;
prédominer.

prevent, v.a. empêcher.

prevention, s. empêche-
ment m.

previous, adj. antérieur
(à).

prey, s. proie f.

price, s. prix m.; cours m.

price-list, s. prix-courant
m., tarif m.

prick, v.a. piquer; —
s. piqûre f.

pride, s. orgueil m.

priest, s. prêtre m.

primary, adj. primaire.

prime, adj. ~ minister
see premier.

primitive, adj. primitif.

prince, s. prince m.

princess, s. princesse f.

principal, adj. principal;
— s. directeur m.,
patron, -ne m.f., princi-
pal m.

principle, s. principe m

print, s. empreinte f.;
impression f.; out of ~
épuisé; — v.a. im-
primer; faire une em-
preinte (sur); (photo)
tirer; ~ed matter im-
primés m. pl.

printing-office, s. imprimerie f.

prison, s. prison f.

prisoner, s. prisonnier,
-ère m. f.

private, adj. particulier;
personel; privé.

privilege, s. privilège m.

prize, s. prix m.

probability, s. probabi-
lité f.

probable, adj. probable.

probably, adv. proba-
blement.

problem, s. problème m.

procedure, s. procédé m.

proceed, v.n. aller (à);
se mettre (à); avan-
cer; passer (à); pro-
céder; ~ with conti-
nuer.

process, s. développe-
ment m.; méthode f.,
procédé m.; — v.n.
aller en procession.

procession, s. cortège m.;
procession f.

proclaim, v. a. proclamer.

proclamation, s. procla-
mation s.

produce, v.a. produire.

producer, s. producteur,
-trice m. f.

product, s. produit m.

production, s. production
f.

profess, v.a. profes-
ser, déclarer.

profession, s. profession f.

professional, adj. professionnel; de profession.

professor, s. professeur m.

profit, s. profit m.; —
v.n. ~ by profiter de.

profitable, adj. profitable.

profound, adj. profond.

programme, s. program-
me m.

progress, s. progrès m.;
marche f.; — v.n.
s'avancer, faire des
progrès.

prohibit, v.a. défendre.

prohibition, s. prohibi-
tion f., défense f.

project, s. projet m.;
— v.a. projeter; v.n.
saillir.

projector, s. projecteur
m.

prolong, v.a. prolonger.

prominent, adj. (pro)émi-
nent.

promise, s. promesse f.;
— v.a. promettre.

promote, v.a. donner de

l'avancement (à); en-
courager.
promotion, s. promotion
f., avancement m.
prompt, adj. prompt; —
v.a. (rheatre) souffler;
inspirer.
pronoun, s. pronom m.
pronounce, v.a. pro-
noncer.
pronunciation, s. prononciation f.
proof, s. preuve f.; é-
preuve f.
propeller, s. hélice f.
proper, adj. propre; convenable.
property, s. propriété f.
prophet, s. prophète m.
proportion, s. proportion
f.
propose, v.a. proposer.
proposition, proposal, s.
proposition f.
prose, s. prose f.
prospect, s. prospective
f.
prospectus, s. prospectus
m.
prosper, v.n. prospérer.
prosperity, s. prospérité
f.
prosperous, adj. prospère.
protest, s. protestation
f.; protêt m.; — v.a.
protester.
Protestant, adj. & s. protestant, -e (m. f.).
proud, adj. fier, -ère.
prove, v.a. prouver; é-
prouver.
proverb, s. proverbe m.
provide, v.a. pourvoi
de; fournir de; v.n.
~ for pourvoir à; ~d
that pourvu que.
providence, s. prévoyance
f.
province, s. province f.
provincial, adj. provincial.

provision, s. provision f.
provoke, v. a. provoquer
(à).
prudent, adj. prudent.
psalm, s. psaume m.
psychological, adj. psychologique.
psychology, s. psychologie f.
public, adj. & s. pu-
blic m.
publication, s. publication f.
publicity, s. publicité f.
publish, v.a. publier.
publisher, s. éditeur m.
pudding, s. pouding m.
pull, v.a. tirer; ~ down
démolir; ~ out arra-
cher; ~ up arrêter; v.
n. tirer; ~ through s'en
tirer; — s. traction f.,
tirage f.
pulpit, s. chaire f.
pulse, s. pouls m.
pump, s. pompe f.; —
v. a. pomper.
punch¹, s. poinçon m.;
— v.a. poinçonner,
percer.
punch², s. punch m.
punctual, adj. ponctuel.
puncture, s. piqûre f.;
(tyre) crevaison f.;
— v.a.& n. crever.
punish, v.a. punir.
punishment,, s. punition
f.
pupil¹, s. élève m. f.
pupil², s. (eye) pupille f.
puppy, s. petit chien m.
purchase, s. achat m.;
— v.a. acheter.
pure, adj. pur.
purge, v.a. purger.
purify, v.a. purifier.
purity, s. pureté f.
purpose, s. but m.
purse, s. porte-monnaie
m., bourse f.
pursue, v.a. (pour)sui-

vre.

pursuit, *s.* poursuite *f.*

push, *v.a. & n.* pousser; ~ *back* repousser; ~ *on* faire avancer; pousser (jusqu'à); — *s.* poussé *f.*; allant *m.*

puss, *s.* minet *m.*

put, *v.a.* mettre; *(express)* dire; ~ *back* remettre; ~ *down* déposer; attribuer; inscrire; ~ *off* remettre; ôter; ~ *on* mettre; ~ *out* tendre; éteindre; ~ *up* ouvrir; loger; ~ *up with* s'accommoder.

puzzle, *v.a.* embarrasser.

pyjamas, *s. pl.* pyjama *m.*

pyramid, *s.* pyramide *f.*

Q

quadrangle, *s.* quadrilatère *m.*; cour *f.*

quake, *v.n.* trembler.

qualification, *s.* qualification *f.*; compétence *f.*

qualify, *v.a.* qualifier; *v.n.* ~ *for* passer l'examen de.

quality, *s.* qualité *f.*

quantity, *s.* quantité *f.*

quarrel, *s.* querelle *f.*; brouille *f.*; — *v.n.* se brouiller; ~ *with* se quereller avec.

quarter, *s.* quartier *m.*; quart *m.*; ~*s* quartiers *m.pl.*

quartet(te), *s.* quatuor *m.*

quay, *s.* quai *m.*

queen, *s.* reine *f.*; *(cards)* dame *f.*

queer, *adj.* bizarre.

quench, *v.a.* éteindre.

question, *s.* question *f.*; — *v.a.* interroger.

queue, *s.* queue *f.*; — *v.n.* ~ *up* faire (la) queue.

quick, *adj.* prompt, rapide; vif.

quick(ly), *adv.* vite.

quiet, *adj.* tranquille; calme; *be* ~ se taire.

quilt, *s.* courtepointe *f.*

quit, *v.a.* quitter.

quite, *adv.* tout à fait.

quiver, *v.n.* trembler.

quiz, *s.* mystification *f.*; persifleur *m.*; *v.a.* railler.

quotation, *s.* citation *f.*

quote, *v.a.* citer.

R

rabbi, *s.* rabbin *m.*

rabbit, *s.* lapin, -e *m. f.*

race[1], *s.* course *f.*; — *v.n.* faire la course; courir; lutter de vitesse.

race[2], *s.* race *f.*

rack, *s.* râtelier *m.*

racket, *s.* raquette *f.*

radiate, *v.n.* rayonner, irradier; *v.a.* dégager.

radiator, *s.* radiateur *m.*

radical, *adj.* radical.

radio, *s.* radio *f.*

radioactive, *adj.* radioactif.

radish, *s.* radis *m.*

rag, *s.* chiffon *m.*

rage, *s.* rage *f.*

raid, *s.* razzia *f.*, rafle *f.*; raid *m.*

rail, *s.* barre *f.*, rampe *f.*; rail *m.*; *by* ~ par chemin de fer.

railway, *s.* chemin *m.* de fer.

rain, *s.* pluie *f.*; — *v.n.* pleuvoir.

rainy, *adj.* pluvieux.

raise, *v.a.* lever, élever; soulever; *(plants)* faire pousser, cultiver.

rake, *s.* râteau *m.*

rally, *v.n.* se rallier; — *s.* ralliement *m.*

ramify, *v.n.* ramifier.

random, *s.* at ~ par hasard.

range, *s.* rangée *f.;* *(mountains)* chaîne *f.;* *(extent)* étendue *f.;* *(kitchen)* fourneau *m.;* — *v.a.* ranger.

rank, *s.* rang *m.;* grade *m.*

ransom, *s.* rançon *f.;* — *v.a.* payer rançon pour.

rap, *s.* tape *f.;* coup *m.;* — *v.a.* frapper.

rapid, *adj.* rapide.

rare, *adj.* rare.

rascal, *s.* coquin *m.*

rash, *adj.* téméraire; inconsidéré.

raspberry, *s.* framboise *f.*

rat, *s.* rat *m.*

rate, *s.* taux *m.,* cours *m.,* tarif *m.;* *(speed)* vitesse *f.,* allure *f.;* *(tax)* taxe *f.;* at the ~ of à la vitesse de; at any ~ en tout cas, quoi qu'il en soit; — *v.a.* estimer; taxer.

rather, *adv.* plutôt; un peu.

ratify, *v.a.* ratifier.

ration, *s.* ration *f.*

rational, *adj.* raisonnable.

rattle, *s.* bruit *m.;* — *v.n.* faire du bruit.

raven, *s.* corbeau *m.*

raw, *adj.* cru; ~ material matière *f.* première.

ray, *s.* rayon *m.*

razor, *s.* rasoir *m.;* safety ~ rasoir de sûreté; electric ~ rasoir électrique.

razor-blade, *s.* lame *f.* de rasoir.

reach, *v.a.* arriver (à); atteindre; *v. n.* atteindre; parvenir (à); — *s.* étendue *f.;* portée *f.;* within ~ à portée.

react, *v.n.* réagir.

reaction, *s.* réaction *f.*

reactor, *s.* réacteur *m.*

read, *v.a.* lire; *(study)* étudier; ~ for *(exam)* préparer.

reader, *s.* lecteur, -trice *m. f.*

reading, *s.* lecture *f.*

ready, *adj.* prêt (à); prompt (à); près (de); get ~ (se) préparer.

real, *adj.* réel; véritable.

reality, *s.* réalité *f.*

realization, *s.* réalisation *f.*

realize, *v.a.* réaliser.

really, *adv.* vraiment.

realm, *s.* royaume *m.;* *fig.* domaine *m.*

reap, *v.a. & n.* moissonner.

reaper, *s.* moissonneur *m.*

rear, *adj.* de derrière; — *s.* arrière *m.;* queue *f.;* — *v.a.* élever; *v. n.* se cabrer.

reason, *s.* raison *f.;* — *v. a. & n.* raisonner.

reasonable, *adj.* raisonnable.

reasoning, *s.* raisonnement *m.*

rebellion, *s.* rébellion *f.*

rebuke, *s.* réprimande *f.;* — *v.a.* réprimander.

recall, *v.a.* rappeler; *(remember)* se rappeler.

receipt, *s.* reçu *m.,* quittance *f.;* recette *f.*

receive, *v.a.* recevoir.

receiver, s. destinataire m. f.; (phone, wireless) écouteur m., récepteur m., poste m.

recent, adj. récent.

recently, adv. récemment.

reception, s. réception f.

receptionist, s. portier m. d'auberge; employé à la réception.

recipe, s. recette f.

recital, s. récit m.; récital m.

recite, v.a. & n. réciter.

reckless, adj. insouciant.

reckon, v.a. compter.

recognize, v.a. reconnaître.

recollect, v. a. se rappeler.

recommend, v.a. recommander.

recommendation, s. recommandation f.

reconcile, v. a. réconcilier.

record, s. rapport m. officiel; souvenir m.; mention f.; archives f. pl.; (gramophone) disque m.; (sport) record m.; — v.a. enregistrer; rapporter.

recount, v.a. raconter.

recover, v.a. recouvrer; v.n. se remettre.

recreation, s. récréation f.

recruit, s. recrue f.; — v.a. recruter.

rectangle, s. rectangle m.

rector, s. recteur m.; curé m.

recur, v. n. revenir.

red, adj. rouge; roux.

redress, v.n. réparer; redresser.

reduce, v.a. réduire.

reduction, s. réduction f.

reed, s. roseau m.

reef, s. ris m.; récif m.

reel, s. dévidoir m.; bo-

bine f.; — v.n. tourner.

refer, v.a. référer; renvoyer; v.n. ~ to se rapporter à, s'en rapporter à, se référer à.

referee, s. arbitre m.; — v.a. arbitrer.

reference, s. renvoi m., référence f.; rapport m.; allusion f.; with ~ to à propos de; have ~ to se rapporter à.

refill, s. recharge f.

reflect, v.a. réfléchir; v.n. méditer (sur).

reflection, s. réflexion f.; image f.

reform, s. réforme f.; — v.a. réformer.

Reformation, s. Réforme f.

refrain, v.n. ~ from se retenir de.

refresh, v.a. rafraîchir.

refreshment, s. rafraîchissement m.; ~ room buffet m.

refrigerator, s. réfrigérateur m.

refuge, s. refuge m.; take ~ se réfugier.

refugee, s. réfugié, -e m. f.

refusal, refus m.

refuse, v.a. refuser.

refute, v.a. réfuter.

regain, v.a. reconquérir; regagner; reprendre.

regard, s. égard m.; with ~ to à l'égard de; kind(est) ~s meilleurs amitiés f. pl.; — v.a. regarder; tenir compte (de); considérer.

regent, s. régent m.

regime, s. régime m.

regiment, s. régiment m.

region, s. région f.

register, v. a. enregistrer.

regret, *v.a.* regretter; — *s.* regret *m.*

regular, *adj.* régulier.

regulate, *v.a.* régler.

regulation, *s.* ordonnance *f.*; réglementation *f.*

rehearsal, *s.* répétition *f.*

rehearse, *v.a.* répéter.

reign, *s.* règne *m.*; — *v. a.* régner

rein, *s.* rêne *f.*

reject, *v.a.* rejeter; refuser.

relate, *v.a.* raconter; be ~ed to être apparenté à; *v.n.* ~ to se rapporter à; *relating to* relatif à.

relation, *s.* relation *f.*, rapport *m.* (à); *(relative)* parent, -e *m. f.*

relative, *s.* parent, -e *m. f.*; — *adj.* relatif; ~ to au sujet de.

relax, *v.n.* se relâcher; *v. a.* relâcher.

relay, *s.* relais *m.*

release, *s.* délivrance *f.*; — *v.a.* libérer; décharger (de).

reliable, *adj.* digne de confiance.

relic, *s.* relique *f.*

relief[1], *s.* délivrance *f.*; soulagement *m.*; secours *m.*

relief[2], *s.* relief *m.*

relieve, *v.a.* soulager; secourir; délivrer.

religion, *s.* religion *f.*

religious, *adj.* religieux.

rely, *v.n.* ~ upon compter sur.

remain, *v.n.* rester.

remark, *s.* remarque *f.*; — *v.a.* remarquer; *v.n.* faire une remarque.

remarkable, *adj.* remarquable.

remedy, *s.* remède *m.*

remember, *v.a.* se souve-nir (de), se rappeler.

remembrance, *s.* souvenir *m.*

remind, *v. a.* ~ of rappeler (à), faire souvenir (de).

remit, *v.a.* remettre.

remittance, *s.* remise *f.*

remorse, *s.* remords *m.*

remote, *adj.* reculé.

removal, *s.* déménagement *m.*; enlèvement; *(dismissal)* renvoi *m.*

remove, *v.a.* déménager; enlever; *(dismiss)* renvoyer, *(from school)* retirer; *v.n.* déménager; s'en aller.

Renaissance, *s.* Renaissance *f.*

render, *v.a.* rendre.

renew, *v.a.* renouveler.

renounce, *v.a.* renoncer (à); dénoncer; répudier.

rent, *s.* *(house)* loyer *m.*; — *v.a.* louer.

repair, *s.* réparation *f.*; — *v.a.* réparer.

repay, *v.a.* rembourser.

repeat, *v.a.* répéter.

repentance, *s.* repentir *m.*

repetition, *s.* répétition *f.*

replace, *v.a.* replacer.

reply, *s.* réponse *f.*; — *v.a. & n.* répondre.

report, *s.* rapport *m.*, compte *m.* rendu; bruit *m.*; bulletin *m.*; — *v.a.* rapporter; rendre compte (de).

reporter, *s.* reporter *m.*

represent, *v.a.* représenter.

representation, *s.* représentation *f.*

representative, *s.* représentant *m.*

reproach, *s.* reproche *m.*

reproduce, *v.a.* reproduire.

reproduction, *s.* reproduction *f.*

reprove, *v.a.* réprimandder.

republic, *s.* république *f.*

repulsion *s.* répulsion *f.*

repulsive, *adj.* repoussant.

reputation, repute, *s.* réputation *f.*

request, *s.* requête *f.;* — *v.a.* demander.

require, *v. a.* demander; exiger.

requirement, *s.* besoin *m.;* exigence *f.*

rescue, *s.* délivrance *f.;* secours *m.;* — *v.a.* délivrer; secourir.

research, *s.* recherche *f.*

resemble, *v.a.* ressembler (à).

resent, *v.a.* être froissé (de); ressentir.

reserve, *s.* réserve *f.;* — *v.a.* réserver.

reside, *v.n.* résider.

residence, *s.* résidence *f.*

resident, *s.* habitant *m.;* — *adj.* résidant.

resign, *v.a.* résigner, se démettre (de); *v.n.* donner sa démission.

resignation, *s.* résignation *f.;* démission *f.*

resist, *v. a.* résister (à).

resistance, *s.* résistance *f.*

resolution, *s.* résolution *f.*

resolve, *v.a.* résoudre; *v.n.* se résoudre (à), se décider (à faire).

resort, *s.* recours *m.;* ressource *f.;* — *v.n.* ~ *to* avoir recours à.

resource, *s.* ressource *f.*

respect, *s.* respect *m.;* rapport *m.; in this* ~ sous ce rapport; *with* ~ *to* concernant ...· — *v.a.* respecter.

respectful, *adj.* respectueux.

respective, *adj.* respectif.

respond, *v.n.* répondre.

response, *s.* réponse *f.*

responsibility, *s.* responsabilité *f.*

responsible, *adj.* responsable (de).

rest¹, *s.* reste *m.; the* ~ les autres.

rest², *s.* repos *m.;* pause *f.;* — *v.n.* se reposer.

restaurant, *s.* restaurant *m.*

restless, *adj.* sans repos; inquiet; agité.

restoration, *s.* restauration *f.*

restore, *v.a.* restaurer.

restrain, *v. a.* retenir; ~ *from* empêcher de.

restraint, *s.* contrainte *f.;* retenue *f.*

restrict, *v.a.* restreindre.

restriction, *s.* restriction *f.*

result, *s.* résultat *m.;* — *v.n.* ~ *from* résulter de; ~ *in* avoir pour résultat.

resume, *v. a.* reprendre.

retain, *v.a.* retenir.

retire, *v. n.* se retirer.

retreat, *s.* retraite *f.*

return, *v.n.* revenir, retourner; *v.a.* rendre; renvoyer; *(answer)* faire; — *s.* retour *m* ; renvoi *m.;* ~ *ticket* billet *m.* d'aller et retour.

reveal, *v.a.* révéler.

revenge, *s.* vengeance *f.;* — *v.a.* venger.

revenue, *s.* revenu *m.*

reverend, *adj.* révérend.

reverse, *adj.* inverse; — *s.* revers *m.*

review, *s.* revue *f.; (of book)* compte *m.* rendu, critique *f.;* — *v.a.* revoir; *(book)* faire la critique (d'un livre).

revision, *s.* révision *f.*

revolt, *s.* révolte *f.*

revolution, *s.* révolution

f.; (motor) tour *m.*

reward, *s.* récompense *f.;* — *v.a.* récompenser.

rheumatism, *s.* rhumatisme *m.*

rhyme, *s.* rime *f.*

rhythm, *s.* rythme *m.*

rib, *s.* côte *f.*

rice, *s.* riz *m.*

rich, *adj.* riche.

rid, *v.a.* get ~ *of* se débarrasser de.

riddle, *s.* énigme *f.*

ride, *v.n.* monter; aller à cheval *or* à bicyclette; *(bus)* voyager; aller (en autobus); *v. a.* monter; — *s.* promenade *f.*

ridge, *s.* crête *f.*

ridiculous, *adj.* ridicule.

rifle, *s.* fusil *m.*

right, *adj.* droit; correct, exact; juste, bon; bien; ~ *side* endroit *m.;* be ~ avoir raison; *that's* ~ c'est ça; — *s.* droit *m.; (opposed to left)* droite *f.;* — *adv.* droit; bien; *(very)* très.

rim, *s.* bord *m.*

ring[1]**,** *s.* anneau *m.;* cercle *m.; (sport)* ring *m.*

ring[2]**,** *v.n. & a.* sonner; ~ *up* appeler (au téléphone); — *s.* son *m.;* coup *m.* de sonnette; *there is a* ~ *at the door* on sonne (à la porte).

rinse, *v.a.* rinser.

riot, *s.* émeute *f.*

rip, *v.a.* déchirer; ~ *up* arracher; *v.n.* aller à toute vitesse.

ripe, *adj.* mûr.

rise, *v. n.* se lever; *(revolt)* se soulever; *(prices)* hausser; *(originate)* naître (de); — *s.* montée *f.; (salary)* augmentation *f.; give* ~ *to* donner lieu à.

risk, *s.* risque *m.;* — *v.a.* risquer.

rival, *adj. & s.* rival, -e *(m. f.);* — *v.a.* rivaliser (avec).

rivalry, *s.* rivalité *f.*

river, *s.* fleuve *m.,* rivière *f.*

road, *s.* route *f.,* chemin *m.*

road-map, *s.* carte *f.* routière. *f.*

roar, *s.* rugissement *m.;* — *v.n.* rugir; hurler.

roast, *v.a. & n.* rôtir; — *s.* rôti *m.*

rob, *v.a.* voler.

robber, *s.* voleur *m.*

robbery, *s.* vol *m.*

robe, *s.* robe *f.*

robin, *s.* rouge-gorge *m.*

rock, *s.* rocher *m.,* roc *m.*

rocket, *s.* fusée *f.*

rocky, *adj.* rocheux.

rod, *s.* baguette *f.*

rogue, *s.* coquin, -e *m. f.*

roll, *s.* rouleau *m.;* liste *f.;* — *v. a.* rouler.

roller-towel, *s.* essuie-mains *m.* à rouleau.

Roman, *adj.* romain; — *s.* Romain, -e *m. f.*

romantic, *adj.* romanesque; romantique.

roof, *s.* toit *m.*

room, *s.* chambre *f.;* salle *f.; (space)* place *f.*

root, *s.* racine *f.;* source *f.*

rope, *s.* corde *f.*

rose, *s.* rose *f.*

rotten, *adj.* pourri, carié.

rough, *adj.* rude; grossier; brut; *(sea)* gros.

roughly, *adv.* approximativement.

round, *adj.* rond; — *adv.* de tour, en rond, autour; *hand* ~ faire circuler; *go* ~ tourner;

turn ~ tourner, se retourner; — *prep.* autour de; — *s.* rond *m.*, cercle *m.*; tournée *f.*; tour *m.*

rouse, *v.a.* réveiller.

route, *s.* route *f.*

routine, *s.* routine *f.*

row¹, *s.* rang *m.*, rangée *f.*; ligne *f.*

row², *v.n.* ramer; *v.a.* faire aller (à la rame); — *s.* promenade *f.* en canot.

row³, *s.* chahut *m.*, vacarme *m.*, querelle *f.*; réprimande *f.*

royal, *adj.* royal.

rub, *v.a.* frotter.

rubber, *s.* caoutchouc *m.*

rubbish, *s.* décombres *m. pl.*; ordure(s) *f. (pl)*, immondices *f. pl.*

ruby, *s.* rubis *m.*

rudder, *s.* gouvernail *m.*

rude, *adj.* rude.

ruffian, *s.* bandit *m.*

ruffle, *s.* ride *f.*; — *v.a.* rider; ébouriffer.

rug, *s.* couverture *f.*; tapis *m.*

ruin, *s.* ruine *f.*; — *v. a.* ruiner.

rule, *s.* autorité *f.*; règle *f.*; *(of the road)* code *m.*; as a ~ généralement; — *v.a.* gouverner; régler; guider; ~ *out* exclure.

ruler, *s.* gouverneur *m.*, souverain *m.*; *(for lines)* règle *f.*

rum, *s.* rhum *m.*

Rumanian, *adj.* roumain; — *s.* Roumain, -e *m. f.*

rumour, *s.* rumeur *f.*

run, *v.n.* courir; fuir, se sauver; *(flow)* couler; *(veh.)* marcher, faire le service; *(engine)* fonctionner; *(play in*

theatre) se jouer; *v.a.* faire fonctionner; mettre en service; faire marcher, faire aller; ~ *after* courir après; ~ *away* s'enfurir; ~ *down* descendre en courant; *(health)* s'affaiblir; ~ *in (motor)* roder; ~ *into* heurter, rencontrer; ~*off* s'enfuir; s'écouler; ~ *out* se terminer; ~ *over* passer dessus; ~ *up (debts)* entasser; — *s.* course *f.*; voyage *m.*

runner, *s.* coureur, -euse *m. f.*

runway, *s.* piste (d envol) *f.*

rupture, *s.* rupture *f.*

rural, *adj.* rural.

rush, *v.n.* se précipiter, se jeter; *v.a.* entraîner à toute vitesse; — *s.* ruée *f.*, hâte *f.*; ~ *hours* heures *f.pl.* d'affluence, coup *m.* de feu.

Russian, *adj.* russe; — *s.* Russe *m. f.*

rust, *s.* rouille *f.*

rustic, *adj.* rustique.

rustle, *s.* bruissement *m.*

rye, *s.* seigle *m.*

S

sabre, *s.* sabre *m.*

sack, *s.* sac *m.*

sacrament, *s.* sacrement *m.*

sacrifice, *s.* sacrifice *m.*

sad, *adj.* triste.

saddle, *s.* selle *f.*

sadness, *s.* tristesse *f.*

safe, *adj.* sûr, en sûreté. sans danger; — *s.* coffre-fort *m.*

safely, *adv.* sain et sauf;

en sûreté.
safety, s. sûreté f.
sail, s. voile f.; — v.n. faire voile, naviguer.
sailor, s. marin m., matelot m.
saint, s. saint, -e m. f.
sake: for the ~ of pour l'amour de.
salad, s. salade f.
salary, s. traitement m., appointements m. pl.
sale, s. vente f.; (auction) vente f. aux enchères.
salesman, s. vendeur m.
saleswoman, s. vendeuse f.
salmon, s. saumon m.
saloon, s. salon m.; ~ bar bar m.
salt, s. sel m.
salt-cellar, s. salière f.
salvation, s. salut m.
same, adj. & pron. même.
sanatorium, s. sanatorium m.
sanction, s. sanction f.; — v.a. sanctionner.
sand, s. sable m.; the ~s la plage.
sandal, s. sandale f.
sandwich, s. sandwich m.
sanitary, adj. sanitaire.
sarcastic, adj. sarcastique.
sardine, s. sardine f.
Satan, s. Satan m.
satellite, s. satellite m.
satire, s. satire f.
satisfaction, s. satisfaction f.
satisfactory, adj. satisfaisant.
satisfy, v.a. satisfaire.
Saturday, s. samedi m.
sauce, s. sauce f.
sausage, s. saucisse f.
save, v. a. sauver; (spare) épargner, gagner; v.n. économiser.
savings-bank, s. caisse f. d'épargne.
Saviour, s. Sauveur m.

saw, s. scie f.; — v.a. & n. scier.
say, v. a. dire; that is to ~ c'est-à-dire.
scale[1], s. plateau (de balance) m.; (pair of) ~s balance f.; — v. a. peser.
scale[2], s. échelle f.; (music) gamme f.
scale[3], s. (fish) écaille f.
scanty, adj. maigre.
scar, s. cicatrice f.
scarce, adj. rare.
scarcely, adv. à peine.
scare, s. panique f.; — v.a. effrayer.
scarf, s. écharpe f., foulard m.
scarlet, adj. écarlate.
scatter, v.a. disperser; éparpiller; dissiper.
scene, s. scène f.; behind the ~s dans les coulisses.
scenery, s. paysage m.; (theatre) décor m.
scent, s. odeur f.; parfum m.; (dog) flair m.
schedule, s. liste f.; cédule f.
scheme, s. plan m.; projet m.
scholar, s. (child) écolier, -ère m. f.; (learned) savant m.
scholarship, s. bourse f.
school, s. école f.; classe f.
schoolboy, -girl, s. écolier, -ère m. f.
schoolmaster, s. instituteur m., maître m. d'école.; (secondary) professeur m.
schoolmistress, s. maîtresse f. d'école; (secondary) professeur m.
schoolroom, s. (salle de) classe f.
science, s. science f.

scientific, *adj.* scientifique.

scientist, *s.* savant *m.*

scissors, *s. pl.* ciseaux *m. pl.*

scold, *v.a.* gronder.

scoop, *s.* écope *f.*

scooter, *s.* scooter *m.*

scope, *s.* portée *f.;* envergure *f.;* carrière *f.*

scorch, *v.a.* roussir, brûler.

score, *s.* entaille *f.; (sum)* compte *m.; (games)* points *m. pl.,* marque *f.,* score *m.; (twenty)* vingtaine *f.; (music)* partition *f.;* — *v.a.* marquer; ~ *out* rayer.

scorn, *s.* mépris *m.*

Scotch, Scottish, Scots, *adj.* écossais.

Scotsman, *s.* Écossais *m.*

scout, *s.* éclaireur *m.*

scrambled: ~ *eggs* œufs *m. pl.* brouillés.

scrap, *s.* morceau *m.;* bout *m.*

scrape, *v.a.* gratter; râcler; ~ *off* décrotter.

scratch, *v.a.* gratter; égratigner; *v. n.* griffer gratter; — *s.* égratignure *f.; m.* coup d'ongle.

scream, *v.n. & a.* crier; — *s.* cri *m.*

screen, *s.* écran *m.*

screw, *s.* vis *f.*

scrub, *v.a.* frotter; nettoyer à la brosse.

scrupulous, *adj.* scrupuleux.

sculptor, *s.* sculpteur *m.*

sculpture, *s.* sculpture *f.;* — *v.a.* sculpter.

scythe, *s.* faux *f.*

sea, *s.* mer *f.; by* ~ par (voie de) mer.

seal[1], *s. (animal)* phoque *m.*

seal[2], *s.* sceau *m.;* — *v.a.* sceller; cacheter.

seam, *s.* couture *f.*

seaport, *s.* port *m.* de mer.

search, *v.a.* chercher; — *s.* recherche *f.*

search-light, *s.* projecteur *m.*

seasickness, *s.* mal *m.* de mer.

seaside, *s.* bord *m.* de la mer.

season, *s.* saison *f.*

seat, *s.* siège *m.;* — *v.a.* asseoir; placer.

second, *adj.* second; deux; deuxième; — *s.* seconde *f.*

secondary, *adj.* secondaire; ~ *school* école *f.* secondaire.

second-hand, *adj.* de seconde main, d'occasion.

secret, *adj. & s.* secret *(m.).*

secretary, *s.* secrétaire *m. f.*

section, *s.* section *f.*

secular, *adj.* séculier.

secure, *adj.* en sûreté, sûr; — *v.a.* mettre en sûreté; obtenir; fixer.

security, *s.* sécurité *f.;* caution *f.;* sûreté *f.; securities* valeurs *f. pl.; social* ~ sécurité *f.* sociale.

sediment, *s.* sédiment *m.*

see, *v.a.* voir; *(understand)* comprendre; *(make sure)* s'assurer; *(accompany)* accompagner; ~ *about* s'occuper de; ~ *out* accompagner jusqu'à la porte; ~ *through* voir à travers, pénétrer; mener à bonne fin; ~ *to* veiller à, s'occuper de.

seed, *s.* semence *f.;* graine *f.*

seek, *v.a.* chercher.

seem, *v.n.* sembler, paraître.

seize, *v.a.* saisir; prendre.

seldom, *adv.* rarement.

select, *v.a.* choisir.

selection, *s.* choix m.

self, *s.* moi *m.*

self-conscious, *adj.* gêné.

self-control, *s.* maîtrise *f.* de soi-même.

selfish, *adj.* égoïste.

selfishness, *s.* égoïsme *m.*

self-respect, *s.* respect *m.* de soi.

self-service, *adj.* ~ *restaurant* restaurant à libre service.

sell, *v.a.* vendre; ~ *out* vendre tout son stock; *v. n.* se vendre.

seller, *s.* vendeur, -euse *m. f.*

semaphore, *s.* sémaphore *m.*

semicolon, *s.* point (et) virgule *m.*

senate, *s.* sénat *m.*

senator, *s.* sénateur *m.*

send, *v.a.* envoyer; *(money)* remettre; ~ *back* renvoyer; ~ *for* envoyer chercher: ~ *forth* exha er; ~ *off* expédier; ~ *on* faire suivre; ~ *out* lancer.

sender, *s.* expéditeur, -trice *m. f.*

sense, *s.* sens *m.*

senseless, *adj.* insensé; sans connaissance.

sensibility, *s.* sensibilité *f.*

sensible, *adj.* sensible; sensé, raisonnable.

sensitive, *adj.* sensible.

sensual, *adj.* sensuel.

sentence, *s.* jugement *m.;* sentence *f.;* phrase *f.;*

— *v. a.* condamner.

sentiment, *s.* sentiment *m.*

sentry, *s.* sentinelle *f.*

separate, *adj,* séparé; à part; — *v.a.* séparer; *v.n.* se séparer.

separation, *s.* séparation *f.*

September, *s.* septembre *m.*

serenade, *s.* sérénade *f.*

sergeant, *s.* sergent *m.*

series, *s.* série *f.*

serious, *adj.* sérieux.

sermon, *s.* sermon *m.*

servant, *s.* serviteur, -vante *m. f.;* domestique *m. f.*

serve, *v. a. & n.* servir.

service, *s.* service *m.;* utilité *f.*

service-station, *s.* station-service *f.*

session, *s.* séance *f.,* session *f.*

set, *v.a.* mettre, placer; *(limb)* remettre; *(fashion)* donner; *(jewels)* monter; *(watch)* régler; *(problem)* donner; *(appoint)* fixer; *(trap)* tendre; — *v.n.* *(sun)* se coucher; — ~ *about* se mettre à; ~ *aside* mettre de côté; ~ *down* déposer; noter; ~ *forth* exposer; ~ *in* commencer; ~ *off, out* partir; ~ *on* pousser (à); ~ *up* dresser; établir; ~ *up for* se donner pour. — *s* ensemble *m.,* assortiment *m.,* collection *f.;* *(tea)* service *m.;* *(radio)* poste *m.;* *(ornaments)* garniture *f.;* *(tennis)* set *m.;* *(gang)* bande *f.;* ~ *of furniture* ameublement *m.;* ~ *of false teeth* dentier *m.*

setting, *s.* mise *f.,* pose *f.;* montage *m.;* installation *f.;* coucher *m.*

settle, *v. a.* fixer; arranger; régler, payer; décider, résoudre; *v.n.* s'établir; se poser (sur); se décider à; ~ *down* s'établir.

settlement, *s.* colonie *f.*

seven, *adj. & s.* sept.

seventeen, *adj.* dix-sept.

seventh, *adj.* septième.

seventy, *adj. & s.* soixante-dix.

several, *adj.* plusieurs; différent.

severe, *adj.* sévère.

sew, *v.a.* coudre.

sewing-machine, *s.* machine *f.* à coudre.

sex, *s.* sexe *m.*

sexual, *adj.* sexuel.

shabby, *adj.* usé, râpé.

shade, *s.* ombre *f.;* ombrage *m.;* — *v.a.* ombrager.

shadow, *s.* ombre *f.*

shady, *adj.* ombreux.

shaft, *s.* bois *m.;* trait *m.;* flèche *f.;* arbre *m.*

shake, *v.a.* secouer; ébranler; *(hands)* serrer; *v.n.* trembler; s'ébranler; — *s.* secousse *f.*

shaky, *adj.* tremblant, branlant; cassé; faible.

shall, *(future see Grammar); (command)* vouloir; *(duty)* devoir.

shallow, *adj.* peu profond.

shame, *s.* honte *f.*

shameless, *adj.* éhonté; honteux.

shampoo, *s.* shampooing *m.*

shank, *s.* jambe *f.*

shape, *s.* forme *f.;* — *v. a.* façonner; former; diriger; *v.n.* se développer; promettre.

shapeless, *adj.* sans forme.

share, *s.* part *f.;* action *f.; have a* ~ *in* contribuer (à); *go* ~*s (in)* partager; — *v. a. & n.* partager.

shareholder, *s.* actionnaire *m. f.*

sharp, *adj.* tranchant; aigu; aigre; piquant; perçant; — *s. (music)* dièse *m.;* — *adv.* net; 9.0 ~ 9 heures précises.

sharpen, *v.a.* aiguiser; tailler.

shatter, *v.a.* fracasser; déranger.

shave, *v.a.* raser; *v.n.* se raser.

shawl, *s.* châle *m.*

she, *pron.* elle.

shear, *v.a.* tondre; couper; — *s. (pair of)* ~*s* cisailles *f. pl.*

sheath, *s.* étui; fourreau *m.*

shed, *v.a.* verser; *(light)* répandre.

sheep, *s.* mouton *m.*

sheer, *adj.* pur; perpendiculaire.

sheet, *s.* drap *m.; (paper)* feuille *f.;* ~ *iron* tôle *f.*

shelf, *s.* rayon *m.*

shell, *s. (egg, nut)* coque *f.; (peas)* cosse *f.*

shelter, *s.* abri *m.; take* ~ s'abriter; — *v.a.* abriter (de); *v. n.* se mettre à l'abri (de).

shepherd, *s.* berger.

shield, *s.* bouclier *m.;* écu *m.*

shift, *s.* changement *m.; (work)* équipe *f.; make* ~ *to* s'arranger (de); — *v. n. & a.* changer de place.

shine, *v. n.* briller; rayonner (de); *the sun is shining* il fait du soleil.

ship, *s.* vaisseau *m.,* navire *m.;* — *v. a.* embarquer.

shipping, s. embarquement m.; navires m. pl.; ~ company compagnie f. de navigation.

shipping-agent, s. agent maritime, m.; (goods) expéditeur m.

shipwreck, s. naufrage m.; — v.a. be ~ed faire naufrage.

shipyard, s. chantier m. de construction.

shirt, s. chemise f.

shiver, v.n. frissonner; (cold) grelotter;

shock, s. choc m.; coup m.; — v.a. choquer; frapper d'horreur.

shocking, adj. affreux; choquant.

shoe, s. soulier m.

shoeblack, s. décrotteur m., cireur m.

shoe-lace, s. lacet m.

shoemaker, s. cordonnier m.

shoot, v.a. tirer, fusiller; lancer; décharger; (game) chasser; (plant) pousser; (rays) darder; (film) tourner; v.n. tirer; se précipiter, se lancer; (plant) pousser; (pain) élancer.

shooting, s. tir m., fusillade f.; (game) chasse f.; — adj. (pain) lancinant.

shop, s. boutique f., magasin m.; — v.n. go ~ping faire des achats or emplettes.

shop-assistant, s. commis m.; demoiselle f., vendeur, -euse m. f.

shopkeeper, s. marchand, -e m. f.; commerçant, -e m. f.

shore, s. rivage m.; rive f.

short, adj. court; petit; bref, brève; (lacking) de manque; — adv. be ~ of manquer de.

shorten, v. a. & n. raccourcir; abréger.

shorthand, s. sténographie f.

shortly, adv. sous peu; bientôt; brièvement.

shot, s. coup m.; trait m.; (bullet) balle f., (cannon) boulet m.

shoulder, s. épaule f.

shout, s. cri m.; — v. a. & n. crier.

shove, v.a. pousser.

shovel, s. pelle f.

show, v.a. montrer; indiquer; manifester; exposer; expliquer; v.n. se montrer; ~ in faire entrer; ~ off étaler; faire ressortir; se donner des airs; ~ out reconduire; ~ up ressortir; — s. blant m.; spectacle m.; parade f.; exposition f.

shower, s. averse f.; — v.a. faire pleuvoir.

shower-bath, s. douche f.

shrill, adj. aigre; aigu, -ë.

shrine, s. châsse f.; lieu saint m.

shrink, v. a. & n. rétrécir; reculer.

shroud, s. linceul m.

shrub, s. arbrisseau m., arbuste m.

shrug, s. haussement m. d'épaules; — v.a. hausser.

shudder, s. frisson m.; — v. n. frissonner (de).

shut, v.a. fermer; (also ~ in) enfermer; ~ off couper; ~ up fermer; se taire.

shutter, s. volet m.

shy, adj. timide.

sick, adj. malade; be ~ vomir; be ~ of être dégoûté de; fall ~

tomber malade.

sickle, *s.* faucille *f.*

sickly, *adj.* maladif; malsain.

sickness, *s.* maladie *f.*

side, *s.* côte *m.;* bord *m.;* *(team)* équipe *f.*

siege, *s.* siège *m.*

sieve, *s.* crible *m.*

sift, *v.a.* cribler.

sigh, *s.* soupir *m.; — v. n.* soupirer.

sight, *s.* vue *f.;* spectacle *m.;* ∼s curiosités *f. pl.*

sightseeing: *go* ∼ visiter les curiosités.

sign, *s.* signe *m.;* enseigne *f.; — v. a. & n.* signer; ∼ *on* engager.

signal, *s* signal *m.; — v.a.* signaler; *v.n.* faire des signaux.

signature, *s.* signature *f.*

significant, *adj.* significatif.

signify, *v.a.* signifier; *v.n.* importer.

signpost, *s.* poteau *m.* indicateur.

silence, *s.* silence *m.*

silent, *adj.* silencieux; muet.

silk, *s.* soie *f.*

silly, *adj.* sot.

silver, *s.* argent *m.; — adj.* d'argent; argenté.

similar, *adj.* semblable.

simple, *adj.* simple.

simultaneous, *adj.* simultané.

sin, *s.* péché *m.; — v.n.* pécher.

since, *adv. & prep.* depuis; *— conj.* depuis que; *(because)* puisque.

sincere, *adj.* sincère.

sinew, *s.* tendon *m.*

sinful, *adj.* pécheur.

sing, *v. a. & n.* chanter.

singer, *s.* chanteur, -euse *m. f.;* cantatrice *f.*

single, *adj.* simple; seul; célibataire; particulier; ∼ *ticket* billet *m.* d'aller.

singular, *s.* singulier *m.; — adj.* remarquable; singulier.

sink, *v. n.* tomber au fond, sombrer; s'enfoncer; baisser; *v. a.* enfoncer; faire baisser; foncer; couler; *— s.* évier *m.*

sinner, *s.* pécheur, -eresse *m. f.*

sir, *s.* monsieur *m.;* Sir *m.*

sister, *s.* sœur *f.; (nurse)* infirmière *f.*

sister-in-law, *s.* belle-sœur *f.*

sit, *v.n.* s'asseoir; être assis; rester; ∼ *down* s'asseoir; se mettre (à); ∼ *for (exam)* se présenter à; ∼ *up* se dresser; *(at night)* veiller.

site, *s.* emplacement *m.;* terrain *m.;* site *m.*

sitting-room, *s.* petit salon *m.*

situation, *s.* situation *f.; (employment)* position *f.;* emploi *m.*

six, *adj. & s.* six *(m.).*

sixteen, *adj. & s.* seize *(m.).*

sixth, *adj.* sixième; six.

sixty, *adj. & s.* soixante.

size, *s.* grandeur *f.,* mesure *f.; (shoes etc.)* pointure *f.;* numéro *m.,* taille *f.; (pers.)* taille *f.*

skate, *v.n.* patiner.

skating, *s.* patinage *m.*

sketch, *s.* croquis *m.;* esquisse *f.; — v.a.* esquisser.

ski, *s.* ski *m.*

skid, *v.n.* déraper.

skier, *s.* skieur *m.*

skiff, *s.* esquif *m.*

skilful, *adj.* adroit.

skill, *s.* adresse *f.*

skim, *v.a.* écrémer.

skin, *s.* peau *f.;* — *v.a.* écorcher; peler.

skip, *v. a. & n.* sauter.

skirt, *s.* jupe *f.*

skull, *s.* crâne *m.*

sky, *s.* ciel *m. (pl.* cieux).

slack, *adj.* lâche; négligent.

slacken, *v.a.* ralentir; relâcher; *v.n.* se relâcher; diminuer.

slacks, *s. pl.* pantalon *m.*

slander, *s.* calomnie *f.;* — *v.a.* calomnier.

slant, *s.* biais *m.;* — *v. a.* faire pencher; *v. n.* être en pente.

slap, *s.* claque *f.;* soufflet *m.;* — *v. a.* claquer; souffleter.

slate, *s.* ardoise *f.*

slaughter, *s.* massacre *m.*

slave, *s.* esclave *m. f.*

sledge, *s.* traineau.

sleep, *s.* sommeil *m.; go to* ~ s'endormir; — *v. a. & n.* dormir.

sleeping-car, *s.* wagon-lit *m.*

sleepy, *adj.* somnolent; *be* ~ avoir sommeil.

sleeve, *s.* manche *f.*

slender, *adj.* mince, faible.

slice, *s.* tranche *f.*

slide, *s.* glissade *f.; (photo)* diapositive *f.*

slight, *adj.* mince; léger.

slim, *adj.* mince, svelte.

sling, *s.* fronde *f.*

slip, *v.n.* glisser; se glisser (dans); *v.a.* filer; pousser, glisser; ~ *off* ôter; ~ *on* mettre; ~ *out* s'esquiver; — *s.* glissade *f.; (mistake)* faux pas *m.; (paper)* fiche *f.; (underwear)* combinaison *f.*

slipper, *s.* pantoufle *f.*

slope, *s.* biais *m.;* pente *f.;* — *v. n.* incliner.

slot, *s.* fente *f.*

slow, *adj.* lent; *(clock)* en retard; *(dull)* peu intelligent; ~ *to* lent à; — *v.n. & a.* ~ *down* ralentir.

slumber, *s.* sommeil *m.;* — *v.n.* sommeiller.

slump, *s.* débâcle *f.;* *(in trade)* mévente *f.;* dépression *f.*

sly, *adj.* rusé.

small, *adj.* petit; faible; peu important; menu.

smart, *adj. (clever)* habile, débrouillard; *(witty)* spirituel; *(dress, pers.)* élégant, chic; pimpant; *(society)* élégant.

smash, *v. a.* briser; *fig.* écraser; — *s.* fracas *m.;* collision *f.*

smear, *v.a.* enduire; — *s.* tache *f.*

smell, *s.* odorat *m.;* odeur *f.;* — *v. a. & n.* sentir; ~ *out* flairer.

smile, *s.* sourire *m.;* — *v.n.* sourire (at à).

smoke, *s.* fumée *f.;* — *v.a. & n.* fumer.

smooth, *adj.* lisse; uni; doux, -ce; *(sea)* calme; — *v.a.* aplanir; lisser.

smuggle, *v.a.* ~ *in* faire passer en contrebande; *v.n.* faire la contrebande.

smuggler, *s.* contrebandier *m.*

snack, *s.* morceau (sur le pouce) *m.; have a* ~ casser la croûte.

snail, *s.* colimaçon *m.*

snake, *s.* serpent *m.*

snap, *s.* fermoir *m.;* coup *m.* de dents; claquement *m.; (photo)* instantané *m.;* — *v. a.* faire claquer; fermer;

~ *at* happer; ~ *off* casser.

snapshot, *s.* instantané *m.*

snatch, *s.* action de saisir, *f.;* accès *m.;* fragment *m.;* — *v. a.* saisir; ~ *at* saisir au vol.

sneeze, *v. n.* éternuer; — *s.* éternuement *m.*

sniff, *v.a.&n.* renifler.

snore, *v. n.* ronfler.

snow, *s.* neige *f.;* — *v.n.* neiger.

snug, *adj.* commode.

so, *adv.* ainsi; si; donc; ~ *that* de sorte que; afin que.

soak, *v.n.* tremper.

soap, *s.* savon *m.*

soar, *v.n.* prendre son essor; *fig.* s'élancer.

sob, *v.n.* sangloter; — *s.* sanglot.

sober, *adj.* sobre; sensé;

social, *adj.* social.

socialism, *s.* socialisme *m.*

society, *s.* société *f.*

sock, *s.* chaussette *f.*

socket, *s.* cavité *f.;* *(electric)* prise *f.* de contact.

soda-water, *s.* eau *f.* de Seltz.

sofa, *s.* canapé *m.*

soft, *adj.* mou, mol molle; doux, -ce.

soil, *s.* terroir; *(stain)* tache; — *v. a.* souiller.

soldier, *s.* soldat *m.*

sole¹, *s.* plante *f.;* semelle *f.;* *(fish)* sole *f.*

sole², *adj.* seul.

solicit, *v. a.* solliciter.

solicitor, *s.* avoué *m.* solicitor *m.*

solidarity, *s.* solidarité *f.*

solitude, *s.* solitude *f.*

solution, *s.* solution *f.*

solve, *v.a.* résoudre.

some, *adj.* quelque; de; — *pron.* quelques-uns; les uns; en *(+ verb)*

— *adv.* environ.

somebody, -one, *pron.* quelqu'un.

somehow, *adv.* d'une façon quelconque; ~ *or other* d'une façon ou d'une autre.

something, *s.* & *pron.* quelque chose *m.*

sometime, *adv.* quelque jour, autrefois.

sometimes, *adv.* quelquefois, parfois.

somewhere, *adv.* quelque part.

son, *s.* fils *m.*

song, *s.* chanson *f.*

son-in-law, *s.* gendre *m.*

soon, *adv.* bientôt.

sore, *adj.* douloureux; *have a* ~ ... avoir mal à ...; — *s.* plaie *f.*

sorrow, *s.* douleur *f.*

sorry, *adj. be* ~ *for* regretter; ~! pardon!

sort, *s.* sorte *f.;* genre *m.;* type *m.;* ~ *of* une espèce de.

soul, *s.* âme *f.*

sound¹, *s.* son *m.;* bruit *m.;* — *v. n.* sonner; — *v.a.* sonner; sonder; *(physician)* ausculter.

sound², *adj.* sain; solide; droit; profond; en bon état.

soup, *s.* potage *m.;(clear)* consommé *m.;* *(thick)* soupe *f.*

sour, *adj.* aigre; acide; *(milk)* tourné.

source, *s.* source *f.*

south, *s.* sud *m.*, midi *m.;* — *adj.* sud; du sud; — *adv.* vers le sud.

southeast, *adj.* & *s.* sud-est *(m.);* — *adv.* vers le sud-est.

southern, *adj.* du sud.

southwest, *adj.* & *s.* sud-ouest *(m.);* — *adv.* vers le sud-ouest.

sovereign, *s.* souverain, -e *m. f.*

sow[1]**,** *v. a.* & *n.* semer (de).

sow[2]**,** *s.* truie *f.*

space, *s.* espace *m.*

space-craft, -ship, -vehicle, *s.* astronef *m.*

space-flight, *s.* navigation *f.* astronautique.

spaceman, *s.* cosmonaute *m.,* astronaute *m.*

spade, *s.* bêche *f.; (cards)* pique *m.*

span, *s.* empan *m.; ouverture; — v.a.* traverser; couvrir.

Spaniard, *s.* Espagnol, -e.

Spanish, *adj.* & *s.* espagnol *(m.).*

spanner, *s.* clef *f.*

spare, *adj.* maigre; disponible; de réserve; ~ *parts* pièces de rechange *f. pl.;* ~ *time* loisir *m.; — v.a.* épargner; économiser; *(evade)* éviter.

spark, *s.* étincelle *f.*

sparrow, *s.* moineau *m.*

speak, *v.n.* parler; *v.a.* dire; ~ *out* parler hardiment; ~ *up* parler plus haut; ... ~*ing* ici ...

spear, *s.* lance *f.*

special, *adj.* spécial.

specialist, *s.* spécialiste *m. f.*

specific, *adj.* spécifique.

specify, *v.a.* spécifier.

speck, *s.* grain *m.;* tache *f.*

spectacles, *s. pl.* lunettes *f.*

spectacular, *adj.* impressionnant.

spectator, *s.* spectateur, -trice *m. f.*

speech, *s.* parole *f.;* langage *m.; (address)* discours *m.*

speed, *s.* vitesse *f.*

speedy, *adj.* rapide;

prompt.

spell[1]**,** *v.a.* & *n.* épeler; orthographier, écrire; *how is it spelt?* comment cela s'écrit-il?

spell[2]**,** *s.* période *f.;* tour *m.*

spelling, *s.* ortographe *f.*

spend, *v.a.* dépenser; *(time)* passer; *v.n.* dépenser.

sphere, *s.* sphère *f.*

spice, *s.* épice *f.*

spider, *s.* araignée *f.*

spill, *v.a.* repandre; renverser.

spin, *v.a.* & *n.* filer; faire tourner.

spinach, *s.* épinards *m. pl.*

spine, *s.* épine (dorsale) *f.*

spinster, *s.* vieille fille *f.;* célibataire *f.*

spiral, *adj.* en spirale.

spire, *s.* flèche *f.*

spirit, *s.* esprit *m.;* âme *f.;* spectre *m.;* caractère *m.,* cœur *m.;* ~*s* spiritueux *m. pl.*

spiritual, *adj.* spirituel.

spit, *s.* crachat *m.; — v. a.* & *n.* cracher.

spite, *s.* dépit *m.; in* ~ *of* malgré.

splash, *s.* éclaboussement *m.; — v. a.* & *n.* éclabousser (de).

spleen, *s.* rate *f.*

splendid, *adj.* splendide.

splinter, *s.* éclat *m.; (bone)* esquille *f.*

split, *v. a.* fendre; (also ~ *up*) partager; *v.n.* se fendre; se diviser.

spoil, *v.a.* gâter; dépouiller (de); endommager; *v.n.* se gâter.

sponge, *s.* éponge *f.*

spontaneous, *adj.* spontané.

spoon, *s.* cuiller *f.*

spoonful, *s.* cuillerée *f.*

sport, s. sport m.; amuse-
ments m. pl.

sportsman, s. sportsman
m.

spot, s. tache f.; (place)
endroit m.; — v.a.
tacher; reconnaître.

spout, s. gouttière f.; bec
m.; — v.a. lancer.

sprain, v.a. donner une
entorse (à).

spray, s. embrun m.,
vaporisateur m.; ato-
miseur m.; — v.a. vapo-
riser, atomiser; arroser.

spread, v.a. étendre; ré-
pandre; (cloth) mettre;
(cover) couvrir; (news)
faire circuler; v.n.
s'étendre; — s. propa-
gation f.; étendue f.

spring¹, s. printemps m.

spring², v.n. sauter;
pousser; jaillir; prove-
nir (de), descendre (de),
naître (de); ~ up se
lever vite; jaillir; — s.
saut m.; (watch etc.)
ressort m.

sprinkle, v.a. répandre;
asperger (de), arroser.

sprout, v. a. & n. germer;
pousser; — s. pousse
f.; Brussels ~s choux
m. pl. de Bruxelles

spur, s. éperon m., aiguillon m.; — v. a. éperon-
ner; ~ on pousser à.

spy, s. espion, -onne
m. f.; — v.n. espionner.

squander, v. a. gaspiller.

square, s. carré m.; (town)
place f.; — adj. carré;
honnête.

squeeze, v.a. serrer; presser.

squint, v.n. loucher; —
s. strabisme m.

squire, s. écuyer m.;
châtelain m.

squirrel, s. écureuil m.

stability, s. stabilité f.

stable, s. écurie f.; — adj.
stable.

stack, s. pile f.; meule f.

stadium, s. stade m.

staff, s. état-major m.;
bâton m.; hampe f.;
(institution) personnel
m.; ~ officer officier
d'état-major m.

stag, s. cerf m.

stage, s. scène f.; (dra-
ma) théâtre m.; (pe-
riod) période f.; (plat-
form) estrade f.; —
v.a. mettre en scène.

stagger, v.n. chanceler;
v.a. bouleverser.

stain, s. tache f.; — v.a.
tacher; salir.

stair, s. marche; ~s
escalier m.

staircase, s. escalier m.

stake, s. pieu m.; at ~
en jeu; — v.a. garnir
de pieux; mettre au
jeu; jouer.

stale, adj. rassis.

stall, s. stalle f.; fauteuil
m.; (books) kiosque m.
à journaux.

stammer, v. n. bégayer.

stamp, s. timbre-poste m.;
estampe f.; contrôle
m.; empreinte f.; —
v.a. timbrer; estamper;
contrôler.

stand, v.n. être debout,
se tenir debout, se
soutenir; (be situated)
se trouver; (remain)
rester; ~ out ressortir;
~ up se lever; — s.
position f.; (vehicles)
station f.; (stall) éta-
lage m.; stand m.

standard, s. étendard m.;
étalon m.; niveau m.;
— adj. régulateur; au
titre; (authors) clas-
sique.

star, s. étoile f.

stare, *v.n.* (also ~ *at*) regarder fixement.

start, *v.n.* partir; commencer; *v. a.* faire partir; faire lever; commencer; lancer; — *s.* commencement *m.;* départ *m.*

starve, *v.n.* mourir de faim; *v. a.* faire mourir de faim.

state, *s.* état *m.;* — *v. a.* affirmer; porter; déclarer.

statement, *s.* déclaration *f.*

statesman, *s.* homme *m.* d'état.

station, *s.* poste *m.;* endroit *m.; (railway)* gare *f.; (police)* poste *m.* de police.

stationer, *s.* papetier *m.;* ~'*s shop* papeterie *f.*

statistic(al), *adj.* statistique.

statistics, *s.* statistique *f.*

statue, *s.* statue *f.*

statute, *s.* statut *m.;* ordonnance *f.*

stay, *v.n.* rester; être installé; ~ *away* rester absent; ~ *up* veiller.

steady, *adj.* ferme; soutenu; *(pers.)* rangé; — *int.* attention!

steak, *s.* tranche *f.;* bifteck *m.*

steal, *v.a.* voler.

steam, *s.* vapeur *f.*

steamboat, *s.* bateau *m.* à vapeur

steam-engine, *s.* locomotive *f.*

steel, *s.* acier *m.*

steep, *adj.* raide, escarpé.

steeple, *s.* clocher *m.*

steer, *v.a.* gouverner; diriger.

steering-gear, *s.* appareil *m.* de direction.

steering-wheel, *s.* volant *m.*

stem, *s.* tige *f.;* queue *f.*

step, *s.* pas *m.; (stair)* marche *f.; (ladder)* échelon *m.; take* ~*s* faire des démarches; — *v.n.* faire un pas; marcher; aller, venir; ~ *in* entrer.

stepmother, *s.* belle-mère *f.*

stereotype, *s.* cliché *m.*

sterile, *adj.* stérile.

stern, *s.* arrière *m.* — *adj.* sévère.

stew, *s.* ragoût *m.; (fruit)* compote *f.;* — *v.a. (meat)* faire un ragout de; *(fruit)* faire une compote de.

steward, *s.* régisseur *m.;* steward *m.*

stewardess, *s.* hôtesse *f.* de l'air.

stick, *s.* bâton *m.,* canne *f.,* petite branche *f.;* — *v.a.* coller; *v.n.* se coller; ~ *on* attacher; ~ *to* rester fidèle à.

sticky, *adj.* gluant.

stiff, *adj.* raide; dur.

still, *adj.* calme — *adv.* toujours; encore; cependant.

sting, *s.* aiguillon *m.;* — *v.a. & n.* piquer.

stink, *v.n.* puer; — *s.* puanteur *f.*

stipulate, *v.a.* stipuler.

stir, *v.a.* remuer; exciter; *v. n.* remuer; bouger; — *s.* remuement *m.*

stirrup, *s.* étrier *m.*

stitch, *s.* point *m.;* — *v.a. & n.* coudre.

stock, *s.* marchandises *f. pl.;* provision *f.; (tree)* tronc *m.; (cattle)* bestiaux *m. pl.; (finance)* valeurs *f. pl.; Stock Exchange* Bourse *f.*

stockholder, *s.* actionnaire *m. f.*

stocking, *s.* bas *m.*

stomach, *s.* estomac *m.*

stone, *s.* pierre; *(fruit)* noyau *m.; — v.a.* lapider.

stony, *adj.* pierreux.

stool, *s.* tabouret *m.*, escabeau *m.*

stop, *v.a.* arrêter; empêcher (de); *(teeth)* plomber; retenir suspendre, *v.n.* s'arrêter; cesser; *— s.* halte *f.;* arrêt *m.; (organ)* jeu *m.; (sign)* signe de ponctuation, *m.*

store, *s.* provision *f.;* ~s grand magasin *m.; — v.a.* emmagasiner.

stork, *s.* cigogne *f.*

storm, *s.* orage *m.*

story[1], *s.* histoire *f.*

story[2], *s.* étage *m.*

stout, *adj.* fort; intrépide.

stove, *s.* poêle *m.;* fourneau *m.*

straight, *adj.* droit; honnête; d'aplomb; *— adv.* juste; droit.

straighten, *v.a.* (re)dresser; *v.n.* se redresser.

strain, *s.* effort *m.;* tension *f.; — v. a.* tendre; *(filter)* passer; *(muscle)* forcer.

strange, *adj.* étrange(r).

stranger, *s.* étranger -ère *m. f.*

strap, *s.* courroie *f.*

straw, *s.* paille *f.*

strawberry, *s.* fraise *f.*

stray, *adj.* égaré; *— v. n.* errer.

streak, *s.* raie *f.;* bande *f.*

stream, *s.* courant *m.; — v.n.* couler, ruisseler.

street, *s.* rue *f.*

strength, *s.* force *f.*

strengthen, *v.a.* fortifier.

stress, *s.* force *f.; (grammar)* accent *m.*

stretch, *s.* effort *m.;* étendue *f.; — v.a.* étendre; élargir.

stretcher, *s.* brancard *m.*

strew, *v.a.* semer.

strict, *adj.* strict.

stride, *s.* enjambée *f.;* grand pas *m.; — v. n.* enjamber.

strike, *v.a.* frapper; *(blow)* asséner; *(work)* cesser; *v.n.* frapper; *(clock)* sonner; *(workers)* se mettre en grève *— s.* grève *f.;* be on ~ être en grève.

striking, *adj.* frappant.

string, *s.* ficelle *f.;* corde *f.*

strip, *s.* bande *f.;* bout *m.; — v. a.* déshabiller; *v.n.* se déshabiller.

stripe, *s.* bande *f.*

strip-lighting, *s.* éclairage *m.* par luminescent.

strive, *v. n.* s'efforcer (de).

stroke, *s.* coup *m.; (swimming)* brasse *f.; (pen)* trait *m.*

strong, *adj.* fort; vigoureux; puissant; solide.

structure, *s.* structure *f.*

struggle, *v.n.* lutter (avec); faire de grands efforts (pour); *— s.* lutte *f.;* mêlée *f.*

stub, *s.* souche *f.;* bout *m.*

stubborn, *adj.* obstiné.

stud, *s.* bouton *m.*

student, *s.* étudiant, -e *m. f.*

studio, *s.* atelier *m.*

study, *s.* étude *f.;* cabinet *m.* de travail —

v. a. & n. étudier.

stuff, *s.* étoffe *f.;* mate-
riaux *m.pl.;* — *v.a.*
remplir; fourrer.

stumble, *v.n.* trébucher;
~ *(up)on* tomber sur;
— *s.* faux pas *m.*

stump, *s.* souche *f.;* —
v.a. estomper.

stupid, *adj.* stupide.

style, *s.* style *m.*

subject, *s.* sujet, -te *m. f.;*
— *adj.* ~ *to* sujet
à; —*v.a.* assujettir (à).

submarine, *s.* sous-marin
m.

submission, *s.* soumission *f.*

submit, *v.a.* soumettre.

subordinate, *adj. & s.*
subordonné; — *v.a.*
subordonner.

subscribe, *v.a. & n.* (~
to) souscrire (à); s'a-
bonner (à).

subscriber, *s.* souscripteur *m.;* abonné; -e
souscripteur *m.;* abon-
né, -e *m. f.*

subscription, *s.* souscription *f.;* abonnement *m.*

subsequent, *adj.* subséquent.

subsequently, *adv.* par
la suite.

subsidy, *s.* subside *m.*

subsist, *v. n.* exister; subsister (de).

subsistence, *s.* subsistance *f.*

substance, *s.* substance *f.*

substantial, *adj.* substantiel.

substantive, *s.* substantif *m.*

substitute, *v.a.* substituer *(for* à).

substitution, *s.* substitution *f.*

subtle, *adj.* subtil.

subtract, *v.a.* soustraire.

subtraction, *s.* soustraction *f.*

suburb, *s.* faubourg *m.;*
~*s* banlieue *f.*

subway, *s.* souterrain *m.;*
métro *m.*

succeed, *v.a.* succéder
(à); *v.n. (be success-
ful)* réussir (à); faire
ses affaires; ~ *to* succéder à.

success, *s.* succès *m.*

successful, *adj.* heureux,
(exam) reçu.

succession, *s.* succession
f.

successive, *adj.* successif.

such, *adj.* tel, -le; ~ *and*
~ tel(le) ou tel(le); —
pron. ~ *as* ceux, cel-
les.

suck, *v.a. & n.* sucer;
— *s. give* ~ *to* allai-
ter.

sudden, *adj.* soudain.

suddenly, *adv.* soudain.

suet, *s.* graisse *f.* de rognon.

suffer, *v. a. & n.* souffrir.

sufficient, *adj.* suffisant.

sufficiently, *adv.* suffisamment.

sugar, *s.* sucre *m.*

suggest, *v.a.* suggérer;
proposer.

suggestion, *s.* suggestion
f.

suicide, *s.* suicide *m.*

suit, *s. (clothes)* complet
m.; (cards) couleur *f.;*
(law) procès *m.; (re-
quest)* requête *f.;* —
v.a. convenir (à);
adapter (à); *v.n.* con-
venir (à); aller (avec).

suitable, *adj.* convenable; ~ *for* adapté à.

suitcase, *s.* mallette *f.,*
valise *f.*

sum, *s.* somme *f.;* ~ *total* somme totale, *f.;*

— *v.a.* ~ up résumer

summary, *s.* résumé *m.*

summer, *s.* été *m.*

summon, *v.a.* convoquer; appeler.

sun, *s.* soleil *m.*

Sunday, *s.* dimanche *m.*

sunny, *adj.* ensoleillé; exposé au soleil.

sunrise, *s.* lever *m.* du soleil.

sunset, *s.* coucher *m.* du soleil.

sunshine, *s.* soleil *m.*

sunstroke, *s.* coup *m.* de soleil.

superannuate, *v. a.* mettre à la retraite.

superficial, *adj.* superficiel.

superfluous, *adj.* superflu.

superior, *s. & adj.* supérieur *(m.).*

supermarket, *s.* supermarché *m.*

supersonic, *adj.* supersonique.

superstition, *s.* superstition *f.*

superstitious, *adj.* superstitieux.

supervise, *v.a.* surveiller.

supervision, *s.* surveillance *f.*

supper, *s.* souper *m.*

supplement, *s.* supplément *m.;* — *v.a.* suppléer (à).

supplementary, *adj.* supplémentaire.

supply, *s.* provision *f.;* approvisionnement *m.;* ~ *and demand* l'offre et la demande; — *v.a.* fourner (de); suppléer.

support, *s.* appui *m.;* support *m.;* — *v.a.* supporter; soutenir; appuyer.

suppose, *v.a.* supposer.

supposition, *s.* supposition *f.*

suppress, *v.a.* supprimer.

suppression, *s.* suppression *f.;* répression *f.*

supreme, *adj.* suprême.

sure, *adj.* sûr; *be* ~ *to* ne pas manquer de; *make* ~ *that* s'assurer que.

surely, *adv.* sûrement.

surface, *s.* surface *f.*

surgeon, *s.* chirurgien *m.*

surgery, *s.* chirurgie *f.*

surname, *s.* nom *m.* de famille.

surpass, *v.a.* surpasser.

surprise, *s.* surprise *f.;* — *v.a.* surprendre.

surprising, *adj.* surprenant.

surrender, *s.* abandon *m.;* reddition *f.;* — *v.a.* rendre; renoncer; *v.n.* se rendre.

surround, *v.a.* entourer (de).

surroundings, *s. pl.* environs *m. pl.;* entourage *m.*

survey, *s.* vue *f.;* examen *m.;* — *v.a.* contempler, regarder; examiner; expertiser.

survive, *v. n. & a.* survivre (à).

suspect, *adj. & s.* suspect, -e *(m. f.);* — *v. a. & n.* soupçonner.

suspenders, *s. pl.* jarretelles *f. pl.*

suspicion, *s.* soupçon *m.*

suspicious, *adj.* soupçonneux; suspect.

swallow[1]**,** *s.* hirondelle *f.*

swallow[2]**,** *v. a.* avaler; gober.

swan, *s.* cygne *m.*

swarm, *s.* essaim *m.;* foule *f.;* — *v.n.* essaimer; s'assembler en foule.

swear, v.a. jurer; prêter; v.n. jurer.

sweat, s. sueur f.; — v.a. exploiter; v.n. suer.

Swede, s. Suédois, -e m. f.

Swedish, adj. & s. suédois (m.).

sweep, v.a. balayer; (chimney) ramoner; — s. coup m. de balai; courbe f.; grand geste m.; (pers.) ramoneur m.

sweet, adj. doux; (pers.) gentil; — s. bonbon m.; entremets m.

sweetheart, s. bien-aimé, -ée m. f.; ~! mon amour!, ma chérie!

swell, v.n. (s')enfler; se gonfler; grossir; v.a. gonfler; bouffir; — s. houle f.; élévation f.

swim, v. n. nager; aller à la nage; flotter; v.a nager; — s. have a ~ aller nager.

swimmer, s. nageur, -euse m. f.

swimming-pool, s. piscine f.

swine, s. cochon m.

swing, s. va-et-vient m.; rythme m.; (for children) escarpolette f. balançoire f.; — v.a. balancer; v. n. osciller; se balancer.

Swiss, adj. suisse; — s. Suisse m. f.

switch, s. badine f.; aiguille f.; interrupteur m., commutateur m.; — v.a. cingler; aiguiller; couper; ~ off couper (le courant); ~ on donner (le courant), tourner (le bouton).

sword, s. épée f.; sa-bre m.

syllable, s. syllabe f.

symbol, s. symbole m.

symmetrical, adj symétrique.

symmetry, s. symétrie f.

sympathy, s. sympathie f.

symphony, s. symphonie f.

synagogue, s. synagogue f.

synthetic, adj. synthétique.

syringe, s. seringue f.

syrup, s. sirop m.

system, s. système m.

systematic(al), adj. systématique.

T

table, s. table f.; clear the ~ desservir; lay the ~ mettre le couvert.

table-cloth, s. nappe f.

table-spoon, s. cuiller f. à soupe.

tablet, s. tablette f.

tack, s. broquette f., petit clou m.

tackle, s. attirail m.; apparaux m. pl.; — v.a. saisir à bras le corps; (problem) essayer de résoudre.

tact, s. tact m.

tag, s. ferret m.; étiquette (volante) f.; bout m.

tail, s. queue f.

tailor, s. tailleur m.

take, v.a. prendre; (carry) porter; (walk) faire; ~ after ressembler à; ~ away enlever; ~ down descendre, (write) prendre (par écrit); ~ in (paper) s'abonner à; ~ off ôter; (v.n.) prendre son élan; ~ on se charger

de; ~ *to* se mettre
à; ~ *up* ramasser,
relever.

tale, *s.* conte *m.*, histoire *f*

talent, *s.* talent *m.*

talk, *v.a. & n.* parler
(*about, of* de); ~*ing of*
à propos de; — *s.*
conversation *f.;* cau-
serie *f.*

tall, *adj.* grand; *how ~ is
he?* quelle est sa taille?

tame, *adj.* apprivoisé.

tan, *s.* tan *m.*

tank, *s.* réservoir *m.;* char
m. d'assaut.

t ankard, *s.* chope *f.*

tap, *s.* robinet *m.; (blow)*
tape *f.;* petit coup *m.;*
— *v.a.* mettre en
perce; *(strike)* frap-
per légèrement, taper.

tape, *s.* ruban *m.* (de coton).

tape-recorder, *s.* magnétophone *m.*

tapestry, *s.* tapisserie *f.*

target, *s.* cible *f.*

tariff, *s.* tarif *m.*

tart, *s.* tart *f.*

task, *s.* tâche *f.; (school)*
devoir *m.*

taste, *s.* goût *m.*

tasteless, *adj.* sans saveur.

tasty, *adj.* savoureux,
de bon goût.

tatter, *s.* lambeau *m.*

tavern, *s.* taverne *f.*

tax, *s.* impôt *m.;* ~ *free*
exempt d'impôts.

taxi, *s.* taxi *m.*

tea, *s.* thé *m.*

teach, *v.a.* enseigner,
instruire; *(how to)* ap-
prendre (à).

teacher, *s.* instituteur,
-trice *m. f.;* professeur
m. f.

teaching, *s.* enseignement
m.

team, *s.* équipe *f.*

tea-pot, *s.* théière *f.*

tear[1], *s. (eye)* larme *f.*

tear[2], *v.a.* déchirer; ~
away, down, out ar-
racher; ~ *up* déchirer;
— *s.* déchirure *f.*

tease, *v.a.* taquiner.

tea-spoon, *s.* cuiller *f.* à
thé.

technical, *adj.* technique.

technique, *s.* technique *f.*

technology, *s.* technologie *f.*

tedious, *adj.* ennuyeux.

teenager, *s.* adolescent,
-e *m. f.*

telecast, *v.a.* téléviser.

telegram, *s.* télégramme
m.

telegraph, *s.* télégraphe
m.

telephone, *s.* téléphone
m.; — *v.a. & n.* télé-
phoner (*to* à).

telescope, *s.* téléscope *m.;*
réfracteur *m.;* — *v.a.*
télescoper.

televise, *v.a.* téléviser.

television, *s.* télévision *f.*

television-set, *s.* appareil *m.* de TV, télé-
viseur *m.*

telex, *s.* télex *m.*

tell, *v.a.* dire; raconter; distinguer; ~ *s.o.*
to do sth. enjoindre,
dire à qn de faire qch.

temper, *s.* colère *f.;*
tempérament *m.*

temperature, *s.* température *f.*

temporary, *adj.* tempo-
raire.

tempt, *v.a.* tenter.

ten, *adj. & s.* dix *(m.).*

tenant, *s.* locataire *m. f.*

tend, *v.n.* tendre (à).

tendency, *s.* tendence *f.*

tender[1], *v.a.* offrir; ~

for soumissionner; — *s.* soumission *f.*

tender[2], *adj.* tendre.

tennis, *s.* tennis *m.*

tension, *s.* tension *f.*

tent, *s.* tente *f.*

tenth, *adj.* dixième; dix.

term, *s.* terme *m.;* (school) trimestre *m.; be on good ~s* être bien (avec); — *v.a.* appeler.

terminate, *v.a.* terminer; *vn.* se terminer.

terminus, *s.* (gare *f.*) terminus *m.*

terrace, *s.* terrasse *f.*

terrible, *adj.* terrible.

territory, *s.* territoire *m.*

test, *s.* épreuve *f.;* examen *m.;* (school) composition *f.,* (oral) épreuve *f.;* orale — *v.a.* mettre à l'épreuve.

testify, *v.a.* affirmer.

testimony, *s.* témoignage *m.*

text, *s.* texte *m.*

text-book, *s.* manuel *m.*

textile, *s.* textile *m.*

than, *conj.* que; (with numbers) de.

thank, *v.a.* remercier; *~ you* merci; — *s.* *~s* remerciements *m. pl.;* merci.

thankful, *adj.* reconnaissant.

that[1], *adj.* ce, cet, cette' ces; — *pron.* celui, celle, ceux; cela; *~'s it* c'est cela.

that[2], *conj.* que.

the, *art.* le, la, les; ce, cet, cette; ces.

theatre, *s.* théâtre *m.*

their, *pron.* leur, leurs.

theirs, *pron.* le leur, la leur, les leurs; à eux, à elles.

them, *pron.* les; leur; eux, elles.

theme, *s.* thème *m.;* sujet *m.*

themselves, *pron.* se; eux-mêmes, elles-mêmes.

then, *adv.* alors; (after that) puis; (consequently) donc.

theology, *s.* théologie *f.*

theoretical, *adj.* théorique.

theory, *s.* théorie *f.*

there, *adv.* là; (with verb) y; *~ is, are* il y a.

therefore *adv.* donc.

thermometer, *s.* thermomètre *m.*

thermos, *s.* thermos *f.*

they, *pron.* ils, elles; *~ say* on dit

thick, *adj.* épais.

thief, *s.* voleur, -euse *m. f.*

thigh, *s.* cuisse *f.*

thimble, *s.* dé *m.*

thin, *adj.* mince; maigre; *fig.* pauvre.

thing, *s.* chose *f.; ~s* effets *m. pl.*

think, *v.a.* croire; concevoir; *v.n.* croire; penser (about, of à); *~ out* élaborer; *~ over* réfléchir à, penser.

third, *adj.* troisième; trois; — *s.* tiers *m.*

thirsty, *adj.* altéré; *be ~* avoir soif.

thirteen, *adj. & s.* treize (m.).

thirty, *adj. & s.* trente (m.).

this, *pl.* these, *pron.* cela, — *adj.* ceci; ce, cet, cette; ces.

thorn, *s.* épine *f.*

thorough, *adj.* profond, complet; consommé.

thoroughfare, *s.* artère *f.* principal, grande rue *f.; no ~* rue barrée, passage interdit.

thoroughly, *adv.* tout à fait, à fond.

though, *conj.* quoique, bien que; — *adv.* tout de même.

thought, *s.* pensée *f.;* idée *f.; (care)* souci *m.*

thoughtful, *adj.* pensif; attentif.

thoughtless, *adj.* étourdi; insouciant.

thousand, *s.* & *adj.* mille *(m.)*

thrash, *v.a.* battre.

thread, *s.* fil *m.;* — *v. a.* enfiler.

threat, *s.* menace *f.*

threaten, *v. a.* & *n.* menacer (de).

three, *adj.* & *s.* trois *(m.).*

threshold, *s.* seuil *m.*

thrifty, *adj.* économe.

thrill, *s.* tressaillement *m.;* — *v. a.be ~ed with* frissonner de.

thrive, *v. n.* prospérer.

throat, *s.* gorge *f.*

throne, *s.* tône *m.*

through, *prep.* à travers; au travers de; par; par suite de; pendant; — *adv.* d'un bout à l'autre; *be ~ with* avoir fini qch.; — *adj.* direct.

throughout, *prep.* & *adv.* d'un bout à l'autre.

throw, *v.a.* jeter; *~ away* jeter, dissiper; *~ down* renverser; jeter à terre; *~ off* se débarrasser de; ôter; *~ out* rejecter; *~ over* abandonner; — *s.* jet *m.*

thrust, *v.a.* fourrer, pousser; enforcer; — *s.* poussée *f.;* botte *f.*

thumb, *s.* pouce *m.*

thunder, *s.* tonnerre *m.;* — *v.n.* tonner.

Thursday, *s.* jeudi *m.*

thus, *adv.* ainsi.

ticket, *s.* billet *m.;* étiquette *f.*

ticket-collector, *s.* contrôleur *m.*

tide, *s.* marée *f.;* courant *m.*

tidy, *adj.* propre; bien rangé; *(pers.)* ordonné; — *v.a.* *(also ~ up)* mettre en ordre.

tie, *v.a.* attacher; lier; nouer; *~ down* lier; *~ up* attacher; — *s.* lien *m.;* cravate *f.;* *(sport)* partie *f.* égale.

tiger, *s.* tigre, -esse *m. f.*

tight, *adj.* serré; tendu.

tighten, *v.a.* serrer.

tile, *s.* tuile *f.*

till, *prep.* jusqu'à; — *conj.* jusqu'à ce que.

tilt, *s.* inclinaison *f.;* — *v. n.* s'incliner, pencher; *v.a.* pencher.

time, *s.* temps *m.;* moment *m.; (clock)* heure *f.; (occasions)* fois; *at ~s* de temps en temps; *by the ~ that* avant que; *for the ~ being* actuellement; *what ~ is it?* quelle heure est-il?; *have a good ~* s'amuser bien; *keep good ~* marcher bien.

timely, *adj.* opportun.

timetable, *s.* horaire *m.;* indicateur *m.; (school)* emploi *m.* du temps.

tin, *s.* étain *m.; (conserve)* boîte *f.* (en fer blanc).

tinned, *adj.* en boîte; conservé.

tint, *s.* teinte *f.*

tiny, *adj.* tout petit.

tip[1], *s.* bout *m.;* — *v.a.*

renverser; *v.n.* (also ~ *over*) se renverser.

tip², *s. (money)* pourboire *m.;* — *v.a.* donner un pourboire (à).

tire¹, tyre, *s.* pneu(matique) *m.*

tire², *v.a.* fatiguer; *v.n.* se fatiguer.

tired, *adj. be* ~ *of* être las de.

tissue, *s.* tissu *m.*

tissue-paper, *s.* papier *m.* de soie.

title, *s.* titre *m.*

to, *prep.* à; vers; en,

toast, *s.* rôtie *f.; (bread, drink)* toast *m.;* — *v.a.* rôtir.

tobacco, *s.* tabac *m.*

tobacconist, *s.* marchand *m.* de tabac; ~'s débit *m.* de tabac.

today, *adv.* aujourd'hui.

toe, *s.* orteil *m.,* doigt *m.* du pied.

together, *adv.* ensemble; en même temps.

toil, *s.* travail *m.;* — *v.n.* travailler.

toilet, *s.* toilette *f.*

toilet-paper, *s.* papier *m.* hygiénique.

tomato, *s.* tomate *f.*

tomb, *s.* tombeau *m.*

tomorrow, *adv.* demain.

ton, *s.* tonne *f.*

tone, *s.* ton *m.*

tongs, *s. pl.* pincettes *f. pl.;* pince *f.*

tongue, *s.* langue *f.*

tonight, *adv.* cette nuit; ce soir.

tonsil, *s.* amygdale *f.*

too, *adv.* trop; *(also)* aussi.

tool, *s.* outil *m.;* instrument *m.*

tooth, *s.* dent *f.*

toothache, *s.* mal *m.* de dents.

toothbrush, *s.* brosse *f.* à dents.

toothpaste, *s.* pâte *f.* dentrifice.

top, *s.* sommet *m.,* faîte *m.;* dessus *m.;* couvercle *m.;* tête *f.;* premier, -ère *m. f.;* — *v.a.* couronner; dépasser.

topic, *s.* sujet *m.;* ~s *of the day* actualités *f. pl.*

torch, *s.* torche *f.*

tortoise, *s.* tortue *f.*

toss, *s.* mouvement *m.;* — *v.a.* jeter; lancer en l'air; ballotter; ~ *up* lancer en l'air.

total, *adj. & s.* total *(m.).*

totter, *v.n.* chanceler.

touch, *s.* toucher *m.;* attouchement *m.;* touche *f.;* légère *f.* attaque,; — *v.a.* toucher.

tough, *adj.* dur; robuste; rude.

tour, *s.* voyage *m.;* tour *m.;* tournée *f.;* — *v.n.* voyager.

tourism, *s.* tourisme *m.*

tourist, *s.* touriste *m.*

tournament, *s.* tournoi *m.*

tow, *s.* étoupe *f.;* remorque *f.;* — *v.a.* remorquer.

toward(s), *prep.* vers; envers; pour.

towel, *s.* essuie-main(s) *m.,* serviette *f.*

tower, *s.* tour *f.*

town, *s.* ville *f.*

town-hall, *s.* hôtel *m.* de ville.

toy, *s.* jouet *m.;* — *v.n.* jouer (avec).

trace, *s.* trace *f.;* trait *m.;* — *v.a.* tracer; ~ *back* remonter à.

track, *s.* traces *f. pl.;* sentier *m.; (railw.)* voie *f.; (running)* piste

f.

tractor, *s.* tracteur *m.*

trade, *s.* commerce *m.;* *(occupation)* métier *m.;* *v.n.* commercer; ~ *in* faire le commerce de.

trade-mark, *s.* marque *f.* de fabrique.

tradesman, *s.* commerçant *m.*

trade(s)-union, *s.* syndicat *m.*

tradition, *s.* tradition *f.*

traditional, *adj.* traditionnel.

traffic, *s.* trafic *m.;* circulation *f.;* ~ *lights* feux *m.pl.* de signalisation.

tragedy, *s.* tragédie

tragic(al), *adj.* tragique.

trail, *s.* trace *f.;* — *v.a.* & *n.* traîner.

train, *s.* train *m.; (series)* suite *f.;* — *v.a.* entraîner; former.

trainer, *s.* entraîneur *m.*

traitor, *s.* traître *m.*

tram, *s.* tramway *m.*

tramp, *v.n.* aller à pied; — *s.* bruit *m.* de pas; *(pers.)* chemineau *m.*

transaction, *s.* transaction *f.*

transfer, *s.* transport *m.;* — *v.a.* transférer.

transform, *v.a.* transformer (en).

transfusion, *s.* transfusion *f.*

transgress, *v.a.* transgresser; *v.n.* pécher.

transistor, *s.* transistor *m.*

transit, *s.* transit *m; in* ~ en cours de route.

translate, *v.a.* traduire.

translation, *s.* traduction *f.*

translator, *s.* traducteur,

-trice *m. f.*

transmission, *s.* transmission *f.*

transmit, *v.a.* transmettre, émettre.

transmitter, *s.* (poste) émetteur *m.*

transparency, *s.* diapositive *f.*

transport, *s.* transport *m.;* — *v.a.* transporter.

trap, *s.* piège *m.*

trash, *s.* rebut *m.;* niaiseries *f. pl.*

travel, *v.n.* voyager; — *s.* voyage *m.*

traveller, *s.* voyageur, -euse *m. f.*

tray, *s.* plateau *m.*

treachery, *s.* trahison *f.*

tread, *s.* pas *m.;* — *v.n.* & *a.* marcher (sur).

treasure, *s.* trésor *m.*

treasury, *s.* trésor *m.;* trésorerie *f.*

treat, *v.a.* traiter.

treatment, *s.* traitement *m.*

treaty, *s.* traité *m.*

tree, *s.* arbre *m.*

tremble, *v.n.* trembler.

tremendous, *adj.* terrible; immense.

trench, *s.* tranchée *f.*

trend, *s.* tendance *f.*

trespass, *v.n.* envahir sans autorisation; ~ *against* offenser; ~ *on* abuser de; — *s.* offense *f.*

trial, *s.* essai *m.;* épreuve *f.; (law)* procès *m.*

tribe, *s.* tribu *f.*

tribute, *s.* tribut *m.*

trick, *s.* ruse *f.;* tour *m.;* truc *m.;* — *v.a.* duper.

trifle, *s.* bagatelle *f.;* *a* ~ un peu; — *v.n.* ~ *with* traiter légèrement.

trim, s. état m.; tenue f.;
— adj. bien tenu; —
v.a. arranger; garnir,
orner; dresser.

trip, s. excursion f.;
voyage m.; — v.a. ~ up
faire trébucher.

triumph, s. triomphe m.;
— v.n. triompher.

triumphant, adj. triom-
phant.

trolley, s. fardier m.,
diable m.; trolley m.

trolley-bus, s. trolleybus
m.

troop, s. troupe f.

trophy, s. trophée m.

tropic(al), adj. tropi-
que.

tropics, s. pl. tropiques
m. pl.

trot, s. trot m.; — v.n.
trotter.

trouble, s. affliction f.;
malheur m.; dérange-
ment m.; difficulté f.;
— v.a. inquiéter; dé-
ranger; affliger.

troublesome, adj. en-
nuyeux.

trousers, s. pl. pantalon m.

trout, s truite f.

truck, s. wagon m.

true, aaj. vrai; exact;
fidèle; come ~ se réali-
ser.

truly, adv. vraiment.

trumpet, s. trompette
f.; — v. a. proclamer.

trunk, s. melle f. (tree)
tronc m.

trunk-call, s. appel m. in-
terurbain.

trust, s. confiance f.;
espoir m.; dépôt m.;
trust m.; — v.a.
se confier (à); faire
crédit (à); v.n. espérer;
compter sur.

truth, s. vérité f.

try, v.a. essayer, éprou-
ver; (law) mettre en
jugement; ~ on essa-
yer; — s. essai m.

tub, s. bac m.; (bath)
tub m.

tube, s. tube m.; tuyau
m.; métro m.

Tuesday, s. mardi m.

tug, s. effort m.; — v.a.
tirer; remorquer.

tug-boat, s. (bateau) re-
morqueur m.

tuition, s. enseignement
m.

tumble, v. n. tomber.

tumour, s. tumeur f.

tune, s. air m.; accord m.;
harmonie f.; in ~ d'ac-
cord; out of ~ faux; —
v.a.&n. accorder; ~
in to mettre sur; ~
up régler; s'accorder.

tunnel, s. tunnel m.

turbine, s. turbine f.

turbo-jet: ~ engine turboréacteur m.

turbo-prop, s. turbopro-
pulseur m.

turkey, s. dindon, din-
de m. f.

Turkish, adj. turc, -que:
— s. Turc, -que m. f.;
(lang.) turc m.

turn, v.a. tourner, dé-
tourner; diriger; v.n.
tourner; se diriger; de-
venir; avoir recours (à);
~ about (se) tourner;
~ back retourner; ~
down plier, baisser;
repousser; ~ upside
down renverser; ~ in
se coucher; ~ off fer-
mer, serrer; éteindre;
~ on ouvrir; allumer;
~ over (se) renverser;
~ up arriver, appa-
raître — s. tour m.; dé-
tour m.; (mind, style)
tournure f.; (tide)
changement m.

turning, *s.* tournant *m.*

turnip, *s.* navet *m.*

turnover, *s.* chiffre *m.* d'affaires.

turret, *s.* tourelle *f.*

turtle, *s.* tortue *f.*

tutor, *s.* précepteur *m.;* — *v.a.* instruire.

twelfth, *adj.* douzième; douze.

twelve, *adj.* & *s.* douze *(m.).*

twentieth, *adj.* vingtième.

twenty, *adj.* & *s.* vingt *(m.).*

twice, *adv.* deux fois.

twig, *s.* brindille *f.*

twin, *adj.* & *s.* jumeau *(m.),* jumelle *(f.).*

twist, *s. (road)* coude *f.;* torsion *f.:* — *v. a.* tordre; dénaturer; *v. n.* s'entortiller.

twitter, *v.n.* gazouiller.

two, *adj.* & *s.* deux *(m.).*

type, *s.* type *m.;* caractère *m.;* — *v.a.* taper (à la machine).

type-script, *s.* manuscrit *m.* dactylographié.

typewriter, *s.* machine à écrire, *f.*

typical, *adj.* typique.

typist, *s.* dactilo(graphe) *m. f.*

tyre *see* tire.

U

udder, *s.* mamelle *f.*

ugly, *adj.* laid.

ulcer, *s.* ulcère *m.*

ultimate, *adj.* final, dernier.

umbrella, *s.* parapluie *m.*

umpire, *s.* arbitre *m. f.*

unable, *adj.* incapable; ~ *to* impuissant à faire qch.; dans l'impossibilité de.

unaccustomed, *adj.* inaccoutumé, peu habitué (à).

unaided, *adj.* sans aide.

unanimous, *adj.* unanime.

unassisted, *adj.* sans aide.

unaware: *be* ~ *of* ignorer.

unbearable, *adj.* insupportable.

uncertain, *adj.* incertain.

uncertainty, *s.* incertitude *f.*

unchangeable, *adj.* immuable.

uncle, *s.* oncle *m.*

uncomfortable, *adj.* peu confortable.

uncommon, *adj.* rare; extraordinaire.

unconditional, *adj.* sans conditions.

unconscious, *adj.* sans connaissance; ~ *of* sans conscience de.

uncover, *v. a.* découvrir.

undamaged, *adj.* non endommagé.

undefined, *adj.* non défini.

undeniable, *adj.* incontestable.

under, *prep* sous; au-dessous de; dans.

undercarriage, *s.* châssis *m.,* train (d'atterrissage) *m.*

underclothes, *s. pl.* vêtements *m. pl.* de dessous.

underdeveloped, *adj.* sous-développe.

underdone, *adj.* pas assez cuit, saignant.

undergo, *v.a.* subir.

undergraduate, *s.* étudiant, -e (non diplomé) *m. f.* ·

underground, *s.* métro(politain) *m.*

underline, *v.a.* souligner.

undermine, *v.a.* miner.

underneath, *prep. & adv.* au-dessous (de).

undersigned, *adj. & s.* soussigné, -e *(m. f.).*

understand, *v.a.&n.* comprendre; *it is understood that* il est convenu que.

understanding, *s.* entendement *m.;* intelligence *f.*

undertake, *v.a.* entreprendre; ~ *to* se charger de, s'engager à.

undertaking, *s.* entreprise *f.*

underwear, *s.* vêtements *m.pl.* de dessous.

undesirable, *adj.* peu désirable.

undo, *v.a.* défaire.

undress, *v. n.* se déshabiller.

undue, *adj.* indu.

uneasy, *adj.* inquiet; mal à l'aise; incommode.

uneducated, *adj.* sans instruction.

unemployed, *adj. & s.* sans travail; *the* ~ les chômeurs *m.*

unemployment, *s.* chômage *m.*

unequal, *adj.* inégal.

uneven, *adj.* inégal; impair.

unexpected, *adj.* inattendu; soudain.

unfair, *adj.* injuste; déloyal.

unfavorable, *adj.* défavorable.

unfortunate, *adj.* malheureux.

unfortunately, *adv.* malheureusement.

unhappy, *adj.* malheureux.

unhealthy, *adj.* maladif; *(place)* insalubre.

uninhabited, *adj.* inhabité.

uninteresting, *adj.* peu intéressant,sans intérêt.

union, *s.* union *f.*

unique, *adj.* unique.

unit, *s.* unité *f.; (motor)* bloc *m.*

unite, *v.a.* unir; *v.n.* s'unir.

unity, *s.* unité *f.;* harmonie *f.*

universal, *adj.* universel.

university, *s.* université *f.*

unjust, *adj.* injuste.

unkind, *adj.* dur; peu aimable.

unknown, *adj.* inconnu.

unless, *conj.* à moins que... ne; à moins de.

unlike, *adj.* dissemblable.

unload, *v.a.* décharger.

unlock, *v.a.* ouvrir.

unmarried, *adj.* célibataire.

unnatural, *adj.* non naturel, dénaturé.

unnecessary, *adj.* inutile.

unnoticed, *adj.* inaperçu.

unoccupied, *adj.* inoccupé; libre; non occupe.

unpack, *v.a.* déballer.

unpaid, *adj.* impayé.

unparalleled, *adj.* incomparable.

unpleasant, *adj.* désagréable.

unprecedented, *adj.* sans exemple. *or.* précédent.

unprejudiced, *adj.* sans préjugés, impartial.

unprepared, *adj.* non préparé; *be* ~ *for* ne pas s'attendre à qch.

unprofitable, *adj.* peu profitable.

unpromising, *adj.* qui s'annonce mal; peu prometteur.

unqualified, *adj.* non qualifié; sans restriction.

unreal, *adj.* irréel.

unreasonable, *adj.* déraisonnable.

unsatisfactory, *adj.* peu satisfaisant.

unseen, *adj.* invisible; inaperçu.

unsettled, *adj.* non réglé; *(in mind)* indécis; incertain.

unskilled, *adj.* non spécialisé.

unsolved, *adj.* non résolu.

unspeakable, *adj.* inexprimable.

unsteady, *adj.* tremblant; peu fixe; chancelant; inconstant.

unsuccessful, *adj.* malheureux; infructueux.

unsuitable, *adj.* inconvenant; peu propre (à).

untidy, *adj.* sans ordre, malpropre; en désordre.

until, *prep.* jusqu'à; — *conj.* jusqu'à ce que; avant que.

unto, *prep.* jusqu'à.

unusual, *adj.* rare, peu commun.

unwell, *adj.* indisposé; souffrant.

unwilling, *adj.* peu disposé (à).

unworthy, *adj.* indigne.

unyielding, *adj.* inflexible.

up, *adv.* en montant, vers le haut; (en) haut; *go* ~ monter; *be* ~ *in* être fort en; *what's* ~? qu'est-ce qu'il y a?; — *prep.* vers le haut de; en haut; — *adj.* montant.

uphill, *adj.* montant; — *adv. go* ~ monter.

uphold, *v.a.* soutenir; appuyer.

upholsterer, *s.* tapissier *m.*

upon, *prep* sur.

upper, *adj.* supérieur; *(deck)* deuxième; *the* ~ *classes* les hautes classes.

upright, *adj.* droit; honnête.

upset, *v.a.* renverser; *fig.* troubler, bouleverser; — *adj.* renversé; *fig.* dérangé; *be* ~ être indisposé.

upside do n, *adv.* sens dessus dessous.

upstairs, *adv.* en haut; *go* ~ monter (l'escalier).

up-to-date, *adj* moderne, à la mode.

upwards, *adv.* en haut, vers le haut, en montant.

urge, *v.a.* prier instamment (de); recommander instamment; pousser en avant.

urgent, *adj.* urgent; pressant.

us, *pron.* nous.

usage, *s.* usage *m.*

use, *v.a.* se servir de; traiter; faire usage (de); consommer; ~ *up* user; consommer; ~*d to* habitué à; *get* ~*d to* s'habituer à; — *s.* usage *m.*; emploi *m.*; utilité *f.*; *be of* ~ être utile (à); *(of) no* ~ inutile; *out of* ~ hors d'usage *or* de service.

useful, *adj.* utile (à).

useless, *adj.* inutile.

usher, *s. (court)* (huissier) audiencier *m.*

usherette, *s. (theatre)* ouvreuse *f.*

usual, *adj.* usuel.

usually, *adv.* ordinaire-

ment.
utensil, *s.* ustensile *m.*
utility, *s.* utilité *f.*
utilize, *v.a.* utiliser.
utmost, *adj.* extrême; le plus grand; — *s.* le plus; tout son possible.
utter¹, *adj.* le plus grand; absolu.
utter², *v.a.* dire, prononcer; pousser.
utterance, *s.* prononciation. *f.*; expression *f.*; parole *f.*

V

vacancy, *s.* vacance *f.*
vacant, *adj.* vacant; vide; sans expression.
vacation, *s.* vacances *f. pl.*
vaccinate, *v.a.* vacciner.
vaccination, *s.* vaccination.
vacuum-cleaner, *s.* aspirateur *m.*
vague, *adj.* vague.
vain, *adj.* vain; vaniteux; *in* ~ en vain.
valid, *adj.* valide.
validity, *s.* validité *f.*
valley, *s.* vallée *f.*
valuable, *adj.* de valeur.
value, *s.* valeur *f.*; — *v.a.* évaluer; priser.
valve, *s.* soupape *f.*; lampe *f.*, tube *m.*
van, *s.* fourgon *m.*; camion *m.* de livraison; wagon *m.*
vanish, *v.n.* disparaître; (*also* ~ *away*) s'évanouir.
vanity, *s.* vanité *f.*
variety, *s.* variété *f.*
various, *adj.* divers.
varnish, *s.* vernis *m.*
vary, *v.a. & n.* varier.

vase, *s.* vase *m.*
vast, *adj.* vaste.
vault, *s.* voûte *f.*; cave *f.*, caveau *m.*
veal, *s.* veau *m.*
vegetable, *s.* légume *m.*
vehicle, *s.* véhicule *m.*
veil, *s.* voile *m.*
vein, *s.* veine *f.*
velvet, *s.* velours *m.*
venison, *s.* venaison *f.*
vent, *s.* ouverture *f.*; *give* ~ *to* donner libre cours à.
ventilation, *s.* ventilation *f.*
ventilator, *s.* ventilateur *m.*
venture, *s.* risque *m.*; hasard *m.*; — *v.a.* risquer; hasarder; *v.n.* ~ (*up-*) *on* se hasarder à, se risquer à.
verb, *s.* verbe *m.*
verdict, *s.* décision *f.*, verdict *m.*
verge, *s.* bord *m.*
verify, *v.a.* vérifier.
verse, *s.* vers *m.*; strophe *f.*
version, *s.* version *f.*
vertical, *adj.* vertical.
very, *adv.* très; ~ *good* très bien; — *adj.* vrai; même.
vessel, *s.* vaisseau *m.*
vest, *s.* gilet *m.*; chemise *f.* américaine.
vestry, *s.* sacristie *f.*; assemblée *f.*
veterinary, *adj.* ~ *surgeon* vétérinaire *m.*
veto, *s.* véto *m.*; — *v.a.* mettre son véto (à).
vex, *v.a.* vexer.
vibrate, *v.n.* vibrer, osciller.
vibration, *s.* vibration *f.*
vicar, *s.* curé *m.*
vice-, *prefix* vice-.

vicinity, *s.* voisinage *m.*
victim, *s.* victime *f.*
victorious, *adj.* victorieux.
victory, *s.* victoire *f.*
victuals, *s. pl.* victuailles *f. pl.*
view, *s.* vue *f.;* avis *m.; on* ∼ exposé; *have in* ∼ se proposer (de); *with a* ∼ *to* en vue de; *point of* ∼ ∼ point *m.* de vue; − *v.a.* voir; regarder; envisager.
viewer, *s.* spectateur, -trice *m. f.*
vigorous, *adj.* vigoureux.
vigour, *s.* vigueur *f.*
village, *s.* village *m.*
villain, *s.* scélérat *m.*
vine, *s.* vigne *f.*
vinegar, *s.* vinaigre *m.*
vineyard, *s.* vignoble *m.*
vintage, *s.* vendange *f.*
violate, *v.a.* violer.
violation, *s.* violation *f.*
violence, *s.* violence *f.*
violent, *adj.* violent.
violet, *s.* violette *f.; (colour)* violet *m.;* − *adj.* violet.
violin, *s.* violon *m.*
violinist, *s.* violoniste *m. f.*
violoncellist, *s.* violoncelliste *m.*
violoncello, *s.* violoncelle *m.*
virgin, *s.* vierge *f.*
virtue, *s.* vertu *f.*
visa, visé, *s.* visa *m.*
visibility, *s.* visibilité *f.*
visible, *adj.* visible.
vision, *s.* vision *f.*, vue *f.*
visit, *s.* visite *f.;* séjour *m.; be on a* ∼ *to* être en visite chez; − *v.a.* visiter.
visitor, *s.* visiteur, -euse *m. f.*
vital, *adj.* vital.
vitamin, *s.* vitamine *f.*
vocabulary, *s.* vocabu-laire *m.*
vocation, *s.* vocation *f.*
voice, *s.* voix *f.;* − *v.a.* exprimer.
voltage, *s.* voltage *m.*
volume, *s.* volume *m.*
voluntary, *adj.* volontaire.
volunteer, *s.* volontaire *m.;* − *v.n.* s'engager (pour).
vomit, *v.a. & n.* vomir.
vote, *s.* voix; − *v.a. & n.* voter (sur).
voucher, *s.* pièce *f.* de dépense ; pièce *f.* de recette; bon *m.*
vow, *s.* vœu *m.;* − *v. a.* vouer; jurer; *v. n.* faire un vœu; jurer.
vowel, *s.* voyelle *f.*
voyage, *s.* voyage *m.;* − *v. n.* voyager (par mer).

vulgar, *adj.* vulgaire.

W

wade, *v.a.* passer à gué.
wafer, *s.* gaufrette *f.;* hostie *f.*
wag, *v.a.* hocher; *(tail)* agiter; *v.n.* s'agiter.
wage(s), *s. (pl.)* salaire *m.*, gages *m. pl.;* − *v.a.* ∼ *war* faire la guerre.
wag(g)on, *s.* wagon *m.*
waist, *s.* taille *f.*
waistcoat, *s.* gilet *m.*
wait, *v. a. & n.* attendre *(for* qn, qch).
waiter, *s.* garçon *m.* (de restaurant); *head*∼ premier garçon *m.*, maître *m.* d'hôtel.
waiting-room, *s.* salle *f.* d'attente.
wake, *v.a.* (also ∼ *up*) réveiller; *v.n.* (also ∼

up) s'éveiller.

waken, *v.a.* éveiller; *v.n.* s'éveiller .

walk, *s.* marche *f.;* promenade *f.; (path)* allée *f.; go for a ~* faire une promenade; — *v.n.* aller à pied; marcher; *(pleasure)* se promener; *~ off* s'en aller; *~ out* sortir.

wall, *s.* mur *m.*

wallet, *s.* portefeuille *m.*

walnut, *s.* noyer *m.; (fruit)* noix *f.*

waltz, *s.* valse *f.*

wander, *v.n.* errer; s'égarer (de); divaguer.

want, *s.* besoin *m.;* manque *m.; for ~ of* faute de; — *v.a.* avoir besoin (de); manquer (de); vouloir; demander; *v.n.* faire défaut; *be ~ing in* manquer de.

war, *s.* guerre *f.*

ward, *s.* pupille *m. f.; (hospital)* salle *f.*

warden, *s.* gouverneur *m.;* directeur *m.*

warder, *s.* gardien, -enne *m. f.*

wardrobe, *s.* armoire *f.*

ware, *s.* marchandise(s) *f. (pl.);* article *m.*

warehouse, *s.* magasin *m.;* dépôt *m.*

warm, *adj.* chaud; *be ~* avoir chaud; — *v.a.* chauffer; *~ up* réchauffer; *v.n.* se chauffer.

warmth, *s.* chaleur *f.*

warn, *v.a.* avertir; prévenir; mettre sur ses gardes (contre).

warning, *s.* avertissement *m.;* avis *m.*

warrant, *s.* autorisation *f.;* mandat *m.;* — *v. a.* garantir; justifier.

wash, *v.a.* laver; *v.n.* se laver; *~ away* effacer; *~ up the dishes* faire la vaisselle; — *s.* lavage *m.;* lotion *f.;* toilette *f.;* lessive *f.*

wash-basin, *s.* cuvette *f.* (de lavabo).

washing-machine, *s.* machine *f.* à laver.

wasp, *s.* guêpe *f.*

waste, *s.* désert *m., (money)* gaspillage *m.; (energy)* déperdition *f.; (loss)* perte *f.;* déchets *m. pl.; ~ of time* perte de temps *f.;* — *adj.* inculte; de rebut; *~ paper* papier *m.* de rebut; —*v.a.* gaspiller; perdre; ravager.

watch, *s.* garde *f.;* gardien *m.,* garde *m.; (to.indicate time)* montre *f.;* — *v. a.* veiller, garder; observer; regarder; *v.n.* veiller; *~ out!* ouvrez l'œil!

watch-maker, *s.* horloger *m.*

water, *s.* eau *f.*

water-closet , *s.* cabinet *m.*

waterfall, *s.* chute *f.* d'eau

watering-place, *s.* station *f.* balnéaire; ville *f.* d'eaux.

waterproof, *adj.* imperméable; — *s.* caoutchouc *m.*

wave, *s.* vague *f.;* onde *f.;* — *v.a.* agiter; *(hair)* onduler; *v. n.* flotter; onduler.

wave-length, *s.* longueur *f.* d'onde.

waver, *v.n.* vaciller.

wax, *s.* cire *f.*

way, *s.* chemin *m.,* route

f.; distance *f.;* côte *m.; (means)* moyen *m.;* façon *f.,* manière *f.; which* ~*?* de quel côté?; *it's a long* ~ *to* il y a loin pour aller (à); *on the* ~ chemin faisant; ~ *in* entrée *f.;* ~ *out* sortie

f.; out of the ~ retiré; extraordinaire; *this* ~ de ce côté-ci, par ici; *by* ~ *of* par; *by the* ~ à propos; *in a* ~ à certains égards; *give* ~ *to* céder à.

we, *pron.* nous.

weak, *adj.* faible.

weakness, *s.* faiblesse *f.*

wealth, *s.* richesse *f.;* profusion *f.*

wealthy, *adj.* riche.

weapon, *s.* arme *f.*

wear, *v.a.* porter; ~ *away, down, out* (s')user; ~ *off* (s')effacer; — *s.* usage *m.;* usure *f.*

weary, *adj.* las, fatigué.

weather, *s.* temps *m.*

weather-forecast, *s.* prévisions *f. pl.* du temps; bulletin *m.* météorologique.

weave, *v. a.* tisser.

web, *s.* tissu *m.; (spider)* toile *f.*

wedding, *s.* mariage *m.*

wedding-ring, *s.* alliance *f.,* anneau *m.* de mariage.

wedge, *s.* coin *m.;* — *v.a.* coincer; caler.

Wednesday, *s.* mercredi *m.*

weed, *s.* mauvaise herbe *f.;* — *v.a.* sarcler.

week, *s.* semaine *f.*

week-day, *s.* jour *m.* de semaine; *on* ~s en semaine.

week-end, *s.* fin *f.* de semaine, week-end *m.*

weekly, *adj.* de la semaine; hebdomadaire; — *s.* (journal) hebdomadaire *m.*

weep, *v.n.* pleurer.

weigh, *v.a. & n.* peser; ~ *down* faire pencher, surcharger, accabler.

weight, *s.* poids *m.;* *put on* ~ prendre du corps.

welcome, *adj.* bienvenu; ~*!* soyez le bienvenu!; — *s.* accueil *m.;* — *v.a.* souhaiter la bienvenue (à); accueillir (avec plaisir).

well[1], *adv.* bien; ~, ~*!* allons, allons!; — *adj.* bien (portant).

well[2], *s.* puits *m.*

well-being, bien-être *m.*

well-informed, *adj.* bien informé, renseigné.

well-to-do, *adj.* aisé; *be* ~ être dans l'aisance

west, *s.* ouest *m.*

western, *adj.* de l'ouest.

westward, *adv.* vers l'ouest.

wet, *adj.* mouillé, humide; pluvieux; ~ *through* trempé jusqu'aux os; — *v.a.* mouiller; tremper.

whale, *s.* baleine *f.*

what, *rel. pron.* ce qui, ce que; — *interrog. pron.* qu'est-ce qui, que; — *int.* quoi!

wheat, *s.* blé *m.,* froment *m.*

wheel, *s.* roue *f.; (steering)* volant *m.*

when, *adv. & conj.* quand.

whenever, *adv.* toutes les fois que.

where, *adv.* où.

whereas, *conj.* tandis que;

vu que.

wherever, *adv.* partout où.

whether, *conj.* soit que; *(if)* si; ~ *or not*... qu'il en soit ainsi ou non...

which, *(interrogative) adj.* quel, quelle; *pron.* lequel; *(relative) adj.* lequel, laquelle; *pron.* qui, que, lequel.

while, *conj.* pendant que; *(whereas)* tandis que; *(as long as)* tant que; — *s.* temps *m.; be worth* ~ *to* cela vaut la peine de; — *v.a.* ~ *away* faire passer.

whip, *s.* fouet.

whisk, *v.a.* fouetter; — *s.* époussette *f.; (eggs)* fouet à œufs, *m.*

whisper, *s.* chuchotement *m.;* murmure *m.; v.a.* dire à l'oreille; *v.n.* chuchoter; murmurer.

whistle, *s.* sifflet *m.;* — *v.a. & n.* siffler.

white, *adj.* blanc, blanche; pâle.

Whit Sunday, dimanche *m.* de la Pentecôte.

who, *pron.* qui.

whole, *s.* tout *m.;* totalité *f.; on the* ~ à tout prendre; — *adj.* tout le, toute la; entier, -ère.

wholesale, *adj. & adv.* en gros.

wholesome, *adj.* sain.

wholly, *adv.* entièrement.

whom, *pron.* que; lequel; *interrog.* qui?, qui est-ce que?

whose, *pron.* dont; *interrog.* de qui?

why, *adv.* pourquoi.

wicked, *adj.* méchant.

wide, *adj.* large; étendue; *6 feet* ~ 6 pieds de largeur.

widow, *s.* veuve *f.*

widower, *s.* veuf *m.*

width, *s.* largeur *f.*

wife, *s.* femme *f.*

wild, *adj.* sauvage; déréglé; impétueux; frénétique.

wilful, *adj.* volontaire.

will, *s.* volonté *f.;* intention *f.;* testament *m.; at* ~ à volonté; *of one's own free* ~ de plein gré; — *v.n. & aux.* vouloir; *(future tense unexpressed, see grammar).*

willing *adj.* bien disposé; *be* ~ vouloir bien.

willingly, *adv.* volontiers.

win, *v. a. & n.* gagner.

winch, *s.* manivelle *f.*

wind[1], *s.* vent *m.;* souffle *m.*

wind[2], *v. a.* enrouler; dévider; ~ *up (clock)* remonter; *fig.* liquider; *v.n.* tourner, serpenter; s'enrouler.

window, *s.* fenêtre *f.; (car)* glace *f.*

windscreen, *s.* pare-brise *m.*

windy, *adj.* venteux.

wine, *s.* vin *m.*

wing, *s.* aile *f.;* vol *m.; take* ~ s'envoler.

wink, *s.* clin d'œil, *m.;* — *v.a.* clignoter.

winner, *s.* gagnant *m.*

winter, *s.* hiver *m.*

wipe, *v.a.* essuyer; ~ *out* effacer; — *s.* coup *m.* de torchon.

wire, *s.* fil *m.* (de fer); télégramme *m.; live* ~ fil *m.* en charge; — *v.a. & n.* télégraphier.

wireless, *s.* T.S.F.; télégraphie sans fil; ~ *set* poste *m.* (de T.S.F.).

wise, *adj.* sage; prudent.

wish, *s.* désir *m.;* ~es vœux *m. pl.;* — *v.a.* désirer (de); souhaiter; *(should like)* vouloir *(in conditional).*

wit, *s.* esprit *m.; (pers.)* bel esprit *m.*

witch, *s.* sorcière *f.*

with, *prep.* avec; *(at)* chez.

withdraw, *v.n.* se retirer; *v.a.* retirer.

within, *adv.* dedans; — *prep. (time)* en; *(place)* dans; à.

without, *prep.* sans; *(place)* en dehors de.

witness, *s.* témoignage *m.; (pers.)* témoin *m.;* — *v.a.* être témoin de; *(attest)* témoigner; *(document)* signer (à).

witty, *adj.* spirituel.

wizard, *s.* sorcier *m.*

wolf, *s.* loup, louve *m. f.*

woman, *s.* femme *f.*

womb, *s.* matrice *f.; fig.* sein *m.*

wonder, *s.* étonnement *m.; (a thing)* merveille *f.;* — *v.n.* ~ at être étonné de; *(curious)* se demander; *I* ~ je me le demande.

wonderful, *adj.* étonnant.

wood, *s.* bois *m.*

wooden, *adj.* de bois.

woodman, *s.* bûcheron *m.*

wool, *s.* laine *f.*

woollen, *adj.* de laine.

word, *s.* mot *m.; (utterance)* parole *f.; (term)* terme *m.; (information* avis *m.; upon my* ~! ma parole!; *have a* ~ *with* avoir deux mots avec.

work, *s.* travail *m.; (achievement)* ouvrage *m.;* ~ *(of art)* œuvre *f.* d'art; ~s *(of s.o.)* œuvres *f.pl., (factory)* usine *f.; set to* ~ se mettre à l'œuvre; — *v.a.* faire travailler; *(wood)* ouvrager; *v.n.* travailler; *(operate)* fonctionner; marcher.

worker, *s.* travailleur, -euse *m. f.,* ouvrier, -ère *m. f.*

workman, *s.* ouvrier *m.*

workshop, *s.* atelier *m.*

world, *s.* monde *m.*

world-war, *s.* guerre *f.* mondiale.

world-wide, *adj.* universel; mondial.

worm, *s.* ver *m.*

worry, *s.* ennui *m.,* tracas *m.;* — *v.a.* tracasser; importuner; *v. n.* se tracasser (de), se tourmenter; *don't* ~! soyez tranquille!

worse, *adj.* pire, plus mauvais; *grow* ~ empirer; — *adv.* pis.

worship, *s.* culte *m.;* — *v.a. & n.* adorer.

worst, *adj.* le, la pire; le, la plus malade; — *adv.* le plus mal; — *s.* pis *m.*

worth, *s.* valeur *f.;* — *adj. be* ~ valoir; *is it* ~ *while?* cela (en) vaut-il la peine?; *it is not* ~ *the trouble* cela ne vaut pas la peine.

worthless, *adj.* sans valeur, indigne.

worthy, *adj.* digne.

wound, *s.* blessure *f.*

wounded, *adj.* blessé; *the* ~ les blessés.

wrap, *s. (garment)* peignoir *m.; v.a.* ~ *up* envelopper; *fig.* être absorbé *(in* dans).

wrapper, *s.* toile d'emballage *f.; (book)* bande *f.*

wreck, *s.* naufrage *m.;* navire *m.* naufragé; *fig.* ruine *f.; v.a.* ruiner: *be ~ed* faire naufrage; être naufragé.

wrench, *s.* torsion *f.; (tool)* clef (à écrous) *f.; — v.a.* tordre; *(ankle)* fouler.

wrestle, *v.n.* lutter (avec).

wrestler, *s.* lutteur *m.*

wrestling, *s.* lutte *f.*

wring, *v.a.* tordre.

wrinkle, *s.* ride *f.; (crease)* faux pli *m.; — v.a.* rider.

wrist, *s.* poignet *m.*

writ, *s.* exploit *m.*

write, *v.a. & n.* écrire; *~ down* noter; *~ off* amortir; *~ out* transcrire.

writer, *s.* écrivain *m.*

writing, *s.* écriture *f.;* écrit *m.; in ~* par écrit.

writing-desk, *s.* bureau *m.*

wrong, *adj.* incorrect, faux; *be ~* avoir tort; se tromper (de); *take the ~ train* se tromper de train; *it is the ~ book* ce n'est pas le livre qu'il faut.

yard, *s.* yard *m.;* cour *f.*

yarn, *s.* fil *m*; histoire *f.*

yawn, *s.* bâillement *m.; — v.n.* bâiller.

year, *s.* an *m.;* année *f.*

yearly, *adv.* annuellement.

yearn, *v.n. ~ for* soupirer après.

yeast, *s.* levure *f.*

yell, *v. n.* hurler.

yellow, *adj.* jaune.

yes, *adv.* oui; *(after negation)* si.

yesterday, *adv.* hier.

yet, *adv.* encore; *not ~* pas encore; *as ~* jusqu'à présent; *— conj.* néanmoins.

yield, *v.a.* produire; accorder; rendre; *v.n.* céder (à); fléchir.

yoke, *s.* joug *m.*

yolk, *s.* jaune *m.*

you, *pron.* tu; vous.

young, *adj.* jeune; *(animal)* petit; *~er* plus jeune. cadet.

your, *adj.* votre, *(pl.)* vos.

yours, *pron.* à vous; le, la vôtre, les vôtres.

yourself, *pron.* vous-même, *-s.*

youth, *s.* jeunesse *f.; (pers.)* jeune homme *m.*

youth-hostel, *s.* auberge *f.* de la jeunesse.

X

Xmas, *s.* Noël *m.*

x-ray, *adj. ~ treatment* radiothérapie *f.; ~photograph* radiograph e *f.*

Y

yacht, *s.* yacht *m.*

Z

zeal, *s.* zèle *m.*

zealous, *adj.* zélé.

zero, *s.* zéro *m.*

zest, *s.* enthousiasme *m.;* goût *m.*

zigzag, *s.* zigzag *m.; — adv.* en zigzag.

zinc, *s.* zinc *m.*
zipper, *s.* fermeture éclair. *f.*

zone, *s.* zone *f.*
zoo, *s.* zoo *m.*
zoology, *s.* zoologie *f.*

FRENCH-ENGLISH

DICTIONARY

A

à, au, *prep*. to; at.

abaisser, *v. a*. lower, let down; s'~ stoop.

abandonner, *v. a*. forsake, abandon.

abat-jour, *s. m*. lampshade.

abbaye, *s. m*. abbey.

abbé, *s. m*. abbot.

abdication, *s. f*. abdication.

abdiquer, *v. n*. abdicate; *v. a*. renounce.

abeille, *s. f* bee.

abject, *adj*. abject, low.

abjurer, *v.a*. abjure; give up.

abolir, *v. a*. abolish.

abondance, *s. f*. plenty, abundance.

abondant, *adj*. abundant.

abonder, *v. n*. abound.

abonner: s'~ subscribe to, take in.

abord, *adv*. d'~ (at) first.

aboutir, *v. n*. end in, come to.

aboyer, *v. n*. bark.

abricot, *s. m*. apricot.

abrupt, *adj*. steep.

absence, *s. f*. absence; ~ d'esprit absence of mind.

absent, *adj*. absent.

absenter: s'~ leave, depart.

absolu, *adj*. absolute.

absorber, *v. a*. absorb;

absoudre*, *v. a*. absolve.

abstraction, *s. f*. abstraction.

abstrait, *adj*. abstract.

absurde, *adj*. absurd.

abus, *s. m*. abuse.

académie, *s. f*. academy.

accélérer, *v. a*. accelerate, hasten.

accent, *s.m*. accent, stress.

accentuer, *v.a*. accent.

accepter, *v. a*. accept; admit.

accès, *s. m*. access; fit.

accessible, *adj*. accessible.

accident, *s. m*. accident; par ~ accidentally.

accidentel, -elle, *adj*. accidental.

acclamer, *v.a*. acclaim.

acclimater, *v.a*. acclimatize; 's'~ become acclimatized.

accommoder, *v. a*. accommodate; fit up; s'~ put up with, come to terms.

accompagner, *v. a*. accompany.

accomplir, *v. a*. accomplish, carry out.

accord, *s. m*. agreement, accord, harmony.

accorder, *v.a*. grant, confer; agree.

accoutumer, *v. a*. accustom; s'~ get accustomed (to).

accréditer, *v. a*. accredit.

accrocher, *v. a*. hang up, hook; run against.

accroître, *v. a*. increase; s'~ increase.

accueil, *s. m*. reception.

accueillir, *v. a*. receive, welcome.

accumuler, *v. a*. accumulate, heap up.

accusation, *s. f*. accusation, charge.

accuser, *v.a*. accuse.

achat, *s. m*. purchase; faire des ~s go shopping.

acheter, *v.a*. purchase, buy.

achèvement, *s. m*. completion.

achever, *v.a.* complete
finish; achieve.

acide, *adj.* acid, sour; —
s. m. acid.

acier, *s. m.* steel.

acoustique, *s. f.* acoustics.

acquérir*, *v.a.* acquire,
purchase; get.

âcre, *adj.* acrid, sour.

acte, *s. m.* action, deed,
act; transaction, docu-
ment, certificate; *(the-
atre)* act.

acteur, *s. m.* actor.

actif, -ive, *adj.* active;
— *s.m.* assets *(pl.);*

action, *s. f.* action; act,
deed; effect; lawsuit;
plot; story.

activité, *s. f.* activity.

actrice, *s. f.* actress.

actualité, *s. f.* topic of
the hour; ∼s current
events; news-reel.

actuel, -elle, present, of
present interest; actual.

adapter, *v.a.* adapt; s'∼
adapt oneself.

addition, *s. f.* addition;
bill.

additionner, *v. a.* add up.

adhérer, *v. a.* adhere,
stick.

adieu, *s. m. (pl. -x)* good-
bye; *faire ses* ∼x take
one's leave.

adjoint, *adj. & s. m.* assistant; deputy.

adjuger, *v. a.* adjuge.

administrateur, -trice,

s. m. f. manager, di-
rector.

administratif, -ive- *adj.*
administrative.

administration, *s. f.* management, direction;
administration.

administrer, *v.a.* administer; manage.

admirable, *adj.* admi-

rable.

admiration, *s. f.* admiration.

admirer, *v. a.* admire,
wonder at.

admission, *s. f.* admission,
admittance.

adolescent, *s. m.* adolescent, youth.

adopter, *v.a.* adopt, pass.

adoption, *s.f.* adoption.

adorer, *v.a.* adore.

adresse, *s. f.* address;
skill, dexterity.

adresser, *v. a.* address,
direct; s'∼ apply (to).

adroit, *adj.* clever, skilful.

adulte, *adj. & s.* adult.

adversaire, *s. m.* adversary.

aérien, -enne, *adj.* aerial.

aérodrome, *s. m.* airport.

aéroport, *s. m.* airport.

affaiblir, *v. a.* weaken.

affaire, *s. f.* business,
affair, matter; lawsuit.

affamé, *adj.* hungry.

affecter, *v. a.* affect,
feign; move; assume.

affection, *s. f.* affection;
disease.

affectueux, -euse, *adj.*
affectionate.

affermir, *v. a.* strengthen;
s'∼ become stronger.

affiche, *s. f.* poster, bill.

afficher, *v. a.* post up,
stick up, placard.

affiler, *v.a.* sharpen.

affirmatif, -ive, *adj.* affirmative.

affirmer, *v. a.* affirm.

affliger, *v. a.* afflict.

affluer, *v. n.* flow into.

affranchir, *v. a.* (set)
free; stamp.

affreux, -euse, *adj.* dreadful, terrible.

affronter, *v.a.* face.

afin, *conj.* ∼ *de* in order
to; ∼ *que* in order

that, so that.

africain (A.), *adj. & s. m. f.* African.

âge, *s. m.* age; period; *quel ~ avez-vous?* how old are you?

agence, *s. f.* agency.

agent, *s. m.* agent; policeman.

aggraver, *v. a.* aggravate.

agile, *adj.* agile, active.

agilité, *s. f.* agility.

agir, *v. n.* act; take effect; behave; *s'~* be in question.

agitation, *s. f.* agitation.

agiter, *v. a.* agitate.

agneau, *s. m.* lamb.

agonie, *s. f.* agony.

agréable, *adj.* agreeable.

agréer, *v. a.* accept, receive favourably.

agrément, *s. m.* consent, approval; pleasure.

agressif, -ive, *adj.* aggressive.

agression, *s. f.* aggression, attack.

agriculture, *s. f.* agriculture.

aide, *s. f.* help.

aider, *v. a.* help.

aïeux, *s. m. pl.* ancestors.

aigle, *s. m.* eagle.

aigre, *adj.* sour, acid.

aigrir: *s'~* turn sour.

aigu, *adj.* pointed, sharp; keen; *accent ~* acute accent.

aiguille, *s. f.* needle; hand, index; point, switch; *grande ~* minute hand.

aiguiser, *v. a.* sharpen.

ail, *s. m.* garlic.

aile, *s. f.* wing; flank; aisle; mudguard.

ailleurs, *adv.* somewhere else, elsewhere; *d'~* in addition, besides.

aimable, *adj.* amiable, pleasant, kindly.

aimer, *v. a. & n.* like, love,
be fond of, care to.

aîné, *adj. & s. m. f.* elder, eldest; senior.

ainsi, *adv. & conj.* so, thus; likewise; *~ de suite* and so on; *~ que* as well as.

air, *s. m.* air; look(s), appearance, manner; *(music)* air.

aisance, *s. f.* ease; comfort; facility; *être dans l'~* be well off.

aise, *s. f.* ease, comfort.

aisé, *adj.* easy; well-off.

ajourner, *v.a.* adjourn.

alcool, *s. m.* alcohol.

alcoolique, *adj.* alcoholic.

algèbre, *s. f.* algebra.

aliment, *s. m.* aliment, food.

alimentation, *s. f.* alimentation; feeding.

alimenter, *v. a.* feed.

aliter, *v. a. être alité* be confined to bed, be laid up.

allaiter, *v. a.* give suck to; nurse.

allée, *s. f.* (garden) path, lane, walk, alley.

alléger, *v.a.* lighten; alleviate, soothe.

allégresse, *s. f.* gaiety, delight.

allemand (A.), *adj. & s. m. f.* German.

aller*, *v. n.* go, proceed; get on; grow, get; *~ à pied* walk; *~ en auto* drive; *~ en avion* fly; *~ bien* be well; *comment allez-vous?* how are you?; *allons!* come on!; *allez!* indeed; *s'en ~* go away, be off.

alliance, *s. f.* alliance, union; wedding-ring.

allié, -e, *s. m. f.* ally; — *adj.* allied.

allier, *v.a.* alloy; match;

unite; s'~ join with, unite.

allonger, *v. a.* lengthen, stretch out, prolong; ~ *le pas* step out; s'~ get longer.

allumer, *v. a.* light (up), set on fire; excite.

allumette, *s. f.* match.

allure, *s. f.* gait, pace; manner, behaviour; direction.

allusion, *s. f.* allusion, hint; reference.

alors, *adv.* then.

alpinisme, *s. m.* mountaineering.

altérer, *v. a.* alter, change; s'~ alter, degenerate.

alternance, *s. f.* alternation.

alternatif, -ive, *adj.* alternate, alternative.

alterner, *v. n. & a.* alternate.

altitude, *s. f.* altitude.

aluminium, *s. f.* aluminium.

amaigrir, *v.a.* make thin; s'~ grow thin.

amant, -e, *s. m. f.* lover.

amas, *s.m.* heap, mass, pile.

amateur, *s. m.* amateur, lover, fancier.

ambassade, *s. f.* embassy.

ambassadeur, *s. m.* ambassador.

ambassadrice, *s.f.* ambassadress.

ambitieux, -euse, *adj.* ambitious.

ambition, *s. f.* ambition.

ambulance, *s. f.* ambulance; ~ *(automobile)* ambulance(-car).

âme, *s.f.* soul; mind.

améliorer, *v. a.* ameliorate, improve; s'~ improve.

aménager, *v.a.* fit up, out.

amender, *v.a.* amend, improve.

amener, *v. a.* bring, draw; bring before, in, out; introduce; induce.

amer, -ère, *adj.* bitter.

américain, -e (A.), *adj. & s. m. f.* American.

ami, -e, *s. m. f.* friend; sweetheart; *bon* ~, *bonne* ~e sweetheart.

amical, *adj.* friendly, kind.

amiral, *s. m.* admiral.

amitié, *s. f.* friendship; affection; *meilleures* ~s kindest regards.

amortir, *v.a.* lessen, soften; pay (off), write off.

amortisseur, *s. m.* shockabsorber.

amour, *s. m.* love; *faire l'*~ court, make love to; *mon* ~ my darling.

amoureux, -euse, *adj.* in love *(de* with), enamoured *(de* of).

amplificateur, *s.m.* amplifier.

amplifier, *v. a.* amplify.

ampoule, *s. f.* blister; bulb.

amulette, *s. f.* amulet.

amusant, *adj.* amusing.

amusement, *s. m.* amusement, pastime, fun.

amuser, *v.a.* amuse, entertain; s'~ enjoy oneself.

an, *s. m.* year; *il y a un* ~ a year ago.

analogie, *s. f.* analogy.

analogue, *adj.* analogous.

analyse, *s. f.* analysis.

analyser, *v. a.* analyse.

ananas, *s. m.* pineapple.

anatomie, *s. f.* anatomy.

ancêtre, *s. m. f.* ancestor.

ancien, -enne, *adj.* ancient, old, antique.

ancre, *s. f.* anchor; *lever l'*~ weigh anchor.

âne, *s. m.* ass.

anéantir, *v. a.* annihilate.

anecdote, *s. f.* anecdote.

ange, *s. m.* angel.

anglais, -e (A.), *adj.* English; — *s. m. f.* Englishman, Englishwoman.

angle, *s. m.* angle, corner; bend.

angoisse, *s.f.* anguish.

animal, *s.m.* animal; beast.

anneau, *s. m.* circle, ring.

année, *s. f.* year; ~ *scolaire* school-year; *bonne* ~ a happy New Year!

annexer, *v. a.* annex.

anniversaire, *s. m.* anniversary, b rthday.

annonce, *s. f.* announcement, advertisement.

annoncer, *v. a.* announce, give notice of; advertise.

annuaire, *s. m.* year-book, annual, directory.

annuel, -elle, *adj.* annual.

annuler, *v. a.* annul.

anonyme, *adj.* anonymous; *société* ~ joint-stock company.

anormal, *adj.* abnormal.

anse, *s. f.* handle; creek.

antécédent, -e, *adj. & s. m.* antecedent.

antenne, *s. f.* aerial.

antérieur, *adj.* anterior, previous.

antibiotique, *s. m.* antibiotic.

antichambre, *s. f.* entrance hall.

anticiper, *v. a. & n.* anticipate; encroach.

antipathie, *s.f.* antipathy.

antiquaire, *s. m.* antiquarian.

antique, *adj.* antique, ancient.

antiquité, *s. f.* antiquity.

antiseptique, *adj. & s. m.* antiseptic.

anxiété, *s. f.* anxiety.

anxieux, -euse, *adj.* anxious.

août, *s.m.* August.

apaiser, *v. a.* appease, pacify, quiet.

apercevoir, *v. a.* perceive, catch sight of; remark, notice.

aplanir, *v.a.* smooth, level, even off; s'~ become level.

aplatir, *v.a.* flatten.

apologie, *s. m.* apology, defence.

apoplexie, *s. f.* apoplexy.

apostolique, *adj.* apostolic(al).

apostrophe, *s. f.* apostrophe.

apôtre, *s. m.* apostle.

apparaître, *v. n.* appear.

appareil, *s. m.* apparatus, device, appliance, gear; camera; ~ *de TV* TV-set; ~ *de direction* steering-gear.

apparence, *s. f.* appearance, look(s); likelihood; *en* ~ apparenty.

apparent, *adj.* apparent.

apparition, *s. f.* appearance; apparition.

appartement, *s.m.* flat; apartment.

appartenir, *v.n.* belong, appertain *(à* to).

appel, *s. m.* call; appeal; *faire l'*~ call the roll.

appeler, *v. a.* call in, out, up, down; ring up; name, term; *en* ~ appeal; *faire* ~ send for; s'~ be called, call oneself.

appendice, *s. m.* appendix.

appendicite, *s.f.* appedicitis.

appesantir, *v.a.* make heavy, weigh down.

appétit, *s. m.* appetite.

applaudir, *v. n.* applaud, clap.

application, *s. f.* application; diligence.

appliquer, *v. a.* apply; lay on.

apporter, *v.a.* bring.

appréciation, *s.f.* appreciation; estimation.

apprécier, *v. a.* value.

appréhension, *s. f.* apprehension, fear.

apprendre, *v. a.* learn, acquire; hear of; teach.

apprentissage, *s. m.* apprenticeship.

apprêter, *v. a.* prepare; season; dress; s'~ prepare oneself, get ready.

approbation, *s. f.* approbation, approval.

approche, *s. f.* approach, advance.

approcher, *v.a.* bring toward, forward.

approprié, *adj.* appropriate.

approprier: s'~ appropriate, take; accommodate, adapt oneself.

approuver, *v. a.* sanction; approve.

approximatif, -ive, *adj.* approximate.

approximation, *s.f.* approximation.

appui, *s. m.* support.

appuyer, *v. a.* support; lean; *v. n.* ~ *sur* lay stress (up)on; s'~ lean, rest, rely (upon).

après, *adv.* after; behind; next (to); ~ *coup* too late; ~ *tout* after all; d'~ after, according to; by.

après-demain, *adv.* & *s. m.* (the) day after tomorrow.

après-midi, *s. m.* afternoon.

à-propos, *adv.* in good time; — *s. m.* timely word; fitness.

apte, *adj.* apt, suitable.

aptitude, *s. f.* aptitude, ability, talent.

aquarelle, *s.f.* water-color.

arabe (A.), *adj.* & *s. m. f.* Arab, Arabian; Arabic.

araignée, *s. f.* spider.

arbitre, *s. f.* arbiter, judge; umpire, referee.

arbre, *s. m.* tree; shaft; ~ *fruitier* fruit-tree; ~ *coudé* crank shaft.

arc, *s. m.* bow; arc(h).

arcade, *s. f.* arcade.

arche, *s. f.* arch, vault.

archet, *s.m.* bow.

archevêque, *s.m.* archbishop.

architecture, *s.f.* architecture.

archives *s. f. pl.* archives.

ardemment, *adv.* ardently.

ardent, *adj.* burning, fiery, ardent, eager.

ardeur, *s. f.* keenness; ardour, zeal.

arête, *s. f.* fish-bone; edge; ridge.

argent, *s. m.* silver; money; ~ *en caisse* cash in hand ~ *comptant* ready money; ~ *de la poche* pocket-money; *à-court* d'~ pressed for money.

argenterie, *s. f.* plate.

argentin[1], *adj.* silvery.

argentin[2], -e (A.), *adj.* & *s. m. f.* Argentine.

argile, *s.f.* clay.

argot, *s. m.* slang.

argument, *s.m.* argument, proof, evidence.

aristocratie, *s.f.* aristocracy.

aristocratique, *adj.* aristocratic.

arme, *s.f.* arm, weapon; ~s *à feu* fire-arms; *faire des* ~s fence.

armée, *s. f.* army.

armer, *v.a.* arm; fortify; s'~ arm oneself.

armoire, *s. f.* cupboard;

wardrobe.

armure, *s. f.* armour; armature.

arracher, *v.a.* pull (out), tear up; extract, draw; remove from.

arrangement, *s. m.* arrangement; agreement, settlement; ~s terms.

arranger, *v. a.* arrange, settle, fix (up); s'~ come to an agreement, make arrangements (for); make shift (to).

arrestation, *s. f.* arrest.

arrêt, *s. m.* stop (of bus, tram etc.); pause; standstill; sentence; arrest; ~ *facultatif* request stop; *sans* ~ non-stop.

arrêter, *v.a.* check, stop; arrest; engage, book; decide, decree; settle; s'~ stop; draw up; leave off.

arrière, *adv.* behind, backward; *en* ~ back(ward); ~ *s. m.* back part, rear.

arriéré, *adj.* overdue; backward; under-developed; — *s.m.* arrears *(pl.).*

arrivée, *s. f.* arrival; *à l'*~ on arrival.

arriver, *v. n.* arrive, come; turn up; happen; occur; ~ *à* attain, arrive at, reach; *le train arrive à* the train is due at.

arrogance, *s. f.* arrogance.

arroser, *v. a.* water, sprinkle; baste.

art, *s. m.* art; *les beaux* ~s the fine arts.

artère, *s.f.* artery; thoroughfare.

article, *s. m.* article; ~s *de grande consommation* consumer(s') goods.

articulation, *s. f.* joint.

articuler, *v.a.* articulate.

artificiel, -elle, *adj.* artificial.

artillerie, *s. f.* artillery.

artisan, *s. m.* craftsman.

artiste, *s. m. & f.* artist; player

ascenseur, *s. m.* lift.

asile, *s. m.* refuge, asylum.

aspect, *s.m.* aspect.

asperge, *s. f.* asparagus.

aspirateur, *s.m.* vacuum-cleaner.

aspiration, *s. f.* aspiration.

aspirer, *v.a.* inspire; *v. n.* aspire *(à to).*

assaillir*, *v. a.* assault.

assaisonner, *v.a.* season; dress.

assassin, *s. m.* assassin.

assassiner, *v. a.* assassinate, murder.

assaut, *s.m.* assault.

assemblage, *s. m.* assemblage, gathering, collection.

assemblée, *s.f.* assembly, meeting.

assembler, *v. a.* assemble; put together; gather; s'~ assemble.

asseoir*, *v. a.* seat; place; s'~ take a seat.

assez, *adv.* enough; pretty, fairly.

assiduité, *s.f.* assiduity.

assiéger, *v.a.* attack, besiege.

assiette, *s. f.* posture; seat; position; plate.

assimiler, *v. a.* assimilate *(à to).*

assistance, *s.f.* presence, attendance; audience; assistance, help.

assister, *v. n.* attend, be present *(à at); v. a.* assist, help.

association, *s. f.* association; partnership, company.

associer, *v.a.* associate, link up; share interests with; s'~ associate oneself *(avec* with).

assommant, *adj.* boring, dull.

assortir, *v.a.* match, assort; s'~ be suitable, go well together.

assoupir, *v. a.* make drowsy, sleepy; s'~ grow sleepy.

assujettir, *v.a.* subject, subjugate.

assumer, *v. a.* assume.

assurance, *s. f.* assurance; insurance; ~ *sur la vie* life-insurance.

assuré, *adj.* assured, confident, sure; insured.

assurer, *v. a.* assure, secure; insure; s'~ make sure (of).

astre, *s. m.* star.

astronaute, *s. m.* astronaut, space man.

astronautique, *s. f.* astronautics, space travel.

astronef, *s. m.* space-craft, space-ship.

atelier, *s.m.* workshop; studio.

athée, *s.m.f.* atheist.

athlète, *s.m.* athlete.

athlétique, *adj.* athletic.

atome, *s.m.* atom.

atomique, *adj.* atomic; *bombe* ~ atom(ic) bomb *énergie* ~ atomic energy.

attache, *s. f.* tie, fastener; bond, strap; *fig.* attachment.

attaché, *s. m.* attaché.

attacher, *v.a.* fasten, tie (up), attach; associate; engage; s'~ attach (to), become attached (to).

attaque, *s. f.* attack.

attaquer, *v.a.* attack.

attarder, *v.a.* delay; *être attardé* be delayed.

atteindre*, *v. a.* attain, reach; hit, stirke.

atteinte, *s. f.* blow, stroke; fit; injury; *hors d'*~ out of reach.

attendre, *v. a. & n.* await, wait for, expect; s'~ hope for, expect.

attendrir, *v. a.* soften; *fig.* move, touch; s'~ be moved.

attendrissement, *s.m.* compassino; tenderness.

attente, *s. f.* waiting; hope

attentif, -ive, *adj.* attentive, considerate.

attention, *s.f.* attention, notice, heed, care; *(pl.)* attentions; *faire* ~ be careful, mind, take notice of, take heed (to); ~*!* look out!

atténuer, *v. a.* extenuate, attenuate.

atterrir, *v. n.* land.

atterrissage, *s. m.* landing; *piste d'*~ landing-strip.

attester, *v.a.* attest.

attirail, *s. m.* implements *(pl.),* utensils *(pl.),* gear; tackle.

attirer, *v.a.* attract.

attitude, *s. f.* attitude.

attraction, *s. f.* attraction.

attrape, *s. f.* trap; catch.

attribuer, *v. a.* assign, allot; attribute, ascribe.

attribut, *s. m.* attribute.

au *(pl.* **aux),** to the, at the.

auberge, *s. f.* inn, tavern; ~ *de la jeunesse* youth hostel.

aucun, *adj. & pron.* no, none, no one, not any.

au-dessous, *adv.* below; ~ *de* under.

au-dessus, *adv. (*~ *de)* above, over.

audience, *s. f.* audience; public; sitting, session.

audiovisuel, -elle, *adj.* audio-visual.

auditeur, -trice, *s. m. f.* listener; auditor.

auditoire, *s. m.* audience;

congregation.

auge, *s.m.* trough; bucket.

augmentation, *s.f.* augmentation, increase; rise.

augmenter, *v. a.* augment, increase; s'~ increase.

aujourd'hui, *adv.* today.

auparavant, *adv.* previously, earlier; before.

auprès, *adv.* near, by, close by; ~ *de* near.

auquel, *rel.pron.* to whom, to which.

aurore, *s.f.* dawn.

aussi, *adv.* also, too; ~ ... *que* as ... as; — *conj.* and so, therefore; ~ *bien que* as well as; ~ *bien* in fact.

austère, *adj.* austere, severe.

autant, *adv. & conj.* as much, as many, as far; ~ *que* as far as, as much as.

autel, *s. m.* altar.

auteur, *s. m.* author.

authentique, *adj.* authentic, genuine.

auto, *s. f.* car.

autobus, *s.m.* (motor-)bus.

autocar, *s. m.* (motor-) coach.

automatique, *adj.* automatic; — *s.m.* dial-telephone.

automne, *s. m. f.* autumn.

automobile, *s. m. f.* motor-car.

autonomie, *s.f.* autonomy.

autorisation, *s. f.* authorization, permission; licence.

autoriser, *v.a.* authorize.

autorité, *s. f.* authority; rule.

autoroute, *s. f.* motor-way.

auto-stop, *s. m.* hitch-hiking.

auto-stoppeur, -euse, *s. m. f.* hitch-hiker.

autour, *adv. & prep.* ~ *de* about, (a)round; *tout* ~ all round.

autre, *adj.* different, other, another, else; *un* ~ another; *d'*~ *part* on the other hand; ~ *part* elsewhere; *de temps* ~ now and then, at times; *l'*~ *jour* the other day; *l'un et l'*~ both; *l'un l'*~ each other.

autrefois, *adv.* formerly, long ago.

autrichien, -enne (A.), *adj. & s.m.f.* Austrian.

autrui, *pron.* others, other people.

avalanche, *s.f.* avalanche.

avaler, *v.a.* swallow; *fig.* endure, pocket.

avance, *s.f.* advance.

avancé, *adj.* advanced.

avancement, *s.m.* advance, progress; promotion.

avancer, *v.a.* advance, bring, put forward; pay in advance; — *v. n.* advance, proceed, move on; s'~ come, move, go forward.

avant, *prep. & adv.* before, in front (of), in advance; ~ *tout* above all, before everything; *en* ~ forward, to the front; *mettre en* ~ bring forward; *en* ~ *de* in front of; — *s.m.* front (part); bow (of ship); forward.

avantage, *s. m.* advantage, benefit, profit; *(tennis)* vantage.

avantageux, -euse, *adj.* advantageous.

avant-hier, *adv.* day before yesterday.

avant-propos, *s. m.* foreword, preface.

avare, *s. m. f.* miser; — *adj.* avaricious, miserly.

avarice, *s.f.* avarice.

avec, *prep.* with.

avenir, *s. m.* future; *à l'~* in the future.

aventure, *s. f.* adventure; chance, luck.

aventurer, *v.a.* risk; **(s'~)** venture.

aventurier, -ère, *s. m. f.* adventurer.

avenue, *s. f.* boulevard; avenue.

averse, *s.f.* shower (of rain).

aversion, *v. f.* aversion, dislike.

avertir, *v.a.* inform, let know; warn; *faire ~ de* give notice of.

avertissement, *s. m.* information, notification; advice; warning.

aveu, *s. m.* admission, confession; consent.

aveugle, *adj.* blind.

aveuglement, *s. m.* blindness.

avide, *adj.* greedy, eager.

avidité, *s.f.* avidity.

avilir, *v.a.* debase, disgrace, degrade.

avion, *s.m.* (aero)plane; *~ de ligne* air-liner; *~ à réaction* jet plane; *par ~* by air-mail.

avis, *s. m.* opinion; advice, counsel; information, notice; hint; mind; *changer d'~* change one's mind.

aviser, *v.a.* perceive; inform; let know; advise; *s'~ de* think, find.

avocat, *s. m.* barrister, advocate, counsel.

avoine, *s.f.* oat(s).

avoir*, *v. a.* have, possess; have on, wear; feel; *~ raison* be right; *~ faim* be hungry; *~ de* take after; *~ à* have to; *il y a* there is, there are; ago.

avorter, *v. n.* miscarry, have a miscarriage.

avorton, *s. m.* abortion.

avoué, *s. m.* attorney, solicitor; lawyer.

avouer, *v. a. & n.* admit, confess; acknowledge; approve.

avril, *s.m.* April.

axe, *s.m.* axis; axle.

azote, *s.m.* nitrogen.

B

baccalauréat, *s. m.* baccalaureate, bachelor's degree.

bachelier, *s. m.* bachelor (of arts etc.).

bacille, *s.m.* bacillus.

bagage, *s. m.* luggage; *plier ~* pack up one's kit.

bague, *s.f.* ring.

bai, *adj.* bay.

baie¹, *s. f.* bay.

baie², *s. f.* berry.

baigner: se ~ bathe.

baignoire, *s.m.* bath, bathtub; pit-box.

bâiller, *v. n.* yawn, gape.

bain, *s. m.* bath; *salle de ~* bath-room.

baïonette, *s.f.* bayonet.

baiser, *v.a.* kiss.

baisse, *s.f.* fall; decline.

baisser, *v.a.* lower, let down; bring down; turn down; cast down; *v.n.* decline, fall; sink; **se ~** stoop.

bal, *s. m.* ball; *~ costumé* fancy-dress ball.

balai, *s.m.* broom, mop; (house-)brush; *donner un coup de ~* sweep.

balance, *s. f.* balance, scales *(pl.).*

balancer, *v.a.&n.* balance; weigh; swing, rock; give the sack; se ~ swing, wave; balance.

balayer, *v.a.* sweep (out), clear away.

balcon, *s. m.* balcony; dress-circle.

baleine, *s.f.* whale.

ballade, *s.f.* ballad.

balle, *s.f.* ball; bullet; bale.

ballon, *s.m.* balloon; (foot-)ball.

balnéaire, *adj.* pertaining to baths; *station ~* watering place.

bambou, *s.m.* bamboo.

ban, *s. m.* ban; *~s de mariage* banns.

banal *adj.* banal, common, ordinary.

banane, *s. f.* banana.

banc, *s. m.* bench, form; bank; pew; stand.

bande, *s.f.* band, strip; bandage; troop, gang, set; ~ *de papier* slip of paper; ~ *transporteuse* conveyer belt.

bander, *v. a.* bind up.

bandit, *s. m.* bandit.

banlieu, *s. f.* outskirts, suburbs *(pl.).*

bannir, *v. a.* banish, exile.

banque, *s. f.* bank; *billet de ~* banknote; *compte en ~* bank-account.

banquet, *s. m.* banquet, feast.

banquier, -ère, *s.m.f.* banker.

baptême, *s. m.* baptism.

baptiser, *v.a.* baptize.

barbare, *adj. & s.m.* barbarian.

barbarie, *s. f.* barbarousness, cruelty.

barbe, *s. f.* beard; *faire la ~ à* shave.

barbet, *s. m.* poodle.

barbier, *s. m.* barber.

baron, *s. m.* baron.

baronne, *s.f.* baroness.

barque, *s.f.* boat, barge.

barrage, *s.m.* barrier, barrage, dam.

barre, *s.f.* bar.

barreau, *s. m.* (small) bar; the Bar.

barrer, *v.a.* fasten, bar; cut off, shut out; steer.

barrière, *s.f.* barrier, town-gate, gate; bar; obstacle.

barrique, *s.f.* barrel, cask.

bas¹, *adj.* low; *à ~ prix* cheap; *terre ~se* lowland; *en ~* (down) below, down(-wards), — *s. m.* bottom, lower part

bas², *s. m.* stocking; ~ *nylons* nylon stockings.

base, *s. f.* base; basis.

basique, *adj.* basic.

basse, *s.f.* bass; bass-viol.

bassesse, *s.f.* lowness, meanness.

basset, *s. m.* basset (dog).

bassin, *s. m.* basin, pool.

bataille, *s.f.* battle.

bataillon, *s. m.* battalion.

bateau, *s. m.* boat.

batelier, *s.m.* boatman.

bâtiment, *s. m.* building; building trade; ship.

bâtir, *v.a.* build, erect.

bâtisseur, -euse *s. m. f.* builder.

bâton, *s. m.* stick, staff.

batte, *s.f.* bat; beater.

battement, *s.m.* clap-(ping); flapping.

batterie, *s.f.* battery; fight, row; percussive instruments *(pl.);* ~ *de cuisine* kitchen utensils *(pl.)*.

battre*, *v. a. & n.* beat, strike, thrash; se ~ fight.

battu, *adj.* beaten.

bavard, -e *s.m.f.* gossip.

bavarder, *v.n.* chat(ter), gossip.

bazar, *s.m.* bazaar.

beau, bel; belle; beaux, belles, *adj.* beautiful, handsome, good-looking, fair; considerable; *il y a ~ temps que* it seems an age since; *un ~ jour* one fine day; — *s.m.* beauty.

beaucoup, *adv.* (~ *de*) a good deal, many, much; plenty (of); *à ~ près, de ~* by far.

beau-frère, *s. m.* brother-in-law.

beau-père, *s. m.* father-in-law.

beauté, *s. f.* beauty

beaux-arts, *s. m. pl.* (the) fine arts.

bébé, *s. m.* baby.

bec, *s. m.* beak, bill nib; mouth-piece; jet; ~ *de gaz* gas-burner, gas-jet.

bêche, *s. f.* spade.

bégayer, *v. n. &a.* stammer, stutter.

belge (B.), *adj. & s. m. f.* Belgian.

belle-fille, *s. f.* daughter-in-law; step-daughter.

belle-mère, *s. f.* mother-in-law; stepmother.

belle-sœur, *s. f.* sister-in-law.

bémol, *s. m. & adj.* flat *(music)*.

bénédiction, *s.f.* benediction, blessing.

bénéfice, *s. m.* benefit, advantage, profit.

bénir, *v. a.* bless; praise.

berceau, *s. m.* cradle; *fig.* origin.

bercer, *v. a.* rock, lull (to sleep); *fig.* lull (with promises).

béret, *s.m.* beret.

berger, *s. m.* shepherd.

bergère, *s. f.* shepherdess; deep easy chair.

bésicles, *s. f. pl.* spectacles; goggles.

besogne, *s. f.* (piece of) work, job, task.

besoin, *s. m.* need, want; requirement; *avoir ~ de* want, need; *être dans le ~* be poor.

bétail, *s. m.* cattle.

bête, *s. f.* beast; animal; — *adj.* foolish, silly, stupid, dull.

bêtise, *s. f.* foolishness, stupidity; nonsense; trifle.

beurre, *s. m.* butter.

biais, *s. m.* bias, slant, slope.

biaiser, *v. n.* slant, slope.

bibelot, *s. m.* trinket, gew-gaw.

biberon, *s. m.* feeding-bottle.

bible, *s. f.* Bible.

bibliothécaire, *s. m. f.* librarian.

bibliothèque, *s. f.* library; bookcase; book-stall.

bicyclette, *s. f.* bicycle, bike.

bicycliste, *s. m. f.* cyclist.

bien, *adv.* well, right, properly, fully; *assez ~* fairly; *faire du ~* benefit; *ou ~* or else; *très ~* very well, all right; *~ avant* long before; very bad indeed; *~ que* (al)though; — *s. m.* good, welfare, benefit; property, goods;

aller à ~ prosper, be successful.

bien-être, *s. m.* welfare, well-being.

bienfaisance, *s. f.* beneficence.

bienfaisant, *adj.* charitable, kind; humane.

bienfait, *s.m.* kindness; benefaction.

bientôt, *adv.* soon, shortly; *à* ~*!* so long!

bienveillance, *s.f.* benevolence, kindness.

bienveillant, *adj.* kind(ly), benevolent, charitable.

bienvenu, *adj.* welcome; *soyez le* ~ welcome!

bière, *s.f.* beer.

bifteck, *s. m.* beef-steak.

bijou, *s. m.* *(pl.* -x) jewel.

bijouterie, *s.f.* jewellery; jeweller's shop.

bijoutier, -ière *s. m. f.* jeweller.

bile, *s. f.* bile; *se faire de la* ~ worry, fret.

bille, *s. f.* billiard-ball.

billet, *s. m.* note; ticket; certificate; ~ *d'aller et retour* return ticket; ~ *d'entrée* admission ticket; ~ *de banque* banknote.

billot, *s. m.* block; yoke.

biographe, *s. m. f.* biographer.

biographie, *s. f.* biography.

biologie, *s. f.* biology.

biologiste, biologue, *s. m. f.* biologist.

bis, *int.* encore!

biscuit, *s. m.* biscuit.

bison, *s. m.* bison.

bistro, *s. m.* pub; wineshop.

bizarre, *adj.* strange, odd.

blague, *s.f.* pouch.

blaireau, *s. m.* badger; shaving-brush.

blâme, *s. m.* blame, reprimand.

blâmer, *v. a.* blame; find fault with.

blanc, blanche, *adj.* white; hoary; blank.

blanchir, *v.a.* whiten, bleach; whitewash; *v.n.* turn white, whiten.

blasphème, *s. m.* blasphemy.

blasphémer, *v.a. & n.* blaspheme.

blé, *s. m.* wheat.

blême, *adj.* pale.

blesser, *v. a.* wound, injure, hurt; offend; se ~ wound oneself; be offended.

blessure, *s. f.* wound, injury; offence.

bleu, *adj. & s. m.* blue; ~ *marine* navy blue.

bloc, *s. m.* block; *en* ~ in the lump.

blond, *adj.* fair, blond.

bloquer, *v.a.* blockade; block (up); tighten.

blouse, *s.f.* blouse, smock.

bobine, *s. f.* bobbin, spool.

bœuf, *s. m.* ox, beef.

bohème, *adj.* bohemian.

boire*, *v. a. & n.* drink; swallow; ~ *à la santé de X* drink X's health; — *s. m.* drink(ing).

bois, *s. m.* wood; timber; *de, en* ~ wood(en).

boisson, *s.f.* drink, beverage.

boîte, *s. f.* box, case; can, tin; ~ *aux lettres* letter-box; ~ *de vitesse* gear-box; *en* ~ tinned.

boiteux, -euse *adj.* lame.

bombardement, *s. m.* bombardment.

bombarder, *v. a.* bombard, shell.

bombe, *s. f.* bomb, shell; ~ *H* H-bomb.

bon, bonne, *adj.* good; kind, nice; right; valid; *c'est ~!* (all) right! ~ *à rien* good for nothing; *~ne année!* happy new year!; *de ~ne heure* early; — *s. m.* good(ness); bond, order.

bonbon, *s. m.* bonbon, sweet.

bond, *s. m.* bound, leap.

bondé, *adj.* crowded.

bonder, *v. a.* load, cram.

bondir, *v. n.* bound, leap, spring.

bonheur, *s. m.* happiness; good fortune; success.

bonhomme, *s. m.* good-natured man; simple man; fellow.

bonjour, *s. m.* good morning; salutation.

bonne, *s. f.* maid-servant; ~ *(d'enfants)* nursery-maid.

bonnet, *s. m.* cap, hood.

bonsoir, *s. m.* good evening.

bonté, *s. f.* goodness, kindness, benevolence.

bord, *s. m.* edge, border, brink, (b)rim, verge; side, board, bank; *à ~* on board; *monter à ~* go on board.

border, *v.a.* border, adjoin.

bordure, *s. f.* border, edging; verge; kerb.

borne, *s. f.* milestone; bound(ary), limit.

borner, *v. a.* bound, limit, restrict.

bosse, *s. f.* bump, protuberance; knob.

botanique, *adj.* botanical; — *s. f.* botany.

botte[1], *s. f.* (high) boot.

botte[2], *s. f.* bottle; truss.

bottine, *s. f.* boot.

bouche, *s. f.* mouth; orifice, muzzle.

boucher, *s. m.* butcher.

boucherie, *s. f.* butcher's (shop).

bouchon, *s. m.* plug, cork, stopper.

boue, *s. f.* mud, dirt.

bouger, *v. n.* stir, budge.

bougie, *s.f.* candle. (sparking-)plug.

bouillir*, *v. n. & a.* (also *faire ~*) boil.

bouillon, *s. m.* bubble; stock; ~ *de bœuf* beef-tea.

bouillotte, *s. f.* kettle.

boulanger, -ère, *s. m. f.* baker; baker's wife.

boulangerie, *s. f.* bakery, baker's (shop).

boule, *s. f.* ball, bowl.

boulevard, *s. m.* boulevard.

bouleverser, *v. a.* overthrow, upset; turn upside down; distract.

boulon, *s. m.* bolt, pin.

bouquet, *s. m.* cluster, bunch; bouquet.

bourdonnement, *s.m.* buzz(ing), humming.

bourdonner, *v.n.* buzz, hum, drone.

bourg, *s. m.* (small) town; village.

bourgeois, e, *s. m. f.* citizen; townsman.

bourgeoisie, *s. f.* citizens *(pl.);* middle class.

bourse, *s. f.* purse; exchange; Stock Exchange; scholarship, bursary.

bousculade, *s. f.* hustling.

bousculer, *v. a.* upset, hustle, jostle; *se ~* hustle each other.

bout, *s. m.* end, extremity, tip, top, button; *un ~ de chemin* a short distance.

bouteille, *s. f.* bottle.

boutique, *s.f.* shop; booth, stall.

bouton, *s. m.* button; stud; bud; nipple; knob; ~s *de manchette* cuff-links.

boutonnière, *s. f.* button-hole.

boxer, *v. n.* box, fight.

boxeur, *s.m.* boxer.

bracelet, *s. m.* bracelet.

braconner, *v. n.* poach.

braconnier, *s. m.* poacher.

brancard, *s. m.* stretcher; shaft.

branche, *s.f.* branch.

branler, *v. a.* shake, totter, waver.

bras, *s. m.* arm; hand; branch.

braser, *v.a.* braze, solder

brasserie, *s. f.* brewery; beershop.

brave, *adj.* brave; honest. worthy, good.

braver, *v. a.* face, brave.

bravoure, *s. f.* bravery, courage.

brebis, *s. f.* ewe, sheep.

brèche, *s. f.* breach, gap.

bref, brève, *adj.* brief, short.

bretelles, *s. f. pl.* braces.

brevet, *s. m.* patent; certificate.

bride, *s. f.* bridle, reins.

brièveté, *s. f.* brevity.

brigade, *s.f.* brigade.

brigadier, *s. m.* corporal, overseer.

brigand, *s. m.* brigand, armed robber.

brillant, *adj.* brilliant, shiny, glittering.

briller, *v.n.* shine, glitter, sparkle.

brin, *s. m.* shoot, sprig, blade (of grass).

brioche, *s. f.* brioche.

brique, *s. f.* brick; bar (of soap).

briquet *s. m.* lighter.

briquette, *s. f.* briquette.

brise, *s. f.* breeze.

briser, *v. a.* break (to pieces), smash; *v. n.* break; se ~ break to pieces.

britannique, *adj.* British.

broche, *s. f.* brooch; knitting-needle; spindle spit.

brochure, *s. f.* pamphlet.

broder, *v.a.* embroider.

broderie, *s. f.* embroidery, braid.

bronchite, *s. f.* bronchitis.

bronze, *s. m.* bronze.

brosse, *s. f.* brush; ~ *à barbe* shaving-brush; ~ *à dents* tooth-brush; ~ *à cheveux* hairbrush; *donner un coup de* ~ *a* brush up.

brosser, *v.a.* brush; se ~ brush oneself.

brouillard, *s. m.* mist, fog.

brouille, *s.f.* quarrel.

brouiller, *v.a.* mingle, mix; confuse, embroil; shuffle (cards).

broyer, *v. a.* crush, pound.

bruire, *v.n.* rustle.

bruit, *s. m.* noise, din; fuss; rumour.

brûlant, *adj.* burning, hot, scorching; fiery.

brûler, *v. a. & n.* burn, schorch, roast; ~ *de* long for.

brume, *s. f.* mist, fog.

brumeux, -euse *adj.* foggy.

brun, *adj.* brown.

brusque, *adj.* sudden, curt, gruff.

brutal, *adj.* brutal, rude savage.

brute, *s. f.* brute.

bruyant, *adj.* noisy, loud.

budget, *s. m.* budget.

buffet, *s. m.* sideboard; buffet; refreshment room.

buisson, *s. m.* bush, shrub.

bulbe, *s. m.* bulb.

bulle, *s. f.* bubble; bull.

bulletin, *s.m.* bulletin.

bureau, *s. m.* (writing-) desk; bureau, office; department; board, committee; ~ *de location* box-office; ~ *de poste* post-office; ~ *de tabac* tobacconist's (shop); ~ *central* exchange.

burlesque, *adj.* burlesque, ridiculous; — *s.m.* burlesque.

but, *s. m.* butt, target; goal; aim, object, purpose; scope.

buter, *v.n.* stumble *(contre* against); se ~ grow obstinate.

butin, *s. m.* booty.

butte, *s. f.* hill, mound, knoll.

C

ça, *pron.* that; *comme* ~ in that way; — *adv.* here; — *int.* now then!

cabaret, *s. m.* tavern; wine-shop; night-club, music-hall.

cabine, *s. f.* cabin, berth; cage, car; ~ *téléphonique* call-box.

cabinet, *s. m.* small room; study; water-closet; office; business; cabinet (council); cabinet; ~ *de consultation* consulting room; surgery.

câble, *s. m.* rope, cable.

cabriolet, *s. m.* cabriolet,

cacao, *s. m.* cocoa.

cacher, *v.a.* hide, conceal; se ~ hide oneself.

cadeau, *s. m.* present, gift.

cadet, *adj. & s.m.* younger, junior; cadet.

café, *s. m.* coffee; café, coffee-house; ~ *au lait* white coffee; ~ *concert* music-hall.

cafetière, *s. f.* coffee-pot.

cage, *s.f.* cage; coop; case, crate.

cahier, *s. m.* exercise book.

caillou, *s.m.* pebble, stone.

caisse, *s.f.* box, case; cash(-box), till; cashier's office; drum; *en* ~ in hand.

caissier, -ère, *s.m.f.* cashier.

calcul, *s. m.* calculation, reckoning; arithmetic.

calculateur, *s. m.* calculator, computer.

calculer, *v.a. & n.* calculate, reckon, compute.

caleçon, *s. m.* pants *(pl.);* ~ *de bain* bathing-drawers *(pl.).*

calendrier, *s. m.* calendar.

calme, *adj.* quiet, calm; *fig.* cool; — *s. m.* calm.

calmer, *v. a.* quiet, calm.

calomnier, *v. a.* calumniate, slander.

calorie, *s. f.* calorie.

calorifère, *s. m.* heating apparatus.

calvaire, *s. m.* Calvary.

camarade, *s. m.* comrade, fellow; ~ *d'école* school-friend.

cambrioler, *v. a.* burgle, break into.

cambrioleur, *s.m.* burglar.

caméra, *s. f.* (cine-)camera.

camion, *s. m.* lorry.

camp, *s. m.* camp; side.

campagnard, *s. m.* countryman, peasant.

campagne, *s. f.* country-(side), fields *(pl.);* campaign, expedition.

camper, *v. n.* camp.

camping, *s. m.* camping;
(terrain de) ~ camping site; *matériel de* ~ camping equipment; *faire du* ~ camp.

canal, *s. m.* canal; channel.

canapé, *s. m.* sofa, couch.

canard, *s. m.* duck, drake.

candidature, *s. f.* candidature, candidacy.

canif, *s. m.* penknife.

canne, *s. f.* stick, cane; ~ *à pêche* fishing-rod.

canon, *s. m.* gun, cannon

canot, *s. m.* boat.

cantine, *s. f.* canteen.

canton, *s.m.* canton, district.

cantonade, *s.f.* wings *(pl.); à la* ~ behind the scenes.

caoutchouc, *s.m.* rubber; waterproof, mackintosh.

capable, *adj.* capable, able; efficient; fit.

capacité, *s. f.* capacity, (cap)ability.

capitaine, *s. m.* captain, leader.

capital, *adj.* capital, chief; —*s.m.* main point; capital, fund.

capitale, *s.f.* capital; capital letter.

capitalisme, *s. m.* capitalism.

capituler, *v. n.* capitulate.

caprice, *s. m.* caprice.

capricieux, *adj.* capricious, fickle.

capsule, *s. f.* capsule.

captif, -ive, *adj. & s. m. f.* captive.

captiver, *v. a.* captivate.

capturer, *v. a.* capture.

car, *conj.* for, because.

caractère, *s. m.* character, temper; nature; type, print, letter.

caractériser, *v.a.* characterize, distinguish.

caractéristique, *adj. & s.f.* characteristic.

cardinal, *s.m.* cardinal; — *adj.* chief, cardinal; *points card naux* cardinal points.

caresser, *v.a.* caress, fondle; foster.

caricature, *s. f.* caricature.

carnaval, *s. m.* carnival.

carnet, *s. m.* note-book, pocket-book; book of tickets; ~ *de chèques* cheque-book.

carotte, *s. f.* carrot.

carreau, *s. m.* square; (paving-)tile; tile flooring; pane; diamond.

carrière, *s.f.* career; race-course; race; quarry.

carrosserie, *s.f.* body.

carte, *s.f.* card; map; ticket; bill (of fare); *partie de* ~s game of cards; ~ *postale* postcard; ~ *routière* road-map; ~ *de visite* visiting-card; ~ *marine* chart; ~ *d'entrée* admission ticket; ~ *grise* driving licence; *à la* ~ à la carte.

carton, *s. m.* pasteboard, cardboard; (paper)box.

cas, *s.m.* case; event; instance, fact; *dans le* ~ *où, en* ~ *de* in case; *en tout* ~ in any case.

caserne, *s.f.* barracks *(pl.).*

casquette, *s. f.* cap.

casser, *v. a. & n.* break; crack, snap; annul; dismiss; *se* ~ break, get broken.

casserole, *s. v.* saucepan

casuel, -elle, *adj.* casual,

accidental.

catalogue, *s. m.* catalogue.

catastrophe, *s. f.* catastrophe, disaster.

catégorie, *s. f.* category, class.

cathédrale, *s. f.* cathedral.

catholicisme, *s. m.* catholicism.

catholique, *adj.* catholic.

cause, *s. f.* cause, reason, ground; case; *à ~ de* on account of, owing to.

causer¹, *v. a.* cause.

causer², *v.n.* talk, converse, chat.

cavalerie, *s. f.* cavalry.

cavalier, *s. m.* horseman, cavalier.

cave, *s. f.* cave; cellar.

caverne, *s. f.* cave(rn).

ce¹, c', *pron.* this, it.

ce², cet; cette; *dem. adj.* *(pl.* ces) this *(pl.* these); that *(pl.* those).

ceci, *pron.* this.

céder, *v. a.* give up, yield, cede, make over; *v. n.* yield, give in, up.

ceinture, *s. f.* belt, girdle.

cela, *pron.* that, it; *c'est ~* that's right.

célébration, *s. f.* celebration.

célèbre, *adj.* celebrated.

célébrer, *v. a.* celebrate.

célibataire, *adj.* unmarried, single.

cellule, *s. f.* cell.

celtique, *adj.* Celtic.

celui, celle, *dem. pron.* *(pl.* ceux, celles) he, she, they, those.

celui-ci, celui-là, celle-ci, celle-là, *dem. pron.* *(pl.* ceux-ci, -là, celles-ci, -là) this one, this person, the latter, these ones.

cément, *s. m* cement.

cendre, *s. f.* ash(es).

cendrier, *s. m.* ash-tray.

cent, *adj. & s. m.* hundred; *pour ~* per cent.

centime, *s. m.* centime.

centimètre, *s. m.* centimetre.

central, *adj.* central.

centrale, *s. f. ~ électrique* power-plant, -station.

centre, *s. m.* centre.

cependant, *conj.* however, yet, still, nevertheless; in the meantime; *~ que* while.

céramique, *s. f.* ceramics; — *adj.* ceramic.

cercle, *s. m.* circle, ring; party, club.

cercueil, *s. m.* coffin.

cérémonie, *s. f.* ceremony.

cerf, *s. m.* stag, hart,

cerise, *s. f.* cherry.

certain, *adj.* certain, sure.

certainement, *adv.* certainly, surely.

certificat, *s. m.* certificate, testimonial.

certifier, *v. a.* certify.

certitude, *s. f.* certainty.

cerveau, *s. m.* brain(s).

ces *see* ce²

cesse, *s. f.* ceasing, pause; *sans ~* unceasingly.

cesser, *v. a. & n.* cease, stop; give up; *faire ~* put an end to.

c'est-à-dire, *conj.* that is to say, viz., i.e.

cet *see* ce².

ceux *see* celui.

chacun, *pron.* each, each one, every one; everybody.

chagrin, *s. m.* grief, sorrow, vexation; — *adj.* sad, sorrowful; sorry; gloomy.

chaine, *s. f.* chain; range (of mountains); *~ de*

montage assembly line.

chair, *s. f.* flesh; pulp (of fruit).

chaire, *s. f.* chair; pulpit; seat, see.

chaise, *s. f.* chair.

châle, *s. m.* shawl.

chaleur, *s. f.* heat; fire.

chambre, *s.f.* room; bedroom; chamber; apartment; hall; ~ à *coucher* bedroom; ~ Haute Upper House; ~ *de commerce* chamber of commerce.

chameau, *s.m.* camel.

champ, *s.m.* field, country; *fig.* space, opportunity, theme.

champagne, *s. m.* champagne.

champignon, *s. m.* mushroom.

champion, -onne, *s.m. f.* champion.

championnat, *s. m.* championship.

chance, *s. f.* chance, fortune, risk; luck.

chancelier, *s. m.* chancellor.

chancellerie, *s.f.* chancery.

chandail, *s. m.* sweater, pullover.

chandelle, *s. f.* candle.

change, *s. m.* change, changing; succession; (foreign) exchange, barter; *agent de* ~ stockbroker; *bureau de* ~ exchange office; *lettre de* ~ bill of exchange.

changer, *v. a.* change, alter; exchange; *se* ~ betransformed; change one's clothes.

chanson, *s. f.* song.

chant, *s. m.* singing; song, tune; chant(ing).

chanter, *v. a. & n.* warble; chant; praise.

chanteur, -euse, *s.m.f.* singer

chantier, *s.m.* yard, timber-yard, work-yard.

chapeau. *s.m.* hat; bonnet; cap.

chapelain, *s. m.* chaplain.

chapelle, *s. f.* chapel.

chapitre, *s.m.* chapter; subject, head.

chaque, *adj.* each, every.

charbon, *s. m.* coal; embers *(pl.);* ~ *de bois* charcoal.

charcuterie, *s. f.* pork-butchery.

charcutier, -ière, *s. m. f.* pork-butcher.

charge, *s. f.* load, burden; post, function, charge, office; attack; accusation.

charger, *v. a. & n.* load; burden; charge; entrust.

charité, *s. f.* charity.

charmant, *adj.* charming.

charme, *s. m.* charm.

charpente, *s.f.* timber-work.

charpentier, *s.m.* carpenter.

charrette, *s:f.* cart, wagon.

charrue, *s. f.* plough.

charte, *s. f.* charter.

chasse, *s. f.* chase, hunt-(ing), shooting.

chasser, *v. a. & n.* chase, pursue, hunt, shoot, go shooting; drive out.

chasseur, *s.m.* hunter; page-boy.

chaste, *adj.* chaste, pure.

chat, *s. m.* (he-)cat.

châtaigne, *s. f.* chestnut.

château, *s.m.* castle; palace.

chatte, *s. f.* (she-)cat.

chaud, *adj. & adv.* hot, warm; ardent.

chauffage, *s. m.* heating,

warming; ~ *central*
central heating.

chauffe-bain, *s. m.* geyser.

chauffer, *v. a. & n.* heat,
warm; urge on; coach.

chauffeur, *s. m.* driver.

chausse, *s.f.* hose

chausser, *v. a. & n.* put
on (shoes etc.), wear;
se ~ put on one's
stockings etc.

chaussette, *s. f.* sock.

chaussure, *s. f.* footwear,
shoes *(pl.).*

chauve, *adj.* bald.

chef, *s. f.* chief; ~ *de train*
guard; ~ *d'orchestre*
conductor.

chemin, *s. m.* road, way;
lane; *se mettre en* ~
start; ~ *de fer* railway.

cheminée, *s. f.* chimney.
fireplace, funnel.

chemise, *s. f.* shirt.

chêne, *s. m.* oak(-tree).

chèque, *s. m.* cheque; ~
en blanc blank cheque;
~ *de voyage* traveller's
cheque.

cher, chère, *adj.* dear.

chercher, *v. a.* seek, look
for, search for.

chéri, -e, *adj.* dear; —
s. m. f. darling.

cheval, *s. m.* horse; *à*
~ on horseback; *monter*
à ~ ride.

chevalerie, *s. f.* chivalry.

chevalier, *s. m.* knight.

chevelure, *s. f.* hair.

cheveu, *s. m.* hair; *en* ~
bareheaded.

cheville, *s.f.* wooden pin,
peg; ankle.

chèvre, *s.f.* (she-)goat.

chevreau, *s.m.* kid-
(leather).

chez, *prep.* at, in, at the
house of; ~ *X* at X's.

chic, *adj.* smart, spruce,
fashionable; — *s. m.*
chic; trick; elegance.

chien, -enne, *s. m. f.* dog.

chiffon, *s. m.* rag, scrap;
chiffon.

chiffre, *s. m.* figure, digit;
number.

chignon, *s.m.* knot (of
hair), bun.

chimie, *s.f.* chemistry.

chimique, *adj.* chemical.

chimiste, *s. m. f.* chemist.

chinois, -e (Ch.), *adj &*
s.m.f. Chinese.

chirurgie, *s. f.* surgery.

chirurgien, -enne, *s.m.f.*
surgeon.

choc, *s.m.* shock, clash,
collision.

chocolat, *s. m.* chocolate.

chœur, *s. m.* chorus; choir.

choisir, *v.a.* choose, pick
out, select.

choix, *s. m.* choice.

chômage, *s. m.* stoppage,
cessation of work;
unemployment.

choquer, *v. a.* run into,
strike against, collide
with; shock, offend;
se ~ come into colli-
sion; be shocked.

chose, *s. f.* thing, object,
matter; goods; event;
quelque ~ something,
anything.

chou, *s. m.* cabbage, cole.

chou-fleur, *s. m.* cauliflower.

chrétien, -enne, *adj. & s.m.*
f. Christian.

christianisme, *s.m.* Christianity.

chronique, *adj.* chronic;
— *s. f.* chronicle.

chuchoter, *v.n.&a.*
whisper.

chute, *s. f.* fall, down-
fall, descent; slope.

ci, *adv.* here.

ci-dessous, *adv.* below,
underneath.

ci-dessus, *adv.* above;
aforesaid.

cidre, *s. m.* cider.

ciel, *s. m. (pl.* **cieux)** heaven; sky; weather; climate.

cierge, *s. m.* wax candle.

cigare, *s. m.* cigar.

cigarette, *s. f.* cigarette.

cigogne, *s. f.* stork.

cil, *s. m.* eyelash.

cime, *s. f.* top, summit.

ciment, *s. m.* cement.

cimetière, *s. m.* cemetery; churchyard.

cinéma, *s. m.* cinema.

cinérama, *s. m.* cinerama.

cinq, *adj. & s. m.* five; fifth.

cinquante, *adj. & s. m.* fifty; fiftieth.

circonstance, *s.f.* circumstance; occurrence, occasion, event.

circuit, *s. m.* circuit.

circulation, *s. f.* circulation; currency; traffic.

circuler, *v. n.* circulate; *circulez!* move on!

cire, *s. f.* wax.

cirer, *v. a.* wax; polish.

ciseau, *s.m.* chisel.

ciseaux, *s. m. pl.* scissors.

citation, *s.f.* citation.

cité, *s. f.* city, town.

citer, *v.a.* cite; quote.

citoyen, **-enne,** *s.m.f.* citizen.

citron, *s. m.* lemon.

citronnade, *s.f.* lemon squash.

civil, *adj.* civil; — *s. m.* civilian.

civilisation, *s. f.* civilization, culture.

clair, *adj.* light, clear.

clapet, *s. m.* valve.

claquement, *s. m.* clap-(ping); snap.

claquer, *v. n. a.* crack, clap; chatter; bang,

clarté, *s. f.* light, brightness; clearness.

classe, *s. f.* class; order, rank; form, class-room.

classer, *v.a.* class, rank.

classifier, *v.a.* classify.

classique, *adj.* classic(al).

clause, *s. f.* clause.

clé, clef, *s. f.* key; spanner, wrench; *fig.* clue; ~ *de contact* ignition key.

clerc, *s. m.* clerk; scholar.

clergé, *s. m.* clergy.

clérical, *adj.* clerical.

client, *s. m.* client, customer, patron.

clientèle, *s. f.* clients *(pl.).*

cligner, *v. a. & n.* wink.

clignotant, *s. m.* indicator.

clignoter, *v.a.&n.* blink, wink.

climat, *s. m.* climate.

clinique, *adj. & s.f.* clinic, clinical.

cloche, *s. f.* bell.

cloître, *s. m.* cloister.

clore*, *v. a.* shut, close.

clos, *adj.* closed.

clôture, *s. f.* enclosure, fence; close.

clou, *s. m.* nail, stud; boil, furuncle.

clouer, *v. a.* nail (down).

club, *s. m.* club.

cocher, *s. m.* coachman, driver.

cochon, *s. m.* pig, swine.

code, *s. m.* code; law, rule.

cœur, *s. m.* heart; *fig.* mind, soul, courage; *par* ~ by heart.

coffre, *s. m.* chest.

coffre-fort, *s. m.* safe.

cognac, *s. m.* cognac.

cogner, *v. n. & a.* beat, knock, strike; **se** ~ knock against.

coiffer, *v. a.* put on (hat); dress, do s.o.'s hair.

coiffeur, **-euse,** *s.m.f.* hairdresser.

coiffure, *s. f.* head-dress, cap; hair-do; *salon de* ~ hairdresser.

coin, *s. m.* corner; angle.

coïncider, *v.n.* coincide.

coke, *s.m.* coke.

col, *s.m.* collar; neck.

colère, *s.f.* anger.

colis, *s.m.* parcel; item (of luggage).

collaborateur, -trice, *s. m. f.* fellow worker; collaborator.

collaborer, *v.n.* work jointly, collaborate.

collectif, -ive, *adj.* collective.

collection, *s. f.* collection.

collège, *s.m.* college; grammar school.

collègue, *s.m.f.* colleague, fellow worker.

coller, *v.a.* stick, paste.

collet, *s.m.* collar; neck.

collier, *s.m.* necklace; collar.

colline, *s.f.* hill.

collision, *s.f.* collision; *entrer en* ~ collide.

colombe, *s. f.* dove.

colonel, *s.m.* colonel.

colonie, *s. f.* colony; dominion.

colonne, *s.f.* column.

coloré, *adj.* coloured; colourful.

colossal, *adj.* colossal.

combat, *s.m.* fight, combat.

combattre, *v.a.&n.* fight (against), combat (with).

combien, *adv.* (~ *de*) how much, how many, how far; ~ *de temps?* how long?

combinaison, *s.f.* combination.

combiner, *v.a.* combine, unite; contrive, devise.

comédie, *s.f.* comedy.

comédien, *s.m.* comedian, actor.

comestible, *adj.* edible.

comique, *adj.* comic; — *s. m.* comic actor.

comité, *s. m.* committee.

commandant, *s. m.* commander.

commande, *s.f.* order.

commandement, *s. m.* command, order; commandment.

commander, *v. a.* command, order; control.

comme, *adv. & conj.* as, like; as . . . as; while; ~ *il faut* decent, proper; *tout* ~ just like; ~ *si* as if, as though.

commémorer, *v.a.* commemorate.

commençant, -e, *s. m. f.* beginner; — *adj.* beginning.

commencement, *s.m.* beginning.

commencer, *v. a. & n.* begin, commence.

comment, *adv.* how, in what manner; why; ~ *allez-vous?* how are you?; ~ *(dites-vous)?* (I beg your) pardon?

commentaire, *s. m.* comment; commentary.

commenter, *v. a.* comment (on); criticize.

commerçant, -e, *s. m. f.* merchant, dealer.

commerce, *s. m.* commerce, trade; *voyageur de* ~ commercial traveller; ~ *de gros* wholesale trade; *faire le* ~ trade.

commercer, *v. n.* trade, deal with, in.

commercial, *adj.* commercial.

commettre, *v. a.* commit; *se* ~ commit oneself.

commis, *s.m.* clerk, employee.

commissaire, *s.m.* commisary; commissioner.

commissariat, *s.m.* police-station.

commission, *s. f.* commission; charge; committee; errand.

commode, *adj.* convenient, handy, comfortable; — *s. f.* chest of drawers.

commun, *adj.* common; joint; usual; vulgar; *peu ~* unusual; — *s.m.* common people.

communauté, *s. f.* community.

commune, *s. f.* district.

communication, *s. f.* communication, message; call.

communier, *v. n.* communicate.

communion, *s.f.* communion.

communiqué, *s. m.* communiquè.

communiquer, *v. a. & n.* communicate.

compact, *adj.* compact.

compagnie, *s.f.* company.

compagnon, *s. m.* companion, fellow.

comparaison, *s. f.* comparison.

comparer, *v. a.* compare.

compartiment, *s. m.* compartment; *~ de fumeurs* smoking compartment; *~ pour non-fumeurs* non-smoker.

compas, *s.m.* compass-(es).

compatriote, *s. m. f.* compartiot, (fellow) countryman.

compensation, *s. f.* compensation.

compenser, *v.a.&n.* com-

pensate.

compétent, *adj.* competent.

compétiteur, -trice, *s. m. f.* competitor.

compétition, *s. f.* competition.

compilation, *s. f.* compilation.

compiler, *v. a.* compile.

complainte, *s.f.* complaint.

complaisance, *s. f.* complaisance, kindness.

complaisant, *adj.* complaisant, obliging, kind.

complément, *s. m.* complement; object.

complémentaire, *adj.* complementary.

complet, -ète, *adj.* complete, full.

compléter, *v.a.* complete.

complexe, *adj.* complex, compound.

complication, *s. f.* complication.

compliment, *s. m.* compliment; congratulation.

compliquer, *v.a.* complicate.

comploter, *v.a.* plot.

composant, -e, *adj. & s. f.* component.

composer, *v. a.* compose, *se ~ de* be composed of, consist of.

compositeur, -trice ,*s. m. f.* composer.

composition, *s. f.* composition; paper.

comprendre, *v. a.* comprehend; unterstand.

comprimé, -e, *adj.* pressed; — *s. m.* tablet.

compromettre, *v. a.* compromise, commit; *se ~* commit oneself.

compromis, *s. m.* compromise.

comptabilité, *s. f.* book-keeping, accounts *(pl.)*

compte, *s.m.* account; amount, sum; ~ *courant* current account; *faire le* ~ *de* count; *régler un* ~ settle an account; ~ *rendu* report, account, statement; review; *tenir* ~ *de* take into account.

compter, *v. a. & n.* count, reckon, calculate.

comptoir, *s. m.* counter.

computer, *v. a.* compute.

comte, *s. m.* count.

comtesse, *s. f.* countess.

concéder, *v. a.* grant.

concentration, *s. f.* concentration; reduction.

concentrer, *v. a.* condense, concentrate.

concept, -tion, *s. m. f.* concept(ion), idea.

concernant, *prep.* concerning.

concerner, *v. a.* concern, relate to.

concert, *s. m.* concert.

concevoir*, *v. a. & n.* conceive; think; imagine; apprehend.

concierge, *s. f. m.* porter.

concile, *s. m.* council.

concis, *adj.* concise.

conclure*, *v.a.&n.* conclude, end.

conclusion, *s.f.* conclusion, end.

concombre, *s. m.* cucumber.

concorder, *v.n.* agree.

concourir, *v. n.* contribute, concur; compte.

concours, *s. m.* concourse; help; assistance; competition.

concret, -ète, *adj.* concrete.

concurrence, *s. f.* competition; rivalry.

concurrent, *s. m.* competitor; rival.

condamnation, *s. f.* condemnation; sentence.

condamner, *v.a.* condemn, sentence.

condenser, *v. a.* condense.

condition, *s. f.* condition, state; service; stipulation, condition; *à* ~ *que* on condition that, provided that.

conditionnel, *adj.* conditional.

conditionnement, *s.m.* ~ *de l'air* air-conditioning.

conducteur, -trice, *s. m. f.* conductor; driver.

conduire*, *v. a. & n.* conduct, lead; drive; show (to), take (to); manage; *permis de* ~ driving licence.

conduit, *s. m.* pipe, tube.

conduite, *s. f.* conducting, leading; driving; behaviour, conduct.

cône, *s. m.* cone.

confection, *s. f.* ready-made clothes *(pl.)*.

confédération, *s. f.* confederation, confederacy.

conférence, *s. f.* comparison; conference; lecture; *maître de* ~s lecturer; *faire une* ~ deliver a lecture.

conférencier, -ère, *s. m. f.* lecturer.

conférer, *v.a.* grant, confer, bestow; compare.

confesser, *v.a.* confess.

confession, *s. f.* confession.

confiance, *s. f.* confidence, trust, reliance; *avoir* ~ count on, trust.

confiant, *adj.* confident.

confidence, *s. f.* confidence.

confidentiel, -elle *adj.*

confidential.

confier, *v.a.* trust; entrust, give in charge.

confinement, *s. m.* imprisonment.

confiner, *v. n. & a.* confine.

confirmation, *s.f.* confirmation.

confirmer, *v.a.* confirm.

confiserie, *s.f.* confectionery, sweet-shop.

confiture, *s.f.* jam, preserve.

conflit, *s. m.* conflict.

confondre, *v. a.* confound.

conformer, *v. a.* conform, adapt; se ~ *à* conform oneself (to).

confort, *s.m.* comfort, ease.

confortable, *adj.* comfortable.

confrère, *s.m.* fellow-worker, colleague.

confronter, *v. a.* confront, compare.

confus, *adj.* confused.

confusion, *s. f.* confusion.

congé, *s. m.* leave, holiday; permission; discharge; warning, notice; *donner* ~ give notice (to); dismiss; *prendre* ~ *de* take leave of; *être en* ~ be on holiday.

congédier, *v. a.* dismiss.

congratulation, *s. f.* congratulation.

congrès, *s.m.* congress, assembly.

conjecture, *s.f.* conjecture.

conjecturer, *v.a.&n.* conjecture, guess.

conjonction, *s.f.* conjunction, union.

connaissance, *s. f.* knowledge; acquaintance; *faire* ~ *avec* get acquainted with.

connaître*, *v.a.* know, understand; be acquainted with.

connexion, *s.f.* connection.

conquérir*, *v. a. & n.* conquer; win (over).

conscience, *s.f.* consciousness; conscience; *avoir la* ~ *de* be conscious of, be aware of.

conscient, *adj.* conscious.

conscrit, *s. m.* conscript.

conseil, *s. m.* counsel, advice; adviser; council, board, staff.

conseiller[1], -**ère**, *s. m. f.* counsellor, councillor.

conseiller[2], *v. a.&n.* advise, counsel.

consentir, *v. n.* consent, agree (*à* to).

conséquence, *s. f.* consequence, result.

conséquent, *adj.* consistent; *par* ~ consequently.

conservatoire, *s. m.* conservatory.

conserver, *v.a.* keep, preserve; tin.

considérable, *adj.* considerable.

considération, *s. f.* consideration; esteem.

considérer, *v. a.* consider; esteem.

consigne, *s. f.* cloak-room, left-luggage office.

consigner, *v.a.* deposit.

consister, *v.n.* consist (of), be made (of).

consoler, *v.a.* console.

consommateur, -**trice**, *s. m. f.* consumer, customer.

consommer, *v.a.* consummate; consume.

consomption, *s.f.* consumption.

consonne, *s. f.* consonant.

conspiration, *s.f.* conspiracy.

conspirer, *v. a. & n.* conspire, plot.

constant, *adj.* constant, firm.

constipation, *s.f.* constipation.

constituer, *v. a.* constitute, compose.

constitution, *s. f.* constitution.

constitutionnel, -elle, *adj.* constitutional.

constructeur, *s. m.* builder.

construction, *s.f.* construction, building.

construire*, *v.a.* build, construct.

consul, *s. m.* consul.

consulat, *s. m.* consulate.

consulter, *v.a.* consult.

consumer, *v. a.* consume.

contact, *s.m.* contact, touch, switch.

contaminer, *v. a.* contaminate.

conte, *s.m.* story, tale.

contemplation, *s.f.* contemplation.

contempler, *v.a. & n.* contemplate.

contemporain, -e, *adj. & s. m. f.* contemporary.

contenance, *s. f.* capacity, contents *(pl.)*.

contenir, *v.a.* contain, hold; restrain; **se ~** restrain oneself.

content, *adj.* content.

contentement, *s. m.* content, satisfaction.

contenter, *v.a.* content, satisfy; **se ~** be contented, do with.

contenu, *s.m.* contents *(pl.)*.

conter, *v.a. & n.* tell, relate.

continent, *s. m.* continent.

continental, *adj.* continental.

continuation, *s.f.* con-

tinuation, continuance.

continuel, -elle, *adj.* continual.

continuer, *v.a. & n.* go on (with), keep on; **se ~** be continued.

contour, *s.m.* contour, outline.

contracter, *v. a.* contract, bargain for.

contradiction, *s. f.* contradiction.

contraindre*, *v. a.* compel, force; **se ~** restrain oneself.

contrainte, *s.f.* constraint.

contraire, *adj. & s. m.* contrary; *au ~* on the contrary.

contrairement, *adv.* **~** *à* contrary to.

contraste, *s. m.* contrast.

contraster, *v. n.* contrast *(avec* with).

contrat, *s.m.* contract.

contre, *prep.* against.

contrée, *s.f.* country.

contrefaçon, *s. f.* counterfeit(ing); forgery.

contrefaire, *v. a.* counterfeit; pirate; forge.

contre-partie, *s. f.* counterpart.

contresigner, *v. a.* countersign.

contribuant, *s. m.* contributor.

contribuer, *v. n.* contribute *(à* to).

contribution, *s.f.* contribution, tax.

contrôle, *s.m.* control, check; hall-mark.

contrôler, *v.a.* control, check.

contrôleur, *s. m.* ticket-collector.

contusion, *s. f.* bruise.

convaincre, *v.a.* convince.

convenable, *adj.* suitable, appropriate.

convenance, *s.f.* suit-ability, convenience.
convenir, *v.n.* suit, be convenient (to), fit.
conventionnel, -elle, *adj.* conventional.
conversation, *s.f.* conversation, talk.
converser, *v. n.* converse.
convertir, *v.a.* convert.
conviction, *s. f.* conviction.
convier, *v.a.* invite.
convive, *s.m.* guest.
convoi, *s.m.* convoy; funeral procession.
convoquer *v.a.* convoke.
coopération, *s. f.* co-operation.
coopérer, *v. n.* co-operate.
copie, *s. f.* (fair) copy.
copier, *v.a.* copy.
coq, *s. m.* cock.
coquille, *s. f.* shell.
coquin, *s.m.* rogue.
corail, *s.m.* coral.
corbeau, *s. m.* raven.
corbeille, *s. f.* basket.
corde, *s.f.* cord, rope.
cordial, *adj.* cordial.
cordonnier, *s.m.* shoe-maker.
corne, *s. f.* horn; hooter.
corneille, *s. f.* crow, rook.
cornet, *s. m.* horn; cornet.
cornichon, *s. m.* gherkin.
corporation, *s. f.* corporation.
corps, *s. m.* body, corpse; corporation, corps.
correct, *adj.* correct.
correction, *s. f.* correction.
correspondance, *s. f.* correspondence; relation; communication; connection.
correspondant, *adj.* corresponding.
correspondre, *v. n.* correspond; communicate.
corriger, *v.a.* correct.

corrompre, *v.a.* corrupt, spoil; se ~ become corrupted.
corruption, *s. f.* corruption.
corset, *s. m.* stays *(pl.)*.
cortège, *s. m.* escort.
cosmétique, *adj.* cosmetic; — *s. m.* ~s cosmetics.
cosmonaute, *s. m.* cosmonaut, spacemen.
costume, *s. m.* dress, costume; ~ de bain(s) bathing-costume.
côte, *s. f.* rib; slope; shore.
côté, *s. m.* side, part; à ~ by the side; de ~ on one side; d'un ~ on the one hand; de l'autre ~ on the other hand; passer à ~ pass by; à ~ de next (door) to; beside.
côtelette, *s. f.* chop.
coton, *s. m.* cotton.
cottage, *s. m.* cottage.
cou, *s. m.* neck.
couche, *s. f.* bed; napkin, diaper; coat; layer; *(pl.)* confinement.
coucher, *v. a.* put to bed; lay; *v.n.* lie down; sleep; *être couché* lie; se ~ go to bed, lie down; — *s. m.* bedtime; setting.
couchette, *s.f.* berth, bunk; napkin.
coude, *s. m.* elbow; angle, bend.
coudre*, *v. a. & n.* sew.
couler, *v.n.* flow, run, stream; leak; sink.
couleur, *s. f.* colour.
coulisse, *s. f.* groove; slip, wings *(pl.)*; dans les ~s behind the scenes.
couloir, *s.m.* passage; corridor; lobby.
coup, *s. m.* blow, stroke, knock; smack; pull;

kick; shot; draught; cast, move; *d'un seul* ~ at once; ~ *de feu* rush hours *(pl.); de froid* chill; ~ *de main* sudden attack; ~ *d'œil* glance, look; ~ *de soleil* sunstroke.

coupe, *s.f.* wine-cup.

couper, *v.a.* cut; cut down, off, up; divide; cross; mix; se ~ cut oneself, cut one's (finger etc.).

couple, *s. f.* pair, brace; *m.* couple.

cour, *s. f.* (court)yard; court; courting, courtship; *faire la* ~ *à* court, make love to.

courage, *s. m.* courage.

courageux, -euse, *adj.* courageous, brave.

courant, *adj.* current; running; — *s.m.* current; stream; course run; ~ *d'air* draught.

courbe, *s. f.* curve, bend.

courbé, *adj.* curved; bent.

courber, *v. a. & n.* bend, bow; se ~ bend, be bent; bow.

courir*, *v. n.* run; hurry; flow; be curent.

couronne, *s.f.* crown.

couronner, *v.a.* crown.

courrier, *s. m.* messenger, courier, post, mail.

cours, *s. m.* course; current, flow; currency.

course, *s. f.* race, run; course; drive.

court, *adj.* short, brief; — *adv.* short; suddenly; — *s. m.* tennis-court.

courtiser, *v. a.* pay court to, court.

courtois, *adj.* courteous, polite.

courtoisie, *s. f.* courtesy.

cousin, -e *s. m. f.* cousin.

coussin, *s.m.* cushion.

coût, *s.m.* cost, price.

couteau, *s.m.* knife.

coûter, *v. n. & a.* cost.

coûteux, -euse, *adj.* costly, expensive, dear; *peu* ~ inexpensive.

coutume, *s.f.* custom, habit; *de* ~ customary.

couture, *s.f.* sewing, seam; needlework; scar.

couturière, *s.m.* dressmaker.

couvent, *s.m.* convent.

couver, *v.a.* brood (on), sit; hatch, breed.

couvercle, *s. m.* cover, lid, cap.

couvert, *adj.* covered; covert, sheltered; cloudy; secret; —

s.m. set (of fork and spoon); cover; protection; *mettre le* ~ lay the table.

couverture, *s. f.* cover-(ing); blanket; ~s bedclothes.

couvrir*, *v.a.* cover; load; protect; be sufficent for.

crabe, *s. m.* crab.

cracher, *v.n. & a.* spit.

craie, *s. f.* chalk.

craindre, *v.a.* fear, be afraid of.

crainte, *s. f.* fear; *de* ~ *de* for fear of; *de* ~ *que* lest.

crampe, *s.f.* cramp.

crampon, *s.m.* cramp.

crâne, *s. m.* skull; — *adj.* bold.

craquer, *v.n.* crack.

cravate, *s. f.* (neck)tie.

crayon, *s. m.* pencil; crayon.

créance, *s. f.* credence, belief, trust.

créancier, -ère, *s. m. f.* creditor.

création, *s. f.* creation.

créature, *s. f.* creature.

crèche, *s. f.* crèche.
crédit, *s. m.* credit; *à ~* on credit.
créditer, *v.a.* credit.
crediteur, *s.m.* creditor.
créer, *v.a.* create, make.
crème, *s. f.* cream, custard; *~ à raser* shaving cream.
crémerie, *s. f.* dairy.
crêpe, *s. m.* crape, crêpe.
creuser, *v. a.* dig; deepen.
creux, *-euse*, *adj.* hollow, empty; *— s. m.* hollow.
crevaison, *s. f.* puncture.
crever, *v. a. & n.* burst; puncture; die.
cri, *s. m.* cry, scream; call, shout.
crible, *s.m.* sieve, screen.
cric, *s. m.* jack.
crier, *v.a. & n.* cry (out).
crime, *s. m.* crime, guilt.
criminel, *-elle*, *adj. & s. m. f.* criminal.
crise, *s. f.* crisis.
crisper, *v.a.* contract, shrivel.
cristal, *s. m.* crystal.
critique, *adj.* critical; *— s.f.* criticism, critique; *s.m.f.* critic, reviewer.
crochet, *s. m.* hook; crochet(-work); hanger.
croire*, *v. a. & n.* believe, credit, trust; think.
croiser, *v.a.* cross; *v.n.* cruise.
croître*, *v.n.* grow, increase; grow up; *v.a.* increase.
croix, *s. f.* cross.
croquis, *s.m.* sketch.
crouler, *v. n.* fall (to pieces), fall in.
croûte, *s. f.* crust; *casser la ~* have a snack.
croyance, *s.f.* belief, faith; creed.
croyant, *-e*, *s. m. f.* believer; *— adj.* faithful.

cru, *adj.* raw; crude.
cruauté, *s. f.* cruelty.
crue, *s. f.* rise, growth.
cruel, *-elle*, *adj.* cruel.
crypte, *s. f.* crypte.
cube, *s. m.* cube.
cueillir*, *v.a.* gather, pick, glean.
cuiller, *-ère*, *s. f.* spoon; *~ à pot* ladle; *~ a café* teaspoon.
cuir, *s. m.* skin; leather.
cuire*, *v. a. & n.* cook; boil; roast; burn; *faire trop ~* overdo.
cuisine, *s. f.* kitchen; cooking, cookery; *batterie de ~* kitchen utensils; *de ~* culinary; *livre de ~* cookery-book.
cuisinière, *s.f.* cook; kitchen range, cooker.
cuisse, *s. f.* thigh; leg.
cuit, *adj.* cooked, baked.
cuivre, *s. m.* copper.
cul, *s. m.* bottom.
culinaire, *adj.* culinary.
culotte, *s. f.* panties; breeches *(pl.)*.
culte, *s. m.* cult, worship.
cultivateur, *-trice*, *s. m. f.* farmer.
cultiver, *v.a.* cultivate, till; *fig.* improve.
culture, *s.f.* culture.
culturel, *-elle*, *adj.* cultural.
cure, *s. f.* care; cure.
curé, *s. m.* priest; vicar.
cure-dent, *s. m.* toothpick.
curieux, *-euse*, *adj.* curious, strange, inquisitive.
curiosité, *s. f.* curiosity; *~s* sights.
cuve, *s. f.* tub, vat.
cuvette, *s. f.* *~ (de lavabo)* wash-basin.
cycle, *s. m.* cycle.
cygne, *s. m.* swan.

cylindre, *s. m.* cylinder.

D

dactylo(graphe), *s. m. f.* typist.

dame, *s.f.* lady; queen.

danger, *s. m.* danger.

dangereux, -euse, *adj.* dangerous.

danois, -e (D.), *adj. & s. m. f.* Dane, Danish.

dans, *prep.* in, into; inside; during; ~ *le temps* formerly.

danse, *s. f.* dance.

danser, *v. n.* dance.

danseur, *s. m.* dancer.

danseuse: *s. f.* ballet-girl, dancer.

date, *s.f.* date; *prendre* ~ fix a day.

dater, *v. a. & n.* date.

datte, *s. f.* date.

davantage, *adv.* more, further; *bien* ~ much more; *pas* ~ no more; *en* ~ some more.

de, *prep.* of, from, out of, on account of.

dé, *s. m.* thimble.

déballer, *v. a.* unpack.

débarquer, *v. a. & n.* land, disembark, arrive.

débarrasser, *v. a.* clear (up), rid, free; *se* ~ get rid (of).

débat, *s. m.* debate.

débattre, *v. a. & n.* debate.

débit, *s. m.* sale; debit; output; utterance; ~ *de tabac* tobbaconist's shop.

déborder, *v. n. & a.* overflow, run over.

débouché, *s. m.* outlet, issue.

déboucher, *v. a.* uncork, open; *v. n.* run into.

débourser, *v. a.* disburse.

debout, *adv.* upright, standing; *être* ~ stand.

début, *s.m.* start, outset; first appearance.

débuter, *v. n.* begin, start; make one's first appearance.

décadence, *s.f.* decadence.

décagramme, *s.m.* decagramme.

décéder, *v.n.* die, decease.

décembre, *s. m.* December.

déception, *s. f.* deception, deceit; disappointment.

décharge, *s. f.* discharge; outlet.

décharger, *v.a.* unload, unburden; release; discharge; *se* ~ unburden oneself.

déchausser, *v.a.* take off (shoes).

déchéance, *s.f.* decadence, decay; decline.

déchiffrer, *v.a.* decipher; make out.

déchirer, *v.a.* tear, rend.

dechoir*, *v.n.* fall off, decay.

décider, *v. a. & n.* decide, settle; *se* ~ make up one's mind; be settled.

décilitre, *s. m.* decilitre.

décimal, -e, *adj. & s. f.* decimal.

décimètre, *s.m.* decimetre.

décisif, -ive, *adj.* decisive, final.

décision, *s.f.* decision.

déclaration, *s.f.* declaration, statement.

déclarer, *v.a.* declare, state; *se* ~ declare itself.

décliner, *v.n.* decline.

décolletage, *s.m.* low neck.

décolleter, *v.a.* cut low

turn; *tour* *a* ~ turning lathe.

décomposer, *v. a.* decompose; spoil; **se** ~ decompose.

décomposition, *s. f.* decomposition.

décompte, *s. m.* discount; particulars *(pl.)*.

décor, *s. m.* decoration; scene, environment; scenery.

décoratif, -ive, *adj.* decorative.

décorer, *v.a.* decorate; trim.

découper, *v.a.* cut out, carve.

décourager, *v.a.* discourage

découverte, *s. f.* discovery.

découvrir*, *v. a.* discover, find out; uncover; **se** ~ uncover oneself, disclose oneself.

décret, *s. m.* decree, order.

décrier, *v.a.* cry down.

décrire, *v.a.* describe.

décrocher, *v.a.* unhook, take down.

décroissance, *s. m.* decrease.

décroître, *v. n.* decrease.

déçu, *adj.* disappointed.

dédain, *s.m.* disdain, scorn.

dedans, *adv.* within, inside; indoors, at home.

dédicace, *s. f.* dedication.

dédier, *v.a.* dedicate.

déduire*, *v.a.* deduct.

défaire, *v. a.* undo; break; unfasten; take off; defeat; **se** ~ come undone.

défaite, *s. f.* defeat

défaut, *s. m.* defect, deficiency, want; fault; flaw; *à* ~ *de* for want of; *sans* ~ faultless.

défavorable, *adj.* unfavourable.

défendre, *v.a.* defend; forbid; **se** ~ defend oneself.

défense, *s.f.* defence, protection; prohibition; tusk; *se mettre en* ~ stand on one's guard.

défiance, *s.f.* distrust, mistrust.

défier, *v. a.* defy.

défigurer, *v. a.* disfigure, deface, spoil.

défiler, *v. n.* defile.

défini, *adj.* definite.

définir, *v. a.* define.

définitif, -ive, *adj.* definitive, final.

définition, *s. f.* definition.

défunt, -e, *adj. & s. m. f.* deceased, defunct.

dégager, *v. a.* redeem, release, disengage; emit.

dégorger, *v.a.* disgorge, discharge; *v.n.* discharge, overflow.

dégoût, *s. m.* disgust.

dégoûtant, *adj.* disgusting.

dégoûter, *v.a.* disgust; **se** ~ get tired of.

dégradation, *s. f.* degradation.

dégrader, *v.a.* degrade; damage.

degré, *s. m.* degree.

déguisement, *s.m.* disguise.

déguiser, *v.a.* disguise, hide.

dehors, *adv.* out, outside, out of doors; *au* ~ outside, abroad; *en* ~ *de* outside of, apart from.

déjà, *adv.* already; previously.

déjeuner, *s. m.* lunch(eon); *petit* ~ breakfast; — *v.n.* have breakfast; take lunch.

delà, *prep.* beyond; *au ~ de* beyond.

délai, *s. m.* delay; *à bref ~* at short notice.

délégation, *s. f.* delegation.

déléguer, *v. a.* delegate.

délibération, *s. f.* deliberation, resolution; *en ~* under consideration.

délibérer, *v. n.* deliberate, ponder; *v.a.* bring under discussion.

délicat, *adj.* delicate; feeble; fastidious, dainty.

délicatesse, *s. f.* delicacy; delicateness; daintiness.

délice, *s. m.* delight.

délicieux, **-euse**, *adj.* delicious, delightful.

délier, *v. a.* untie; loosen.

délivrance, *s. f.* deliverance.

délivrer, *v.a.* deliver, (set) free.

déloyal, *adj.* disloyal, unfair.

demain, *adv.* tomorrow.

demande, *s.f.* request, application, inquiry, call, request, demand.

demander, *v.a.* ask, inquire (after); beg, demand; request, require; *se ~* wonder.

démanger, *v.n.* itch.

démarche, *s. f.* walk, gait; proceeding.

démasquer, *v. a.* unmask.

déménagement, *s. m.* removal, moving.

déménager, *v.n.&a.* move (house); remove.

démesuré, *adj.* immoderate, excessive.

demeure, *s.f.* delay; home, dwelling.

demeurer, *v.n.* live; stay.

demi, -e, *adj.* half; *à ~* by half; *une heure et ~e* half past one; an hour and a half; — *s. f.* half-hour.

demi-cercle, *s. m.* semi-circle.

demi-heure, *s. f.* half an hour.

demi-jour, *s. m.* twilight.

démobiliser, *v.a.* demobilize.

démocratie, *s. f.* democracy.

démocratique, *adj.* democratic.

démodé, *adj.* old-fashioned.

demoiselle, *s.f.* young lady, miss.

démolir, *v. a.* demolish, pull down.

démon, *s. m.* demon.

démonstratif, **-ive**, *adj.* demonstrative.

démonstration, *s.f.* demonstration.

démontrer, *v. a.* demonstrate.

dénaturé, *adj.* unnatural.

dénombrer, *v. a.* number.

dénomination, *s. f.* denomination.

dénoncer, *v. a.* denounce.

dénoter, *v. a.* denote; indicate.

dense, *adj.* dense, compact.

densité, *s. f.* density.

dent, *s. f.* tooth; *mal de ~s* toothache.

dental, *adj.* dental.

dentelle, *s. f.* lace.

dentier, *s. m.* set of (false) teeth, denture.

dentifrice, *s. m.* *pâte ~* tooth-paste.

dentiste, *s. m. f.* dentist.

dénué, *adj.* destitute.

dénuement, *s. m.* destitution.

départ, *s. m.* departure.

département, *s. m.* department; territory.

départir, *v. a.* grant, allot; se ~ give up

dépasser, *v. a. & n.* pass, exceed, go beyond.

dépêche, *s. f.* despatch, wire, telegram.

dépêcher, *v. a.* dispatch; *v. n. &* se ~ hurry.

dépendance, *s. f.* dependance.

dépendant, -e, *adj.* dependent; — *s. m. f.* dependant.

dépendre, *v. n.* depend.

dépense, *s. f.* expense; larder.

dépenser, *v. a. & n.* spend; waste.

dépit, *s. m.* spite; *en* ~ *de* in spite of.

déplacement, *s. m.* displacement; shift.

déplacer, *v.a.* displace, move, shift; se ~ move.

déplaire, *v.n.* displease.

déplier, *v.a.* unfold, lay out.

déplorer, *v. a.* deplore.

déportation, *s. f.* transportation, deportation.

déposer, *v. a.* put down, set down; deposit; — se ~ settle.

dépôt, *s.m.* deposit; store-room, warehouse; lock-up.

dépourvu, *adj.* needy.

dépraver, *v. a.* deprave.

déprécier, *v. a.* depreciate.

dépression, *s. f.* depression.

déprimer, *v. a.* depress.

depuis, *prep.* since, from; ~ *longtemps* long since.

députation, *s. f.* deputation.

député, *s.m.* deputy; member of the French parliament.

dérangé, *adj.* deranged; upset.

déranger, *v. a.* upset, put out of order.

déraper, *v. n.* skid.

dérèglement, *s. m.* irregularity; disorder.

dérivation, *s. f.* derivation.

dériver, *v.n.* drift; be derived.

dernier, -ère, *adj. & s. m. f.* latter, last, latest; *le* ~ the latter.

dernièrement, *adv.* lately.

dérober, *v. a.* rob, steal. se ~ steal away.

déroger, *v.n.* derogate (from).

dérouler, *v.a.* unroll, unfold.

déroute, *s.f.* defeat.

derrière, *adv. & prep.* behind, back; — *s. m.* back (part); bottom.

dès, *prep.* from, as early as, since; ~ *que* as soon as.

désagréable, *adj.* disagreeable, unpleasant.

désarmer, *v.a.* disarm.

désastre, *s.m.* disaster.

désavantage, *s. m.* disadvantage.

descendance, *s.f.* descent.

descendant, *adj.* descending; *en* ~ downward, downhill.

descendre, *v. n.* descend, come down, go down; alight; ~ *terre* land; — *v.a.* take down.

descente, *s.f.* descent; landing.

description, *s. f.* description.

désert[1], *s. m.* desert.

désert[2], *adj.* deserted, desolate.

déserter, *v. n. & a.* leave, desert.

désespérer, *v.n.* despair,

give up.

désespoir, *s. m.* despair.

déshabiller, *v. a.* undress; take off clothes.

déshonneur, *s.m.* dishonour, disgrace.

déshonorer, *v.a.* dishonour, disgrace.

désigner, *v. a.* designate; denote; appoint.

desinfecter, *v. a.* disinfect.

désir, *s. m.* desire.

désirable: *adj.* desirable.

désirer, *v. a. & n.* desire, long for.

désireux, -euse, *adj.* desirous, anxious.

désobéir, *v.n.* disobey.

désobéissance, *s.f.* disobedience.

désobéissant, *adj.* disobedient.

désœuvré, *adj.* idle, unoccupied.

désolation, *s. f.* devastation; desolation.

désoler, *v.a.* desolate; afflict, distress; **se ~** grieve, be sorry.

désordre, *s.m.* disorder.

dessert, *s. m.* dessert.

dessin, *s.m.* drawing, sketch; design; **~** *animé* cartoon.

dessiner, *v.a.* draw; sketch; design.

dessous, *adv. & prep.* under, underneath, below, beneath; **—** *s. m.* under-part; undies *pl.*

dessus, *adv. & prep.* on, upon, over, above, on top; **—** *s. m.* upper part, top.

destin, *s. m.* destiny, fate.

destinataire, *s. m. f.* receiver, addressee.

destination, *s. f.* destination.

destinée, *s.f.* destiny.

destiner, *v.a.* destine;

mean (for); **se ~** be destined (*à* for).

détachement, *s. m.* disengagement; detachment.

détacher, *v.a.* loose(n), unfasten; detach; **se ~** get loose, come undone.

détail, *s.m.* detail, particular; retail; *en* **~** in detail.

détention, *s. f.* detention.

détermination, *s.f.* determination.

déterminé, *adj.* definite, determinate; resolute; limited.

déterminer, *v.a.* determine, fix; limit; settle.

détestable, *adj.* hateful.

détester, *v.a.* detest.

détonation, *s.f.* detonation.

détour, *s.m.* turning, winding, turn; roundabout way; evasion.

détourner, *v.a.* turn aside; lead astray.

détroit, *s. m.* strait, pass.

détruire*, *v.a.* destroy, ruin; do away with.

dette, *s. f.* debt.

deuil, *s.m.* mourning.

deux, *adj. & s. m.* two; both.

deuxième, *adj.* second.

devancer, *v. a.* precede; anticipate.

devant, *prep. adv.* before; in front of; opposite to; **~** *que* before; *au-***~** *de* **~** in front of; **—** *s. m.* front; foreground.

dévaster, *v. a.* devastate, destroy.

développement, *s. m.* development, growth.

développer, *v.a.* (*also* **se ~**) develop.

devenir, *v.n.* become, get, turn, grow.

dévier, *v. a. & n.* deviate, turn away.

devise, *s. f.* device.
dévoiler, *v. a.* unveil, reveal.
devoir*, *v.a.* owe, be in debt for; have to, must, be bound to, ought to; — *s. m.* duty; task; work., prep.
dévorer, *v. a.* devour, eat up.
dévouement, *s. m.* devotion.
dévouer, *v. a.* devote, dedicate; se ~ devote oneself.
diable, *s. m.* devil; trolley, truck.
diacre, *s. m.* deacon.
diadème, *s. m.* diadem.
diagnostic, *s. m.* diagnosis.
dialecte, *s. m.* dialect.
dialogue, *s. m.* dialogue.
diamant, *s. m.* diamond.
diapositive, *s. f.* transparency, slide.
diarrhée, *s. f.* diarrhoea.
dictée, *s. f.* dictation.
dicter, *v. a.* dictate.
dictionnaire, *s. m.* dictionary.
diesel, *s. m.* diesel engine.
dieu, *s. m.* *(pl. -x)* God.
différence, *s. f.* difference.
différent, *adj.* different.
différer, *v.a.* defer, put off; *v.n.* differ, be different, vary.
difficile, *adj.* difficult, hard.
difficulté, *s. f.* difficulty, trouble.
diffusion, *s. f.* diffusion.
digne, *adj.* worthy; ~ *de* ... worthy of ...
dignité, *s.f.* dignity.
diligence, *s.f.* diligence.
diligent, *adj.* diligent.
dimanche, *s. m.* Sunday.
dimension, *s.f.* dimension.
diminuer, *v.a.* & *n.*

diminish, lessen, reduce.
dindon, *s.m.* turkey.
dîner, *s. m.* dinner; — *v. n.* dine.
diplomate, *s. m.* diplomat.
diplomatie, *s. f.* diplomacy.
diplomatique, *adj.* diplomatic.
diplôme, *s.m.* diploma.
dire*, *v.a.* say, tell; speak; ~ *à qn de faire qch.* tell s.o. to do sth.; *c'est à* ~ that is to say; *pour ainsi* ~ as it were; *vouloir* ~ mean; *dites donc!* look here!
direct, *adj.* direct.
directeur, *s.m.* director, manager; head master.
direction, *s.f.* direction; management; guidance; streering-gear.
directrice, *s. f.* directress; head mistress.
diriger, *v.a.* direct; lead, guide; manage; turn; steer.
disciple, *s.m.* disciple, follower.
discipline, *s. f.* discipline.
discorde, *s.f.* discord.
discours, *s.m.* discourse, speech.
discrédit, *s.m.* discredit.
discréditer, *v. a.* discredit.
discret, -ète *adj.* discreet; discrete.
discrètement, *adv.* discreetly.
discrétion, *s. f.* discretion.
discussion, *s. f.* discussion.
discuter, *v.a.* discuss, debate.
disparaître, *v.n.* disappear.
dispenser, *v. a.* dispense; se ~ *de* dispense with.
disposer, *v. a.* & *n.* dispose, lay out; se ~ prepare (to), be about

(to); *bien disposé* willing.

disposition, *s. f.* disposition, arrangement; *la ~ de qn.* at s.o.'s disposal.

dispute, *s. f.* dispute.

disputer, *v. a. & n.* dispute, contest, argue; se ~ quarrel, dispute.

disqualifier, *v.a.* disqualify.

disque, *s. m.* disc, record; discus; *~ microsillon* or *longue durée* long playing record.

dissimulation, *s. f.* dissimulation, dissembling.

dissimuler, *v.a. & n.* dissemble, conceal; se ~ conceal oneself.

dissolution, *s. f.* dissolution; undoing, breaking up.

dissoudre*, *v. a.* dissolve, disperse.

distance, *s. f.* distance; *à quelle ~ est-ce?* how far is it?

distant, *adj.* distant, far.

distiller, *v.a. & n.* distil.

distinct, *adj.* distinct, clear.

distinction, *s.f.* distinction.

distinguer, *v.a.* distinguish, discriminate; make out, tell.

distraction, *s. f.* abstraction; recreation; entertainment; distraction.

distraire, *v.a.* subtract; divert, distract; amuse, entertain.

distrait, *adj.* inattentive, absent-minded.

distribuer, *v. a.* distribute; deal out.

district, *s.m.* district.

divan, *s.m.* sofa, divan.

divergence, *s.f.* divergence; difference.

divers, *adj.* diverse, different, miscellaneous.

diversion, *s. f.* diversion.

divertir, *v. a.* divert, entertain; se ~ enjoy oneself.

divertissement, *s. m.* diversion; entertainment.

divin, *adj.* divine.

diviser, *v.a.* divide, separate.

division, *s.f.* division, department.

divorce, *s. m.* divorce.

divorcer, *v n. & n.* divorce, be divorced.

dix, *adj. s. m.* ten.

dix-huit, *adj. & s.m.* eighteen.

dixième, *adj. & s.f.* tenth.

dix-neuf, *adj. & s.m.* nineteen.

dix-sept, *adj. & s.m.* seventeen.

dizaine, *s. f.* ten.

docteur, *s. m.* doctor.

document, *s.m.* document.

documentaire, *s. m.* documentary (film).

dogme, *s. m.* dogma.

doigt, *s.m.* finger; toe.

dollar, *s.m.* dollar.

domaine, *s.m.* domain; landed property.

dôme, *s. m.* dome.

domestique, *adj. & s. m. f.* domestic, servant.

domicile, *s. m.* domicile, dwelling.

domination, *s. f.* domination, rule.

dominer, *v. a. & n.* dominate, rule.

dommage, *s. m.* damage; pity.

dompter, *v. a.* subdue, master, tame.

don, *s. m.* present, gift.

donateur, *s.m.* giver.

donc, *conj.* therefore, then, so; of course.

donne, *s. f.* deal.

donner, *v. a.* give, grant, present with, afford, hand over; ~ *congé* give notice to; se ~ *pour* claim to be.

dont, *pron.* whose, of whom; of which.

dormir*, *v.n.* sleep.

dortoir, *s. m.* dormitory.

dos, *s. m.* back.

dose, *s. f.* dose.

dossier, *s. m.* back-piece; record, file.

dot, *s. f.* dowry.

doter, *v. a.* endow.

douane, *s.f.* customs; custom-house; duty; *déclaration de* ~ customs declaration; *droits de* ~ customs duties; *la visite de la* ~ customs formalities.

douanier, *s.m.* custom-house officer.

double, *s.m.* double; *en* ~ duplicate; — *adj.* double, dual.

doubler, *v. a.* double (up); line; dub.

doublure, *s.f.* lining; understudy.

douce *see* doux.

douceur, *s. f.* sweetness; gentleness.

douche, *s. f.* shower-bath.

douer, *v. a.* endow, gift.

douleur, *s. f.* pain, ache.

douloureux, -euse, *adj.* painful.

doute, *s. m.* doubt; *sans* ~ no doubt, undoubtedly.

douter, *v. n.* doubt; se ~ suspect.

douteux, -euse, *adj.* doubtful, dubious.

doux, douce, *adj.* sweet; mild, soft.

douzaine, *s.f.* dozen.

douze, *adj. & s. m.* twelve; twelfth.

douzième, *adj.* twelfth.

dramatique, *adj.* dramatic; *l'art* ~ drama.

drame, *s.m.* drama.

drap, *s.m.* cloth, sheet.

drapeau, *s.m.* flag.

dresser, *v. a.* set up, erect; prepare; se ~ stand up, get up.

drogue, *s. f.* drug.

droguerie, *s. f.* drugs *pl.*

droit, *s. m.* right; law; duty, due; *avoir* ~ *à* be entitled to; ~ *de cité* citizenship; ~ *d'auteur*, copyright; *exempt de* ~s duty-free; ~*(s) de sortie*, export duty; — *adj.* right, direct, straight.

droite, *s. f.* right hand.

drôle, *adj.* droll, funny, strange; — *s. m.* rogue.

du, *art.* of the, some, any.

dû, *adj. & s. m.* due.

duc, *s. m.* duke.

duchesse, *s.f.* duchess.

duel, *s. m.* duel.

duplicata, *s. m.* duplicate, copy.

dur, *adj.* hard, tough.

durable, *adj.* lasting.

durant, *prep.* during, for.

durcir, *v. a. & n.* harden.

durée, *s.f.* duration, term.

durer, *v.n. & a.* last, endure, hold out.

dureté, *s. f.* hardness.

dynastie, *s.f.* dynasty.

E

eau, *s. f. (pl. -x)* water;

~ *de mer* salt water;
~ *de* S*eltz* soda-water.

ébaucher, *v.a.* sketch; outline.

ébouriffer, *v.a.* ruffle.

ébullition, *s.f.* boiling.

écaille, *s.f.* scale.

écailler, *v.a.* scale.

écart, *s.m.* deviation; *à l'*~ aside, apart.

écarter, *v.a.* set aside; dispel, take away; s'~ turn aside.

ecclésiastique, *adj. & s. m.* ecclesiastic.

échafaud, *s. m.* scaffold-(ing).

échange, *s. m.* exchange.

échanger, *v. a.* exchange.

échapper, *v. n.* escape, get away.

échauder, *v.a.* scald.

échauffer, *v. a.* heat; s'~ get hot.

échéance, *s. f.* expiration.

échéant, *adj.* due.

échec, *s. m.* check.

échecs, *s. m. pl.* chess.

échelle, *s.f.* ladder; scale.

échine, *s.f.* backbone.

écho, *s.m.* echo.

échoir*, *v.n.* expire, fall due; happen.

éclabousser, *v. a.* splash, spatter with mud.

éclair, *s.m.* lightning; flash.

éclairage, *s. m.* lighting; ~ *au néon* strip-lighting.

éclaircir, *v. a.* make clear, clear up; clarify; throw light on; s'~ become clear, clear up.

éclairer, *v. a.* light, illuminate; enlighten.

éclaireur, *s. m.* boy scout.

éclat, *s.m.* splinter; burst; brightness.

éclatant, *adj.* bright.

éclater, *v. n.* split; burst; break out; flash.

éclipser, *v. a.* eclipse; s'~ be eclipsed; take French leave.

école, *s.f.* school; *maître d'*~ schoolmaster; ~ *normale* teachers' training college; ~ *secondaire* grammar-school.

écolier, *s. m.* schoolboy.

écolière, *s. f.* schoolgirl.

économe, *adj.* economical; — *s. m.* bursar.

économie, *s. f.* economy; thrift; ~ *politique* political economy; ~*s* savings; *faire des* ~*s* save up.

économique, *adj.* economic; economical.

économiser, *v. a. & n.* economize, save, spare.

écorce, *s. f.* bark; rind.

écossais, *adj.* Scottish, Scotch.

Écossais, *s. m.* Scotsman.

écouler, *v.a.* sell.

écouter, *v.a.* listen to; hear.

écouteur, *s.m.* headphone; receiver.

écran, *s.m.* screen; *le petit* ~ television.

écrier: s'~ cry out.

écrire*, *v. a.* write (down); *machine à* ~ typewriter.

écrit, *adj.* written; — *s. m.* writing; *par* ~ in writing.

écriture, *s.f.* writing, handwriting; style.

écrivain, *s.m.* writer, author.

écuelle, *s. f.* bowl, basin, dish.

écume, *s.f.* foam.

écureuil, *s.m.* squirrel.

écurie, *s.f.* stable.

édifice, *s.m.* building.

édifier, *v.a.* build, erect; edify.

édit, *s.m.* edict, decree.

éditer, *v. a.* publish; edit.

éditeur, *s. m.* publisher.

édition, *s. f.* publication; edition.

éducation, *s. f.* education; training.

effacer, *v. a.* efface, rub out; wipe out.

effectif, -ive *adj.* actual, real.

effectuer, *v.a.* effect, carry out.

effet, *s. m.* effect, result; impression; bill (of exchange); *(pl.)* clothes, belongings.

efficacité, *s. f.* efficacy.

effondrer: s'~ fall in, collapse.

effort, *s. m.* effort, exertion, endeavour.

effrayant, *adj.* frightful.

effrayé, *adj.* afraid.

effrayer, *v.a.* frighten; s'~ be frightened.

effroi, *s.m.* fright.

effroyable, *adj.* frightful.

effusion, *s.f.* effusion, gush.

égal, *adj.* equal, like, alike; (all the) same; even.

également, *adv.* equally.

égaler, *v.a.* equal.

égalité, *s.f.* equality.

égard, *s. m.* regard; *à cet ~* on that account; *à l'~ de* with regard to; *en ~ à* considering.

égarer, *v. a.* mislead, misguide; s'~ lose one's way.

égayer, *v. a.* cheer (up); s'~ cheer up.

église (É), *s. f.* church.

égoïste, *adj.* egoistic, selfish.

egyptien, -enne (E.), *adj.* & *s.m.f.* Egyptian.

eh, *int.* ah!;~ *bien!* well!

élaborer, *v. a.* work out, think out, elaborate.

élan, *s.m.* dash; run; élan, zest.

élancé, *adj.* slim.

élancer, *v. n.* shoot; s'~ bound, dash, rush; soar.

élargir, *v. a.* make wider, enlarge; set at liberty.

élastique, *adj.* & *s. m.* elastic.

électeur, -trice, *s. m. f.* voter.

élection, *s.f.* election.

électricien, -enne, *s. m. f.* electrician.

électricité, *s.f.* electricity; *usine d'~* powerplant, -station.

électrique, *adj.* electric(al).

électron, *s.m.* electron.

électronique, *adj.* electronic.

élégance, *s.f.* elegance.

élégant, *adj.* elegant.

élément, *s. m.* element.

élémentaire, *adj.* elementary.

éléphant, *s. m.* elephant.

élévation, *s.f.* elevation.

élève, *s.m.f.* pupil.

élevé, *adj.* educated.

élever, *v. a.* raise, lift up; increase; bring up, educate; rear; s'~ rise; exalt oneself.

éliminer, *v. a.* eliminate.

élire, *v. a.* choose; elect.

elle, *pron.* *(pl.* elles*)* she, it, her; they.

elle-même, *pron.* herself.

éloigné, *adj.* far, distant.

éloigner, *v.a.* remove; take away; set aside.

émail, *s. m.* enamel.

émaner, *v.n.* emanate.

emballer, *v.a.* pack up; pack off.

embarquement, *s. m.* embarking; shipment.

embarquer, *v.a.* ship, embark; *v.n.* go on board.

embarrasser, *v. a.* embarrass.

embellir, *v. a.* embellish.

embêter, *v.a.* bore; annoy.

emblème, *s. m.* emblem.

embouchure, *s. f.* mouthpiece; mouth (of river).

embranchement, *s.m.* branchline; junction.

embrasser, *v. a.* embrace; kiss; s'~ kiss.

embrayage, *s. m.* clutch, coupling.

embrouillement, *s.m.* tangle; muddle.

embrouiller, *v. a.* embroil, entangle; muddle; s'~ become confused.

émetteur, *s. m.* transmitter.

émettre *v. a.* emit; transmit, broadcast.

émigration, *s. f.* emigration.

émigré, -e, *s.m.f.* emigrant.

émigrer, *v.n.* emigrate.

éminent, *adj.* eminent.

emmener, *v.a.* take away.

émotion, *s.f.* emotion; feeling.

émouvoir, *v.a.* move, touch; s'~ be moved.

emparer: s'~ *de* get hold of, seize.

empêchement, *s. m.* hindrance.

empêcher, *v.a.* keep from; prevent; hinder.

empire, *s.m.* empire.

emplette, *s. f.* purchase.

emplir, *v.a.* fill (up).

emploi, *s.m.* employment, job; use.

employé, -e, *s.m.f.* employee; clerk; attendant.

employer, *v.a.* employ; use.

empoigner, *v.a.* grasp, grip; lay hands on.

empoisonner, *v. a.* poison.

emporter, *v.a.* carry, take away, carry off, remove; s'~ get angry, lose one's temper.

empreinte, *s. f.* stamp, print, impression.

empresser: s'~ hurry, hasten.

emprisonnement, *s.m.* imprisonment.

emprisonner, *v.a.* imprison.

emprunter, *v. a.* borrow.

en, *prep.* in; to; into; at; like, as; by, through;

— *pron.* of him, of her, of it, of them, their; any, some.

encan, *s.m.* auction.

enceinte, *adj.* pregnant.

enchaîner, *v.a.* chain; link up; detain.

enchantement, *s. m.* spell; delight.

enchanter, *v.a.* charm, delight.

enclore, *v.a.* enclose.

enclose, *s. m.* enclosure; close.

enclume, *s.f.* anvil.

encombrement, *s. m.* stoppage; (traffic) jam.

encombrer, *v. a.* block up, jam.

encore, *adv.* yet, still; again; *pas* ~ not yet; ~ *une fois* once again; ~ *que* although; ~ *du* some more; ~ *quelque chose, Madame?* anything else, madam?

encouragement, *s. m.* encouragement.

encourager, *v. a.* encourage; cheer.

encre, *s.f.* ink.

encyclopédie, *s. f.* encyclopaedia.

endommager, *v.a.* dam-
age; injure.

endormir, *v.a.* put to
sleep; s'~ go to sleep,
fall asleep.

endosser, *v.a.* endorse.

énergie, *s. f.* energy; ~ *a-
tomique* atomic energy.

énergique, *adj.* energe-
tic.

enfance, *s.f.* infancy,
childhood.

enfant, *s. m. f.* infant,
child; *chambre d'~s*
nursery; *d'~s* juvenile.

enfermer, *v.a.* shut in,
up, lock up.

enfin, *adv.* at last; finally; in short.

enflammer, *v. a.* set on
fire; s'~ take fire.

enfler, *v. a.* swell (up);
s'~ swell.

enflure, *s. f.* swelling.

engagement, *s. m.* obli-
gation; commitment;
engagement.

engager, *v. a. & n.* pledge;
pawn; engage, sign on.

engloutir, *v. a.* swallow
up, devour.

engraisser, *v.a.* fatten;
v.n. grow fat.

enlèvement, *s.m.* removal.

enlever, *v.a.* remove,
clear away, take away.

ennemi, *s.m.* enemy.

ennui, *s. m.* bore(dom);
vexation; nuisance.

ennuyer, *v. a.* bore, weary; s'~ be bored.

ennuyeux, -euse, *adj.*
boring, tedious.

énoncer, *v.a.* state.

énorme, *adj.* enormous.

enquérir: s'~ *de* inquire
about.

enrager, *v. n.* be enraged.

enregistrer, *v. a.* register,
enter, record.

enrhumer, *v.a.* *être
enrhumé* have a cold;
s'~ catch a cold.

enrôler, *v. a.* enrol, draft.

enroué, *adj.* hoarse.

enrouler, *v. a.* roll (up).

enseignement, *s. m.* in-
struction, tuition.

enseigner, *v.a. & n.*
teach, instruct (in).

ensemble, *adv.* together;
— *s. m.* whole, mass;
unity; two-piece suit;
set of furniture, suite.

ensuite, *adv.* then; next.

ensuivre: s'~ follow, en-
sue.

entasser, *v.a.* heap up.

entendement, *s. m.* understanding.

entendre, *v. a. & n.* hear;
understand; ~ *parler
de* hear of; *ne pas ~*
miss; *qu'entendez-vous
par là?* what do you
mean by that?; *bien
entendu* of course;
c'est entendu! that's
settled!, agreed!

entente, *s.f.* meaning;
understanding; agree-
ment.

enterrement, *s. m.* burial.

enterrer, *v.a.* bury.

enthousiasme, *s. m.* en-
thusiasm.

enthousiaste, *adj.* enthusiastic; keen.

entier, -ère, *adj.* entire.

entièrement, *adv.* entirely,
wholly.

entorse, *s.f.* sprain;
donner une ~ a sprain
one's (foot, ankie).

entourage, *s. m.* circle of
friends; surroundings
(pl.); attendants *(pl.)*.

entourer, *v.a.* surround;
encircle.

entracte, *s. m.* interval.

entrailles, *s. f. pl.* entrails.

entraîner, *v.a.* draw

along; carry away; involve, entail; coach.

entraîneur, s. m. trainer, coach.

entre, prep, between, among; into, in.

entrée, s. f. entry, entrance, beginning; free access; duty.

entremets, s. m. second course.

entreprendre, v.a. attempt, undertake, contract for; worry.

entrepreneur, s.m. contractor.

entreprise, s. f. undertaking, enterprise.

entrer, v. n. enter; come in, go in; get in; get into; faire ~ show in.

enveloppe, s. f. envelope; wrapper, cover.

envelopper, v. a. wrap up, do up; envelop.

envers, prep. towards, to.

enviable, adj. enviable.

envie, s. f. envy; desire.

envier, v. a. envy; desire.

environ, adv. & prep. about.

environner, v.a. surround.

environs, s. m. pl. surroundings.

envoi, s. m. sending; consignment, shipment.

envoler: s'~ fly away, take wing.

envoyer*, v.a. send, dispatch, forward.

envoyeur, s.m. sender.

épais, -aisse, adj. thick.

épaisseur, s. f. thickness.

épargne, s.f. savings (pl.).

épargner, v. a. save (up).

épaule, s.f. shoulder.

épée, s.f. sword.

éperon, s.m. spur.

épice, s. f. spice.

épicerie, s.f. grocery, grocer's (shop).

épicier, -ère, s. m. f. grocer.

épidémie, s. f. epidemic.

épinard, s.m. spinach.

épine, s. f. thorn; spine, backbone; obstacle.

épingle, s. f. pin; ~ de sûreté safety-pin.

épisode, s.m. episode.

éplucher, v. a. peel; pick; sift, preen, thin out.

éponge, s.f. sponge.

éponger, v. a. sponge; mop (up).

époque, s. f. period, age, epoch, time.

épouse, s.f. wife.

épouser, v.a. marry.

épouvante, s.f. fright.

époux, s. m. husband.

épreuve, s. f. test, trial; proof; print.

éprouver, v. a. test, prove; feel; experience.

épuisé, adj. exhausted; out of print.

épuiser, v. a. exhaust; use up; wear out.

équation, s.f. equation.

équilibre, s.m. balance, equilibrium.

équipage, s. m. suite, retinue; carriage; crew.

équipe, s. f. gang, shift; crew, team, side; train.

équipement, s. m. equipment.

équiper, v.a. equip.

équivalent, adj. equivalent.

ère, s.f. era.

errant, adj. wandering.

errer, v. n. stray; err.

erreur, s. f. error, mistake.

érudit, adj. learned.

érudition, s.f. learning.

escalateur, s. m. escalator.

escale, s.f. port; landing; sans ~ non-stop.

escalier, s. m. stairs (pl.), staircase; ~ de sauve-

tage fire-escape; ~ *de service* backstairs *(pl.)*; ~ *roulant* escalator.

escargot, *s.m.* snail.

escarpins, *s. m. pl.* pumps.

esclavage, *s.m.* slavery.

esclave, *s. m. f.* slave; — *adj.* slavish.

escrime, *s.f.* fencing; *faire de l'*~ fence.

escrimer, *v.n.* fence.

espace, *s. m.* space; room.

espagnol, -e (E.), *adj.* Spanish; — *s. m. f.* Spaniard; Spanish.

espèce, *s. f.* species, kind.

espérance, *s. f.* hope, expectation.

espérer, *v. a.* hope (for).

espion, -onne, *s.m.f.* spy.

espionnage, *s. m.* espionage, spying.

espoir, *s.m.* hope.

esprit, *s. m.* spirit; mind; character; wit; sense.

esquille, *s.f.* splinter.

esquiver, *v.a.* evade.

essai, *s.m.* trial, test; essay; attempt.

essayer, *v. a.* try, attempt; essay; assay.

essence, *s.f.* essence; petrol.

essentiel, -elle, *adj.* essential.

essieu, *s.m.* axle.

essor, *s.m.* flight.

essoreuse, *s. f.* spin-drier.

essuie-glace, *s. m.* windscreen wiper.

essuie-main(s), *s. m. (pl.)* towel; ~ *à rouleau* roller-towel.

essuyer, *v.a.* dust; wipe; dry; mop up.

est, *s.m.* cast.

esthétique, *adj.* aesthetic.

estime, *s.f.* esteem.

estimer, *v.a. & n.* estimate, value; esteem, regard; consider.

estomac, *s.m.* stomach.

estrade, *s.f.* platform.

estuaire, *s.m.* estuary.

et, *conj.* and; ~ ...~ both ... and.

étable, *s.f.* cow-shed; ~ *à porcs* pigsty.

établi, *s.m.* (joiner's) bench.

établir, *v.a.* establish, found, settle, set up; build; prove; s'~ settle (down).

établissement, *s. m.* establishment.

étage, *s. m.* floor, stor(e)y.

étagère, *s. f.* shelf.

étaler, *v.a.* display; spread (out); show off; s'~ stretch oneself out.

étang, *s.m.* pond.

étape, *s.f.* stage.

état, *s.m.* state; condition; profession, station office; statement; *homme d'*~ statesman; *coup d'*~ revolt.

été, *s.m.* summer.

éteindre*, *v. a.* put out, extinguish; turn off; s'~ be extinguished.

étendre, *v. a.* spread out; stretch out; extend; s'~ lie down; stretch one-self out.

étendu, *adj.* wide, vast, extensive.

étendue, *s.f.* expanse, reach, range; extent.

éternel, -elle, *adj.* eternal.

éternuement, *s. m.* sneeze.

éternuer, *v.n.* sneeze.

étincelle, *s.f.* spark.

étiquette, *s.f.* ticket, label; etiquette.

étoffe, *s.f.* cloth, material.

étoile, *s.f.* star.

étonnant, *adj.* astonishing, amazing.

étonnement, *s. m.* astonishment, wonder.

étonner, *v.a.* astonish,

amaze; s'~ be astonished.

étouffer, *v.a.* choke.

étrange, *adj.* strange.

étranger, -ère, *adj.* foreign, strange; — *-s.m.f.* foreigner; *à l'*~ abroad.

être*, *v.n.* be, exist; *il est... it is...; ~ bien* be good-looking; be well; *c'est que* the fact is; ~ belong to; — *s.m.* being.

étreindre*, *v.a.* clasp; press; embrace.

étreinte, *s.f.* embrace.

étrier, *s. m.* stirrup.

étroit, *adj.* narrow, strait; close.

étude, *s. f.* study; chambers *(pl.)*.

étudiant, -e, *s.m.f.* student, undergraduate.

étudier, *v. a.* study, read; practise.

étui, *s.m.* case, box.

étuver, *v.a.* stew, steam.

eucharistie, *s.f.* eucharist.

européen, -enne, *adj.* European.

eux, *pron. m.* they, them.

évader: s'~ escape; get away.

évaluer, *v. a.* value, estimate.

évangélique, *adj.* evangelical.

évangile, *s.m.* gospel.

évaporer, *v. a.* evaporate; s'~ evaporate.

éveil, *s. m. en* ~ on the lookout.

éveiller, *v. a.* awaken; s'~ wake up.

événement, *s.m.* event.

éventail, *s.m.* fan.

éventuel, -elle, *adj.* eventual.

évêque, *s.m.* bishop.

évidemment, *adv.* evidently, obviously.

évidence, *s.f.* evidence.

évident, *adj.* evident, obvious.

éviter, *v. a.* avoid, evade.

évoluer, *v.n.* evolve.

évolution, *s. f.* evolution.

exact, *adj.* exact, accurate.

exactement, *adv.* exactly.

exactitude, *s.f.* exactitude, precision.

exagérer, *v. a.* exaggerate.

examen, *s. m.* exam(ination); test.

examiner, *v. a.* examine; investigate, look into.

excédent, *s.m.* surplus; ~s *de bagages* excess luggage.

excéder, *v. a.* exceed, surpass; tire out.

excellence, *s. f.* excellence; excellency.

excellent, *adj.* excellent.

excepté, *adj.* excepted; — *prep.* except(ing), but.

excepter, *v.a.* except.

exception, *s. f.* exception.

exceptionnel, -elle, *adj.* exceptional.

excès, *s. m.* excess.

excessif, -ive, *adj.* excessive.

excitation, *s.f.* excitement.

exciter, *v.a.* excite, stir up; urge on.

exclamation, *s.f.* exclamation.

exclure*, *v.a.* exclude.

exclusif, -ive, *adj.* exclusive.

excursion, *s. f.* excursion.

excursionniste, *s.m.f.* holiday-maker, tourist.

excuse, *s. f.* excuse; apology; *faire des* ~s apologize.

excuser, *v.a.* excuse; pardon; apologize for; s'~ apologize; ask to be excused; *excusez-moi* I beg your pardon; excuse me.

exécuter, *v.a.* execute, carry out, perform.

exécutif, -ive, *adj.* executive.

exécution, *s. f.* execution.

exemplaire, *s.m.* copy.

exemple, *s. m.* example; *par* ~ for example; *sans* ~ unprecedented.

exempt, *adj.* exempt, free *(de* from).

exemption, *s.f.* exemption.

exercer, *v.a.* exercise; practise; carry on; s'~ practise.

exercice, *s.m.* exercise.

exhibition, *s.f.* exhibition; display.

exigence, *s.f.* demand; exigency.

exil, *s.m.* exile.

existence, *s. f.* existence.

exister, *v. n.* exist.

expansif, -ive, *adj.* expansive.

expansion, *s.f.* expansion.

expédient, *s.m.* expedient, device.

expédier, *v.a.* forward, send off.

expéditeur, -trice, *s. m. f.* sender, shipping-agent.

expédition, *s. f.* consignment; expedition, forwarding, dispatch.

expérience, *s. f.* experience; experiment; *faire des* ~s to experiment.

expérimental, *adj.* experimental.

expert, *adj.* expert.

expirer, *v.n.* expire; die.

explication, *s. f.* explanation.

expliquer, *v.n.* explain, account for, show.

exploration, *s. f.* exploration.

explorer, *v.a.* explore.

explosion, *s. f.* explosion.

exportateur, *s.m.* exporter.

exportation, *s. f.* export, exportation.

exporter, *v. a.* export.

exposé, *s.m.* statement.

exposer, *v.a.* expose, show; state; set forth.

exposition, *s. f.* exhibition, display; statement, exposure; exposition.

exprès, *adv.* on purpose.

express, *adj.* express; *s.m.* express (train).

expression, *s. f.* expression

exprimer, *v.a.* express.

expulser, *v.a.* expel.

expulsion, *s.f.* expulsion.

extension, *s. f.* extension; extent.

exténuer, *v.a.* tire out, exhaust.

extérieur, *s. m.* exterior; outside; *à l'*~ outwards — *adj.* outward.

extinction, *s.f.* extinction; quenching.

extraire, *v. a.* extract; draw, pull out.

extraordinaire, *adj.* extraordinary, unusual.

extravagant, *adj.* extravagant.

extrême, *adj.* extreme.

extrêmement, *adv.* extremely, very.

extrémité *s. f.* extremity; last moment.

F

fabricant, *s.m.* manufacturer, maker.

fabrication, *s.f.* manufacture; fabrication.

fabrique, *s.f.* factory, works.

fabriquer, *v.a.* manufacture, make.

façade, *s.f.* front.

face, *s.f.* face; look; *en ~ de* opposite, in front of.

facétieux, **-euse,** *adj.* facetious; humorous.

fâché, *adj.* offended.

fâcher, *v. a.* offend; make angry; se ~ get angry.

facile, *adj.* easy; fluent.

facilité, *s.f.* ease; facility; convenience.

faciliter, *v.a.* facilitate; make easy.

façon, *s. f.* making; fashion, shape; way, manner; *de ~ a* so as to; *de ~ que* so that; *en aucune ~* by no means; *d'une ~ quelconque* somehow.

facteur, *s.m.* factor; postman; porter, carrier; *fig.* circumstance.

faction, *s.f.* faction; sentry, watch.

facture, *s.f.* bill, invoice.

facultatif, **-ive,** *adj.* optional.

faculté, *s.f.* faculty.

fade, *adj.* flat, insipid.

faible, *adj.* weak; feeble.

faiblesse, *s. f.* weakness.

faiblir, *v. n.* become weak.

faillir, *v. n.* fail, fall short; err; ~ + *inf.* nearly; *j'ai failli manquer le train* I nearly missed the train.

faim, *s.f.* hunger; *avoir ~* be hungry.

faire*, *v.a.* make; do; build; cause; ~ *allusion* refer to; ~ *attention (a)* pay attention (to); ~ *une chambre* do a room; ~ *le commerce* trade; ~ *la cuisine* do the cooking; ~ *ses*

études study; be at school; ~ *la guerre* make war; ~ *un lit* make a bed; ~ *mal à* hurt; ~ *part à* let know; ~ *des progrès* make progress; ~ *une promenade* take a walk; ~ *queue* queue; ~ *savoir* let know, inform (of); ~ *usage (de)* make use (of); ~ *voir* show; *que ~?* what's to be done?; *qu'est-ce que cela fait?* what does it matter?; *n'avoir rien a ~* have nothing to do; *deux et deux font quatre* two and two make four; ~ *70 km. a l'heure* do 70 km. an hour; *il fait du vent* it is windy; *il fait chaud* it is warm; *il fait jour* it is daylight; — *se ~* be made, be done; get used (to).

faisan, *s. m.* pheasant.

fait, *s. m.* fact; *en ~* in fact, after all, as a matter of fact.

falloir*, *v. impers.* be necessary, be required; must, have to, should, ought to; *comme il faut* proper, decent; *s'en ~* be wanting.

fameux, **-euse,** *adj.* famous.

familier, **-ière,** *adj.* familiar.

famille, *s. f.* family.

faner, *v.n.* fade.

fantaisie, *s.f.* fancy.

fantastique, *adj.* fantastic.

fardeau, *s.m.* burden.

farine, *s.f.* flour, meal.

fatal, *adj.* mortal, fatal.

fatigant, *adj.* fatiguing.

fatigue, *s.f.* fatigue.

fatigué, *adj.* tired, weary.

fatiguer, *v. a.* tire, weary,

fatigue.

faubourg, *s.m.* suburb.

faucher, *v.a.* mow, cut.

faucheuse, *s.f.* ~ *(a moteur)* (lawn-)mower.

faucille, *s. f.* sickle.

faucon, *s.m.* falcon.

faute, *s. f.* mistake, error, fault; lapse; want; *faire* ~ fail.

fauteuil, *s. m.* arm-chair, easy chair; stall, dress-circle seat.

fauve, *s.m.* wild beast.

faux¹, fausse, *adj.* false.

faux², *s. f.* scythe.

faveur, *s. f.* favour; *en* ~ *de* in favour of, on behalf of.

favorable, *adj.* favourable.

favori, -ite, *adj.* favorite.

fécond, *adj.* fertile.

féconder, *v.a.* fertilize.

fédéral, *adj.* federal.

fédération, *s.f.* federation.

fédéré, -e, *adj. & s. m. f.* federate.

feindre*, *v. a. & n.* feign.

félicitation, *s.f.* congratulation.

félicité, *s.f.* happiness.

féliciter, *v.a.* congratulate.

féminin, *adj.* feminine.

femme, *s.f.* woman; wife.

fendre, *v. a.* split; rend.

fenêtre, *s. f.* window.

fente, *s. f.* crack, split.

fer, *s. m.* iron; ~ *à cheval* horseshoe.

férié, *adj. jour* ~ holiday.

ferme¹, *adj.* firm; — *adv.* fast; firmly.

ferme², *s. f.* farm.

fermé, *adj.* closed.

fermer, *v. a.* close, shut; se ~ close, be shut.

fermeté, *s. f.* firmness.

fermeture, *s. f.* shutting; shutter; ~ *éclair* zip fastener, zipper.

fermier, *s. m.* farmer.

féroce, *adj.* wild, cruel.

férocité, *s. f.* ferocity.

ferronnerie, *s.f.* iron-works.

fertile, *adj.* fertile.

fervent, *adj.* fervent.

ferveur, *s. f.* fervour.

fesse, *s.f.* buttock.

festin, *s.m.* feast.

fête, *s. f.* feast, holiday; birthday.

fêter, *v. a.* observe; celebrate.

fêteur, -euse, *s. m. f.* holiday-maker.

feu, *s. m.* fire, flame; light; *mettre le* ~ *à* set on fire; *prendre* ~ take fire; ~ *d'artifice* fireworks *(pl.);* ~*x de circulation* traffic lights; ~*x d'arrière* tail lights.

feuillage, *s.m.* foliage.

feuille, *s.f.* leaf; sheet.

février, *s.m.* February.

fiancé, -e, *s. m. f.* fiancè, -e.

fiancer, *v.a.* engage; se ~ be engaged.

fibre, *s. f.* fibre.

ficelle, *s. f.* string.

fiche, *s. f.* pin, peg; slip (of paper).

ficher, *v. a.* drive in, fix; do, work; deal (a blow).

fidèle, *adj.* faithful.

fidélité, *s. f.* fidelity.

fier: se ~ trust, count on.

fierté, *s. f.* pride.

fièvre, *s. f.* fever.

figue, *s. f.* fig.

figure, *s. f.* form, shape; face; figure.

figurer, *v.a.* figure, represent; se ~ imagine.

fil, *s.m.* thread, yarn; edge; clue; ~ *(de fer)* wire.

file, *s. f.* row, file, line.
filer, *v.a. & n.* spin.
filet, *s.m.* net; fillet; rack.
fille, *s. f.* daughter; girl; maid; *jeune ∼* young lady.
fillette, *s.f.* little girl.
filleul, -e, *s. m. f.* godson, god-daughter.
film, *s. m.* film; *le grand ∼* feature film; *∼ avec* film featuring ...; *∼ annonce* trailer.
fils, *s. m.* son.
fin[1], *s.f.* end; close; *à la ∼* in the end, finally; *mettre ∼ à* put an end to; *tirer à sa ∼* come to an end; *∼ de semaine* week-end.
fin[2], *adj.* fine; nice.
final, *adj.* final.
finance, *s. f.* finance.
financier, *adj.* financial.
fini, *adj.* finished; ended; over.
finir, *v. a. & n.* end, finish, put an end to; eat up.
finlandais, -e (F.), *adj.* Finnish; — *s. m. f.* Finn; Finnish.
fixe, *adj.* fixed, firm.
fixer, *v.a.* fix, fasten; stare at; settle.
flacon, *s. m.* flagon, bottle.
flagrant, *adj.* flagrant.
flairer, *v. a.* smell, scent.
flambeau, *s. m.* torch.
flamboyer, *v.n.* flame, flare.
flamme, *s.f.* flame.
flanelle, *s. f* flannel.
flanquer, *v.a.* fling.
flatter, *v. a.* caress; flatter.
flatterie, *s.f.* flattery.
flèche. *s. f.* arrow.
fléchir, *v. a.* bend, bow; *fig.* move.
fleur, *s. f.* flower, blossom.
fleurir, *v.n.* flower, blossom.

fleuve, *s. m.* river.
flirter, *v. n.* flirt.
flocon, *s. m.* flake *(snow etc.)*.
flot, *s. m.* wave; flood; *être à ∼* be floating.
flottant, *adj.* floating.
flotte, *s.f.* fleet; navy.
flotter, *v.n. & a.* float.
fluide, *s. m. & adj.* fluid.
flute, *s. f.* flute.
foi, *s.f.* faith, belief; credit.
foie, *s. m.* liver.
foin, *s.m.* hay; grass.
foire, *s.f.* fair, market.
fois, *s.f.* time; *une ∼* once; *encore une ∼* again; *deux ∼* twice; *à la ∼* at same time; *chaque ∼* every time.
folie, *s. f.* folly, madness.
folle *see* fou.
foncer, *v. a.* sink; darken, deepen.
fonction, *s.f.* function, duty.
fonctionnaire, *s.m.f.* functionary, official.
fonctionner, *v.n.* function, operate, work.
fond, *s. m.* bottom, ground, foundation; *à ∼* thoroughly.
fondamental, *adj.* fundamental, basic.
forcer, *v. a.* force; break open; compel, impel.
forêt, *s. f.* forest.
forger, *v. a.* forge.
formalité, *s. f.* formality.
forme, *s. f.* form, shape.
formel, -elle, *adj.* formal, express; flat.
former, *v. a.* form, shape.
formidable, *adj.* formidable, terrible.
formule, *s.f.* formula.
formuler, *v. a.* formulate, draw up.
fort, *adj.* strong, robust; fat; stout, stiff; skil-

ful; heavy; *être* ~ *en* be well up in; — *adv.* very (much), highly, hard; ~ *bien* very well; — *s. m.* strong man; stronghold.

forteresse, *s.f.* fortress.

fortification, *s. f.* fortification.

fortifier, *v. a.* strengthen, fortify.

fortune, *s.f.* fortune; chance; luck; wealth, property.

fou, fol, folle, *adj.* mad, foolish; crazy.

foudre, *s.f.* lightning, thunderbolt.

fouille, *s. f.* excavation.

fouiller, *v. a. & n.* dig, excavate.

fouillis, *s.m.* muddle, mess.

foule, *s. f.* crowd, mass.

four, *s. m.* oven, furnace.

fourchette, *s.f.* fork *(table)*.

fourgon, *s. m.* (delivery) van; wagon; ~ *(aux bagages)* luggage-van.

fourmi, *s.f.* ant.

fourneau, *s.m.* stove, range; ~ *à gaz* gas-ring, -stove; ~ *électrique* electric cooker.

fourniment, *s.m.* outfit, kit.

fournir, *v.a.* furnish (with), supply; provide (with).

fourreau, *s.m.* sheath, case, scabbard.

fourreur, *s.m.* furrier.

fourrure, *s.f.* fur.

foyer, *s.m.* fireside, home; foyer, lounge.

fracas, *s.m.* crash; uproar; fuss; noise.

fracasser, *v.a.* shatter, smash.

fraction, *s.f.* fraction; portion; instalment.

fracture, *s.f.* fracture.

fragile, *adj.* fragile.

frais[1], fraîche, *adj.* fresh, cool; chilly.

frais[2], *s. m. pl.* expenses, charges, fees.

fraise, *s.f.* strawberry.

framboise, *s. f.* raspberry.

franc, franche, *adj.* frank, free, open.

français (F.), *adj.* French; — *s. m.* Frenchman; French (language).

Française, *s.f.* French-woman.

franchir, *v.a.* clear, jump over. cross.

franchise, *s. f.* exemption; frankness.

frapper, *v.a.* strike, hit, knock; impress; surprise.

frein, *s. m.* bit (of bridle); brake; *fig.* check.

frêle, *adj.* weak, frail.

fréquent, *adj.* frequent.

frère, *s.m.* brother.

fricassée, *s.f.* fricassee.

friction, *s.f.* friction.

frigidaire, *s.m.* refrigerator.

frigo, *s.m.* fridge.

frileux, -euse, *adj.* chilly.

frire*, *v.n. & a.* fry.

friser, *v.a. & n.* curl.

frissonner, *v. n.* shiver, tremble.

frivole, *adj.* frivolous, flimsy.

froid, *s. m.* cold; *avoir* ~ feel cold; — *adj.* cold, cool; *il fait froid* it is cold.

froisser, *v.a.* rumple, crumple; bruise; *fig.* offend, hurt; *se* ~ take offence.

frôler, *v.a.* graze.

fromage, *s.m.* cheese.

front, *s.m.* forehead; face; front (part).

frontière, *s.f.* frontier, border.

frotter, *v. a.* rub.

fruit, *s.m.* fruit; produce.

fruitier, *s.m.* fruiterer, greengrocer.

fuir*, *v. n. & a.* run away, flee.

fuite, *s. f.* flight; leakage, leak.

fumée, *s.f.* smoke.

fumer, *v. a. & n.* smoke.

fumeur, -euse *s.m.f.* smoker.

fumier, *s.m.* dung.

funèbre, *adj.* funereal.

funérailles, *s.f.pl.* funeral.

funiculaire, *s.m.* rope railway.

fureur, *s.f.* fury, rage.

furie, *s. f.* fury.

furieux, -euse, *adj.* furious.

furoncle, *s.m.* boil, furuncle.

fusée, *s.f.* fuse; rocket.

fusil, *s.m.* gun.

fusillade, *s.f.* firing, shooting.

futur, *adj. & s. m.* future.

fuyant, *adj.* flying, fleeing; passing.

G

gâchis, *s.m.* mortar; mire; *fig.* muddle, mess.

gaffe, *s. f.* blunder.

gage, *s. m.* pledge; security; ~s wages.

gagner, *v. a.* gain; win.

gai, *adj.* gay, cheerful.

gaieté, *s.f.* gaiety.

gain, *s.m.* gain, profit.

galant, *adj.* courteous.

galerie, *s. f.* gallery.

galop, *s. m.* gallop.

gamin, *s.m.* urchin.

gamme, *s. f.* scale; range.

gant, *s. m.* glove.

garage, *s.m.* garage; siding.

garantie, *s. f.* guarantee.

garantir, *v. a.* guarantee.

garçon, *s. m.* boy; young man; fellow; bachelor; waiter.

garde[1], *s. f.* guard; watch; police; nurse.

garde[2], *s.m.* warden, guardian; watch.

garde-bébé, *s. m.* babysitter, sitter-in.

garde-boue, *s.f.* mudguard.

garde-chasse, *s. m.* gamekeeper.

garder, *v.a.* keep, take care of; attend (to).

garde-robe, *s.f.* wardrobe.

gardien, -enne, *s.m. f.* guardian, keeper; warden; watch(man); ~ de la paix constable; ~ (de but) goalkeeper.

gare, *s. f.* station; depot; ~ des marchandises goods station; *aller recevoir qn à la* ~ meet sy at the station.

garni, *s.m.* furnished lodgings *(pl.)*, digs.

garnir, *v. a.* furnish; fit up, trim.

garnison, *s. f.* garrison.

garniture, *s.f.* fittings *(pl.)*; set; garnishing.

gâteau, *s. m.* cake.

gâter, *v. a.* waste, impair; spoil.

gauche, *adj.* left.

gaz, *s. m.* gas; *usine à* ~ gas-works.

gazon, *s. m.* grass; lawn.

géant, *s. m.* giant.

gelée, *s. f.* jelly.

gémir, *v. n.* groan.

gênant, *adj.* inconvenient, annoying.

gendre, *s. m.* son-in-law.

gêne, *s. f.* inconvenience;

trouble; *être dans la* ~ be hard-up.

gêné, *adj.* uneasy; stiff; embarrassed.

gêner, *v.n.* inconvenience; be in the way of; interfere with.

général, *adj. & s. m.* general; *en* ~ in general, generally.

généraliser, *v.a. & n.* generalize.

générateur, *s.m.* generator.

génération, *s.f.* generation.

généreux, **-euse,** *adj.* generous.

générosité, *s.f.* generosity.

génie, *s. m.* genius; corps of engineers.

genou, *s.m.* *(pl. -x)* knee; *(pl.)* lap; *se mettre à* ~s kneel down.

genre, *s. m.* genus, kind.

gens, *s.m. f.* people; attendants.

gentil, -ille, *adj.* gentle.

géographie, *s.f.* geography.

géographique, *adj.* geographic(al).

géologie, *s. f.* geology.

géométrie, *s. f.* geometry.

géométrique, *adj.* geometric(al).

gérant, -e, *s. m. f.* manager; manageress.

gérer, *v. a.* manage.

germanique, *adj.* Germanic.

germe, *s.m.* germ.

gésir*, *v.n.* lie.

geste, *s.m.* gesture.

gesticuler, *v. n.* gesticulate.

gibier, *s. m.* game.

gifle, *s. f.* slap, box on the ear.

gifler, *v. a.* give s.o. a slap (in the face).

gilet, *s.m.* waistcoat, vest.

girafe, *s. f.* giraffe.

glace, *s. f.* ice; ice-cream; mirror; *mer de* ~ glacier.

glacer, *v. a.* freeze, chill.

glacial, *adj.* icy, glacial.

glacier, *s. m.* glacier.

glissade, *s. f.* slide; slip.

glissant, *adj.* slippery.

glisser, *v.n.* slide; slip; glide over; **se** ~ slip, creep (into).

globe, *s. m.* globe; earth.

gloire, *s. f.* glory, fame.

glorieux, **-euse,** *adj.* glorious; proud.

gober, *v.a.* swallow.

golfe, *s. m.* gulf.

gomme, *s. f.* gum; india-rubber.

gommer, *v. a.* gum.

gonfler, *v.a.* inflate.

gorge, *s.f.* throat, gullet.

gorgée, *s. f.* gulp.

gosse, *s.m.* kid, brat.

gothique, *adj.* Gothic.

goudron, *s. m.* tar.

gourmand, *adj.* greedy.

goût, *s. m.* taste; savour.

goûter, *v. a.* taste; relish, enjoy; — *s.m.* tea *(meal)*.

goutte, *s. f.* drop.

gouvernail, *s. m.* rudder, helm.

gouvernante *s. f.* governess.

gouvernement, *s.m.* government.

gouverner, *v. a.* govern, control, rule; manage; steer.

gouverneur, *s. m.* governor; tutor, preceptor.

grâce, *s. f.* grace; pardon; thanks *(pl.)*; favour.

gracieux, **-euse,** *adj.* graceful; gracious.

grade, *s. m.* rank, grade.

grain, s. m. grain, berry, corn; a touch (of).

graine, s. f. seed, berry.

graissage, s. m. lubrication.

graisse, s. f. fat, grease, lard.

graisser, v.a. grease, lubricate.

grammaire, s. f. grammar.

grammatical, adj. grammatical.

gramme, s. m. gramme.

gramophone, s. m. gramophone.

grand, adj. great; large; big; tall; grand.

grandeur, s.f. size; length; breadth; greatness.

grandir, v.n. grow (up); grow big, tall.

grand'mère, s. f. grandmother.

grand-père, s. m. grandfather.

granit, s. m. granite.

grappe, s. f. bunch; ~ de raisin bunch of grapes.

gras, grasse, adj. fat; thick.

gratitude, s.f. gratitude.

gratter, v. a. & n. scratch, overtake; brush.

gratuit, adj. free (of charge).

grave, adj. grave; heavy.

graver, v.a. engrave.

gravure, s.f. engraving.

grec, grecque (G.), adj. & s. m. f. Greek.

grêle, adj. slender, delicate, slim.

grelotter, v.n. shiver.

grenier, s. m. loft; granary.

grenouille, s. f. frog.

grève, s. f. strike; beach.

grief, s. m. grievance.

griffe, s. f. claw; clutch.

grill, s. m. grill, gridiron.

grille, s. f. iron railing, grating.

griller, v.a. grill, toast.

grimace, s.f. grimace.

grimacer, v.n. grimace.

grimper, v. n. & n. climb.

grincer, v. n. & a. grind, grate; creak.

grippe, s.f. influenza.

gris, adj. gray.

grogner, v.n. groan; grunt, grumble.

gronder, v. n. roar; rumble; v.a. scold.

gros, grosse, adj. large, big; stout; great; thick: — s. m. bulk; wholesale; en ~ roughly; wholesale.

grossier, adj. coarse, gross.

grossir, v. a. make bigger; increase; v. n. grow bigger.

grotesque, adj. grotesque.

groupe, s.m. group.

grouper, v.a. group.

grue, s.f. crane.

gué, s. m. ford (across river).

guêpe, s. f. wasp.

guérir, v.a. cure, heal; v. n. & se ~ be cured, get well again.

guerre, s. f. war.

gueule, s. f. mouth, jaws (pl.); opening.

guichet, s.m. ticket window; counter; booking-office.

guide, s. m. guide; conductor; guide-book.

guider, v. a. guide, lead.

guillemets, s. m. pl. inverted commas.

guise, s. f. way, manner; à votre ~ as you like.

guitare, s. f. guitar.

gymnastique, s. f. gymnastics.

H

habile, *adj.* able, clever.

habileté, *s. f.* skill, cleverness; ability.

habiller, *v. a.* clothe; dress (up); s'~ dress, put on one's clothes.

habit, *s. m.* (dress-)suit; coat; ~s clothes.

habitant, -e, *s.m.f.* inhabitant.

habitation, *s. f.* habitation, dwelling.

habiter, *v. a. & n.* inhabit, live in, dwell in.

habitude, *s. f.* habit, use.

habituel, -elle, *adj.* habitual, usual.

habituer, *v. a.* accustom; s'~ *à* get accustomed to, get used to.

hache, *s. f.* axe.

hacher, *v.a.* chop, cut up, hack, mince.

hachis, *s. m.* hash.

haine, *s. f.* hate, hatred.

haïr*, *v.a.* hate.

haleine, *s. f.* breath.

hall, *s. m.* lounge; ~ de montage erecting shop.

halle, *s.f.* market-hall.

hanche, *s.f.* haunch, hip.

hangar, *s. m.* shed, hangar.

happer, *v.a.* snap up.

harasser, *v.a.* harass.

hardi, *adj.* bold, daring.

hareng, *s.m.* herring.

haricot, *s.m.* bean; ~s verts French-beans.

harmonie, *s. f.* harmony.

harmonieux, -euse, *adj.* harmonious.

harnais, *s.m.* harness.

harpe, *s.f.* harp.

hasard, *s. m.* hazard, risk; par ~ by chance.

hasarder, *v.a.* hazard, risk, stake.

hasardeux, -euse, *adj.* risky; unsafe.

hâte, *s. f.* haste, hurry, rush; *à la* ~ in a hurry.

hâter, *v. a.* hasten, urge on; se ~ hurry (up).

hausse, *s. f.* rise.

hausser, *v. a. & n.* raise, lift; se ~ rise.

haut, *adj.* high; elevated; upright; loud; upper; terre ~e highland; à voix ~e aloud: — *adv.* high, highly, up; aloud; en ~ at the top; upstairs; — *s. m.* top, height, summit.

hauteur, *s.f.* height, altitude.

haut-parleur, *s. m.* loudspeaker.

havresac, *s.m.* haversack, knapsack.

hebdomadaire, *adj. & s. m.* weekly.

hébreu (H.), *adj. & s. m.* Hebrew.

hectare, *s.m.* hectare.

hélice, *s.f.* air-screw, propeller.

hélicoptère, *s.m.* helicopter.

herbe, *s.f.* herb, grass; pot-herb.

herbeux, -euse, *adj.* grassy.

hérédité, *s.f.* heredity.

hérisser, *v.a.* bristle; ruffle; se ~ bristle up, stand on end.

hérisson, *s. m.* hedgehog.

héritage, *s. m.* inheritance, heritage.

hériter, *v.a. & n.* inherit.

héritier, *s.m.* heir.

héritière, *s.f.* heiress.

heroïne, *s.f.* heroine.

héros, *s. m.* hero.

hésitation, *s.f.* hesitation.

hésiter, *v.n.* hesitate.

heure, *s. f.* hour, time; *quelle ~ est-il?* what time is it?; *il est dix ~s moins le quart* it's a quarter to ten; *dix ~s* ten o'clock; *dix ~s et quart* a quarter past ten; *dix ~s et demie* half past ten; *de bonne ~* early; *~s de pointe* rush hours; *~s d'ouverture* business hours; *~s supplémentaires* overtime.

heureux, -euse, *adj.* happy, fortunate, successful.

heurter, *v. a. & n.* knock against, hit, run into, against; **se ~** run, hit, dash against, collide.

hibou, *s. m. (pl. -x)* owl.

hideux, -euse, *adj.* hideous, terrible.

hier, *adv.* yesterday; *~ soir* last night.

hirondelle, *s. f.* swallow.

histoire, *s. f.* (hi)story,

historique, *adj.* historic.

hiver, *s.m.* winter.

hollandais, -e (H.), *adj. & s. m. f.* Dutch(man), Dutch-woman.

homard, *s.m.* lobster.

homme, *s.m.* man; *~ d'affaires* business man; *~ d'état* statesman.

hongrois, -e, (H.), *adj. & s.m.f.* Hungarian.

honnête, *adj.* honest.

honnêteté, *s. f.* honesty.

honneur, *s.m.* honour; credit.

honorable, *adj.* honourable.

honoraires, *s. m. pl.* fee(s).

honorer, *v.a.* honour.

honte, *s.f.* shame; *avoir ~ de* be ashamed of.

honteux, -euse, *adj.* shameful, disgraceful.

hôpital, *s. m. (pl. -aux)* hospital.

hoquet, *s.m.* hiccup.

horaire, *s.m.* time-table.

horizon, *s.m.* horizon.

horizontal, *adj.* horizontal.

horloge, *s.f.* clock.

horloger, *s.m.* watchmaker.

horreur, *s.f.* horror.

horrible, *adj.* horrible.

hors, *adv.* out, outside; *— prep.* out of, outside.

hospitalité, *s. f.* hospitality.

hostie, *s.f.* wafer *(Church).*

hostile, *adj.* hostile.

hostilité, *s.f.* hostility.

hôte, *s.m.* host; guest.

hôtel, *s.m.* hotel; large house; *~ de ville* town-hall.

hôtesse, *s. f.* hostess; *~ de l'air* air-hostess.

houe, *s. f.* hoe.

houillère, *s.f.* colliery.

hublot, *s.m.* window.

huile, *s. f.* oil.

huissier, *s. m.* usher.

huit, *adj. & s. m.* eight.

huitième, *adj.* eighth.

huître, *s. f.* oyster.

humain, *adj.* human.

humanité, *s. f.* humanity.

humble, *adj.* humble.

humecter, *v.a.* wet.

humer, *v. a.* inhale, suck in.

humide, *adj.* humid, wet.

humidité, *s. f.* humidity.

humiliation, *s. f.* humiliation.

humilier, *v. a.* humiliate.

humilité, *s. f.* humility.

humoristique, *adj.* humorous.

humour, *s. m.* humour.

hurlement, *s. m.* howl(ing), roar(ing).

hurler, *v.n.* howl, roar.

hutte, *s.f.* hut, cabin.

hydrogène, *s. m.* hydrogen.

hygiène, *s. f.* hygiene.
hymne, *s. m.* hymn.
hypocrite, *s. m. f.* hypocrite; — *adj.* hypocritical.
hypothèse, *s. f.* supposition; hypothesis.
hystérique, *adj.* hysterical.

I

ici, *adv.* here; *d'~* from here; *par ~* this way.
idéal, -e, *adj.* ideal.
idéalisme, *s. m.* idealism.
idéaliste, *s. m. f.* idealist.
idée, *s. f.* idea, notion; *il m'est venu à l'~* it occurred to me.
identique, *adj.* identical.
identité, *s.f.* identity.
idiome, *s. m.* language, dialect.
idiot, *adj.* idiotic; — *s. m.* idiot.
idiotisme, *s. m.* idiom.
ignition, *s. f.* ignition.
ignorance, *s. f.* ignorance.
ignorant, *adj.* ignorant.
ignorer, *v.a.* not know, be ignorant of, be unaware of.
il, elle, *pron. (pl.* ils, elles) he, she, it; they; there.
île, *s. f.* island.
illégal, *adj.* illegal.
illicite, *adj.* illicit, unlawful.
illumination, *s. f.* illumination; *~ par projecteurs* flood-lighting.
illuminer, *v. a.* illuminate, light up; *~ par projecteurs* flood-light.
illusion, *s.f.* illusion, delusion.
illustration, *s. f.* illustration.
illustrer, *v.a.* illustrate, explain.

image, *s. f.* image, picture, likeness.
imagé, *adj.* vivid.
imaginaire, *adj.* imaginary, fantastic.
imaginatif, -ive, *adj.* imaginative.
imagination, *s. f.* imagination, fancy.
imaginer, *v.a.* s'~ imagine.
imbécile, *s.m. f.* fool, idiot; — *adj.* foolish.
imitation, *s.f.* imitation, copy.
imiter, *v. a.* imitate, copy.
immédiat, *adj.* immediate.
immense, *adj.* immense.
immeuble, *s. m.* real estate, landed property.
immigrant, -e, *adj.* & *s. m. f.* immigrant.
immigration, *s.f.* immigration.
immigrer, *v. a.* immigrate.
immobile, *adj.* immobile.
immoral, *adj.* immoral.
immortel, -elle, *adj.* immortal.
imparfait, *adj.* & *s. m.* imperfect.
impartial, *adj.* impartial.
impatience, *s. f.* impatience.
impatient, *adj.* impatient.
impayé, *adj.* unpaid.
impératif, -ive, *adj.* & *s. m.* imperative.
impératrice, *s. f.* empress.
imperfection, *s.f.* imperfection.
impérial, *adj.* imperial.
impérialisme, *s.m.* imperialism.
imperméable, *adj.* impermeable; waterproof.
impertinent, *adj.* impertinent.
impétueux, -euse, *adj.* impetuous, headlong.
impliquer, *v. a.* implicate,

involve, imply.

implorer, v.a. implore, beg.

impoli, adj. impolite.

impopulaire, adj. unpopular.

importance, s.f. importance.

important, adj. important.

importateur, -trice, s.m.f. importer.

importation, s.f. importation; ~s imports.

importer, v.n. matter, be of moment; n'importe it does not matter.

importun, adj. troublesome, importunate.

importuner, v.a. annoy, molest, worry.

imposer, v.a. impose, inflict, lay (on); levy.

impossible, adj. impossible.

impôt, s.m. tax, duty.

impression, s.f. impression; print, edition; faute d'~ misprint.

impressionner, v.a. impress, affect.

imprimé, s.m. printed matter.

imprimer, v.a. (im)print, impress; publish.

imprimerie, s.f. printing; printing office.

impropre, adj. unfit, improper.

imprudent, adj. imprudent.

impuissant, adj. powerless, ineffectual, helpless.

impulsion, s.f. spur, impulse.

inaccoutumé, adj. unaccustomed.

inachevé, adj. unfinished.

inanimé, adj. inanimate.

inapplicable, adj. inapplicable, irrelevant.

inattendu, adj. unexpected.

inattentif, -ive, adj. inattentive, heedless.

incapable, adj. incapable, unable, inefficient.

incendie, s.m. fire.

incendier, v.a. set fire to.

incertain, adj. uncertain.

incessant, adj. incessant.

incident, s.m. incident; — adj. incidental.

inciter, v.a. incite, urge.

inclinaison, s.f. inclination, gradient.

inclination, s.f. inclination; bent; love.

incliner, v.a. & n. incline, bend; slope; slant; s'~ bow down, bend.

inclusif, -ive adj. inclusive.

incommode, adj. inconvenient, uncomfortable.

incommoder, v.a. inconvenience, annoy.

incomparable, adj. incomparable.

incompatible, adj. incompatible.

incompétent, adj. incompetent.

incomplet, adj. incomplete, imperfect.

inconscient, adj. unconscious.

inconséquent, adj. inconsistent.

inconvenant, adj. improper, unsuitable.

inconvénient, s.m. inconvenience.

incorrect, adj. incorrect.

incroyable, adj. incredible.

incurable, adj. incurable.

indécis, adj. uncertain.

indécision, s.f. indecision.

indéfini, adj. indefinite,

undefined.

indépendance, s.f. independence.

index, s.m. forefinger, index.

indicateur, s. m. indicator, gauge; time-table.

indication, s. f. indication; direction; sign.

indice, s. m. sign, token, mark; index.

indien, -enne (I.), adj. & s.m.f. Indian.

indifférent, adj. indifferent.

indigestion, s. f. indigestion.

indignation, s. f. indignation.

indiquer, v.a. indicate, point out, show.

indirect, adj. indirect.

indiscret, -ète, adj. indiscreet.

indiscrétion, s. f. indiscretion.

indispensable, adj. indispensable, essential.

indisposé, adj. unwell; upset.

individu, s. m. individual, person.

individuel, -elle, adj. individual.

indulgence, s. f. indulgence.

indulgent, adj. indulgent.

industrie, s. f. industry.

industriel, -elle, adj. industrial; — s. m. manufacturer.

inefficace, adj. inefficient.

inégal, adj. unequal.

inégalité, s. f. inequality.

inerte, adj. inert; dull.

inévitable, adj. inevitable.

inexpérimenté, adj. inexperienced.

inexplicable, adj. inexplicable.

infâme, adj. infamous.

infanterie. s. f. infantry.

infection, s. f. infection.

inférieur, adj. inferior.

infinitif, s. m. infinitive.

infirmerie, s. f. infirmary.

infirmier, -ère, s. m. f. nurse.

influence, s. f. influence.

influencer, v. a. influence.

information, s.f. information.

informer, v. a. inform, let know; s'~ de inquire about.

infructueux, -euse, adj. unsuccessful.

ingénieur, s. m. engineer.

ingénieux, -euse, adj. ingenious.

ingéniosité, s. f. ingenuity.

ingrat, adj. ungrateful.

ingrédient , s. m. ingredient.

inhabité, adj. uninhabited.

inintéressant, adj. uninteresting.

initial, -e, adj. & s. f. initial.

initiative, s. f. initiative; syndicat d'~ tourist office.

injection, s. f. injection.

injure, s.f. injury.

injurier, v.a. insult.

injurieux, -euse, adj. injurious.

injuste, adj. unjust.

injustice, s. f. injustice.

innocence, s. f. innocence.

innocent, adj. innocent.

innombrable, adj. innumerable, countless.

inoccupé, adj. unoccupied.

inoculer, v.a. inoculate.

inondation, s. f. flood.

inonder, v. a. flood.

inquiet, -ète, adj. anxious, restless, uneasy.

inquiéter, v.a. worry.

insecte, s.m. insect.

insensé, adj. insane, mad.

insensible, *adj.* insensible.

inséparable, *ad.j* inseparable.

insigne, *s. m.* badge.

insignifiant, *adj.* insignificant.

insipide, *adj.* dull, flat.

insister, *v. a.* insist, lay stress on.

insolence, *s. f.* insolence.

insolent, *adj.* insolent.

insouciant, *adj.* careless.

inspecter, *v.a.* inspect, survey.

inspiration, *s. f.* inspiration.

inspirer, *v.a.* inspire, suggest; inhale.

installation, *s. f.* installation; fitting up.

installer, *v.a.* install; fit up; *v.n.* s'~ to settle down.

instant, *adj.* instant, pressing; — *s.m.* instant, moment; *a l'~* instantly, at once.

instantané, *s.m.* snap-(shot).

instinct, *s. m.* instinct.

instituer, *v.a.* institute.

institut, *s.m.* institute.

institution, *s. f.* institution; boarding-school.

instruction, *s. f.* instruction, tuition; knowledge, learning; direction; inquiry.

instruire*, *v.a.* instruct, teach.

instrument, *s. m.* instrument, implement, tool.

instrumental, *adj.* instrumental.

insuffisance, *s. f.* insufficiency.

insuffisant, *adj.* insufficient, deficient.

insulte, *s. f.* insult.

insulter, *v. a. & n.* insult.

insupportable, *adj.* intolerable, unbearable.

intact, *adj.* intact, entire.

intégral, *adj.* integral.

intégrité, *s.f.* integrity.

intellectuel, -elle, *adj. & s.m.* intellectual.

intelligence, *s. f.* intelligence, understanding.

intelligent, *adj.* intelligent, clever.

intendant, *s. m.* manager.

intense, *adj.* intense.

intensité, *s. f.* intensity.

intention, *s. f.* intention, purpose; *avoir l'~* intend, mean.

interdire, *v. a.* forbid.

intéressant, *adj.* interesting; *peu* ~ uninteresting.

intéressé, *adj.* interested, concerned.

intéresser, *v. a. & n.* interest; concern; s'~ take an interest (*à* in); be concerned.

intérêt, *s.m.* interest; concern; share; *avoir* ~ *à* have an interest in.

intérieur, *s.m.* inside, interior; *à l'~* inside, indoors; *Ministre de l'Intérieur* Home Secretary.

intermédiaire, *adj.* intermediate; — *s. m. f.* intermediary.

international, *adj.* international.

interne, *adj.* internal, inward.

interpellation, *s. f.* interpellation.

interpeller, *v. a.* interpellate, question.

interposer, *v. a.* interpose.

interprétation, *s. f.* interpretation.

interprète, *s. m. f.* interpreter.

interpréter. *v.a.* interpret; render.

interrogation, *s. f.* interrogation; inquiry.

interrogatoire, *s.m.* (cross-)examination.

interroger, *v.a.* interrogate, cross-examine, question.

interrompre, *v.a.* interrupt.

interrupteur, *s. m.* interrupter; switch.

interruption, *s. f.* interruption.

intervalle, *s.m.* interval; *dans l'~* in the meantime.

intervenir, *v.n.* intervene, interfere, go between.

intervention, *s. f.* intervention.

interview, *s. f. m.* interview.

intime, *adj.* intimate.

intimité, *s.f.* intimacy.

intolérable, *adj.* intolerable.

intrigue, *s.f.* intrigue.

intriguer, *v.n. & n.* intrigue.

introduction, *s. f.* introduction.

introduire, *v.a.* introduce; show in.

inutile, *adj.* useless.

invalide, *adj.* invalid, disabled.

invasion, *s. f.* invasion.

inventer, *v.a.* make up.

inventeur, *s. m.* inventor.

invention, *s. f.* invention.

investigation, *s. f.* investigation, inquiry.

invisible, *adj.* invisible.

invitation, *s.f.* invitation.

invité, -e, *s. m. f.* guest.

inviter, *v. a.* invite.

iris, *s. m.* iris.

irlandais (I.), *adj.* Irish;

— *s. m.* Irishman.

ironie, *s. f.* irony.

ironique, *adj.* ironical.

irradier, *v. a.* (ir)radiate.

irréel, *adj.* unreal.

irrésistible, *adj.* irresistible.

irritation, *s. f.* irritation.

irriter, *v.a.* irritate.

isolement, *s. m.* isolation.

isoler, *v.a.* isolate.

isotope, *s.m.* isotope.

issue, *s. f.* issue, outlet, way out.

italien, -enne (I.), *adj. & s. m. f.* Italian.

itinéraire, *adj.* itinerary; — *s.m.* guide-book.

ivre, *adj.* drunk.

J

j' *see* **je.**

jadis, *adv.* once, long ago, formerly.

jalousie, *s.f.* jealousy; blind.

jaloux, -se, *adj.* jealous.

jamais, *adv.* never, ever.

jambe, *s. f.* leg, shank.

jambon, *s. m.* ham.

janvier, *s. m.* January.

japonais, -e (J.), *adj. & s. m. f.* Japanese.

jardin, *s. m.* garden.

jardinier, -ère, *s. m. f.* gardener.

jarre, *s. f.* jar.

jarretière, *s. f.* garter.

jauge, *s. f.* gauge.

jauger, *v. a.* gauge.

jaune, *adj.* yellow; — *s. m.* yolk.

je, j', *pron.* I.

jersey, *s. m.* jersey.

jet, *s.m.* throw(ing).

jeter, *v.a.* throw, throw away, down; cast,

fling; shoot; discharge;
se ~ rush.

jeton, *s. m.* counter.

jeu, *s.m.* game, play, set.

jeudi, *s. m.* Thursday.

jeune, *adj.* young.

jeûne, *s.m.* fast(ing).

jeûner, *v.n.* fast.

jeunesse, *s. f.* youth.

joie, *s. f.* joy, delight

joindre*, *v. a. & n.* join,
unite; se ~ join.

joint, *s. m.* joint, articulation.

jointure, *s. f.* joint.

joli, *adj.* pretty, nice.

jonction, *s. f.* junction.

jongleur, *s. m.* juggler.

joue, *s. f.* cheek *(face)*.

jouer, *v. a. & n.* play;
gambol; gamble.

jouet, *s. m.* toy.

joueur, -euse, *s. m. f.*
player; gambler.

joug, *s. m.* yoke.

jouir, *v.n.* (~ *de*) enjoy.

jouissance, *s.f.* enjoyment, pleasure, joy.

jour, *s. m.* day; daylight,
light; life; ~ *de fête*
holiday; ~ *de semaine*
week-day; *un* ~ some
day; *tous les* ~s every
day; *à* ~ up to date.

journal, *s. m.* (news)paper; journal; diary.

journalier, -ère, *adj.* daily;
— *s.m.* day-labourer.

journaliste, *s. m. f.* journalist.

journée, *s. f.* day; day's
wages *(pl.)*; day's
work.

joyau, *s. m.* jewel.

joyeux, -euse, *adj.* joyful, merry.

judiciaire, *adj.* judicial,
legal.

judicieux, -euse, *adj.* judicious, sensible, reasonable.

juge, *s. m.* judge.

jugement, *s. m.* judg(e)ment; sentence.

juger, *v. a. & n.* judge.

juif, -ive (J.), *adj.* Jewish; — *s. m. f.* Jew.

juillet, *s. m.* July.

juin, *s. m.* June.

jumeau, -elle *adj. s. m. f.*
twin; *f. pl.* binoculars.

jungle, *s. f.* jungle.

jupe, *s. f.* skirt.

juré, *s. m.* juryman.

jurer, *v. a. & n.* swear.

jurisprudence, *s..f* jurisprudence.

juron, *s. m.* oath.

jury, *s. m.* jury.

jus, *s.m.* juice.

jusque, jusqu'à, *prep.*
till; as far as.

juste, *adj.* just, right;
fair.

justice, *s.f.* justice.

justification, *s.f.* justification.

justifier, *v.a.* justify.

juvénile, *adj.* juvenile.

K

kangourou, *s. m.* kangaroo.

kayak, *s. m.* kayak.

képi, *s. m.* cap.

kilogramme, *s.m.* kilogram(me).

kilomètre, *s.m.* kilometre.

kiosque, *s. n.* kiosk.

L

l' = le or la.

la, *art.* the; —*pron.* her, it.

là, *adv.* there; here.

labeur, *s.m.* labour, work.

laboratoire, *s.m.* laboratory.

laborieux, -euse, *adj.* laborious, hard-working.

labourer, *v.a.* plough.

lac, *s. m.* lake.

lacer, *v. a.* lace.

lacet, *s. m.* lace; braid; bowstring; shoe-lace.

lâche, *adj.* loose; cowardly; — *s. m.* coward.

lâcher, *v.a.* loosen, slacken; let go.

lactation, *s. f.* lactation.

laid, *adj.* ugly; plain.

laideur, *s. f.* ugliness.

lainage, *s.m.* woollen goods *(pl.)*; wool.

laine, *s. f.* wool; *pure* ~ all wool.

laïque, *adj.* lay.

laisser, *v.a.* leave, quit; give up; let alone; leave behind, off; ~ *aller* let go, neglect.

lait, *s. m.* milk.

laiterie, *s. f.* dairy.

laitier, *s. m.* milkman, dairyman.

laitière, *s. f.* dairymaid.

laitue, *s. f.* lettuce.

lambeau, *s. m.* rag, strip.

lame, *s. f.* blade; plate, sheet; ~ *de rasoir* razor-blade.

lamentation, *s. f.* lamentation.

lampe, *s. f.* lamp.

lancement, *s.m.* throwing; launching.

lancer, *v. a.* throw, fling; se ~ dart, rush.

langage, *s. m.* language, tongue; speech, way of speaking.

lange *s. m.* baby's nappy.

langue, *s. f.* tongue; language; ~ *maternelle* mother-tongue.

laper, *v. a.* lap (up).

lapin, *s. m.* rabbit.

laps, *s. m.* lapse, space (of time).

lapsus, *s. m.* lapse, slip.

laque, *s. f.* lacquer.

lard, *s. m.* bacon.

large, *adj.* broad, wise; generous; liberal; — *s.m.* room, breadth.

largeur, *s. f.* width.

larme, *s. f.* tear.

las, lasse, *adj.* weary.

lasser, *v.a.* tire, wear out; se ~ *de* get tired of.

latéral, *adj.* lateral, side.

latin, -e, *adj. & s. m. f.* Latin.

latitude, *s.f.* latitude; scope, freedom.

lavable, *adj.* washable.

lavabo, *s. m.* wash-basin; lavatory.

lavage, *s.m.* washing; ~ *de vaisselle* washing-up.

lavande, *s. f.* lavender.

laver, *v. a.* wash; se ~ wash (oneself); *machine à* ~ washing-machine.

layette, *s. f.* baby-linen.

le, la, l', *art.* the; —*pron. (pl.* **les)** him, her, it; them.

lécher, *v. a.* lick, lap.

leçon, *s. f.* lesson; lecture.

lecteur, -trice, *s. m. f.* reader; lector.

lecture, *s. f.* reading.

légal, *adj.* legal, lawful.

légende, *s. f.* legend.

léger, -ère, *adj.* light, slight; loose.

légèreté, *s. f.* lightness; ease.

légion, *s. f.* legion.

législation, *s.f.* legislation.

législature, *s. f.* legislature.

légitime, *adj.* legitimate, lawful.

légume, *s.m.* vegetable.

lendemain, *s.m.* next day, day after.

lent, *adj.* slow; tardy.

lenteur, *s.f.* slowness.

lentille, *s.f.* lentil; lens.

léopard, *s.m.* leopard

lequel, laquelle, *rel. pron. (pl.* lesquels, lesquelles*)* who, whom; which, that.

lettre, *s.f.* letter; type character; ~s literature; arts; *à la* ~ literally, word for word; ~ *de change* bill of exchange; ~ *de crédit* letter of credit; ~ *recommandée* registered letter; *boîte aux* ~s letter-box.

lettré, *adj.* learned; literary.

leur, *poss. adj. (pl.* -s*)* their; — *pron.* to them, them; le or la ~, les ~s theirs, their own.

levée, *s. f.* raising; removal; levy.

lever, *v. a.* lift (up), raise; hoist; *v. n.* rise; se ~ rise get up.

levier, *s. m.* lever; ~ *des vitesses* gear-lever.

lèvre, *s. f.* lip.

lexique, *s.m.* lexicon.

liaison, *s.f.* joining, junction; union; connection; tie; liaison.

libéral, *adj.* liberal.

libérer, *v.a.* liberate.

liberté, *s.f.* liberty.

libraire, *s.m. f.* bookseller.

librairie, *s. f.* bookshop.

libre, *adj.* free; unoccupied.

licence, *s.f.* licence, degree.

licencié, -e, *s. m. f.* licenciate; licensee.

licencieux, -euse, *adj.* licentious.

lie, *s. f.* dregs, grounds *(pl.).*

liège, *s.m.* cork.

lien, *s.m.* tie, bond; band, strap, cord; link.

lier, *v. a.* bind, tie (up); fasten; link up.

lieu, *s. m.* place; *au* ~ *de* instead of; *avoir* ~ take place.

lieutenant, *s. m.* lieutenant.

lièvre, *s. m.* hare.

ligne, *s. f.* line; ~ *aérienne* air-line.

lilas, *s. m.* lilac.

limace, *s. f.* slug.

limaçon, *s. m.* snail.

lime, *s. f.* file.

limer, *v. a.* file.

limite, *s.f.* bound(s), border, limit.

limiter, *v.a.* limit, restrict.

limon, *s.m.* mud, silt.

limonade, *s. f.* lemonade.

lin, *s. m.* flax.

linge, *s. m.* linen.

linger, -ère, *s.m.f.* linendraper.

lingerie, *s. f.* ladies' underclothing, lingerie.

lion, *s. m.* lion.

liqueur, *s. f.* liqueur.

liquide, *adj.* liquid.

liquider, *v.a.* liquidate.

lire*, *v.a.* read.

liste, *s. f.* list, roll; panel.

lit, *s. m.* bed.

litre, *s. m.* litre.

littéraire, *adj.* literary.

littérature, *s.f.* literature.

livraison, *s.f.* delivery; part (of book).

livre[1], *s. m.* book; work; *teneur de ~s* book-keeper.

livre[2], *s. f.* pound.

livrer, *v.a.* deliver; give up.

local, *s.m.* spot, premises; — *adj.* local.

localité, *s. f.* place, spot.

locataire, *s. m. f.* tenant, lodger.

location, *s. f.* letting out; hiring, renting; *prendre en ~* hire; *bureau de ~* box-office; *~ des places* seat reservation.

locomotive, *s.f.* (railway) engine.

loge, *s. f.* hut. cabin; box.

logement, *s. m.* lodging.

loger, *v.a.* accommodate, lodge; house; *v. n.* reside, live (in).

logeur, *s. m.* landlord.

logeuse, *s. f.* landlady.

logique, *s. f.* logic; — *adj.* logical.

loi, *s.f.* law, statute; *projet de ~* bill, draft.

loin, *adv.* far, far off, away; *au ~* far off.

lointain, *adj.* far, remote.

loisir, *s. m.* spare time, leisure.

long, **longue**, *adj. & s. m. f.* long; *être ~ à* be long in.

longitude, *s. f.* longitude.

longtemps, *adv.* long, a long time; *depuis ~* for a long time, long since.

longueur, *s. f.* length.

loquet, *s. m.* latch.

lors, *adv.* then; *dès ~* from that time.

lorsque, *conj.* when.

lot, *s. m.* lot, fate; prize.

loterie, *s. f.* lottery.

lotion, *s. f.* lotion.

louage, *s.m.* hiring; hire.

louche, *s.f.* ladle.

louer[1], *v.a.* hire (out); let; *à ~* for hire; to let.

louer[2], *v. a.* praise.

loup, *s. m.* wolf.

lourd, *adj.* heavy; clumsy.

louve, *s. f.* she-wolf.

loyal, *adj.* loyal, true.

loyauté, *s.f.* honesty.

loyer, *s. m.* rent; hire.

lubrifier, *v.a.* lubricate.

lucratif, **-ive**, *adj.* lucrative.

luge, *s. f.* sledge.

lugubre, *adj.* dismal.

lui, *pron.* (to) him, (to) her, (to) it.

lui-même, *pron.* himself.

luire*, *v. n.* shine, gleam.

lumière, *s. f.* light, daylight.

lumineux, **-euse**, *adj.* luminous, bright.

lundi, *s. m.* Monday.

lune, *s. f.* moon; *~ de miel* honeymoon.

lunette, *s. f* telescope; *(pl.)* spectacles, specs; *~s de soleil* sun-glasses.

luthérien, **-enne**, *adj. & s. m. f.* Lutheran.

lutte, *s. f.* wrestling; fight, struggle.

lutter, *v.n.* wrestle, fight.

lutteur, *s. m.* wrestler.

luxe, *s. m.* luxury.

luxeux, **-euse**, *adj.* luxurious.

lycée, *s.m.* secondary

school,grammar-school.

M

m' *see* me.
ma *see* mon.
mâcher, *v. a.* chew.
machine, *s. f.* machine, engine, apparatus; ~ *à coudre*, sewing-machine.
mâchoire, *s. f.* jaw.
maçon, *s m.* mason.
madame, *s. f. (pl.* mesdames) madam.
mademoiselle, *s. f. (pl.* mesdemoiselles) miss.
magasin, *s.m.* shop; store; warehouse; *grand* ~ department store.
magique, *adj.* magic.
magnétique, *adj.* magnetic.
magnétophone, *s.m.* tape-recorder.
magnifique, *adj.* magnificent.
mai, *s. m.* May.
maigre, *adj.* lean, thin.
maigrir, *v.n.* grow lean, get thin.
maille, *s. f.* stitch; knot.
maillot, *s.m.* tights *(pl.);* ~ *(de bain)* bathing-costume.
main, *s. f.* hand; lead; *en* ~ in hand; *se donner la* ~ shake hands; *tenir la* ~ *à* see to, see that; *de seconde* ~ second-hand.
maintenant, *adv.* now, at present
maintenir, *v. a.* (up)hold, support, keep (up), maintain.
maintien, *s. m.* maintenance.
maire, *s. m.* mayor.
mais, *conj.* but.
maïs, *s. m.* maize.
maison, *s. f.* house, residence; home; firm; *à la* ~ at home, indoors; *tenir* ~ keep house.
maître, *s.m.* master; proprietor; teacher; ~ *d'école* schoolmaster; ~ *de maison* host.
maîtresse, *s. f.* mistress; (land)lady; sweetheart; ~ *d'école* schoolmistress.
maîtrise, *s.f.* mastery, control.
maîtriser, *v.a.* master.
majesté, *s. f.* majesty.
majeur, *adj.* major; main; chief; — *s. m.* major.
majorité, *s. f.* majority.
majuscule, *s. f.* capital letter.
mal, *s. m.* ill, evil, wrong; pain, harm; trouble, hardship; *avoir* ~ *à* have a pain in; — *adv.* wrong, badly, ill.
malade, *adj.* sick, ill; *tomber* ~ fall ill, be taken ill; — *s. m. f.* invalid, patient.
maladie, *s.f.* illness; sickness; disease.
maladroit, *adj.* awkward, clumsy.
malaise, *s. m.* uneasiness.
malchance, *s.f.* bad luck.
mâle, *s. m.* male.
malentendu, *s. m.* misunderstandig.
malgré, *prep.* in spite of; ~ *tout* for all that.
malheur, *s.m.* misfortune, ill luck; mischance; accident.
malheureux, -euse, *adj.* unfortunate, unlucky.
malice, *s. f.* malice.
malin, maligne, *adj.* malicious, malignant; evil.
malle, *s. f.* trunk; mail;

faire la ~ pack.

mallette, *s.f.* suit-case.

malpropre, *adj.* dirty, filthy; untidy.

malsain, *adj.* unhealthy.

malveillant, *adj.* male-volent, evil-minded.

maman, *s.f.* mamma.

manche[1]**,** *s.m,* handle. holder.

manche[2]**,** *s. f.* sleeve.

Manche, *s.f.* English Channel.

manchette, *s. f.* cuff.

mandat, *s. m.* mandate; money-order.

manger, *v.a.* eat; *donner à* ~ feed; *salle à* ~ dining-room; — *s. m.* eating; food.

manicure, *s. m. f.* mani-cure.

manier, *v.a.* handle.

manière, *s. f.* manner, way, fashion; *(pl.)* man-ners.

manifestation, *s. f.* man-ifestation.

manifester, *v.a.* mani-fest, show; **se** ~ man fest oneself.

manipuler, *v. a.* manip-ulate, operate.

manœuvre, *s.f.* action; proceeding; manœu-vre; *s. m.* labourer.

manœuvrer, *v. a. & n.* handle, manœuvre, work.

manoir, *s. m.* manor.

manque, *s.m.* want; de-ficiency.

manquer, *v. a.* miss; *v. n.* fail; be missing, be wanting.

mansarde, *s.f.* garret.

manteau, *s. m.* coat.

manuel, -elle, *adj.* manu-al; — *s. m.* manual, handbook.

manufacture, *s. f.* manu-facture; factory.

manufacturer, *v. a.* manu-facture.

manuscrit, *s. m.* manu-script.

maquillage, *s.m.* make-up.

marbre, *s. m.* marble.

marchand, -e, *s. m. f.* merchant, tradesman; shopkeeper.

marchandise, *s. f.* mer-chandise, goods *(pl.)*.

marche, *s. f.* walk; march; progress; move.

marché, *s. m.* market; bargain; agreement: *bon* ~ cheap.

marcher, *v.n.* walk; travel; march; work; run; proceed.

mardi, *s. m.* Tuesday; ~ *gras* Shrove Tuesday.

mare, *s.f.* pool, pond.

maréchal, *s. m.* marshal.

marée, *s.f.* tide, flood.

margarine, *s. f.* marga-rine.

marge, *s. f.* margin.

mari, *s.m.* husband.

mariage, *s. m.* marriage.

marié, -e, *adj.* married; — *s. m. f.* bridegroom, married man; bride, married woman.

marier, *v. a.* marry; match; — **se** ~ marry, get married.

marin, *adj.* marine; — *s.m.* seaman, sailor, mariner.

marmelade, *s. f.* marma-lade.

marque, *s. f.* mark, im-print; trade-mark.

marquer, *v.a.* mark; stamp; brand.

marron, *s. m.* chestnut.

mars, *s. m.* March.

marteau, *s. m.* hammer.

martyr, -e, *s.m.f.* mar-tyr.

masque, *s. m.* mask.
masquer, *v.a.* mask.
massacre, *s. m.* massacre.
massage, *s. m.* massage.
masse, *s. f.* mass; heap.
massif, -ive, *adj.* massive, bulky, clumsy.
mât, *s. m.* mast.
match, *s. m.* match.
matelas, *s. m.* mattress.
matelot, *s.m.* sailor, seaman.
matérialisme, *s. m.* materialism.
matériaux, *s.m.pl.* material(s).
matériel, -elle, *adj.* material; — *s. m.* matter; material; implements *(pl.).*
maternel, -elle, *adj.* maternal; motherly; *école* ~*le* infant-school.
mathématicien, -enne, *s. m. f.* mathematician.
mathématique, *adj.* mathematical; — *s. f.* mathematics.
matière, *s.f.* matter; material; substance; ~ *première* raw material.
matin, *s.m.* morning; *le* ~ in the morning; *du* ~ a.m.
matinal, *adj.* morning.
matinée, *s.f.* morning; matinée.
matrice, *s. f.* womb.
maturité, *s. f.* maturity.
maudire*, *v.a.* curse.
mauvais, *adj.* bad, ill, evil; — *s. m.* bad.
me, m' *pron.* (to) me; (to) myself.
mécanicien, *s. m.* mechanic; engine-driver.
mécanique, *adj.* mechanic(al); — *s.m.* mechanics; machine; mechanism.

mécaniser, *v. a.* mechanize.
mécanisme, *s. m.* mechanism; machinery.
méchant, *adj.* evil, bad.
mécontent, *adj.* displeased, dissatisfied, unhappy.
mécontenter, *v. a.* dissatisfy.
médaille, *s. f.* medal.
médecin, *s.m.* doctor, physician.
médecine, *s. f.* medicine.
médical, *adj.* medical.
médicament, *s. m.* medicament; medicine.
médiéval, *adj.* medieval.
méditation, *s. m.* meditation.
méditer, *v. a. & n.* meditate.
méfiance, *s. f.* mistrust.
méfier: se ~ be suspicious *(de* of); mistrust.
meilleur, -e, *adj.* better; — *s. m. f.* the best.
mélancolie, *s. f.* melancholy, gloom.
mélancolique, *adj.* melancholy, sad.
mélange, *s.m.* mixture, blend.
mélanger, *v.a.* mix, blend.
mêler, *v.a.* mix (up), mingle; se ~ mingle, be mixed; interfere with.
mélodie, *s. f.* melody.
melon, *s.m.* melon.
membre, *s.m.* member, limb.
même, *adj.* same; self; — *adv.* even, also, likewise; *de* ~ in the same way; *de* ~ *que* as well as; *quand* ~ even if.
mémoire, *s.f.* memory; *s.m.* memorandum; bill; *(pl.)* memoirs.

menace, *s.f.* menace.

menacer, *v.a.* threaten.

ménage, *s. m.* housekeeping; household.

ménager, *v. a.* be sparing of; take care of; manage.

ménagère, *s.f.* housewife, housekeeper.

mendiant, -e, *s.m.f.* beggar.

mendier, *v. a. & n.* beg.

mener, *v.a.* guide, conduct, lead.

mensonge, *s.m.* lie.

mensuel, *adj.* monthly.

mental, *adj.* mental.

mention, *s.f.* mention.

mentionner, *v. a.* mention.

mentir*, *v.n.* lie, tell a lie.

menton, *s.m.* chin.

menu, *adj.* slim; small; minute; — *s. m.* bill of fare, menu.

menuisier, *s. m.* joiner, carpenter.

méprendre: se ~ make a mistake, be mistaken.

mépris, *s.m.* contempt.

mer, *s.f.* sea; *par* ~ by sea; *bord de la* ~ seaside.

mercerie, *s. f.* haberdashery.

merci, *s. f.* mercy; — *int.* thanks!, (no) thank you!

mercredi, *s. m.* Wednesday.

mercure, *s.m.* mercury.

mère, *s.f.* mother.

mérite, *s. m.* merit, worth.

mériter, *v.a.* merit, deserve.

merveille, *s.f.* wonder.

merveilleux, -euse, *adj.* wonderful.

message, *s.m.* message.

messe, *s.f.* mass.

mesure, *s.f.* measure,

gauge, measurement; size; metre.

mesurer, *v.a.* measure.

métal, *s.m.* metal.

métallique, *adj.* metallic.

météorologie *s. f.* meteorology.

méthode, *s.f.* method.

méthodique, *adj.* methodical, systematic.

métier, *s. m.* trade; business; employment, occupation.

mètre, *s. m.* metre.

métro, *s. m.* tube, underground.

métropolitain, *adj.* metropolitan; underground.

mets, *s.m.* dish, food.

mettre*, *v.a.* put, set, place; put in, on; bring; ~ *de c té* set aside, save; ~ *en ordre* set in order, tidy up; se ~ sit down; se ~ *à* set about, take to.

meuble, *s. m.* (piece of) furniture; — *adj.* movable; *biens* ~s personal property.

meubler, *v.a.* furnish, fit up.

meunier, *s.m.* miller.

meurtre, *s.m.* murder.

meurtrier, *s. m.* murderer.

meurtrir, *v.a.* bruise, injure.

mi-, half, mid.

microbe, *s. m.* microbe.

microphone, *s. m.* microphone.

microscope, *s. m.* microscope.

midi, *s. m.* noon, midday; south.

miel, *s. m.* honey.

mien, *pron.* mine, my own.

miette, *s. f.* crumb.

mieux, *adv.* better.

mignon, -onne, *adj.* tiny; — *s.m.f.* darling.

migraine, *s. f.* headache.

milieu, *s.m.* middle, centre; environment.

militaire, *adj.* military; — *s. m.* soldier.

mille[1], *adj.* & *s.m.* thousand.

mille[2], *s. m.* mile (= 1609 metres).

millier, *s.m.* thousand.

million, *s.m.* million.

millionaire, *s. m. f.* millionaire.

mince, *adj.* thin, slim.

mine[1], *s.f.* mine.

mine[2], *s.f.* look(s); *de bonne ~* good-looking.

miner, *v. a.* (under)mine.

mineral, *s.m.* ore.

minéral, *adj.* mineral.

mineur[1], *s.m.* miner.

mineur[2], -e, *adj. & s. m. f.* minor.

ministère, *s. m.* ministry.

ministre, *s. m.* minister; *premier ~* prime minister, premier.

minorité, *s. f.* minority.

minuit, *s.m.* midnight.

minuscule, *s.f.* small letter.

minute, *s.f.* minute; instant.

miracle, *s.m.* miracle.

miraculeux, -euse, *adj.* miraculous, wonderful.

miroir, *s.m.* mirror.

misérable, *adj.* miserable.

misère, *s. f.* misery.

miséricorde, *s. f.* mercy.

mission, *s.f.* mission.

missionnaire, *adj. & s. m. f.* missionary.

mite, *s. f.* moth.

mobile, *adj.* movable, mobile.

mobilier, *s. m.* furniture, suite.

mobilisation, *s. f.* mobilization.

mobiliser, *v.a.&n.* mobi-lize.

mode[1], *s.f.* fashion, vogue; *à la ~* in vogue, in fashion.

mode[2], *s. m.* mode, way; mood.

modèle, *s.m.* model.

modération, *s. f.* moderation.

modérer, *v.a.* moderate.

moderne, *adj.* modern.

modeste, *adj.* modest.

modestie, *s.f.* modesty.

modification, *s. f.* modification, change.

modifier, *v.a.* modify.

modiste, *s.f.* milliner.

moelleux, -euse, *adj.* soft, mellow.

mœurs, *s. f. pl.* manners, customs, ways.

moi, *pron.* me, to me.

moi-même, *pron.* myself.

moindre, *adj.* less, lesser, smaller; *le ~* the least.

moineau, *s. m.* sparrow.

moins, *adv. & s. m.* less (*que, de* than); fewer (*de* than); minus; *le ~* the least; *à ~ que* unless; *au ~* at least.

mois, *s. m.* month; *par ~* monthly; a month.

moisson, *s.f.* harvest, crop.

moissonner, *v. a.* harvest, reap.

moitié, *s.f.* half.

molécule, *s. f.* molecule.

mollet, *s. m.* calf *(of leg)*.

moment, *s. m.* moment, instant.

mon, ma, *pron.* *(pl.* mes) my.

monarchie, *s. f.* monarchy

monastère, *s. m.* monastery, convent.

mondain, *adj.* worldly.

monde, *s.m.* world; people, company; *mettre au ~* give birth to; *tout le ~* everybody.

monnaie, *s.f.* money, coin, change; currency; ~ *légale* legal tender; ~ *étrangère* foreign currency.

monopole, *s.m.* monopoly.

monotone, *adj.* monotonous.

monseigneur, *s.m.* my lord, your lordship.

monsieur, *s. m.* gentleman; M. Mr.

monstrueux, -euse, *adj.* monstrous.

mont, *s. m.* mountain.

montage, *s. m.* carrying up; mounting, setting; wiring.

montagne, *s. f.* mountain.

montagneux, -euse, *adj.* mountainous.

montant, *adj.* ascending, uphill; *en* ~ upwards.

monte-charge, *s. m.* goods lift.

montée, *s. f.* rise, slope.

monter, *v.n.* go up, come up, ascend, climb; mount; ride; amount *(à* to); equip, fit up; ~ *à cheval* ride; *faire* ~ *qn. (dans sa voiture)* give s.o. a lift.

montre[1], *s.f.* watch.

montre[2], *s.f.* display, show; show-window.

montrer, *v.a.* show, display, point out; se ~ show oneself.

montueux, -euse, *adj.* hilly, steep.

monument, *s. m.* monument.

monumental, *adj.* monumental.

moquerie, *s. f.* mockery.

moral, *adj.* moral.

morale, *s. f.* ethics; morality.

moralité, *s. f.* morality, morals *(pl.)*.

morceau, *s. m.* piece, morsel, bit; snack.

mordre, *v. a.* bite; gnaw.

mors, *s. m.* bit; *fig.* check.

mort, *s. f.* death; — *adj.* dead, lifeless.

mortel, -elle, *adj.* mortal; boring, tedious.

mot, *s. m.* word; short note; ~s *croisés* crossword (puzzle).

motel, *s. m.* motel.

moteur, *s. m.* motor, engine.

motif, *s. m.* motive; cause.

motion, *s.f.* motion, movement.

motocyclette, *s. f.* motor-(bi)cycle, motor-bike.

mou, mol, molle, *adj.* soft; loose.

mouche, *s. f.* fly.

moucher: se ~ blow one's nose.

mouchoir, *s. m.* handkerchief.

moudre*, *v.a.* grind.

mouette, *s.f.* gull.

mouiller, *v.a.* & *n.* soak, wet.

moule, *s. m.* mould, cast.

moulin, *s. m.* mill; ~ *à vent* windmill; ~ *à café* coffee-mill.

mourant, *adj.* dying, expiring.

mourir*, *v. n.* die, expire.

mousse, *s. f.* foam, froth, lather; moss.

moustache, *s. f.* moustache.

moustique, *s.m.* mosquito.

moutarde, *sf.* mustard.

mouton, *s.m.* sheep; mutton.

mouvement, *s. m.* movement, motion, move.

mouvoir*, *v.a.* move; start; se ~ move, stir.

moyen, -enne, *adj.* mean, middle, average; *le* ~ *âge* the Middle Ages; — *s. m.* means, way, manner; *au* ~ *de* by means of; *avoir les* ~s *de* can afford.

moyenne, *s. f.* average, mean; *en* ~ on the average.

muet, -ette, *adj.* dumb, mute; speechless.

multiplication, *s. f.* multiplication.

multiplier, *v.a.&n.* multiply.

multitude, *s. f.* multitude, crowd.

municipal, *adj.* municipal, city.

munir, *v.a.* provide *(de* with).

munition, *s. f.* (am)munition.

mur, *s. m.* wall.

mûr, *adj.* ripe; mature.

mûrir, *v. a. & n.* ripen.

murmure, *s.m.* murmur.

murmurer, *v.n.* murmur.

muscle, *s.m.* muscle.

muse, *s. f.* muse.

museau, *s. m.* muzzle. musician; — *adj.* musical.

musical, *adj.* musical.

musicien, -enne, *s. m. f.*

musique, *s.f.* music; *instrument de* ~ musical instrument.

mutuel, -elle, *adj.* mutual.

myope, *adj.* short-sighted.

mystère, *s.m.* mystery.

mystérieux, -euse, *adj.* mysterious.

mystification, *s. f.* mystification.

mystique, *adj.* mystic.

N

nacre, *s.f.* mother-of-pearl.

nage, *s.f.* swimming; rowing, paddling.

nager, *v.n.* swim; float; row.

nageur, -euse, *s. m. f.* swimmer.

naïf, -ïve, *adj.* naïve.

nain, -e, *s. m. f.* dwarf.

naissance, *s. f.* birth; *lieu de* ~ birth-place.

naître*, *v. n.* be born; arise (from).

nappe, *s.f.* table-cloth.

narine, *s.f.* nostril.

nasal, *adj.* nasal.

natal, *adj.* natal, native, birth.

natif, -ive, *adj. & s. m. f.* native.

nation, *s.f.* nation.

national, *adj.* national.

nationalité, *s.f.* nationality.

naturaliser, *v.a.* naturalize.

nature, *s.f.* nature.

naturel, -elle, *adj.* natural, native.

naturellement, *adv.* naturally, of course.

naufrage, *s. m.* shipwreck; *faire* ~ be shipwrecked.

nausée, *s.f.* nausea.

nautique, *adj.* nautical.

naval, *adj.* naval.

navigateur, *s.m.* navigator.

navigation, *s.f.* navigation; sailing; *compagnie de* ~ shipping company; ~ *spatiale* space-flight.

naviguer, *v. a. & n.* navigate.

navire, *s.m.* ship; ~s

shipping.

ne, n', *adv.* not; ~ ... *pas* not; ~ ... *que* only.

né, -e, *adj.* born; née.

nécessaire, *adj.* necessary.

nécessité, *s. f.* necessity.

nécessiter, *v.a.* necessitate, make necessary.

nef, *s. f.* ship, vessel; nave; ~ *latérale* aisle.

négatif, -ive, *adj. & s. m.* negative.

négative, *s. f.* negative.

négligence, *s. f.* neglect, negligence.

négligent, *adj.* negligent.

négliger, *v.a.* neglect.

négociant, -e, *s. m. f.* merchant, trader.

négociation, *s. f.* negotiation, transaction.

nègre, *s.m.* negro.

neige, *s.f.* snow.

neiger, *v.n.* snow.

neigeux, -euse, *adj.* snowy

néon, *s. m.* neon.

nerf, *s. m.* nerve; sinew.

nerveux, -euse, *adj.* nervous.

net, nette, *adj.* clean, neat, clear, tidy; net; — *adv.* flatly, point-blank.

nettoyage, *s. m.* cleaning, cleansing.

nettoyer, *v.a.* clean, cleanse, clear.

neuf¹, *adj. & s. m.* nine.

neuf², **neuve**, *adj.* new.

neutre, *adj.* neutral.

neuvième, *adj.* ninth.

neveu, *s.m.* nephew.

nez, *s.m.* nose.

ni, *conj.* ~ ... ~ (n)either ... (n)or; ~ *l'un* ~ *l'autre* neither (one).

nid, *s.m.* nest; berth.

nièce, *s.f.* niece.

nier, *v.a.* deny.

niveau, *s. m.* level.

noble, *adj.* noble.

noblesse, *s.f.* nobility.

noce, *s. f. (often pl.)* wedding; *(sing.)* revelry.

Noël, *s. m.* Christmas; *veillée de* ~ Christmas eve.

nœud, *s. m.* knot, bow, tie.

noir, *adj.* black.

noix, *s. f.* (wal)nut; ~ *de coco* coconut.

nom, *s. m.* name, surname; fame; noun; ~ *de famille* surname.

nombre, *s.m.* number.

nombreux, -euse, *adj.* numerous.

nomination, *s. f.* nomination, appointment.

nommer, *v. a.* name, give name to; appoint, nominate.

non, *adv.* no, not.

nonne, *s. f.* nun.

nord, *s. m.* north; *du* ~, *au* ~ northern.

nord-est, *s. m.* northeast.

nord-ouest, *s. m.* northwest.

normal, *adj.* normal.

norvégien, -enne (N.), *adj. & s. m. f.* Norwegian.

nos, *poss. adj.* our.

notable, *adj.* notable, remarkable.

notaire, *s. m.* notary (-public).

note, *s. f.* note, mark; bill, account; note *(music)*; ~ *(au bas de la page)* foot-note.

noter, *v.a.* note, jot down; notice.

notice, *s. f.* notice.

notion, *s. f.* notion, idea.

notre, *poss. adj.* our.

nôtre, *pron. poss.* ours, our own.

nourrir, *v.a.* nourish, feed.

nourriture, *s. f.* nourishment food.

nous, *pron.* we; us.

nous-mêmes, *pron.* our-selves.

nouveau, -el, -elle, *adj.* new; further; *de* ~ again.

nouvelle, *s. f.* news; short story.

novembre, *s. m.* November.

noyau *s.m.* stone, kernel; nucleus, core.

noyer¹, *v. a.* drown; *se* ~ be drowning; drown oneself.

noyer², *s. m.* walnut-tree.

nu, *adj.* naked, bare.

nuage, *s. m.* cloud.

nuageux, -euse, *adj.* cloudy, clouded.

nuance, *s. f.* shade, tint, nuance.

nucléaire, *adj.* nuclear.

nuire*, *v. n.* hurt, harm, be harmful.

nuit, *s. f.* night; *il (se) fait* ~ it is night, it is getting dark; *de* ~ by night; *la* ~ at night, *bonne* ~! good night!

nul, nulle, *adj.* not one, not any; null, nil; — *pron.* no one, nobody.

numéro, *s. m.* number, size; ticket; copy, issue.

nu-pied, *adv.* barefoot.

nylon, *s. m.* nylon.

O

obéir, *v.n.* obey.

obéissance, *s. f.* obedience.

objectif, -ive, *adj.* objective; — *s. m.* object, purpose; lens.

objection, *s. f.* objection.

objet, *s. m.* object, thing, article; purpose; ~

d'art work of art.

obligation, *s. f.* obligation.

obligatoire, *adj.* compulsory, obligatory.

obliger, *v.a.* oblige, compel.

obscur, *adj.* dark, dim.

obscurité, *s. f.* darkness, dimness; *dans l'*~ in the dark.

observation, *s. f.* observation; remark.

observer, *v. a. & n.* observe, watch; keep.

obstacle, *s. m.* obstacle; hindrance; bar.

obstine, *adj.* obstinate.

obtenir, *v. a.* obtain, get.

occasion, *s. f.* occasion, chance, event; *a l'*~ if need be, eventually; *d'*~ second-hand.

occidental, *adj.* western, occidental.

occupant, -e, *s. m. f.* occupier, occupant.

occupation, *s. f.* occupation; pursuit.

occupé, *adj.* occupied, busy, engaged; *non* ~ unoccupied.

occuper, *v.a.* occupy, employ; *s'*~ occupy oneself *(de* with), be engaged; think *(de* of).

occurrence, *s.f.* occurrence; *en l'*~ in this case.

océan, *s.m.* ocean.

octobre, *s.m.* October.

odieux, -euse, *adj.* odious.

œil, *s. m. (pl.* yeux) eye, sight; *coup d'*~ glance; *au premier coup d'*~ at first sight, at a glance; *ouvrez l'*~! look out!

œillet, *s.m.* carnation; eyelet.

œuf, *s.m.* egg; ~ *à la coque* boiled egg; ~s

brouillés scrambled eggs; ~*s durs* hard-boiled eggs; *blanc d'*~ white of egg; *jaune d'*~ egg-yolk.

œuvre, *s. f.* work; composition; ~ *d'art* work of art.

offense, *s. f.* offence, insult; trespass.

offenser, *v.a.* offend, shock, injure; s'~ take offence, be offended *(de* with), be angry.

office, *s.m.* office; service; post; agency; *exercer un* ~ hold an office.

officiel, -elle, *adj.* official.

officier, *s.m.* officer.

offre, *s. f.* offer, tender.

offrir*, *v. a.* offer, present, hold out; s'~ offer, propose oneself.

oh!, *int.* oh!, O!, indeed!

oie, *s.f.* goose.

oignon, *s. m.* onion; bulb.

oiseau, *s. m.* bird.

olympique, *adj.* Olympic; *les jeux* ~ the Olympic games.

ombre, *s.m.* shade; ghost; obscurity, darkness.

ombreux, -euse, *adj.* shady, shaded.

omelette, *s.f.* omelet.

omettre, *v. a.* omit.

omission, *s. f.* omission, oversight.

omnibus, *s. m.* bus; — *adj.* slow; *train* ~ slow train.

on, *pron.* one, we, people *(pl.);* you; they; somebody; some one; ~ *dit* they say, it is said, people say; *ferme!* closing time!

oncle, *s.m.* uncle.

onde, *s. f.* wave; undulation;

ondulation, *s. f.* undulation; waving.

onduler, *v. a. & n.* undulate, wave; ripple.

ongle, *s. m.* nail *(finger).*

onze, *adj. & s. m.* eleven; eleventh.

opéra, *s. m.* opera; opera-house; ~ *comique* comic opera.

opérateur, *s. m.* operator; cameraman.

opération, *s. f.* operation; *salle d'*~ operating-theatre.

opérer, *v. a. & n.* operate (on); *se faire* ~ undergo an operation.

opérette, *s.f.* operetta.

opinion, *s.f.* opinion.

opportun, *adj.* opportune, timely.

opposer, *v.a.* oppose.

opposition, *s. f.* opposition.

oppression, *s. f.* oppression.

opprimer, *v. a.* oppress.

optimiste, *adj.* optimistic; — *s. m. f.* optimist.

optique, *adj.* optic(al); — *s. f.* optics.

or, *s. m.* gold; *d'*~, *en* ~ golden.

orage, *s.m.* storm.

orange, *s.f.* orange.

orateur, *s.m.* speaker.

orbite, *s. f.* orbit.

orchestre, *s. m.* orchestra.

ordinaire, *adj.* ordinary, usual, common.

ordinairement, *adv.* usually, generally.

ordonnance, *s. f.* order; statute; prescription.

ordonner, *v.a.* order, command.

ordre, *s. m.* order, command; *mettre en* ~ arrange, clear up.

ordure, s. f. refuse, rubbish.

oreille, s. f. ear; hearing; *prêter l'~ a* listen to, lend an ear to.

oreiller, s. m. pillow.

organe, s. m. organ.

organique, adj. organic.

organisation, s. f. organization, arrangement.

organiser, v. a. organize.

organisme, s. m. organism, system.

orgue, s. m. organ.

orgueil, s. m. pride.

orient, s. m. the East; *de l'~* eastern.

oriental, adj. oriental, eastern.

original, adj. original.

origine, s. f. origin, source; *avoir ~* come from.

ornement, s. m. ornament, adornment.

orner, v. a. adorn, ornament, trim, decorate.

orphelin, -e, s. m. f. orphan.

orthographie, s. f. spelling.

os, s. m. bone.

osciller, v. n. oscillate.

oser, v. a. & n. dare, venture.

ôter, v. a. take away, take off, remove, pull off; s'~ remove oneself.

ou, conj. or, either, else.

où, adv. where; whence; at which, in which; *n'importe ~* anywhere.

ouate, s. f. cotton-wool

oublier, v. a. & n. forget; overlook.

ouest, s. m. west; *à l'~* to, in the west, westward; *de l'~* western.

oui, adv. yes.

ouragan, s. m. hurricane.

ours, s. m. bear.

ourse, s. f. she-bear.

outil, s. m. tool.

outré, adj. exaggerated.

ouvert, adj. open; free; open-hearted; *à bras ~s* with open arms.

ouverture, s. f. opening; overtures *(pl.)*, proposal; overture.

ouvrage, s. m. (piece of) work.

ouvre-boîte, s. m. tin-opener.

ouvreuse, s. f. box-opener, attendant.

ouvrier, -ère, s. m. f. workman, worker; workwoman; hand; *premier ~* foreman.

ouvrir*, v. a. & n. open (up); break open; s'~ be opened, open.

oxygène, s. m. oxygen.

P

pacifique, adj. pacific, peaceful; *l'Océan ~* the Pacific Ocean.

pacte, s. m. pact.

page[1], s. f. page; *être à la ~* be up to date.

page[2], s. m. page *(boy)*.

paiement see payement.

paille, s. f. straw, chaff.

pain, s. m. bread, loaf; cake, tablet.

pair[1], adj. equal, even; *au ~* at par; "au pair".

pair[2], s. m. peer.

paire, s. f. pair; couple.

paisible, adj. peaceful.

paître*, v. a. & n. graze, feed.

paix, s. f. peace; calm.

palais[1], s. m. palace.

palais[2], s. m. palate.

pâle, adj. pale.

paletot, s. m. overcoat.

pâleur, *s. f.* pallor.

pâlir, *v. n.* & *a.* (grow) pale.

palmier, *s.m.* palm-tree.

palpiter, *v.n.* palpitate.

pamphlet, *s.m.* pamphlet.

pamplemousse, *s. m.* grapefruit.

pan, *s. m.* flap; coat-tail.

panache, *s.m.* plume.

panier, *s. m.* basket.

panique, *s. f.* panic.

panne, *s. f.* break-down; power-cut.

panneau, *s. m.* panel.

panorama, *s. m.* panorama.

pansement, *s. m.* dressing, bandage.

pantalon, *s. m.* trousers *(pl.)*.

pantoufle(s), *s. f. (pl.)* slipper(s).

papa, *s. m.* dad, daddy.

papauté, *s. f.* papacy.

pape, *s. m.* pope.

papeterie, *s. f.* paper-mill; stationery.

papetier, *s. m.* stationer.

papier, *s. m.* paper; ～ *hygiénique* toilet-paper; ～ *peint* wallpaper.

papillon, *s. m.* butterfly.

pâques, *s. m. pl.* Easter.

paquet, *s.m.* packet, parcel.

par, *prep.* by, by way of, by means of; across; through; per; for.

parade, *s. f.* parade, show.

paragraphe, *s. m.* paragraph.

paraître*, *v.n.* appear, come in sight; come out; *faire* ～ publish.

parallèle, *adj.* & *s. f.* parallel.

paralysie, *s. f.* paralysis.

paralytique, *s. m. f.* paralytic.

parapluie, *s. m.* unbrella.

paratonnerre, *s. m.* lightning-conductor.

parbleu, *int.* indeed!

parc, *s. m.* park; fold.

parce que, *conj.* because, on account of.

parcourir, *v.n.* travel through, go over; cover; run over, look over.

parcours, *s.m.* course, run; distance; mileage.

pardessus, *s. m.* overcoat.

par-dessus, *prep.* above.

pardon, *s. m.* pardon; *je vous demande* ～! I beg your pardon!; pardon me!; excuse me!; ～? (I beg your) pardon?

pardonner, *v.a.* pardon.

pare-boue, . *s.m.* mud-guard.

pare-brise, *s.m.* windscreen.

pare-choc, *s. m.* bumper.

pareil, -eille, *adj.* like, similar; such; same.

parent, *s. m. f.* relative, relation; ～s parents; relatives.

parer, *v. a.* adorn, trim; parry, ward off.

paresseux, -euse, *adj.* lazy, idle.

parfait, *adj.* & *s. m.* perfect.

parfaitement, *adv.* perfectly; ～! quite so!

parfois, *adv.* sometimes.

parfum, *s. m.* perfume.

parfumer, *v. a.* perfume.

parfumerie, *s. f.* perfumery.

parier, *v. a.* bet, stake.

parisien, -enne, *adj.* & *s. m. f.* Parisian.

parlement, *s. m.* parliament.

parlementaire, *adj.* parliamentary.

parler, *v. n.* & *a.* speak, talk; — *s. m.* speech, utterance; parlance.

parmi, *prep.* among.

paroi, *s. f.* wall, partition.

paroisse, *s. f.* parish.

parole, *s. f.* speech, utterance; language; word.

parquet, *s. m.* parquet.

part, *s. f.* part, share; side; *prendre ~ à* take part in, participate; *faire ~ a* inform (of), let know; *à ~* apart; *d'une ~ ... d'autre ~* on the one hand ... on the other (hand).

partager, *v.a.* divide, share out; share.

partenaire, *s. m. f.* partner.

parterre, *s. m.* flower-bed; pit.

parti, *s. m.* party; side.

participant, -e, *s. m. f. & adj.* participant.

participation, *s. f.* participation, share.

participe, *s. m.* participle; *~ passé* past participle.

participer, *v.n.* participate, take part (*à* in).

particulier, -ère, *adj.* particular, special, specific; peculiar; private; — *s. m. f.* private person; *en ~* in particular.

partie, *s. f.* part; match, game; party; *en ~* partly, in part.

partir*, *v. n.* start, leave, go (away), set out.

partisan, *s. m.* partisan, follower.

partition, *s. f.* score.

partout, *adv.* everywhere.

parure, *s. f.* ornament; set.

parvenir, *v. n.* attain (*à* to), reach.

pas[1], *s. m.* step, pace.

pas[2], *adv.* no, not, not any; *~ du tout* not at all; *~ nécessaire* unnecessary.

passage, *s. m.* passing; passage; corridor; crossing; thoroughfare; *~ clouté* pedestrian crossing; *~ à niveau* level-crossing; *~ interdit* no thoroughfare.

passager, -ère, *adj.* passing, transient, fugitive; — *s. m. f.* passenger.

passant, -e, *adj. en ~* by the way, cursorily; — *s. m. f.* passer-by.

passe, *s. f.* pass, passage; channel; permit.

passé, *adj.* past; — *prep.* after, beyond.

passeport, *s. m.* passport.

passer, *v. n. & a.* pass; pass along, by; cross; go on, pass on; hand; pass away; omit; forgive; strain; *en ~ par là* submit to it; *~ un examen* take an examination; *~ la nuit* spend the night; se *~* happen; disappear; do without.

passif, -ive, *adj.* passive — *s.m.* liabilities *(pl.)*.

passion, *s. f.* passion.

passionné *adj.* passionate.

pastel, *s. m.* pastel.

pastille, *s.f.* pastille.

pâte, *s. f.* paste; dough.

pâté, *s. m.* pie, pasty; block (of buildings); blot.

patente, *s.f.* patent, licence.

patience, *s. f.* patience.

patient, -e, *adj. & s. m. f.* patient.

patin, *s. m.* skate.

patinage, *s. m.* skating.

patiner, *v.n.* skate.

patinoire, *s.f.* skating-rink.

pâtisserie, *s.f.* pastry; pastry-shop, cake-shop.

pâtissier, -ère, s. m. f. pastry-cook.

pâtre, s. m. shepherd.

patrie, s. f. country.

patriote, adj. patriotic; — s. m. f. patriot.

patron[1], -onne, s. m. f. patron; employer, boss.

patron[2], s. m. model, pattern.

patronage, s. m. patronage, support.

patronner, v. a. patronize, protect.

patrouille, s. f. patrol.

patte, s. f. paw, foot.

pâture, s. f. fodder, pasture.

paume, s. f. palm.

paupière, s. f. eyelid.

pause, s. f. pause, stop, break; rest.

pauvre, adj. poor.

pauvreté, s. f. poverty.

pavé, s. m. paving-stone; pavement; street.

paver, v. a. pave.

pavillon, s. m. pavilion, summer-house; flag.

payable, adj. payable, due.

paye, s. f. pay, wages pl.

payement, paiement, s. m. payment.

payer, v. a. pay; pay down, for, off; repay.

pays, s. m. country, land; home; nation; district, region.

paysage, s. m. landscape; scenery.

paysan, -anne, s. m. f. peasant, countryman; countrywoman.

peau, s. f. skin; hide; leather.

pêche[1], s. f. peach.

pêche[2], s. f. fishing; angling; ~ à la ligne angling.

péché, s. m. sin, trespass.

pécher, v. n. sin, trespass.

pêcher, v. a. & n. fish, angle.

pécheur, -eresse, s. m. f. sinner.

pêcheur, s. m. angler, fisher.

pécuniaire, adj. pecuniary.

pédagogie, s. f. pedagogy.

pédale, s. f. pedal.

pédant, adj. pedant.

pédicure, s. m. pedicure.

peigne, s. m. comb.

peigner, v. a. comb.

peignoir, s. m. wrapper, dressing-gown.

peindre*, v. a. paint.

peine, s. f. punishment; pain, grief; trouble.

peintre, s. m. painter.

peinture, s. f. painting.

pêle-mêle, adv. pell-mell, in a muddle.

pelle, s. f. shovel, spade.

pellicule, s. f. film.

pelote, s. f. ball.

pelouse, s. f. lawn.

pelure, s. f. rind, peel.

pénalité, s. f. penalty.

penchant, s. m. slope, slant; bent, liking.

pencher, v. a. & n. incline, bend; stoop; lean (towards).

pendant[1], adj. hanging, pendent; — s. m. pendant; match.

pendant[2], prep. during; ~ que while.

pendre, v. a. & n. hang (up), suspend; hang down; be hanging.

pendule, s. f. clock.

pénétrer, v. a. & n. penetrate, go through; search; see through.

pénitence, s. f. penitence.

pensée, s. f. thought, thinking; mind; pansy.

penser, v. n. & a. think.

pension, s. f. pension; board (and lodging);

boarding-house; boarding-school; life annuity; ~ *et chambre(s)* board and lodging; ~ *pour étudiants* hostel.

pensionnaire, *s.m.f.* boarder; paying guest.

pensionnat, *s. m.* boarding-school.

pente, *s. f.* slope, descent; *en* ~ downhill.

Pentecôte, *s. f.* Whitsuntide; *dimanche de la* ~ Whit Sunday.

pépier, *v.n.* chirp.

pépin, *s. m.* pip, stone.

perçant, *adj.* piercing.

perception, *s.f.* perception.

percer, *v. a. & n.* pierce, bore; punch; tap.

percevoir, *v. a.* perceive, understand.

perdre, *v. a. & n.* lose; waste; be the ruin of; *se* ~ get lost, disappear; be ruined.

perdrix, *s. f.* partridge.

père, *s. m.* father.

perfection, *s.f.* perfection.

perforation, *s. f.* perforation.

perforer, *v.a.* perforate.

peril, *s.m.* peril, danger.

période, *s. f.* period, term.

périodique, *adj.* periodic, periodical.

périr, *v. n.* perish.

perle, *s. f.* pearl, bead.

permanent, *adj.* permanent.

permanente, *s. f.* perm.

permettre, *v.a.* allow, permit, let; *permettez-moi de* allow me to; *vous permettez?* may I?

permis, *s.m.* permit, licence.

permission *s. f.* permission, leave (of absence).

perron, *s. m.* stair, steps *(pl.).*

perroquet, *s. m.* parrot.

persan, -e (P.), *adj. & s. m. f.* Persian.

persécuter, *v. a.* persecute.

persécution, *s. f.* persecution.

persil, *s. m.* parsley.

persister, *v.n.* persist.

personnage, *s. m.* personage, person.

personnalité, *s. f.* personality.

personne, *s.f.* person; *grande* ~ grown-up; — *pron.* any one; anybody; no one.

personnel, -elle, *adj.* personal; — *s. m.* personnel, staff.

perspective, *s. f.* perspective, prospect, outlook.

persuader, *v. a.* persuade, convince.

persuasion, *s. f.* persuasion, conviction.

perte, *s. f.* loss; ruin.

pertinent, *adj.* pertinent.

peser, *v. a.* weigh; ponder.

pessimiste, *s. m. f.* pessimist; — *adj.* pessimistic.

petit, *adj.* small, little.

petite-fille, *s.f.* granddaughter.

petit-fils, *s. m.* grandson.

pétition, *s.f.* petition, request.

petits-enfants, *pl.* grandchildren.

pétrole, *s.m.* petroleum.

peu, *adv. & s. m.* little, bit, few; ~ *a* ~ little by little, bit by bit; *un (petit)* ~ a (little) bit; *quelque* ~ somewhat; ~ *abondant* scanty; ~ *commun* unusual; ~ *confortable* uncomfortable; ~ *nécessaire* unnecessary.

peuple, *s. m.* people.

peur, *s. f.* fear; fright; *avoir* ~ *(de)* be afraid (of); *de* ~ *que* for fear that.

peut-être, *adv.* perhaps.

phare, *s. m.* lighthouse; headlight.

pharmacie, *s. f.* pharmacy, chemist's (shop).

pharmacien, -enne, *s. m. f.* chemist.

phase, *s. f.* phase.

phénomène, *s. m.* phenomenon.

philologie, *s. f.* philology.

philosophe, *s. m.* philosopher.

philosophie, *s. f.* philosophy.

philosophique, *adj.* philosophical.

phono(graphe), *s.m.* gramophone.

photo, *s. f.* photo, snap.

photographe, *s.m.* photographer.

photographie, *s. f.* photograph; photography.

photographier, *v. a.* photograph.

photographique, *adj.* photographic; *appareil* ~ camera.

phrase, *s. f.* phrase; sentence.

phtisie, *s. f.* consumption.

physicien, -enne, *s. m. f.* physicist.

physique, *adj.* physical; — *s. f.* physics; ~ *nucléaire* nuclear physics; — *s. m.* physique, constitution.

pianiste, *s. m. f.* pianist.

piano(forte), *s. m.* piano.

pièce, *s. f.* piece, part, bit, coin; play; room; joint.

pied, *s. m.* foot, leg; *à* ~ on foot; *aller à* ~ walk.

pierre, *s. f.* stone; rock.

piéton, *s. m.* pedestrian.

pieu, *s. m.* stake, post.

pieux, -euse, *adj.* pious.

pigeon, -onne, *s. m. f.* dove, pigeon.

pile, *s. f.* pile, heap; battery.

pilier, *s. m.* pillar, post, column.

piller, *v. a. & n.* pillage.

pilot, *s. m.* pile.

pilote, *s. m.* pilot.

piloter, *v.a.* pilot, guide.

pilule, *s. f.* pill.

pin, *s. m.* pine(-tree).

pince, *s. f.* pinch; pincers, pliers, tongs *(pl.)*.

pincer, *v. a.* pinch.

pipe, *s. f.* pipe.

piquant, *adj.* pungent, sharp; piquant.

pique, *s. f.* pike; *s. m. (cards)* spade.

pique-nique, *s. m.* picnic.

piquer, *v. a. & n.* prick, sting; lard; goad, spur.

piqûre, *s. f.* prick, sting; puncture; injection.

pirate, *s. m.* pirate.

pire, *adj.* worse.

pis, *adv.* worse.

piscine, *s. f.* swimming-pool.

piste, *s. f.* track; trace; runway.

pistolet, *s. m.* pistol.

pitié, *s. f.* pity.

placard, *s. m.* placard, poster; cupboard.

place, *s. f.* place; room; seat; square.

placement, *s. m.* placing; investment; *bureau de* ~ labour-exchange.

placer, *v. a.* place, put, set; invest; sell.

plafond, *s. m.* ceiling.

plage, *s. f.* beach.

plaider, *v. a. & n.* plead.

plaindre, *v. a.* pity, feel compassion for; **se** ~ complain.

plaine, *s. f.* plain.

plainte, *s. f.* complaint.

plaire*, *v. n.* please; *vous plaît-il de?* would you like to?; *s'il vous plaît* (if you) please; se ~ take pleasure, enjoy.

plaisant, *adj.* pleasant, pleasing.

plaisanterie, *s.f.* joke,jest; *par* ~ as a joke.

plaisir, *s. m.* pleasure.

plan, *s. m.* plan; design; plane.

planche, *s.f.* board, plank.

plancher, *s. m.* floor.

planer, *v. a.* plane.

plante, *s. f.* plant; sole.

planter, *v. a.* plant; set.

planteur, *s. m.* planter.

plaque, *s. f.* plate; slab; plaque; ~ *de police* number-plate.

plaquer, *v. a.* plate; lay on.

plastique, *adj.* plastic, — *s. f.* plastic art; figure; — *s. m.* plastics *pl.*

plastron, *s. m.* (shirt-) front; plastron; stiff shirt.

plat, *adj.* flat; plain; dull; — *s. m.* flat (part); blade.

plateau, *s.m.* tray; scale (of balance); plateau.

plate-bande, *s. f.* flowerbed.

plate-forme, *s.f.* platform.

plâtre, *s. m.* plaster.

plein, *adj.* full; filled; *en* ~ fully, entirely.

pleurer, *v. n.* cry, weep.

pleuvoir: *il pleut* it rains.

pli, *s. m.* fold, crease.

pliant, *adj.* flexible, pliant; folding.

plier, *v. a. & n.* fold (up), bend; se ~ submit (*a* to).

plisser, *v. a. & n.* plait, fold, tuck; wrinkle.

plomb, *s.m.* lead.

plombage, *s. m.* filling.

plombier, *s. m.* plumber.

plonger, *v. a. & n.* plunge, immerse, dip, dive.

pluie, *s. f.* rain.

plume, *s. f.* feather, plume, pen.

plupart, *s. f.* most, the greatest part, majority.

pluriel, *s. m.* plural.

plus, *adv.* more, most; further, longer; any more; *de* ~ *en* ~ more and more; *en* ~ *de* in addition to; *ne . . .* ~ no more, no longer.

plusieurs, *adj.* several, many, some, a few; — *pron.* several people.

plutôt, *adv.* rather, preferably.

pluvieux, -euse, *adj.* rainy, wet.

pneu(matique), *s. m.* tyre.

pneumonie, *s. f.* pneumonia.

poche, *s. f.* pocket; pouch.

poêle¹, *s. m.* stove.

poêle², *s. f.* frying pan.

poème, *s. m.* poem.

poésie, *s. f.* poetry; poesy.

poète, *s. m.* poet.

poétique, *adj.* poetic(al).

poids, *s. m.* weight.

poignant, *adj.* poignant.

poigne, *s. f.* grip, grasp.

poignée, *s. f.* handle; hilt; handful.

poignet, *s. m.* wrist; cuff.

poil, *s. m.* hair; bristle; coat.

poinçon, *s.m.* punch, bodkin.

poinçonner, *v. a.* punch, clip; stamp.

poing, *s.m.* fist.

point, *s. m.* point, dot; full stop; *deux* ~s colon; ~ *et virgule* semicolon; *à* ~ just in time; *être sur le* ~ *de* be about to; ~ *de vue* point of view.

pointe, *s. f.* point, head, tip.

pointer, *v. a. & n.* point.

pointu, *adj.* sharp, pointed.

poire, *s. f.* pear.

pois, *s. m.* pea.

poison, *s. m.* poison.

poisson, *s. m.* fish.

poissonnier, -ère, *s. m. f.* fishmonger.

poitrine, *s. f.* chest, breast.

poivre, *s. m.* pepper.

pôle, *s. m.* pole.

poli, *adj.* polished; polite.

police, *s. f.* police; policy; *agent de* ~ policeman.

policier, *s. m.* policeman.

policlinique, *s.f.* out-patients' department.

polir, *v. a.* polish, refine.

politesse, *s. f.* politeness.

politicien, -enne, *s. m. f.* politician.

politique, *s. f.* politics.

polonais, -e (P.), *adj.* Polish; — *s. m.* Pole; *s. f.* Polish woman; polonaise.

pomme, *s. f.* apple; ~ *de terre* potato.

pommier, *s. m.* apple tree.

pompe[1], *s. f.* pomp, ceremony.

pompe[2], *s. f.* pump; ~ *à incendie* fire-engine; ~ *à essence* petrol pump.

pompier, *s. m.* fireman; *les* ~*s* fire-brigade.

ponctuel, -elle, *adj.* punctual.

pont, *s. m.* bridge; deck; ~ *suspendu* suspension-bridge; ~ *inférieur* lower deck.

populaire, *adj.* popular; vulgar, common.

popularité, *s. f.* popularity.

population, *s. f.* popula-tion.

populeux, -euse, *adj.* populous.

porc, *s. m.* pig, hog; pork.

porcelaine, *s. f.* porcelain, china(ware).

pore, *s. m.* pore.

poreux, -euse, *adj.* porous.

port[1], *s.m.* harbour (sea-)port; *arriver à bon* ~ arrive safely.

port[2], *s. m.* bearing, gait; carriage; postage; ~ *payé* postage paid.

portable, *adj.* portable.

porte, *s. f.* door(way), entrance; ~ *d'entrée* front-door.

porte-cigarettes, *s. m. pl.* cigarette-case.

portée, *s. f.* litter; range, scope; *à* ~ within reach.

portemanteau, *s.m.* coat-stand; suit-case.

porter, *v. a. & n.* bear; carry; convey; wear, have on; hold; ~ *intérêt* yield interest; show interest; ~ *la santé de B* drink B's health; *se* ~ be worn, be carried; *comment vous portez-vous?* how are you?

porteur, *s. m.* porter, carrier; bearer.

portier, -ère, *s. m. f.* porter, door-keeper.

portière, *s. f.* door (on vehicle); (door-)curtain.

portion, *s. f.* portion, part, share; helping.

portrait, *s. m.* portrait.

portugais, -e (P.), *adj. & s. m. f.* Portuguese.

posemètre, *s. m.* light-meter.

poser, *v. a. & n.* place, lay down, put; state.

positif, -ive, *adj. & s. m. f.* positive.

position, *s.f.* position, situation; attitude.

posséder, *v.a.* possess.

possession, *s.f.* possession; property.

possibilité, *s.f.* possibility.

possible, *adj.* possible; *faire tout son* ~ do one's best.

postal, *adj.* postal; post; *carte* ~e post-card.

poste[1], *s. f.* post(-office), mail; *mettre à la* ~ post (a letter); *bureau de* ~ post-office; *timbre* ~ stamp; ~ *aérienne* airmail.

poste[2], *s. m.* post, station, office; police-station; receiver, set; ~ *de T. S. F.* wireless-set.

postulant, -e, *s. m. f.* applicant, candidate.

pot, *s. m.* pot, can, jug, vessel, pitcher.

potager, *s.m.* kitchen garden.

poteau, *s. m.* post.

poterie, *s. f.* pottery.

potin, *s. m.* noise; (piece of) gossip.

poubelle, *s. f.* dustbin.

pouce, *s.m.* thumb.

pouding, *s. m.* pudding.

poudre, *s. f.* powder, dust.

poudrier, *s. m.* compact.

poule, *s.f.* hen; fowl.

poulet, *s.m.* chicken, fowl.

pouls, *s. m.* pulse.

poumon, *s. m.* lung(s).

poupée, *s. f.* doll.

pour, *prep.* for; ~ *cent* per cent; ~ *que* in order that.

pourboire, *s. m.* tip.

pourquoi, *conj. & adv.* why; what for; for what reason.

poursuite, *s. f.* pursuit, chase; ~s suit, action.

poursuivre, *v. a.* pursue, chase, prosecute.

pourtant, *adv.* however, still.

pourvoir, *v. n. & a.* provide (*à* for), supply, cater (*à* for).

pousser, *v. a. & n.* push; shove; urge; impel; grow; utter.

poussière, *s. f.* dust

poussiéreux, -euse *adj.* dusty.

pouvoir*, *v. a. & n.* be able, may; *se* ~ be possible; *cela se peut* that may be; — *s. m.* power.

pratique, *s. f.* practice, execution; experience; customers (*pl.*); — *adj.* practical, convenient.

pratiquer, *v. a.* practise, carry out; exercise.

préalable, *adj.* previous, *au* ~ first of all.

précédent, *adj.* precedent, previous; — *s. m.* precedent.

précéder, *v. a. & n.* precede; come before.

prêcher, *v.a. & n.* preach.

prêcheur, *s. m.* preacher.

précieux, -euse, *adj.* precious, valuable, costly.

précipice, *s. m.* precipice.

précipitation, *s.f.* precipitation, haste, hurry.

précipité, *adj.* hasty.

précipiter, *v.a.* precipitate; hasten, hurry.

précis, *adj.* exact, precise; — *s. m.* summary.

préciser, *v.a.* specify.

prédécesseur, *s. m.* predecessor.

prédire, *v.a.* foretell.

préfabriqué, *adj.* prefabricated.

préface, *s.f.* preface.

préférable, *adj.* preferable, better.

préférer, *v.a.* prefer; like

better.

préfet, *s.m.* prefect.

préjugé, *s. m.* prejudice, presumtion.

prélat, *s.m.* prelate.

préliminaire, *adj.* preliminary.

premier, **-ère**, *adj.* first, former; ~ *plan* foreground; close-up; *de* ~ *ordre* first-rate; ~ — *s. m.* first floor.

première, *s. f.* first night; first class (in a carriage).

prendre*, *v. a.* take, take up, seize; receive, accept; put on, wear; charge; catch; ~ *place* take a seat: *à tout* ~ on the whole; ~ *pour* mistake for; ~ *du corps* put on weight; ~ *l'air* take a walk; se ~ be taken, be caught.

prénom, *s. m.* Christian name.

préoccuper, *v. a.* preoccupy, engross; worry; se ~ trouble oneself.

préparatifs, *s.m.pl.* preparations.

préparation, *s. f.* preparation.

préparer, *v. a.* prepare, make ready; read for; se ~ prepare oneself, get ready.

préposition, *s. f.* preposition.

prérogative, *s. f.* prerogative, privilege.

près, *adv.* & *prep.* near, close by, close to; nearly; *à peu* ~ nearly (so); *de* ~ closely.

prescription, *s.f.* prescription.

prescrire*, *v. t.* prescribe.

présence, *s. f.* presence, attendance; *en* ~ *de* in the presence of.

présent[1], *s. m.* present, gift; *faire* ~ *de* give as a present.

présent[2], *s. m.* present (time); present tense; — *adj.* present, current *à* ~ at present; *jusqu'à* ~ till now, as yet; *pour le* ~ for the time being.

présentation, *s. f.* presentation, introduction.

présenter, *v. a.* present, offer; introduce; se ~ appear.

préserver, *v. a.* preserve.

président, *s. m.* president.

présomption, *s. f.* presumption; conceit.

presque, *adv.* almost.

pressant, *adj.* pressing.

presse, *s. f.* press; printing-press; haste; crowd.

pressé, *adj.* pressing; *être* ~ be in a hurry.

pressentiment, *s. m.* presentiment; misgiving.

pressentir, *v.a.* have a presentiment of.

presser, *v. a.* press, crush; hurry; *pressez-vous!* hurry up!; se ~ hurry (up).

pression, *s.f.* pressure.

pressurer, *v.a.* press, squeeze; oppress.

prestige, *s.m.* marvel; influence, prestige.

présumer, *v. a.* suppose, expect; presume.

prétendre, *v. a.* & *n.* pretend, claim; intend.

prétention, *s.f.* pretension, claim.

prêter, *v.a.* lend, attribute; se ~ lend oneself (*à* to).

prétexte, *s. m.* pretext.

prêtre, *s. m.* priest.

preuve, *s. f.* proof; *faire*

~ *de* show.

prévaloir, *v.n.* prevail.

prévenir, *v. a.* anticipate, inform, let know.

préventif, -ive, *adj.* preventive.

prévention, *s.f.* bias, prejudice.

prévision, *s. f.* prevision, anticipation; forecast.

prévoir, *v.a.* foresee, anticipate, forecast.

prévoyance, *s. f.* foresight.

prier, *v. a.* pray, beg; ask.

prière, *s.f.* prayer; request.

primaire, *adj.* primary.

prime, *adj.* first, early.

primer, *v. a.* surpass, excel; award a prize to.

primeur, *s. f.* early vegetables *(pl.)*.

primitif, -ive, *adj.* primitive, original.

prince, *s. m.* prince.

princesse, *s. f.* princess.

principal, *adj.* principal.

principalement, *adv.* principally, mainly.

principe, *s. m.* principle.

printemps, *s. m.* spring-(time); *au* ~ in spring.

priorité, *s.f.* priority.

prise, *s.f.* taking; capture, catch; ~ *de courant* (electric) plug.

prisme, *s. m.* prism.

prison, *s. f.* prison.

prisonnier, -ère, *s. m. f.* prisoner.

privation, *s. f.* privation.

privé, *adj.* private.

priver, *v. a.* deprive.

privilège, *s. m.* privilege.

prix, *s. m.* price, cost, charge; prize; *au* ~ *de* at the cost of; ~ *de la course* fare; ~ *par mille* mileage; ~*courant* market-price; ~ *fixe* fixed price.

probabilité, *s. f.* probability.

probable, *adj.* probable.

probablement, *adv.* probably.

problématique, *adj.* problematic(al).

problème, *s. m.* problem.

procédé *s. m.* proceeding.

procéder, *v. n.* proceed.

procédure, *s. f.* procedure.

procès, *s.m.* (law-)suit, trial; *faire un* ~ *u* bring an action against.

procession, *s.f.* procession.

prochain, *adj.* near(est), next. — *s. m.* neighbour

prochainement, *adv.* shortly, soon.

proche, *adj.* near, neighbouring, close at hand.

proclamer, *v. a.* proclaim.

procurer, *v. a.* procure.

procureur, *s. m.* attorney.

prodigieux, -euse, *adj.* wonderful, prodigious.

producteur, -trice, *s. m. f.* producer; — *adj.* producing.

production, *s. f.* production.

produire*, *v. a.* produce, bring forth, yield.

produit, *s. m.* produce; product.

professer, *v. a. & n.* profess; teach.

professeur, *s. m.* teacher; professor; lecturer.

profession, *s.f.* profession.

professionnel, -elle, *adj. & s. m. f.* professional.

profil, *s. m.* profile.

profit, *s. m.* profit, gain.

profitable, *adj.* pro'itable.

profiter, *v. n.* profit (by).

profond, *adj.* deep, profound.

profondeur, s. f. depth; dix pieds de ~ ten feet deep.

programme, s. m. program(me); scheme.

progrès, s. m. progress, improvement; faire des ~ make progress.

prohiber, v.a. prohibit.

projecteur, s. m. headlight; searchlight; projector.

projectile, s. m. projectile, missile.

projection, s. f. projection.

projet, s. m. project, plan; scheme; ~ de loi bill.

projeter, v.a. project throw; scheme, plan.

prolonger, v.a. prolong.

promenade, s.f. walk; promenade.

promener: se ~ go for a walk; se ~ en voiture go for a drive.

promesse, s. f. promise.

promettre, v. a. promise.

promotion, s. f. promotion.

prompt, adj. prompt.

pronom, s. m. pronoun.

prononcer, v.a. &n. pronounce; utter; deliver.

prononciation, s. f. pronunciation; delivery.

propagande, s. f. propaganda.

propager, v.a. propagate.

prophète, s.m.f. prophet.

prophétie, s. f. prophecy.

proportion, s. f. proportion; ratio.

propos, s. m. talk, remark; à ~ in good time; by the way.

proposer, v.a. propose, offer.

proposition, s. f. proposal, proposition.

propre, adj own, peculiar; proper, fit.

propriétaire, s.m.f. owner, proprietor; landlord, landlady.

propriété, s. f. ownership; property.

propulsion, s. f. propulsion; ~ à réaction jet propulsion.

prosaïque, adj. prosaic.

proscrire*, v. a. proscribe.

prose, s. f. prose.

prospectus, s.m. prospectus.

prospère, adj. prosperous.

prospérer, v. n. prosper, get on (well).

prospérité, s.f. prosperity.

protecteur, s. m. protector, patron.

protection, s.f. protection, support.

protéger, v.a. protect; patronize.

protestant, -e, s. m. f. & adj. Protestant.

protestation, s.f. protest(ation).

protester, v. n. & a. protest.

prouver, v.a. prove.

provenir, v.n. come (from), issue, arise.

province, s. f. province, country, district.

provincial, adj. provincial, country.

provision, s. f. provision.

provisoire, adj. provisional, temporary.

provoquer, v. a. provoke; stir up.

proximité, s.f. proximity.

prudence, s. f. prudence, caution.

prudent, adj. prudent, cautious.

prune, s. f. plum.

pruneau, s. m. prune.

prunelle, s. f. pupil.

psaume, *s. m.* psalm.

psychologie, *s. f.* psychology.

psychologique, *adj.* psychological.

public, publique, *adj.* public, common; — *s. m.* public, audience.

publication, *s.f.* publication.

publicité, *s. f.* publicity.

publier, *v. a.* publish.

puce, *s. f.* flea:

puer, *v. n.* stink.

puéril, *adj.* childish.

puis, *adv.* then, after that.

puiser, *v. a.* draw up, fetch up.

puisque, *conj.* as, since.

puissance, *s.f.* power, might, force.

puissant, *adj.* powerful, strong; *tout* ~ almighty.

puits, *s. m.* well; pit.

punaise, *s. f.* drawing-pin; bug.

punch, *s.m.* punch *(drink)*.

punir, *v. a.* punish.

punition, *s.f.* punishment.

pupille, *s.m.f.* ward, pupil; — *s. f.* pupil (of the eye).

pupitre, *s. m.* desk.

pur, *adj.* pure, clean.

purée, *s. f.* mash, purèe.

purement, *adv.* purely, merely.

pureté, *s. f.* purity.

purgatif, -ive, *adj.* & *s. m.* purgative.

purger, *v. a.* purge.

purifier, *v.a.* purify, cleanse.

puritain, -e, *adj.* & *s. m. f.* Puritan.

pyramide, *s. f.* pyramid.

Q

qual, *s. m.* quay; wharf; platform; *billet de* ~ platform ticket.

qualification, *s. f.* qualification.

qualifié, *adj.* qualified.

qualifier, *v.a.* qualify.

qualité, *s.f.* quality.

quand, *adv. & conj.* when; while; ~ *même* all the same.

quant à, *prep.* as for, with regard to.

quantité, *s. f.* quantity; amount; ~ *de* plenty of.

quarante, *adj. & s. m.* forty.

quart, *s.m.* quarter, fourth part; quart.

quartier, *s. m.* quarter; piece, slice; district; ~ *général* headquarters *(pl.)*.

quatorze, *adj. & s.m.* fourteen.

quatre, *adj. &s.m.* four; fourth:

quatre-vingt-dix, *adj. & s. m.* ninety.

quatre-vingts, *adj. & s. m.* eighty.

quatrième, *adj. & s. m.* fourth; fourth floor; — *s. f.* third form.

quatuor, *s. m.* quartet(te).

que, qu', *rel. pron.* whom, which, that; of which, at which; — *adv.* how much, how many; — *conj.* that; than; as; if; as though.

quel, quelle, *adj.* what, which.

quelque, *adj.* some, any; a few; ~ *chose* something, anything; ~ *part* somewhere; ~ *peu* somewhat — *adv.* about, some.

quelquefois, *adv.* sometimes.

quelqu'un, -e, *pron.*

somebody; anybody.

querelle, *s. f.* quarrel.

quereller, *v. a. & n.* quarrel with.

question, *s.f.* question; point, matter, issue.

questionner, *v.a.* question, interrogate.

queue, *s.f.* tail; rear; queue; handle.

qui, *rel. pron.* who, whom; which; that; *à* ~ to whom.

quille, *s. f.* keel, skittle.

quincaillerie, *s. f.* hardware (shop).

quintal, *s. m.* hundredweight.

quinze, *adj. & s. m.* fifteen; fifteenth; ~ *jours* fortnight.

quittance, *s. f.* receipt.

quitte, *adj.* quit, free.

quitter, *v. a.* leave, give up, quit.

quoi, *rel. pron.* what, which; *à propos de* ~ what is it about?; ~ *qu'il en soit* at any rate.

quoique, *conj.* (al)though.

quotidien, -enne, *adj. & s. m.* daily.

R

rabais, *s. m.* reduction in price, rebate.

rabaisser, *v. a.* lower.

rabattre, *v.a.* beat down, pull down; reduce.

raccommoder, *v. a.* mend, repair.

raccourcir, *v.a. & n.* shorten, abridge.

raccrocher, *v.a.* hang up again.

race, *s. f.* race; stock; breed.

racine, *s. f.* root; *prendre* ~ take root.

raconter, *v.a.* tell, relate.

radar, *s. m.* radar.

radiateur, *s. m.* radiator.

radiation *s. f.* radiation.

radical, *adj.* radical.

radieux, -euse, *adj.* radiant, beaming.

radio, *s. f.* radio.

radio-actif, -ive, *adj.* radioactive.

radiodiffuser, *v.a.* broadcast.

radiodiffusion, *s. f.* broadcasting.

radiogramme, *s. m.* X-ray photograph; radiogram.

radiographie, *s. f.* X-ray photograph(y).

radioreportage, *s. m.* running commentary.

radioscopie, *s. f.* radioscopy.

radioscopique, *adj.* *examen* ~ X-ray examination.

radis, *s.m.* radish.

raffermir, *v.a.* strengthen, fortify.

raffinage, *s.m.* refining.

raffiné, *adj.* refined.

raffinement, *s. m.* refinement.

raffiner, *v. a.* refine.

rafraîchir, *v. a.* refresh, cool; *se* ~ cool down.

rafraîchissement, *s.m.* refreshment; ~*s* refreshments.

rage, *s.f.* rage, fury.

ragoût, *s. m.* ragout, stew.

raide, *adj.* stiff, rigid.

raidir, *v. a.* make stiff.

raifort, *s.m.* horse radish.

rail, *s. m.* rail.

railler, *v.a.* mock, rail at.

raillerie, *s.f.* raillery, mocking.

raisin, *s. m.* grape(s);

~ *sec* raisin.

raison, *s.f.* reason; judgement; *à ~ de* at the rate of; *avoir ~* be right.

raisonnable, *adj.* reasonable.

raisonnement, *s. m.* reasoning.

raisonner, *v. n. & a.* reason, argue.

ralentir, *v. a. & n.* slow down.

ramasser, *v.a.* gather up, pick up; take up.

rame, *s. f.* oar; prop.

ramener, *v.a.* bring back, take back.

ramer, *v. n.* row.

rampe, *s.f.* banister; footlights *(pl.)*.

ramper, *v.n.* crawl, creep.

rance, *adj.* rancid.

rancune, *s.f.* spite, grudge.

randonneur, -euse, *s. m. f.* excursionist, hiker.

rang, *s.m.* row, line; rank.

rangé, *adj.* tidy.

rangée, *s.f.* row, line, range.

ranger, *v. a.* put in order; arrange; range; *se ~* settle down; make room.

ranimer, *v.a.* revive, restore to life, refresh.

râpe, *s.f.* rasp, grater.

râpé, *adj.* shabby.

rapide, *adj.* rapid, fast; steep.

rapidité, *s.f.* rapidity, speed.

rappel, *s.m.* recall.

rappeler, *v. a.* recall, call back; bring back; *se ~* remember.

rapport, *s.m.* product, yield; report, account; connection, relation; reference; *sous ce ~* in this respect.

rapporter, *v.a.* bring back; produce, yield; report, state; *se ~* relate to, refer to.

rapprochement, *s. m.* drawing closer.

rapprocher, *v. a.* bring closer; *se ~* draw nearer.

raquette, *s. f.* racket.

rare, *adj.* rare.

raser, *v. a.* shave, graze; pull down; bore; *v.n. se ~* shave.

rasoir, *s. m.* razor; *~ électrique* electric razor; *~ de sûreté* safety razor.

rassembler, *v. a.* gather, assemble, collect.

rassis, *adj.* settled; stale.

rassurer, *v.a.* reassure, comfort.

rat, *s. m.* rat.

râteau, *s. m.* rake.

ratelier, *s. m.* rack; set of false teeth.

rater, *v. n. & a.* miss fire; fail.

ratification, *s. f.* ratification.

ration, *s. f.* ration.

rattacher, *v.a.* tie up again, join.

rattraper, *v.a.* catch again; catch up; overtake.

rauque, *adj.* hoarse.

ravager, *v. a.* ravage, lay waste.

ravir, *v. a.* delight.

ravissant, *adj.* ravishing, charming.

rayer, *v. a.* scratch (out); cross out.

rayon, *s.m.* ray, beam; spoke; radius; shelf.

rayonnement, *s. m.* radiation; radiance.

rayonner, *v.n.* radiate, shine.

razzia, *s. f.* raid.
réacteur, *s.m.* reactor.
réactoin, *s.f.* reaction.
réagir, *v.n.* react.
réalisation, *s.f.* realization; carrying out.
réaliser, *v.a.* realize.
réaliste, *adj.* realistic.
réalité, *s. f.* reality; *en ~* in fact.
rebelle, *adj.* rebellious; — *s. m. f.* rebel.
rébellion, *s. f.*, rebellion.
rebord, *s.m.* edge, brim.
rébus, *s.m.* riddle.
récemment, *adv.* recently, lately.

récent, *adj.* recent.
récepteur, *s. m.* receiver.
réception, *s. f.* reception, receipt; at-home.
recette, *s.f.* receipt; recipe.
receveur, *s.m.* receiver; conductor *(bus).*
recevoir*, *v.n.* receive; admit, take in; accept; *v. n.* entertain; *aller ~ qn. à la gare* meet s.o. at the station.
rechange, *s. m. pièces de ~* spare parts.
recharge, *s. f.* refill.
réchaud, *s.m.* dishwarmer.
réchauffer, *v. a.* warm up again.
recherche, *s.f.* research; inquiry.
rechercher, *v. a.* look for, search for; research into.
récipé, *s.m.* recipe.
réciproque, *adj.* reciprocal, mutual.
récit, *s. m.* recital, account.
récital, *s. m.* recital.
récitation, *s. f.* recitation.
réciter, *v.a.* recite.
réclamation, *s. f.* claim, complaint.
réclame, *s. f.* advertisement; *faire de la ~ (pour)* advertise.
réclamer, *v.a.* demand, claim.
recommandation, *s. f.* recommendation.
recommander, *v. a.* recommend; introduce; request; register.
recommencer, *v. a. & n.* begin again.
récompense, *s. f.* reward.
récompenser, *v. a.* reward, repay.
réconcilier, *v. a.* reconcile.
reconnaissance, *s. f.* recognition, gratitude.
reconnaître, *v. a.* recognize, know; acknowledge; explore.
reconstruction, *s. f.* reconstruction.
reconstruire*, *v.a.* rebuild.
record, *s.m.* record *(sport etc.).*
recourir, *v. n. ~ a* have recourse to.
recouvrir, *v.a.* cover again, hide.
récréation, *s. f.* recreation, amusement, pastime.
recrue, *s. f.* recruit.
recteur, *s.m.* rector, chancellor.
rectifier, *v.a.* rectify, correct.
reçu, *s. m.* receipt; *au ~ de* on receipt of.
recueil, *s. m.* collection.
recueillir, *v.a.* collect; *se ~* collect oneself.
reculer, *v.a.* put back; *v. n.* draw back, recoil.
rédacteur, -trice, *s. m. f.* editor; writer.
rédaction, *s. f.* drawing up; composition; editorial staff.

rédemption, *s. f.* redemption.

rédiger, *v.a.* draw up; edit.

redingote, *s.f.* frock-coat.

redire, *v. a.* repeat, say again; *trouver à ~ à* find fault with.

redoubler, *v.a.* redouble.

redoutable, *adj.* formidable, dreaded.

redouter, *v.a.* dread, be afraid of.

redresser, *v. a.* & *se ~* straighten (up).

réduction, *s. a.* reduction, cut.

réduire*, *v. a.* reduce, cut down.

réduit, *adj.* reduced.

réel, réelle, *adj.* real, actual.

réélection, *s.f.* re-election.

réélire, *v. a.* re-elect.

refaire, *v.a.* do (over) again.

réfectoire, *s. m.* refectory, dining-hall.

référence, *s. f.* reference.

référer, *v. a.* refer; *se ~ à* refer to; *nous référant à* referring to.

réfléchir, *v.a.* reflect; consider, think over.

réflecteur, *s. m.* reflector.

reflet, *s. m.* reflection.

refléter, *v. a.* reflect.

réflexe, *adj.* reflex.

réflexion, *s. f.* reflection, consideration.

reflux, *s. m.* ebb.

réformation, *s.f.* reformation.

réforme, *s.f.* reform, improvement.

Réforme, *s. f.* Reformation.

réformer, *v. a.* reform.

refrain, *s. m.* refrain.

refréner, *v. a.* bridle, curb.

réfrigérateur, *s.m.* refrigerator.

réfrigérer, *v. a.* refrigerate.

refroidir, *v. a.* chill, cool.

refuge, *s. m.* refuge; lay-by.

refugié, -e, *s. m. f.* refugee.

réfugier: se ~ take shelter, take refuge.

refus, *s. m.* refusal, denial.

refuser, *v. a.* refuse, deny; *~ de connaître* ignore; *être refusé* fail.

regagner, *v.a.* regain, recover; return to.

regard, *s. m.* look.

regarder, *v. a.* look at; concern; regard.

régime, *s. m.* (form of) government; diet.

régiment, *s. m.* regiment.

région, *s. f.* region, area.

régional, *adj.* local.

régir, *v.a.* rule, administer.

régisseur, *s. m.* steward; stage-manager.

registre, *s.m.* register; record.

règle, *s. f.* rule; ruler.

réglé, *adj.* regular; punctual; steady; ruled.

règlement, *a.m.* rule, regulation.

régler, *v. a.* rule; regulate; time; settle.

règne, *s.m.* reign.

régner, *v.a.* reign.

regret, *s. m.* regret.

regretter, *v. a.* regret, be sorry for.

régulariser, *v. a.* regularize.

régularité, *s. f.* regularity.

régulateur, *s. m* regulator.

régulier, -ière, *adj.* regular; correct.

rein, *s.m.* kidney.

reine, *s.f.* queen.

reine-claude, *s. f.* greengage.

rejeter, *v. a.* reject, throw out.

rejoindre, *v.a.* rejoin; overtake, catch up; **se ~** meet.

réjouir, *v. a.* give joy to, cheer up, delight; **se ~** rejoice.

relâche, *s. f.* relaxation; respite.

relâcher, *v.a.* slacken, loosen; relax; **se ~** relax.

relatif, -ive, *adj.* relative; **~ à** relating to.

relation, *s.f.* relation, connection; report; *entrer en ~ avec* get in touch with.

relever, *v. a.* lift, take up, pick up; set off; *v. n.* recover.

relief, *s.m.* relief.

relier, *v. a.* bind (a book); hoop (casks).

religieux, -euse, *adj.* religious; — *s. m.* monk; *s. f.* nun.

religion, *s.f.* religion.

relique, *s.f.* relic.

relire, *v.a.* read (over) again.

remarquable, *adj.* remarkable, noticeable.

remarque, *s. f.* remark, observation, notice.

remarquer, *v. a.* remark, notice, observe; *faire ~* point out.

rembourser, *v.a.* repay, reimburse.

remède, *s.m.* remedy; medicine.

remerciement, *s. m.* thanks *(pl.).*

remercier, *v.a.* thank *(de* for).

remettre, *v. a.* put back; put on again; post-

pone; **se ~** recover (oneself).

remilitariser, *v. a.* rearm.

remise, *s. f.* remittance; delivery; allowance; revival, restoration.

remonter, *v. n. & a.* go up, remount; bring up again; set up again.

remords, *s. m.* remorse.

remorque, *s. f.* tow(ing), trailer.

remorqueur, *s. m. (bateau) ~* tug-boat.

remous, *s. m.* eddy(-water), whirl.

remplacer, *v. a.* replace, substitute.

remplir, *v. a.* fill; fill up; fulfil; carry out.

remporter, *v.a.* take away, carry off; get, obtain.

remuer, *v. a. & n.* move, fidget about; **se ~** be busy, move.

rémunération, *s. f.* remuneration.

renaissance, *s. f.* renascence; revival; *la Renaissance* the Renaissance.

renaître, *v.n.* be born again, revive.

renard, *s.m.* fox.

rencontre, *s. f.* meeting, encounter; collision.

rencontrer, *v.a.* meet, meet with; come across; run into; **se ~** *avec* meet, be met with.

rendement, *s. m.* output.

rendez-vous, *s. m.* appointment, rendezvous.

rendormir: se ~ go to sleep again.

rendre, *v.a.* give back, return; yield; render; convey; *~ un arrêt* issue a decree; *~ compte* render an account, realize; *~ visite* pay a visit.

renfermer, *v. a.* lock up again, confine; contain, include.

renfler, *v.a.&n.* swell.

renforcer, *v. a.* strengthen, reinforce.

renfort, *s. m.* reinforcement; help.

renier, *v. a.* deny.

renom, *s.m.* reputation.

renommée, *s. f.* renown.

renoncer, *v.n.&a.* renounce, give up.

renouveler, *v.a.* renew, renovate.

renseignement, *s. m.* information; indication; *bureau des ~s* inquiry office.

renseigner, *v. a.* give information to; *se ~* inquire, ask *(sur* about).

rente, *s. f.* income; rent.

rentrée, *s. f.* return; reopening.

rentrer, *v. n.* reenter, go in; get back, return home.

renversé, *adj.* reversed, upset.

renverser, *v.a.* upset; overthrow; turn upside down; **se ~** be upset, tip over.

renvoi, *s.m.* return; (cross-)reference.

renvoyer, *v.a.* return; dismiss; refer.

réorganiser, *v.a.* reorganize.

répandre, *v.a.* pour; spread, scatter, diffuse.

réparation, *s.f.* repair, amends.

réparer, *v. a.* repair, mend; make up for.

repartir*, *v.a.* answer.

repas, *s. m.* meal.

repasser, *v. n.* pass again.

répéter, *v. a.* repeat; say again; rehearse.

répétition, *s. f.* repetition; rehearsal.

réplique, *s. f.* retort, reply, answer.

répliquer, *v. a. & n.* reply, answer.

répondre, *v. a. & n.* answer, reply; respond to.

réponse *s.m.* answer; response; *~ payée* reply paid.

reporter, *v. a.* carry back, take back.

repos, *s. m.* rest; *sans ~* restless.

reposer, *v. a.* lay again; *v. n.* rest, lie.

repoussant, *adj.* repulsive.

repousser, *v. a.* push back; repulse; drive back.

reprendre, *v.a. & n.* take back, get back; take up, go on; *~ sa parole* go back on one's word.

représentant, -e, *s. m. f.* representative.

représentation, *s. f.* show, production; performance; display; representation.

représenter, *v. a.* represent; show, display.

reprise, *s.f.* renewal.

reproche, *s. m.* reproach, blame.

reprocher, *v. a.* reproach (with); blame for.

reproduction, *s.f.* reproduction.

reproduire*, *v. a.* reproduce.

républicain, -e, *adj. & s. m. f.* republican.

république, *s. f.* republic.

répulsion, *s.f.* repulsion.

réputation, *s. f.* reputation.

requête, *s.f.* request,

demand.

réserve, *s.f.* reserve; reservation; caution; *de* ~ spare; *mettre en* ~ lay by.

réserver, *v. a.* reserve, lay by; book (in advance).

réservoir, *s.m.* tank *(petrol etc.).*

résidence, *s. f.* residence, dwelling.

résident, *s. m.* résident.

résignation, *s. f.* resignation; submission.

résigner, *v. a.* resign; se ~ *à* resign oneself, make up one's mind.

résistance, *s. f.* resistance.

résister, *v. n.* resist.

résolu, *adj.* resolute.

résolution, *s. f.* resolution.

résonance, *s. f.* resonance.

résonner, *v. n.* resound, ring.

résoudre*, *v.a.* resolve; solve; settle; se ~ resolve, make up one's mind (to).

respect, *s. m.* respect.

respectable, *adj.* respectable, decent.

respecter *v. a.* respect.

respectif, -ive, *adj.* respective.

respectueux, -euse, *adj.* respectful.

respiration, *s. f.* respiration, breath(ing).

respirer, *v. n. & a.* breathe.

responsabilité, *s. f.* responsibility.

responsable, *adj.* responsible.

ressaisir, *v. a.* seize again.

ressemblance, *s. f.* resemblance, likeness.

ressemblant, *adj.* like, similar.

ressembler, *v* emble.

ressentiment, *s. m.* resentment, grudge.

ressentir, *v.a.* feel; resent; se ~ be hurt; feel still.

resserrer, *v.a.* tighten; bind.

ressort, *s.m.* spring; energy.

ressortir, *v. n.* come out again; stand out.

ressource, *s. f.* resource.

restaurant, *s. m.* restaurant; ~ *à libre service* self-service restaurant.

restaurateur, -trice, *s. m. f.* restorer; restaurant keeper.

restauration, *s.f.* restoration.

restaurer, *v. a.* restore.

reste, *s. m.* rest, remainder.

rester, *v. n.* remain, be left, keep; ~ *en arrière,* lag behind.

restituer, *v. a.* restore.

restreindre*, *v. a.* restrict.

restriction, *s. f.* restriction.

résultat, *s.m.* result, issue; *avoir pour* ~ result in.

résulter, *v. n.* result *(de* from).

résumé, *s.m.* summing up.

résumer, *v.a.* sum up.

rétablir, *v.a.* restore.

retard, *s. m.* delay; *être en* ~ be late; be overdue.

retarder, *v.a.* delay, retard.

retenir, *v.a.* keep back, hold back; hinder.

retirer, *v.a.* draw back, pull back; extract, get, derive; se ~ retire.

retomber, *v. n.* fall again, fall back; relapse.

retour, *s. m.* return; *en* ~ homeward bound; *être*

de ～ be back.

retourner, *v. n.* turn back; return, go back; **se** ～ turn round.

retracer, *v.a.* retrace; relate, tell.

retraite, *s.f.* retreat; retirement; *mettre à la* ～ superannuate.

retrancher, *v. a.* retrench.

rétrécir, *v.a.* contract; make narrower; shrink.

retrousser, *v. a.* turn up.

retrouver, *v. a.* find again, recover.

rétroviseur, *s. m.* (rear-vision) mirror.

réunion, *s.f.* reunion.

réunir, *v.a.* reunite; join again.

réussi, *adj.* successful.

réussir, *v. n.* succeed.

réussite, *s. f.* success.

revanche, *s. f.* revenge; return match; *en* ～ in return.

rêve, *s. m.* dream.

réveil, *s. m.* waking.

réveille-matin *s. m.* alarm-clock.

réveiller, *v.a.* & **se** ～ wake (up).

révéler, *v.a.* reveal; **se** ～ come to light.

revenir, *v. n.* return, come back; recur; cost.

revenu, *s. m.* income.

rêver, *v. n.* dream.

révérence, *s. f.* reverence; curtsey.

révérend, *adj.* reverend.

rêverie, *s.f.* reverie, fancy.

revers, *s. m.* back, reverse, wrong side.

revêtir, *v.a.* put on; clothe; cover.

révision, *s. f.* revision.

revivre, *v. n.* live again; *faire* ～ revive.

revoir, *v. a.* see again, look over; *au* ～ good-bye (for the present).

révolte, *s. f.* revolt.

révolter, *v. a.* revolt; **se** ～ revolt, rebel.

révolution, *s. f.* revolution; turn.

révolutionnaire, *adj.* & *s. m. f.* revolutionary.

revolver, *s. m.* revolver.

revue, *s. f.* review; magazine.

rez-de-chaussé, *s. m.* ground floor.

rhétorique, *s. f.* rhetoric.

rhum, *s. m.* rum.

rhumatisme, *s. m.* rheumatism.

rhume, *s. m.* cold (in the head).

ricaner, *v. n.* sneer, grin.

riche, *adj.* rich, well off.

richesse, *s.f.* wealth, riches *(pl.)*.

ride, *s. f.* wrinkle.

rideau, *s. m.* curtain.

rider, *v. a.* wrinkle.

ridicule, *adj.* ridiculous; — *s. m.* ridicule.

rien, *pron.* nothing; not ... anything; trifle.

rigoureux, -euse, *adj.* rigorous, severe.

rigueur, *s. f.* rigour.

rime, *s. f.* rhyme.

rincer, *v. a.* rinse.

rire*, *v. n.* laugh; *pour* ～ for fun; — *s.m.* laugh(ing), laughter.

risque, *s. m.* risk.

risquer, *v.a.* risk, run the risk of.

rivage, *s. m.* beach, shore.

rival, -e, *adj.* & *s. m. f.* rival.

rivalité, *s. f.* rivalry.

rive, *s. f.* bank, shore, beach.

rivière, *s. f.* river, stream.

riz, *s. m.* rice.

robe, *s. f.* gown, dress,

frock; robe; ~ *de*
chambre dressing-gown.
robinet, *s. m.* tap, cock.
robuste, *adj.* robust;
strong, sturdy.
roc, *s. m.* rock.
roche, *s.f.* rock, boulder.
rocher, *s. m.* rock, crag.
roder, *v. a.* run in.
rôder, *v.n.* rove.
rogner, *v. a.* clip, pare.
rognon, *s. m.* kidney.
roi, *s. m.* king.
rôle, *s. m.* roll; part, rôle.
romain, -e (R.), *adj. & s.*
m. f. Roman.
roman, *s. m.* novel; ~s
fiction.
romancier, -ère, *s. m. f.*
novelist.
romanesque, *adj.* romantic.
romantique, *s. m.* romantic.
romantisme, *s. m.* roman-
ticism.
rompre, *v. a. & n.* break.
rond, *adj.* round; — *s. m.*
round, circle.
ronde, *s. f.* round; patrol; *à la* ~ round
about, around.
rondelle, *s. f.* ring, collar,
washer.
ronfler, *v. n.* snore; roar.
ronger, *v.a.* gnaw, eat.
rose, *s. f.* rose; — *adj.*
rosy, pink.
roseau, *s. m.* reed.
rosée, *s. f.* dew.
rosier, *s.m.* rose-tree,
rose-bush.
rossignol, *s. m.* nightingale.
rôti, *s. m.* roast (meat).
rôtir, *v.a.* roast; toast;
faire ~ roast, bake.
roucouler, *v. n.* coo.
roue, *s.f.* wheel; ~ *de*
secours spare wheel;
~ *dentée* cog-wheel.
rouge, *adj.* red; — *s. m.*

red (colour); *bâton de*
~ lipstick.
rougeur, *s.f.* redness,
blush.
rougir, *v.n. & a.* turn
red, make red; blush.
rouille, *s. f.* rust.
rouiller, *v. n. & a.* rust,
get rusty.
roulage, *s.m.* rolling;
carriage (of goods);
haulage.
rouleau, *s.m.* roll;
roller; scroll.
roulement, *s. m.* roll(ing),
rotation; ~ *a billes*
ball-bearings.
rouler, *v. a. & n.* roll;
roll up, wind up; turn,
revolve.
roulotte, *s.f.* ~ *(de cam-*
ping) caravan.
roumain, -e (R.), *adj. &*
s. m. f. Rumanian.
route, *s. f.* road; highway;
course; way; *en* ~ on
the way; *en* ~ *pour*
bound for; *code de*
la ~ highway code.
routine, *s. f.* routine.
roux, rousse, *adj.* red-
(dish).
royal, *adj.* royal.
royaliste, -e, *adj. & s. m.*
f. royalist.
royaume, *s. m.* kingdom.
ruban, *s m.* ribbon; band.
rubis, *s m.* ruby.
ruche, *s. f.* hive.
rude, *adj.* rough, rude.
rue, *s. f.* street; ~ *bar-*
rée no thoroughfare;
~ *de traverse* crossroad.
ruée, *s. f.* rush.
ruelle, *s. f.* lane.
ruer; se ~ rush, dash.
rugissement, *s. m.* roar.
ruine, *s. f.* ruin; wreck.
ruiner, *v.a.* ruin, destroy.
ruisseau, *s. m.* stream,
brook; gutter.

ruisseler, v.n. stream, run, flow.

rumeur, s. f. noise; rumour.

ruminer, v. a. & n. ruminate, chew (the cud).

rupture, s. f. rupture.

ruse, s. f. craft, cunning.

rusé, adj. cunning, sly.

russe (R.), adj. & s. m. f. Russian.

russien, -enne (R.), adj. & s. m. f. Russian.

rustique, adj. rustic, rural.

rythme, s. m. rhythm.

rythmique, adj. rhytmical.

S

s' see se.

sa, adj. poss. his, her, its.

sable, s. m. sand.

sablonneux, -euse, adj. sandy.

sabre, s. m. sabre.

sac, s. m. bag, sack; ~ a main handbag; ~ de couchage sleeping-bag.

saccager, v. a. plunder.

sacré, adj. sacred, holy.

sacrement, s. m. sacrament.

sacrifice, s.m. sacrifice.

sacrifier, v.a. sacrifice.

sacristain, s.m. sexton.

sage, adj. wise, well-behaved.

sagesse, s. f. wisdom.

saignant, adj. bleeding; underdone.

saigner, v. a. & n. bleed.

saillant, adj. projecting.

saillir, v. n. stand out, project.

sain, adj. sound; ~ et sauf safe and sound.

saint, -e. adj. holy, sacred; — s. m. f. saint

saisir, v.a. seize.

saison, s. f. season.

salade, s. f. salad.

salaire, s. m. wages (pl.), pay, salary.

sale, adj. dirty, filthy.

saler, v. a. salt.

saleté, s. f. dirt.

salière, s. f. salt-cellar.

salir, v. a. soil, dirty.

salle, s. f. hall; assembly room; house; ~ d'attente waiting-room; ~ de classe schoolroom; ~ (de cours) auditorium; ~ familiale, ~ de séjour living-room.

salon, s. m. drawing-room; saloon; petit ~ sitting-room.

saluer, v. a. & n. bow to; greet.

salut, s. m. salvation; bow, greeting.

samedi, s. m. Saturday.

sanatorium, s. m. sanatorium.

sanction, s. f. sanction.

sanctuaire, s. m. sanctuary.

sandale, s. f. sandal.

sang, s. m. blood.

sanglier, s. m. wild boar.

sanitaire, adj. sanitary.

sans, prep. without.

santé, s. f. health.

sapin, s. m. fir(-tree).

sarcasme, s. m. sarcasm.

sarcastique, adj. sarcastic.

sardine, s. f. sardine.

satellite, s. m. satellite.

satire, s. f. satire.

satisfaction, s. f. satisfaction.

savoir*, v. n. know, be aware; be trained in; understand; be able to; — s. m. knowledge, learning.

savon, s. m. soap.

savourer, *v. a.* taste, relish.

savoureux, -euse, *adj.* savoury, tasty.

scandale, *s. m.* scandal.

scaphandre autonome, *s. m.* skin diver.

scaphandrier, *s. m.* diver.

scarabée, *s. m.* beetle.

sceau, *s. m.* seal.

sceller, *v. a.* seal; fix.

scénario, *s. m.* scenario.

scène, *s. f.* scène; scenery; *fig.* stage; *mettre en* ~ produce (a play).

sceptre, *s. m.* sceptre.

scie, *s. f.* saw.

satisfaire, *v. a. & n.* satisfy, please.

satisfaisant, *adj.* satisfactory.

satisfait, *adj.* satisfied.

sauce, *s. f.* sauce.

saucisse, *s. f.* sausage.

sauf, sauve, *adj.* safe; — *prep.* except, save.

saumon, *s. m.* salmon.

saut, *s. m.* jump, leap.

sauter, *v. n.* leap, jump; spring; *faire* ~ blow up.

sauvage, *adj.* savage, wild.

sauver, *v. a.* save, rescue; *se* ~ run away.

sauveur, *s. m.* Saviour.

savant, -e, *adj.* learned, clever; expert; — *s. m. f.* scholar.

saveur, *s. f.* savour, taste.

science, *s. f.* science, knowledge; *homme de* ~ scientist.

scientifique, *adj.* scientific.

scier, *v. a.* saw.

scolaire, *adj.* school; *année* ~ school year.

scooter, *s. m.* motor-scooter.

scrupule, *s. m.* scruple.

sculpter, *v. a.* carve, sculpture.

sculpteur, *s. m.* sculptor.

sculpture, *s. f.* sculpture.

se, s' *pron.* himself, herself, itself; each other.

séance, *s. f.* sitting, meeting.

seau, *s. m.* pail.

sec, sèche, *adj.* dry, dried up.

sécher, *v. a. & n.* dry (up).

sécheresse, *s. f.* dryness.

second, *adj.* second.

secondaire, *adj.* secondary.

seconde, *s. f.* second.

seconder, *v. a.* back.

secouer, *v. a.* shake.

secourir, *v. a.* help.

secours, *s. m.* help, succour, aid; *au* ~ help!

secousse, *s. f.* shake, jolt, jerk.

secret, -ète, *adj. & s. m.* secret.

secrétaire, *s. m. f.* secretary; — *s. m.* writing-desk.

secrétariat, *s. m.* secretariate.

secteur, *s. m.* sector, section; ~ *(de courant)* mains.

section, *s. f.* section

sécurité, *s. f.* security.

sédatif, -ive, *adj. & s. m.* sedative.

sédiment, *s. m.* sediment.

séduire, *v. a.* seduce.

seigle, *s. m.* rye.

seigneur, *s. m.* lord, squire.

seize, *adj. & s. m.* sixteen; sixteenth.

seizième, *adj.* sixteenth.

séjour, *s. m.* stay, visit; (place of) residence.

séjourner, *v. n.* stay, sojourn.

sel, *s. m.* salt.

selle, *s. f.* saddle.

selon, *prep.* according to; after.

semaine, *s. f.* week.

semblable, *adj.* (a)like.

semblant, *s. m.* semblance; appearance.

sembler, *v. n.* appear, look, seem.

semelle, *s. f.* sole *(footwear)*.

semer, *v. a.* sow.

semestre, *s. m.* half year; semester.

séminaire, *s. m.* seminary.

sénat, *s. m.* senate.

sénateur, *s. m.* senator.

sens, *s. m.* sense; judgement, opinion; direction.

sensation, *s. f.* feeling; sensation.

sensé, *adj.* sensible, reasonable.

sensibilité, *s. f.* sensibility, feeling.

sensible, *adj.* sensible, perceptible; sensitive.

sentence, *s. f.* sentence.

senteur, *s. f.* scent, smell.

sentier, *s. m.* path.

sentiment, *s. m.* feeling, sense, sentiment.

sentimental, *adj.* sentimental.

sentinelle, *s. f.* sentry, sentinel.

sentir*, *v. a.* feel, perceive; experience; smell; se ~ feel.

séparation, *s. f.* separation.

séparer, *v. a.* separate, divide; se ~ part.

sept, *adj.* & *s. m.* seven; seventh.

septembre, *s. m.* September.

septième, *adj.* seventh.

sérénade, *s. f.* serenade.

sérénité, *s. f.* serenity.

sergent, *s. m.* sergeant.

série, *s. f.* series.

sérieux, -euse, *adj.* grave, serious.

serin, -e, *s. m. f.* canary.

seringue, *s. f.* syringe.

serment, *s. m.* oath.

sermon, *s. m.* sermon.

serpent, *s. m.* snake, serpent.

serpenter, *v. n.* wind, meander.

serre, *s. f.* claw; hot-house.

serré, *adj.* tight, close, serried.

serrer, *v. a.* press, crush, jam, tighten.

serre-tête, *s. m.* crash-helmet, headband.

serrure, *s. f.* lock.

serrurier, *s. m.* locksmith.

servante, *s. f.* servant.

service, *s. m.* service, duty; favour; set; *être de* ~ be on duty; *à votre* ~ at your disposal.

serviette, *s. f.* napkin; towel; briefcase.

servir*, *v. a. & n.* serve; be in the service of; ~ *à* be used for; *ne se* ~ *à rien* be of no use; *Mme est servie* dinner is ready; se ~ use, make use of, help oneself.

serviteur, *s. m.* servant.

servitude, *s. f.* servitude.

ses, *adj. poss.* his, her, its; one's.

session, *s. f.* session.

seuil, *s. m.* threshold.

seul, *adj.* alone, single, sole, only.

sévère, *adj.* severe, hard.

sévir, *v. n.* punish; rage.

sexe, *s. m.* sex.

sexuel, -elle, *adj.* sexual.

shampooing, *s. m.* shampoo.

si, *conj,* if, whether; — *adv.* so, so much, such.

siècle, *s. m.* century.

siège, *s. m.* seat.

sien, -enne, *poss. adj.* his, hers; its; one's.

siffler, *v. n.* whistle, hiss.

sifflet, *s. m.* whistle.

signal, *s. m.* signal; ~ *d'alarme* communication-cord.

signaler, *v. a.* signal.

signalisation, *s. f.* signals *(pl.); feux de* ~ traffic-lights.

signature, *s. f.* signature.

signe, *s. m.* sign.

signer, *v. a. & n.* sign.

significatif, -ive, *adj.* significant.

signification, *s. f.* signification; meaning.

signifier, *v. a.* signify.

silence, *s. m.* silence.

silencieux, -euse, *adj.* silent.

silhouette, *s. f.* outline, silhouette.

sillon, *s. m.* furrow.

simple, *adj.* simple.

simplicité, *s. f.* simplicity.

simplifier, *v. a.* simplify.

simultané, *adj.* simultaneous.

sincère, *adj.* sincere.

sincérité, *s. f.* sincerity.

singe, *s. m.* monkey.

singulier, -ère, *adj.* singular, strange.

sinon, *conj.* (or) else, otherwise.

sire, *s. m.* sir, lord.

sirène, *s. f.* siren; hooter, fog-horn.

site, *s. m.* site, place.

sitôt, *adv.* as soon; ~ *que* as soon as; ~ ... ~ no sooner... than.

situation, *s. f.* situation; state; office, position.

situer, *v. a.* place, locate.

six, *adj. & s. m.* six; sixth.

sixième, *adj.* sixth.

ski, *s. m.* ski; *faire du* ~ ski.

skieur, *s. m.* skier, ski-runner.

smoking, *s. m.* dinner-jacket.

sobre, *adj.* sober.

social, *adj.* social.

socialisme, *s. m.* socialism.

socialiste, *adj. & s. m. f.* socialist.

société, *s. f.* society; company; ~ *anonyme* limited liability company.

sœur, *s. f.* sister.

soi, *pron.* oneself; himself, herself; itself.

soi-disant, *adj.* so-called.

soie, *s. f.* silk.

soif, *s. f.* thirst; *avoir* ~ be thirsty.

soigner, *v. a.* take care of, look after.

soigneux, -euse, *adj.* careful.

soin, *s. m.* care; *prendre* ~ *de* take care of; *aux bons* ~s *de* c/o.

soir, *s. m.* evening.

soirée, *s. f.* evening (party).

soit, *conj.* say; suppose; either ... or; ~ *que* whether.

soixante, *adj. & s. m.* sixty.

soixante-dix, *adj. & s. m.* seventy.

sol, *s. m.* soil; ground.

soldat, *s. m.* soldier.

soleil, *s. m.* sun; *il fait du* ~ the sun is shining.

solennel, -elle, *adj.* solemn.

solennité, *s. f.* solemnity.

solidarité, *s. f.* solidarity.

solide, *adj.* solid.
solidité, *s. f.* solidity.
solitaire, *adj.* solitary.
solitude, *s. f.* solitude.
solliciter, *v. a.* solicit, entreat.
sollicitude, *s. f.* care.
soluble, *adj.* soluble.
solution, *s. f.* solution.
sombre, *adj.* dark; dim.
sombrer, *v.n.* founder, sink.
sommaire, *adj. & s. m.* summary.
somme, *s. f.* sum, amount.
sommeil, *s. m.* sleep; *avoir ~* be sleepy.
sommeiller, *v. n.* slumber.
sommer, *v. a.* summon.-
sommet, *s. m.* top, summit.
sommier, *s. m.* spring mattress.
somnifère, *s. m.* sleeping-pill.
somnolent, *adj.* sleepy.
son[1], **sa**, *adj. poss. (pl. ses)* his, her, its; one's.
son[2], *s. m.* sound.
songe, *s. m.* dream.
songer, *v. n.* dream.
sonner, *v. a. & n.* ring, sound; *on sonne (à la porte)* there is a ring at the door.
sonnette, *s. f.* bell.
sonore, *adj.* sonorous.
sorcier, *s. m.* sorcerer, wizard.
sorcière, *s. f.* witch, sorceress.
sornette, *s. f.* nonsense.
sort, *s. m.* fate, lot.
sorte, *s. f.* sort, kind.
sortie, *s. f.* going out; way out, exit; *~ secours* emergency exit.
sortir*, *v. n.* go out, walk out, leave; *ne*

pas ~ keep indoors;
v.a. take out, bring out.
sot, **sotte**, *adj.* foolish, silly.
sottise, *s. f.* foolishness, nonsense.
sou, *s. m.* sou, copper, penny.
souci, *s. m.* care, concern.
soucier: se ~ de care for.
soucieux, -euse, *adj.* full of care, anxious.
soucoupe, *s. f.* saucer.
soudain, *adj.* sudden; — *adv.* suddenly.
soude, *s. f.* soda *(chemical)*.
souffle, *s. m.* breath.
souffler, *v.a. & n.* breathe; blow (out).
soufflet, *s. m.* box (on the ear); bellows *(pl.)*.
souffrance, *s. f.* pain, suffering.
souffrir*, *v. a. & n.* suffer, bear.
souhaiter, *v. a.* desire.
soulever, *v. a.* lift, raise; *se ~* rise (in rebellion).
soulier, *s. m.* shoe.
souligner, *v. a.* underline.
soumettre, *v. a.* submit, subdue; *se ~* submit.
soumission, *s. f.* submission.
soupçon, *s. m.* suspicion.
soupçonner, *v. a.* suspect.
soupe, *s. f.* soup.
souper, *s. m.* supper; — *v. n.* have supper.
soupir, *s. m.* sigh.
soupirer, *v.n.* sigh; *~ après* long for.
souple, *adj.* supple, flexible.
source, *s. f.* source, spring.
sourcil, *s. m.* eyebrow.
sourd, *adj.* deaf.
sourd-muet, **sourde-muette**, *adj. & s. m. f.* deaf and dumb (per-

son).

sourire, *v. n.* smile.

souris, *s. f.* mouse.

sous, *prep.* under; beneath; before.

souscripteur, *s. m.* subscriber.

souscription, *s. f.* subscription.

souscrire, *v. a.* & *n.* sign, subscribe (to).

sousdéveloppé, *adj.* under-developed.

sous-marin, *s. m.* submarine.

soussigné, -e, *adj.* & *s. m. f.* undersigned.

sous-sol, *s. m.* basement.

sous-titre, *s. m.* subtitle, caption.

soustraction, *s. f.* subtraction.

soustraire, *v. a.* take away; subtract.

soutenir, *v. a.* support, sustain, maintain.

souterrain, *adj.* underground; — *s. m.* subway.

soutien, *s. m.* support.

soutien-gorge, *s. m.* bra.

souvenir*, *s. m.* remembrance; souvenir; memory; — *v. reflex.* se ~ remember.

souvent, *adv.* often.

souverain, -e, *s. m. f.* sovereign.

spatial, *adj. vaisseau* ~, *véhicule* ~ space-craft, space-vehicle.

speaker, *s. m.* announcer.

speakerine, *s. f.* lady announcer.

spécial, *adj.* special.

spécialement, *adv.* specially, particularly.

spécialiser, *v. a.* specialize.

spécialiste, *s. m. f.* specialist.

spécialité, *s. f.* special(i)ty.

spécifier, *v. a.* specify.

spécifique, *adj.* specific.

spectacle, *s. m.* spectacle, sight.

spectateur, -trice, *s. m. f.* spectator, spectatress, onlooker; bystander.

spéculation, *s. f.* speculation.

spéculer, *v. n.* speculate.

sphère, *s. f.* sphere.

spirale, *adj.* spiral.

spirituel, -elle, *adj.* spiritual; witty.

splendeur, *s. f.* splendour.

splendide, *adj.* splendid.

spontané, *adj.* spontaneous.

sport, *s. m.* sport.

sportif, -ive, *adj.* sporting; sportsmanlike.

squelette, *s. m.* skeleton.

stade, *s. m.* stadium; *fig.* stage.

stalle, *s. f.* stall; box.

station, *s. f.* standing; stay; station, stop; ~ *balnéaire* watering-place, spa.

stationnement, *s. m.* stationing; parking; ~ *interdit* no parking.

stationner, *v. n.* stop; park.

station-service, *s. f.* service-station.

statistique, *s. f.* statistics; — *adj.* statistical.

statue, *s. f.* statue.

statut, *s. m.* statute.

sténographie, *s. f.* shorthand.

stérile, *adj.* sterile.

stimuler, *v. a.* stimulate.

stipuler, *v. a.* stipulate.

store, *s. m.* (Venetian) blind.

strabisme, *s. m.* squint-

(ing).

stratégie, *s. f.* strategy.

structure, *s. f.* structure.

studieux, -euse, *adj.* studious.

stupéfier, *v. a.* stupefy.

stupide, *adj.* stupid, dull.

stupidité, *s. f.* stupidity.

style, *s. m.* style.

stylo, *s.m.* ~ *à bil'e* ball(-point) pen.

stylo(graphe), *s. m.* fountain-pen.

suave, *adj.* soft, gentle.

subjonctif, *s.m.* subjunctive.

subjuguer, *v.a.* subjugate, overcome.

submerger, *v. a.* submerge, flood.

subordonné, *adj.* subordinate.

subordonner, *v. a.* subordinate.

subséquent, *adj.* subsequent.

subsistance, *s. f.* subsistence.

subsister, *v. n.* subsist.

substance, *s. f.* substance.

substantiel, -elle, *adj.* substantial.

substantif, *s.m.* substantive.

substituer, *v.a.* substitute.

substitution, *s. f.* substitution.

subtil, *adj.* subtle.

subvention, *s. f.* subvention, subsidy.

succéder, *v. n.* succeed *(à* to), follow; **se** ~ follow one another.

succès, *s. m.* success; result.

success'*, -ive, *adj.* successive.

succession, *s. f.* succession.

sucer, *v. a.* suck (in).

sucre, *s. m.* sugar.

sucré, *adj.* sweet(ened).

sud, *adj. & s. m.* south; *du* ~ southern; *au* ~ southward.

sud-est, *adj. & s.m.* south-east.

sud-ouest, *adj. & s. m.* south-west.

suédois, -e, (S.), *adj.* Swedish; — *s. m. f.* Swede; Swedish (language).

suer, *v. n. & a.* sweat.

sueur, *s. f.* sweat.

suffire*, *v.n.* be sufficient, be enough.

suffisamment, *adv.* sufficiently, enough.

suffisant, *adj.* sufficient, enough; conceited.

suffoquer, *v.a. & n.* suffocate, choke.

suggérer, *v.a.* suggest, propose.

suggestion, *s. f.* suggestion, hint.

suicide, *s. m.* suicide.

suisse (S.), *adj. & s. m. (f.* **Suissesse)** Swiss.

suite, *s. f.* retinue; suite, sequence, result; *a la* ~ after; *tout de* ~ at once, directly; *par* ~ consequently; *par* ~ *de* due to.

suivant, *adj.* following, next; — *prep.* according to.

suivre*, *v.a. & n.* follow; *comme suit* as follows; *ce qui suit* the following.

sujet, -ette, *s. m. f.* subject; *s. m.* subject.

superficie, *s. f.* surface, area.

superficiel, -elle, *adj.* superficial.

superflu, *adj.* superfluous.

supérieur, *adj.* superior, upper.

supériorité, s. f. superiority.

supermarché, s. m. supermarket.

supersonique, adj. supersonic.

superstitieux, -euse, adj. superstitious.

superstition, s. f. superstition.

suppléer, v.a. supply; substitute, do duty for; v. n. make up for.

supplément, s. m. supplement; extra charge; excess.

supplémentaire, adj. supplementary, extra.

suppliant, -e, adj. suppliant; — s. m. f. supplicant.

supplier, v.a. beseech.

support, s.m. prop; support.

supporter, v.a. bear, support.

supposer, v. a. suppose.

supposition, s. f. supposition, conjecture.

suppression, s. f. suppression.

supprimer, v. a. suppress, abolish, do away with.

suprême, adj. supreme.

sur, prep. on; over; concerning.

sûr, adj. certain, sure; secure, safe; pour ~! to be sure!

surcharger, v.a. & n. overload; weigh down.

sûrement, adv. surely, certainly.

sûreté, s. f. safety; security.

surface, s.f. surface.

surgir, v. n. arise, spring up, emerge.

surmonter, v.a. surmount, overcome.

surnaturel, -elle, adj. supernatural.

surpasser, v. a. surpass, outdo.

surpeuplé, adj. overcrowded.

surplus, s.m. surplus, excess.

surprendre, v. a. surprise.

surprise, s.f. surprise.

surseoir*, v.n. & a. postpone, delay, put off.

surtaxe, s. f. surtax.

surtout, s. m. overcoat.

surveillance, s. f. supervision.

surveiller, v.a. supervise.

survenir, v. a. arrive unexpectedly; happen, occur.

survivant, -e, s.m.f. survivor.

survivre, v.n. survive, outlive.

susceptible, adj. susceptible.

suspect, adj. suspicious, suspect.

suspendre, v· a. hang up; suspend.

suspension, s. f. suspension.

svelte, adj. slender, slim·

syllabe, s. f. syllable.

symbole, s. m. symbol.

symétrie, s. f. symmetry.

symétrique, adj. symmetrical.

sympathie, s. f. sympathy.

symphonie, s.f. symphony.

symptome, s.m. symptom.

synagogue, s.f. synagogue.

syndical, adj. trade.

syndicat, s. m. syndicate; trade-union; ~d'initiative tourist information office.

synthétique, adj. synthetic(al).

systématique, adj. systematic.

système, *s. m.* system.

T

tabac, *s.m.* tobacco; *bureau de* ~ tobacconist's (shop).

table, *s. f.* table; board; food; ~ *des matières*, table of contents.

tableau, *s.m.* picture; scene; board, panel.

tablette, *s. f.* tablet.

tablier, *s.m.* apron; dash-board.

tabouret, *s. m.* stool.

tache, *s. f.* spot, stain; *sans* ~ spotless.

tâche, *s. f.* task, job.

tacher, *v.a.* spot, stain.

tâcher, *v.n.* try.

tact, *s. m.* touch.

tactique, *s.f.* tactics.

taille, *s.f.* cut; height, stature, size; waist.

tailler, *v.a.* hew, trim; cut.

tailleur, *s. m.* tailor.

taire*, *v.a.* be silent about, conceal; se ~ be quiet.

talent, *s. m.* talent, attainment(s).

talon, *s. m.* heel; counterfoil.

talus, *s. m.* slope, bank.

tambour, *s. m.* drum.

tamis, *s. m.* sieve.

tamiser, *v. a.* sift, sieve.

tampon, *s. m.* plug; tampon.

tamponner, *v. a.* plug.

tandis que, *conj.* whereas, while.

tangible, *adj.* tangible.

tant, *adv.* so much, so many, such, so.

tante, *s. f.* aunt.

tantôt, *adv.* shortly, by and by; ~ ... ~ now ... now.

tapage, *s. m.* noise, fuss.

taper, *v.a. & n.* tap, strike, knock; type.

tapis, *s. m.* carpet, rug.

tapisser, *v. a.* upholster.

tapisserie, *s. f.* tapestry.

tapissier, *s. m.* upholsterer.

tard, *adv.* late.

tarder, *v.n.* delay, put off; be long.

tardif, -ive, *adj.* late.

tarif, *s.m.* tariff, rate; price-list; fare.

tarte, *s. f.* tart.

tas, *s. m.* heap, pile; mass; crowd.

tasse, *s. f.* cup.

tâter, *v.a. & n.* feel, taste, handle.

tâtonner, *v.n.* grope.

taureau, *s.m.* bull.

taux, *s.m.* price, rate (of exchange); tax.

taverne, *s. f.* tavern.

taxe, *s. f.* tax.

taxer, *v. a.* tax, rate.

taxi, *s. m.* taxi; *station de* ~s taxi-rank.

tchèque (T.), *adj. & s. m. f.* Czech.

te, *pron.* you; to you.

technicien, -enne, *s. m. f.* technician.

technique, *adj.* technical; *s. f.* technique, technics.

technologie, *s. f.* technology.

teindre*, *v.a.* dye, stain.

teint, *s. m.* complexion; dye.

teinte, *s. f.* tint, shade.

teinter, *v. a.* tint.

teinture, *s. f.* dye; tincture.

teinturerie, *s.f.* dye-works, dyer.

tel, telle, *adj.* such, like, similar.

télécommunication, *s.f.* telecommunication.

téléférique, *s.m.* rope-way.

télégramme, *s.m.* telegram, wire.

télégraphe, *s.m.* telegraph.

télégraphie, *s.f.* telegraphy.

télégraphier, *v.a. & n.* wire.

télégraphique, *adj.* telegraphic.

télémètre, *s.m.* range-finder.

téléphone, *s.m.* telephone.

télescope, *s. m.* telescope.

téléspectateur, -trice, *s. m. f.* (tele)viewer.

téléviser, *v. a.* televise, telecast.

téléviseur, *s.m.* television-set.

télévison, *s. f.* television.

télex, *s. m.* telex.

tellement, *adv.* so (much).

témoigner, *v.a. & n.* testify; give evidence.

témoin, *s.m.* witness; testimony.

tempe, *s.f.* temple *(forehead).*

tempérament, *s. m.* temper(ament), constitution.

température, *s.f.* temperature.

tempête, *s. f.* storm.

temple, *s. m.* temple, church; chapel; lodge.

temporel, -elle, *adj.* temporal, transient.

temps¹, *s. m.* time; opportunity; *à ~* in time; *pendant ce ~ l* in the meantime; *en ~ voulu* in due time; *combien de ~?* how long?; *la plupart du ~* mostly; *de ~ en ~* at times.

temps², *s.m.* weather; *prévisions du ~* weather-forecast.

tenaille, *s.f.* pincers, pliers, tongs *(pl.).*

tendance, *s.f.* tendency, trend.

tendon, *s.m.* tendon, sinew.

tendre¹ ¹*adj.* tender, soft.

tendre², *v.a.* stretch; strain; bend; hang.

tendresse, *s. f.* tenderness.

tendu, *adj.* tense, taut.

ténébreux, -euse, *adj.* dark, gloomy, dismal.

tenir*, *v. a. & n.* hold; get hold of; hold on; take, contain; keep; *se ~* stay, remain.

tennis, *s. m.* tennis.

tension, *s.f.* tension.

tentation, *s. f.* temptation.

tentative, *s. f.* attempt.

tente, *s. f.* tent.

tenter, *v.a.* attempt; try; tempt.

ténu, *adj.* thin, slender.

tenue, *s. f.* holding; session; behaviour.

terme, *s. m.* term; expression; goal, aim.

terminer, *v. a.* terminate, end, close; *se ~* (come to an) end.

terminus, *s. m.* terminus.

terne, *adj.* dull, dim.

terrain, *s. m.* soil, earth; site; ground; *~ de jeux* sports-ground.

terrasse, *s.f.* terrace.

terre, *s.f.* earth, land.

terreur, *s.f.* fear.

terrible, *adj.* terrible.

terrifier, *v.a.* terrify, frighten.

territoire, *s. m.* territory.

testament, *s.m.* will, testament.

tête, *s. f.* head.

têtu, *adj.* stubborn.
texte, *s.m.* text; type.
textile, *s.m.* textile.
textuel, -elle, *adj.* textual.
texture, *s. f.* texture.
thé, *s. m.* tea.
théâtral, *adj.* theatrical.
théâtre, *s.m.* theatre, stage; drama; *pièce de* ~ play.
théière, *s. f.* tea-pot.
thème, *s. m.* theme, topic; prose.
théologie, *s. f.* theology.
théologique, *adj.* theological.
théorie, *s. f.* theory.
théorique, *adj.* theoretic, theoretical.
thermal, *adj.* thermal.
thermomètre, *s. m.* thermometer.
thermos, *s. f.* thermos.
thèse, *s. f.* thesis.
thon, *s. m.* tunny.
tien, -enne, *poss. adj.* yours.
tiers, tierce, *adj.* third; — *s.m.* third party.
tige, *s. f.* stem, stalk.
tigre, *s. m.* tiger.
tigresse, *s. f.* tigress.
timbre, *s. m.* bell; sound; (postage-)stamp.
timbre-poste, *s. m.* postage-stamp.
timide, *adj.* timid, shy.
timidité, *s. f.* timidity.
tir, *s.m.* shooting.
tirage, *s.f.* draught, pull(ing); impression; issue.
tire-bouchon *s. m.* corkscrew.
tirer, *v. a. & n.* draw, pull, drag; extract; derive; fire, shoot; print.
tiroir, *s.m.* drawer.
tison, *s.m.* brand.
tisonnier, *s.m.* poker.

tisser, *v.a.* weave.
tisserand, *s.m.* weaver.
tissu, *s. m.* texture, fabric; tissue.
titre, *s. m.* title; heading; right.
titrer, *v.a.* give a title to.
toast, *s. m.* toast.
toi, *pron.* you.
toile, *s. f.* linen; cloth.
toilette, *s.f.* dress, clothes *(pl.);* dressing-table; *faire sa* ~ dress; *cabinet de* ~ dressing-room.
toison, *s. f.* fleece.
toit, *s. m.* roof.
tolérance, *s. f.* tolerance, toleration.
tolérer, *v.a.* tolerate, bear.
tomate, *s.f.* tomato.
tombe, *s. f.* tomb, grave.
tombeau, *s. m.* tomb.
tombée, *s.f.* fall.
tomber, *v.n.* fall, fall down; tumble; decay; ~ *sur* meet, run into; *faire* ~ push down; *laisser* ~ drop.
tome, *s. m.* volume.
ton¹, ta, *poss. adj. (pl.* **tes)** your.
ton², *s. m.* tone; colour; manner.
tondeuse, *s.f.* lawn-mower.
tondre, *v.a.* shear, clip, mow.
tonnage, *s. m.* tonnage.
tonne, *s. f.* barrel, tun; ton.
tonneau, *s.m.* barrel.
tonner, *v.n.* thunder.
tonnerre, *s.m.* thunder(bolt).
toqué, *adj.* crazy.
torche, *s. f.* torch.
torcher, *v.a.* wipe, rub.
torchon, *s.m.* duster; dish-cloth.
tordre, *v. a.* twist, wring

(out).

torpille, *s. f.* torpedo.

torrent, *s. m.* torrent.

tort, *s. m.* wrong, harm, injury; *avoir* ~ be wrong.

tortue, *s. f.* tortoise.

torture, *s. f.* torture.

torturer, *v. a.* torture.

tôt, *adv.* soon, quickly; early.

total, *adj.* total, whole.

totalement, *adv.* totally, entirely.

touchant, *prep.* about.

touche, *s. f.* touch; key; hit.

toucher, *v. n. & a.* touch; feel; strike, hit; concern; — *s. m.* touch; feeling.

touffe, *s. f.* tuft.

toujours, *adv.* always, ever; still.

toupet, *s. m.* tuft, lock.

tour¹, *s.f.* tower.

tour², *s.m.* turn; tour, trip; feat, trick; (turning-)lathe; revolution; ~ *à* ~ in turns; *à son* ~ in turn; *faire le* ~ *de* go round.

tourelle, *s. f.* turret.

tourisme, *s. m.* tourism; touring; *faire du* ~ *à pied* hike.

touriste, *s. m. f.* tourist, hiker.

tourment, *s. m.* torment, torture.

tourmenter, *v. a.* torment; se ~ worry.

tournant, *adj.* turning; — *s. m.* turn(ing).

tourné, *adj.* turned; sour.

tournée, *s. f.* tour, walk; circuit.

tourner, *v. a.* turn, twist, wind; turn round; *v. n.* turn, revolve; turn out; turn sour.

tournevis, *s.m.* screwdriver.

tournoi, *s.m.* tournament.

tournure, *s.f.* shape, figure; turn; cast; appearance.

tous *see* **tout.**

tousser, *v.n.* cough.

tout, -e, *adj. (pl.* **tous, toutes)** all, every, any, whole, full; ~ *le monde* everybody; ~ *son possible* one's utmost; *à* ~*e force* at any cost; — *adv.* wholly, entirely; ~ *coup* suddenly; ~ *fait* thoroughly; ~ *de suite* directly; ~ *à l'heure* just now; ~ *au moins* at least; — *pron. & s.m.* everything, all; *pas du* ~ not at all.

toutefois, *adv.* yet, nevertheless, however.

tout-puissant, *adj.* almighty.

toux, *s. f.* cough.

tracas, *s. m.* bustle, stir; worry.

tracasser, *v. n. & a.* worry, bother; fuss; se ~ worry.

trace, *s. f.* trace, track; footprint.

tracer, *v. a.* trace, draw; lay out.

tracteur, *s. m.* tractor.

traction, *s.f.* traction, pull.

tradition, *s. f.* tradition.

traditionnel, -elle, *adj.* traditional.

traduction, *s. f.* translation.

traduire*, *v. a.* translate.

trafic, *s. m.* traffic; trade, commerce.

trafiquer, *v.n.* traffic;

traducteur, -trice, *s. m. f.* translator.

trade, deal.

tragédie, s. f. tragedy.

tragédien, -enne, s. m. f. tragedien.

tragique, adj. tragic.

trahir, v. a. betray; deceive, mislead.

trahison, s. f. treason, treachery.

train, s.m. pace, rate; train; ~ couloir corridor-train; ~ direct through train; ~ de marchandises goods train.

traîne, s.f. train (of a dress).

traîneau, s. m. sledge.

traîner, v.a. drag, draw; lead (to); delay; v.n. drag; lie about; lag behind.

train-poste, s.m mail-train.

traire*, v.a. milk.

trait, s.m. arrow; dart; flash; line; trait, feature.

traite, s.f. journey; stretch; export; draft, bill.

traité, s. m. treaty.

traitement, s. m. treatment; usage; reception; salary.

traiter, v.a. treat, use, deal with; call; entertain.

traître, s. m. traitor; — adj. treacherous.

trajet, s.m. passage, journey, course, crossing.

tram, s.m. tram(-car).

trammer, v. a. weave; plot; devise.

tramway, s. m. tram.

tranchant, adj. sharp, keen.

tranche, s. f. slice, chop, steak.

trancher, v.a. & n. cut; cut off; carve; break off.

tranquille, adj. quiet, calm; soyez ~! don't worry!

tranquilliser, v. a. soothe, calm; se ~ keep calm.

transaction, s. f. compromise, transaction.

transalpin, adj. transalpine.

transatlantique, adj. transatlantic; — s. f. deckchair.

transfert, s. m. transfer.

transformation, s. f. transformation, change.

transformer, v.a. transform, convert.

transfusion, s.f. transfusion.

transistor, s. m. transistor.

transit, s.m. transit.

transition, s.f. transition.

transmettre, v. a. transmit; forward; pass on.

transmission, s. f. transmission.

transparent, adj. transparent.

transpiration, s.f. perspiration.

transpirer, v. n. perspire.

transport, s. m. transport, conveyance; enterprise de ~ forwarding agency.

transporter, v.a. transport, convey; transfer; enrapture.

trappe, s. f. trap; trapdoor.

travail, s. m. (pl. -aux) work, job, employment; task; piece of work; workmanship; petits travaux odd jobs; sans ~ unemployed.

travailler, v.n. & a. work, labour; take pains.

travailleur, -euse, s. m. f. worker, workman, workwoman.

travers, s. m. breadth; à ~ across, through; au ~ de through; en ~ across.

traverse, s.f. traverse; obstacle; crossing.

traversée, s.f. crossing, passage.

traverser, v. a. traverse, cross, go through; run through.

trayeuse, s. f. milking-machine.

trébucher, v. n. stumble; turn the scale.

tréfle, s. m. clover; club (cards).

treille, s. f. vine arbour.

treize, adj. & s.m. thirteen;

tremblant, adj. tembling, shaky.

tremblement, s. m. trembling, shaking; ~ de terre earthquake.

trembler, v. n. tremble, shake.

tremper, v. a. soak, wet; dip; il est tout trempé he is wet through.

tremplin, s.m. spring-board.

trentaine, s.m. thirty.

trente, adj. & s. m. thirty; thirtieth.

très, adv. very, most, very much; ~ bien very well; all right.

trésor, s. m. treasure.

trésorie, s. f. treasury.

trésorier, s. m. treasurer

tresse, s. f. plait, tress, braid.

trêve, s. f. truce, rest; faire ~ stop, cease.

triangle, s. m. triangle.

tribu, s. f. tribe.

tribunal, s. m. tribunal, law-court.

tribune, s.f. tribune, platform; grand-stand.

tributaire, adj. tributary.

tricher, v. n. & a. cheat; trick (s.o. out of).

tricot, s.m. (knitted) jersey.

tricoter, v. a. & n. knit.

triomphant, adj. triumphant.

triomphe, s. m. triumph.

triompher, v. n. triumph.

triple, adj. triple.

tripot, s.m. gambling-den.

triste, adj. sad.

tristesse, s. f. sadness.

trivial, adj. trivial.

trois, adj. & s. m. three; third.

troisième, adj. & s. m. third.

trolley, s.m. trolley (-pole).

trolleybus, s. m. trolley-bus.

trompe, s.f. trumpet, horn.

tromper, v. a. deceive, cheat, take in; se ~ mistake, be mistaken; be wrong; se ~ de train take the wrong train.

trompette, s. f. trumpet; trumpeter.

tronc, s. m. trunk; stock; collecting box.

trône, s.m. throne.

trop, adv. too; too much.

trophée, s. m. trophy.

tropical, adj. tropical.

tropique, s. m. tropic.

trot, s. m. trot.

trotter, v. n. trot.

trottoir, s. m. pavement; footway.

trou, s.m. hole; gap; opening.

trouble, s. m. disorder; confusion; misunderstanding; dispute; — adj. troubled; muddy.

troubler, v.a. stir up,

disturb; make muddy; muddle; confuse, perplex; upset; trouble.

troué, *s. f.* opening, gap.

trouer, *v. a.* make a hole in; pierce; bore.

troupe, *s. f.* troop, band.

troupeau, *s.m.* herd, drove; flock.

trouvaille, *s. f.* find(ing)

trouver, *v. a.* find, discover; find out; think; contrive; se ~ be, be found to be, prove; turn out, happen; *je me trouvais là* I happened to be there.

truite, *s. f.* trout.

trust, *s. m.* trust.

T.S.F., *s. f.* (=*télégraphie sans fil)* wireless (set).

tu, toi, *pron.* you.

tube, *s. m.* tube; pipe; ~ *de télévision* TV tube.

tuberculose, *s. f.* tuberculosis.

tuer, *v. a.* kill; slay.

tuile, *s. f.* tile.

tumeur, *s. f.* tumour.

tunnel, *s. m.* tunnel.

turbine, *s. f.* turbine.

turbopropulseur, *s. m.* turbo-prop aircraft.

turboréacteur, *s.m.* turbo-jet engine.

turc, turque (T.), *adj.* Turkish (language), Turk.

tuteur, -trice, *s.m.f.* guardian, trustee.

tutoyer, *v. a.* to 'thee-and thou' s. o.

tuyau, *s. m.* pipe, tube; flue; ~ *d'échappement* exhaust-pipe.

tympan, *s. m.* ear-drum.

type, *s. m.* type.

typique, *adj.* typical.

typographie, *s. f.* typography; printing.

tyran, *s. m.* tyrant.

tyrannie, *s. f.* tyranny.

tyranniser, *v. a.* tyrannize (over); oppress.

U

ulcère, *s. m.* ulcer.

ultérieur, *adj.* ulterior; further.

ultime, *adj.* ultimate, last, final.

ultra-violet-, -ette, *adj.* ulra-violet.

un, une, *art. & pron.* a, an; any, some; one; *l'~ ou l'autre* either one or the other; *ni l'~ ni l'autre* neither one; *l'~ et autre* both; *~e fois* once; *~ à ~* one by one.

unanime, *adj.* unanimous.

uni, *adj.* smooth, even, level; united.

unification, *s. f.* unification.

unifier, *v. a.* unify; unite.

uniforme, *adj.* uniform.

union, *s. f.* union; agreement; match, marriage.

unique, *adj.* unique, sole, only.

uniquement, *adv.* solely, only.

unir, *v.a.* unite; level, smooth; s'~ join.

unité, *s.f.* unity; unit.

univers, *s. m.* universe.

universel, -elle, *adj.* universal; world-wide.

universitaire, *adj.* academic, university.

université, *s.f.* university.

urbain, *adj.* urban.

urgence, *s.f.* urgency; *d'~* urgent; *en cas d'~* in case of emergency.

urgent, *adj.* urgent, pressing.

uriner, *v. n. & a.* urinate.

urne, *s. f.* urn.

usage, *s. m.* use, custom;

habit, way; wear; *d'*~ usual, habitual; *en* ~ in use.

usé, *adj.* worn-out, shabby.

user, *v. n. & a.* use, make use of; wear out; use up; — *s.m.* wear, service, use; *être d'un bon* ~ wear well.

usine, *s. f.* factory, works.

ustensile, *s. m.* utensil; implement, tool.

usuel, -elle, *adj.* usual, customary.

usure[1], *s. f.* usury.

usure[2], *s. f.* wear (and tear).

usurper, *v.a.* usurp.

utile, *adj.* useful, of use, profitable; *être* ~ ( ) be of use.

utilisation, *s.f.* utilization.

utiliser, *v.a.* utilize.

utilité, *s. f.* utility, use.

V

va *int.* agreed!, indeed.

vacance, *s. f.* vacancy; *(pl.),* holiday(s), vacation; *être en* ~s be on holiday.

vacant, *adj.* vacant.

vacarme, *s.m.* noise, uproar.

vaccin, *s.m.* vaccine.

vacciner, *v. a.* vaccinate.

vache, *s.f.* cow.

vaciller, *v.n.* vacillate; reel; waver.

vacuum, *s. m.* vacuum.

vagabond, *s. m.* trampe.

vague[1], *adj.* vague.

vague[2], *s.f.* wave.

vaillant, *adj.* valiant.

vain, *adj.* vain; empty; *en* ~ in vain.

vaincre*, *v. a. & n.* conquer, defeat.

vainqueur, *s.m.* conqueror, victor; — *adj.* conquering, victorious.

vaisseau, *s. m.* vessel; ship.

vaisselle, *s. f.* plates and dishes, table-service; *laver la* ~ wash up the dishes; *lavage de* ~ washing-up.

valet, *s. m.* valet; knave, jack.

valeur, *s. f.* value, worth; price; courage; ~*s* securities.

valide, *adj.* valid; able-bodied.

validité, *s.f.* validity.

valise, *s. f.* valise, (travelling-)bag; suitcase; ~ *diplomatique* dispatch-box, diplomatic bag.

vallée, *s. f.* valley.

valoir*, *v.n. & a.* be worth, be as good as; deserve; procure; yield.

valse, *s.f.* waltz.

vanille, *s.f.* vanilla.

vanité, *s.f.* vanity.

vaniteux, -euse, *adj.* vain, conceited.

vanter, *v. a.* extol, cry up; se ~ boast.

vapeur[1], *s.f.* steam; vapour.

vapeur[2], *s.m.* steamer.

vaporeux, -euse, *adj.* vaporous.

vaquer, *v. n.* be vacant.

variable, *adj.* variable, changeable.

variante, *s.f.* variant.

variation, *s.f.* variation.

varier, *v. n. & a.* vary; ~ *de* ... *a* range from ... to.

variété, *s. f.* variety.

vase, *s. m.* vase; vessel.

vaseline, *s. f.* vaseline.

vassal, *s. m.* vassal.

vaste, *adj.* vast; spacious.
vautour, *s. m.* vulture.
veau, *s. m.* veal; calf.
vedette, *s.f.* mounted sentinel; motor-boat; (film) star.
végétal, *s. m.* vegetable; plant.
végétation, *s. f.* vegetation.
végéter, *v. n.* vegetate.
véhémence, *s. f.* vehemence.
véhément, *adj.* vehement.
véhicule, *s. m.* vehicle.
véhiculer, *v. a.* transport.
veille, *s. f.* waking; vigil; eve.
veiller, *v. n.* sit up, keep watch; *v.a.* watch.
veine, *s. f.* vein; luck.
vélo, *s.m.* bike.
vélocité, *s.f.* velocity.
velours, *s.m.* velvet.
velouté, *adj.* velvety, soft.
velu, *adj.* hairy.
venaison, *s.f.* venison.
vendange, *s.f.* vintage, grape-harvest.
vendeur, -euse, *s. m. f.* salesman, shop assistant; saleswoman.
vendre, *v. a.* sell; *à ~* for sale.
vendredi, *s. m.* Friday; *le ~ saint* Good Friday.
vénéneux, -euse, *adj.* poisonous.
vénérable, *adj.* venerable.
vengeance, *s. f.* vengeance, revenge.
venger, *v.a.* avenge, revenge; *se ~* avenge oneself.
venin, *s.m.* poison.
venir*, *v. n.* come, arrive; grow; occur; arise; *~ de* come from; *~ à bout de* manage.
vent, *s. m.* wind; *grand ~* gale; *~ alizé* trade-wind.

vente, *s. f.* sale; auction; *en ~* for sale.
venteux, -euse, *adj.* windy.
ventilateur, *s. m.* ventilator.
ventilation, *s. f.* ventilation.
ventre, *s. m.* belly.
venue, *s.f.* coming, arrival.
ver, *s.m.* worm.
verbal, *adj.* verbal, oral.
verbe, *s.m.* verb.
verdeur, *s.f.* greenness; harshness.
verdict, *s.m.* verdict.
verdure, *s.f.* verdure; greenness.
verger, *s.m.* orchard.
vergue, *s.f.* yard.
vérification, *s.f.* verification; check(ing).
vérifier, *v.a.* verify; check; confirm.
vérité, *s.f.* truth.
vermicelle, *s.m.* vermicelli.
vernir, *v. a.* varnish; polish.
vernis, *s.m.* varnish; polish.
verre, *s.m.* glass.
verrou, *s.m.* bolt.
verrouiller, *v.a.* bolt.
vers[1], *s.m.* line; verse.
vers[2], *prep.* towards, to; about.
verser, *v. a.* pour (out) spill, upset; *v. n.* overturn.
version, *s. f.* translation; version.
vert, *adj.* green; hearty; sharp.
vertical, *adj.* vertical, upright.
vertige, *s. m.* dizziness.
vertu, *s.f.* virtue.
vessie, *s.f.* bladder.
veste, *s. f.* coat, jacket.
vestiaire, *s. m.* cloakroom.

vestibule, *s.m.* lobby, hall; *grand* ~ lounge.

veston, *s. m.* coat; *complet* ~ lounge-suit.

vêtement, *s.m.* clothes (pl.); ~*s de dessous* underwear, underclothes.

vétéran, *s.m.* veteran.

vétérinaire, *s. m.* veterinary surgeon, vet.

vêtir*, *v. a.* clothe, dress.

véto, *s.m.* veto.

veuf, *s.m.* widower.

veuve, *s.f.* widow.

vexer, *v. a.* vex, annoy.

via, *prep.* via.

viaduc, *s. m.* viaduct.

viande, *s. m.* meat; ~ *réfrigérée* chilled meat.

vibration, *s. f.* vibration.

vibrer, *v. n.* vibrate.

vicaire, *s.m.* curate.

vice, *s.m.* vice, evil.

vice-, *prefix* vice-

vicieux, -euse, *adj.* vicious; faulty.

vicomte, *s. m.* viscount.

victime, *s.f.* victim.

victoire, *s.f.* victory.

victorieux, -euse, *adj.* victorious.

victuailles, *s. f. pl.* victuals.

vide, *adj.* empty; void; vacant; — *s.m.* space.

vider, *v. a.* empty; drain.

vie, *s.f.* life.

vieillard, *s.m.* old man.

vieillesse, *s.f.* old age.

vieillir, *v.n.* grow old.

vierge, *s. f.* virgin, maid.

vieux, vieil, vieille, *adj.* old.

vif, vive, *adj.* live; quick; lively; full of life; bright, vivid; fiery, ardent.

vigilant, *adj.* watchful.

vigne, *s.f.* vine; vineyard.

vignoble, *s.m.* vineyard.

vigoureux, -euse, *adj.* vigorous.

vigueur, *s.f.* vigour force.

vilain, *s. m.* villain, cad

village, *s.m.* village.

ville, *s. f.* town, city; *hôtel de* ~ town hall.

vin, *s. m.* wine.

vinaigre, *s. m.* vinegar.

vingt, *adj.* & *s.m.* twenty; twentieth.

vingtième, *adj.* twentieth.

violation, *s.f.* violation.

violence, *s.f.* violence.

violent, *adj.* violent; excessive.

violer, *v. a.* violate, ravish.

violette, *s.f.* violet.

violon, *s.m.* violin.

violoncelle, *s. m.* (violon-) cello.

violoniste, *s. m f.* violinist.

vipère, *s.f.* viper.

virgule, *s.f.* comma; *point et* ~ semicolon.

virtuose, *s. m. f.* virtuoso.

vis, *s. f.* screw.

visa, *s.m.* visa, visé.

visage, *s. m.* face.

vis-à-vis, *prep.* opposite; facing.

viser, *v.a.* aim (at); aspire to.

viseur, *s. m.* view-finder.

visibilité, *s. f.* visibility.

visible, *adj.* visible.

vision, *s.f.* sight.

visite, *s. f.* visit; *faire* ~ *à* pay a visit to, call on.

visiter, *v. a.* visit; ~ *les curiosités* go sightseeing.

visiteur, -euse, *s. m. f.* visitor.

visser, *v. a.* screw (down, in).

visuel, -elle, *adj.* visual.

vital, *adj.* vital.

vitalité, *s.f.* vitality.

vitamine, s. f. vitamin.

vite, adj. fast; swift; — adv. fast, rapidly.

vitesse, s. f. speed; rate (of speed); gear; à toute ~ at top speed; boîte de ~ gear-box; ~ de croisière cruising speed.

vitrail s. m. church window.

vitre, s. f. pane.

vitrier, s.m. glazier.

vivant, adj. alive, living: full of life; de mon ~ in my lifetime.

vivement, adv. quickly, fast.

vivre*, v. n. live, be alive.

vocabulaire, s. m. vocabulary.

vocation, s.f. vocation, calling.

vœu, s. m. (pl. -x) wish, desire; vow.

vogue, s. f. vogue, fashion; avoir la ~ be in vogue.

voici, prep. here (is); le ~! here he is!

voie, s.f. way, road; route; line, track; means, channel.

voilà, prep. there (is).

voile¹, s.m. veil.

voile², s.f. sail.

voiler, v.a. veil, cover, hide.

voilier, s. m. sailing-ship.

voir*, v. a. see; look at; view; faire ~ show; ne pas ~ miss.

voire, adv. even.

voisin, adj. neighbouring, adjoining, next (door).

voisinage, s.m. neighbourhood.

voiture, s.f. vehicle, conveyance; carriage; car; coach; van; wagon; aller en ~ drive.

voiture-ambulance, s. f. ambulance(-car).

voix, s. f. voice; sound; à haute ~ aloud.

vol¹, s. m. flying, flight.

vol², s. m. theft, robbery.

volaille, s.f. poultry, fowl.

volant, s.m. steering-wheel.

volcan, s.m. volcano.

volée, s.f. flight.

voler¹, v. n. fly; run at top speed.

voler², v. a. & n. steal, rob.

volet, s.m. shutter.

voleur, s. m. thief, robber.

volontaire, adj. voluntary; — s. m. f. volunteer.

volonté, s. f. will; à ~ at will.

volontiers, adv. willingly.

volt, s.m. volt.

voltiger, v.n. flutter about, fly about.

volume, s. m. volume; bulk.

voluptueux, -euse, adj. voluptuous.

vomir, v. a. & n. vomit, be sick.

vos, adj. poss. your.

vote, s. m. vote; voting.

voter, v. n. ~ & a. vote.

votre, adj. yours.

vouer, v. a. vow; dedicate.

vouloir*, v. a. want, require, demand; ~ bien be willing; je voudrais + inf. I should like to; comme vous voulez as you please.

vous, pron. you; to you.

vous-même, pron. yourself.

voûte, s.f. vault, arch.

voyage, s.m. journey; voyage; bon ~! a pleasant journey (to you)!; *partir en* ~ set off on a journey; *fair e un* ~ make a journey.

voyager, *v.n.* travel, make a trip.

voyageur, -euse, *s. m. f.* traveller, passenger.

voyelle, *s.f.* vowel.

voyou, *s.m.* hooligan.

vrai, *adj.* real, true, right; *être* ~ hold (good); — *s. m.* truth; *être dans le* ~ be right.

vraiment, *adv.* truly, really; indeed.

vraisemblable, *adj.* likely, credible, probable.

vu, *prep.* considering.

vue, *s. f.* sight; vision; view; *à* ~ at sight; *en* ~ *de* with a view to; *point de* ~ point of view; *avoir la* ~ *courte* be short-sighted; *être en* ~ be in the limelight.

vulgaire, *adj.* vulgar; common; coarse.

W

wagon, *s. m.* coach, carriage, car.

wagon-lit, *s. m.* sleeping-car.

wagonnet, *s.m.* tub; truck.

wagon-poste, *s. m.* mail-van.

wagon-restaurant, *s. m.* dining-car.

water-closet, *s. m.* W. C.

water-polo, *s. m.* water-polo.

wattman, *s.m.* tram-driver.

week-end, *s.m.* week-end.

whisky, *s.m.* whisky.

X

xérès, *s. m.* sherry.

xylographie, *s. f.* xylography.

xylophages, *s.m.* *pl.* xylophages.

Y

y, *adv.* here, there; *il* ~ *a* there is, there exists; *s'*~ *connaître* well informed.

yacht, *s. m.* yacht.

yeux *see* œil.

yogourt, yoghourt, *s. m.* yoghourt, yaourt.

yougoslave, *adj.* Yugoslav.

youyou, *s.m.* dinghy.

Z

zèbre, *s.m.* zebra.

zébrer, *v.a.* stripe.

zèle, *s.m.* zeal.

zélé, *adj.* zealous.

zénith, *s.m* zenith.

zéro, *s.m.* zero.

zézayer, *v.n.* lisp.

zigzag, *s.m.* zigzag.

zinc, *s.m.* zinc.

zone, *s.f.* zone, belt.

zoo, *s.m.* zoo.

zoologie, *s.f.* zoology.

zoologique, *adj.* zoological.

zut, *int.* ~*!* damn it!